ALSO BY A. J. LANGGUTH

Union 1812: The Americans Who Fought the Second War of Independence (2006)

Our Vietnam: The War 1954–1975 (2000)

A Noise of War: Caesar, Pompey, Octavian and the Struggle for Rome (1994)

Patriots: The Men Who Started the American Revolution (1988)

Saki: A Life of Hector Hugh Munro (1981)

Hidden Terrors (1978)

Macumba: White and Black Magic in Brazil (1975)

Marksman (1974)

Wedlock (1972)

Jesus Christs (1968)

Driven West

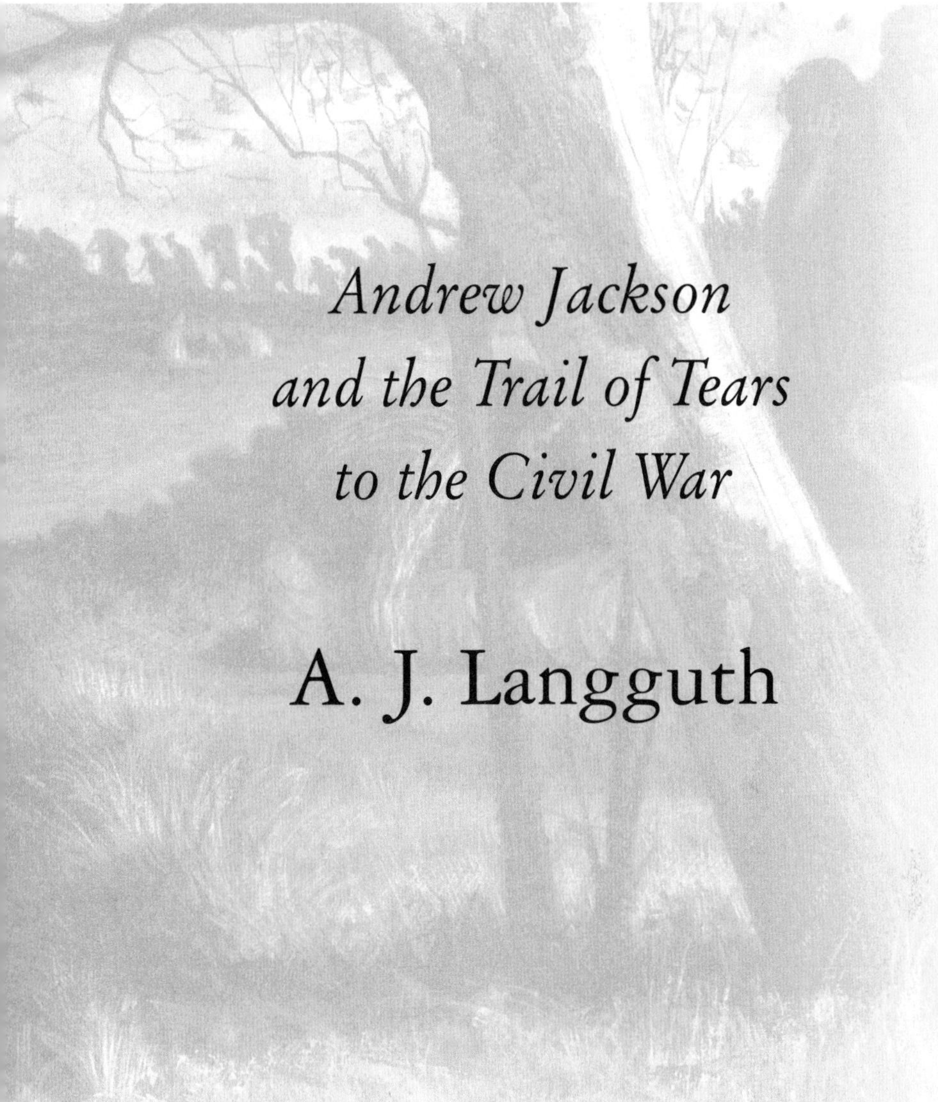

Driven West

Andrew Jackson and the Trail of Tears to the Civil War

A. J. Langguth

Simon & Schuster
NEW YORK LONDON TORONTO SYDNEY

Simon & Schuster
1230 Avenue of the Americas
New York, NY 10020

First Simon & Schuster hardcover edition November 2010
SIMON & SCHUSTER and colophon are registered trademarks of Simon & Schuster, Inc.

For information about special discounts for bulk purchases, please contact Simon & Schuster Special Sales at 1-866-506-1949 or business@simonandschuster.com.

The Simon & Schuster Speakers Bureau can bring authors to your live event. For more information or to book an event contact the Simon & Schuster Speakers Bureau at 1-866-248-3049 or visit our website at www.simonspeakers.com.

Manufactured in the United States of America

Text designed by Paul Dippolito

1 3 5 7 9 10 8 6 4 2

Library of Congress Cataloging-in-Publication Data

Langguth, A. J., 1933–
Driven West : Andrew Jackson's trail of tears to the Civil War / A. J. Langguth.
p. cm.
Includes bibliographical references and index.
1. United States History—1815–1861. I. Title.
E338.L36 2011
973.5'6—dc22 2010020455

ISBN 978-1-4165-4859-1
ISBN 978-1-4391-9327-3 (ebook)

ILLUSTRATION CREDITS

Henry Clay: The Granger Collection; John Quincy Adams: Library of Congress; Elias Boudinot: Courtesy of the Oklahoma Historical Society; Harriet Boudinot: Courtesy of the Oklahoma Historical Society; Sequoyah: Library of Congress; Cherokee Alphabet: Private Collection/Peter Newark, American Pictures/The Bridgeman Art Library International; *Cherokee Phoenix*: American Antiquarian Society, Worcester, Massachusetts, USA/The Bridgeman Art Library International; John Calhoun: National Portrait Gallery, Smithsonian Institution/Art Resource, NY; Margaret Eaton: The Granger Collection; John Henry Eaton: The Granger Collection; Theodore Frelinghuysen: The Granger Collection; John Marshall: National Portrait Gallery, Smithsonian Institution/Art Resource, NY; Daniel Webster: The Granger Collection; Sam Houston: The Granger Collection; John Howard Payne: Michael Nicholson/Corbis; Chief John Ross: Smithsonian American Art Museum, Washington, DC/Art Resource, NY; General Winfield Scott: The Granger Collection; Trail of Tears Painting: Gilcrease Museum, Tulsa, OK; Rose Cottage: Courtesy of the Oklahoma Historical Society; William Henry: The Metropolitan Museum of Art/Art Resource, NY, The Metropolitan Museum of Art, New York, NY, USA; John Tyler: Library of Congress; James Polk: Library of Congress; Zachary Taylor: Library of Congress; Millard Fillmore: Library of Congress; Franklin Pierce: Library of Congress; James Buchanan: Library of Congress; Stand Watie: The Granger Collection.

For Franklin D. Woodson
1933–2000

Contents

Driven West

Henry Clay

1 · Henry Clay (1825)

At 6 p.m. on Sunday, January 9, 1825, Henry Clay, one of his nation's shrewdest political minds, made a miscalculation that helped to end his chance of ever becoming president of the United States.

Over the next three decades, Clay's decision set off repercussions that transformed the character of his young country, uprooted the earliest Americans from their homes in the Southeast, and led ultimately to massive bloodshed.

But at the moment, Clay was only trying to achieve his lifelong goal.

During the prior thirteen years, Henry Clay had evolved from firebrand to peacemaker. The transformation came during the quixotic War of 1812, when an overmatched United States took on Great Britain for a second time. Clay had been one of the most fervent congressional "War Hawks," pressing President James Madison to strike back against Great Britain's aggressiveness. Madison's opposition party, the Federalists of New England, had vehemently resisted the call to arms and had staged an antiwar convention that was seen as a threat to secede from the Union.

But the Federalist timing could not have been worse. As they met in Hartford, Connecticut, Henry Clay was already playing a crucial role at a peace conference in Belgium, and Britain and the United States reached terms on Christmas Eve, 1814. Given the lag in communication with Europe, news of that agreement arrived in America only after Andrew Jackson had scored his epic victory over the redcoats in New Orleans.

Flustered and discredited, the Federalists tried to explain away their actions, but they were finished as a political force. When Madison's secretary of state, James Monroe, ran to succeed him, he won 183 of 217 electoral votes. Four years later, the Federalists did not bother to put forward a candidate. Except for a single protest vote, Monroe swept to reelection unanimously.

Men who knew him agreed that Monroe did not have the intellectual heft of Jefferson and Madison, but he was adroit at avoiding controversy. When he toured the country to promote harmony, a Boston editor conferred on Monroe's years in the White House an enduring label—the Era of Good Feelings.

But Henry Clay saw himself as the man who had repeatedly defused divisive issues during that era and believed that he deserved the presidency as a reward for the nation's tranquility.

The fifth son of a Baptist minister from Hanover County, Virginia, Clay was not preordained to rise to political prominence. He was four years old when his father died and left Henry as his inheritance only a fine speaking voice. The boy's early education was entrusted to a hard-drinking English schoolmaster until Henry's widowed mother married a former army captain, and her husband landed his stepson a clerk's job in Virginia's High Court of Chancery.

The teenager already possessed a charm that compensated for a somewhat equine homeliness. He caught the attention of George Wythe, whose law office had once produced Thomas Jefferson and John Marshall, and he spent four years as Wythe's secretary before studying law with Virginia's attorney general. For an ambitious young man, however, Richmond's entrenched gentry constituted a barrier to rapid advancement. When his mother and stepfather moved to Kentucky, Clay went with them.

From Lexington, he was appointed to the U.S. Senate in 1806 at the age of twenty-nine, a year younger than the age stipulated in the

Constitution. Clay was already a tall and rangy campaigner with every talent to ensure success. When he switched legislative chambers five years later, his nervy vitality led to a unique honor: On the first day of his first session in the House of Representatives, Clay was elected its Speaker.

Now, thirteen years later, Clay at forty-seven was still finding men eager for his all-night card games and women for kisses from his generous mouth. Clay understood both his appeal and the reticence that Americans expected from their politicians.

"Kissing is like the presidency," he said. "It is not to be sought, and not to be declined."

Assessing the United States as the presidential election approached, Clay had been convinced that 1824 was destined to be his year. The percentage of Americans living west of the Appalachians had been expanding rapidly as Congress granted land rights to settlers who made improvements on the property they claimed. The country seemed ready to turn away from the Virginians who had monopolized the presidency for the past twenty-four years—Monroe, and before him, Madison and Jefferson. As a Kentuckian now, Clay was poised to reap the benefit of a fervor along the frontier for one of their own.

He had already surmounted one unlikely obstacle. With his gifts so widely acknowledged in Congress, Clay had assumed that Monroe would appoint him secretary of state, the accepted way station on the road to the presidency. Instead, inexplicably, Monroe had chosen John Quincy Adams, who had often wrangled with Clay when they served together on the peace delegation that ended the War of 1812. Adams was a New Englander and the son of the nation's second president, but he had proved his political independence from his father's Federalist Party by voting as a matter of conscience with the Jeffersonians.

No one who knew John Quincy Adams would suggest that his defection from the Federalists had been prompted by political expediency. And yet when Andrew Jackson scored his improbable victory in New Orleans, the country had exploded with patriotic fervor, and the Jeffersonians became unstoppable.

With the collapse of the party system, voters were again assessing the personal qualities of the candidates rather than their political affiliation, a tendency that would not seem to favor the dour and unbending John Quincy Adams. When Monroe named him secretary of state, Adams had lived abroad as a diplomat for the preceding eight years. After representing the United States in Russia, he had gone on to the peace negotiations in Belgium and, most recently, had served as America's ambassador to England. Even Adams's wife, Louisa, worried that returning to domestic politics in America would reinforce the grim and compulsive aspects of his nature.

Despite those drawbacks, Adams's eight years as Monroe's secretary of state had proved successful. He took advantage of a rash and unauthorized invasion of Florida by Andrew Jackson to negotiate a treaty with Spain that expanded the boundaries of the United States west to the Pacific Ocean. Adams rightly considered his treaty a great achievement and was chagrined when Clay found a major oversight in its original terms. The error was corrected, but Adams never forgot the way Clay had "snickered" over the mistake made by this man notorious for his pedantry.

During his second term at the State Department, Adams had turned his attention south of the equator. He considered it America's moral duty to thwart Spanish colonialism by supporting the revolutionary movements that had sprung up throughout the hemisphere.

Thomas Jefferson took a more pragmatic view. Writing to President Monroe from Monticello, he first apologized for having "so long ceased to take any interest" in politics, but he was convinced that steering the proper course in Latin America was the nation's greatest challenge since Independence. Jefferson argued that an alliance with Great Britain would shut out other European predators from the hemisphere.

As secretary of state, Adams drafted a warning for Monroe to include in his seventh annual State of the Union address in December 1823: Americans would regard any attempt by Europe to extend its influence in the hemisphere "as dangerous to our lives and safety." In time, that message became known as the Monroe Doctrine.

In Latin America, Simón Bolívar and the revolutionaries of Colombia, Argentina, and Mexico welcomed the symbolic support from the United States but were aware that policing the doctrine would require the British navy.

It was during those same years that Clay had enjoyed his own domestic triumphs. He had watched the original thirteen states grow steadily from Vermont—admitted to the Union in 1791—through Kentucky, Tennessee, Ohio, Louisiana, Indiana, Mississippi, and Illinois. By admitting Alabama on December 14, 1819, Congress had struck a balance between eleven free states and eleven slave states. But when the Missouri Territory sought admission, the nation was sharply divided over whether slavery should be sanctioned there.

Southern slave owners were adamantly opposed to a proposal that would bar slavery throughout the area of the Louisiana Purchase. They still resented the Northwest Ordinance of 1787, which had outlawed slavery north of the Ohio River. Now Northern abolitionists were attempting to restrict another great swath of the nation.

Clay's position was equivocal. At home in Kentucky, he owned slaves, and yet he had denounced the evils of slavery. But he had also demanded of his Northern colleagues whether "they would set their wives and daughters to brush their boots and shoes"—performing the chores best left to slaves.

Clay seemed to expect the institution of slavery to wither away gradually without a formal deadline. When that day came, he anticipated that the emancipated families would return to Africa, and in 1816 he had been a founder of the American Colonization Society. Its members promoted the migration of former slaves to a settlement named for America's current president—Monrovia, in the country of Liberia.

Jefferson was attuned more viscerally to slavery than Clay was and less sanguine about a peaceful resolution to what he termed the "momentous question." To a friend, Jefferson wrote that coming to terms with slavery had, "like a firebell in the night, awakened me and filled me with terror."

For the short term, however, Clay formulated a three-part compromise to deal with Missouri: Maine would be detached from Massachusetts and enter the Union as a free state. Missouri would enter as a slave state. To satisfy the antislavery faction, Congress would prohibit slavery from all territory—except for Missouri—north of the parallel at thirty-six degrees, thirty feet. When Northerners dropped their demand for restrictions against slavery in Missouri itself, those terms were taken up individually and passed into law.

A serious setback then arose, however, when Missouri proposed a state constitution that would keep out "free negroes and mulattoes." In response, Clay drafted deliberately ambiguous language that seemed to protect the privileges of every U.S. citizen. Both sides in the debate granted that Clay's motive was less to win political advantage than to preserve the Union. They listened respectfully as Clay—mild and supplicating—went among them to broker his latest compromise.

The Missouri question had aroused such animosity that it clouded even the counting of votes during James Monroe's reelection. Since the Federalists had not fielded a candidate, Missouri's three votes mattered not at all. Yet the question of whether to count them ignited more havoc on the Senate floor.

By the time Clay's compromise was approved and Missouri was admitted on August 10, 1821, congressmen were exhausted and a grateful country gave thanks to Henry Clay. Missouri's new senator, Thomas Hart Benton, said that Clay had saved the Constitution.

Clay's second notable crusade came in the wake of a severe economic depression termed the Panic of 1819. As bankruptcies and unemployment roiled the nation, the future of the Second Bank of the United States seemed in danger. It took a ruling from U.S. Chief Justice John Marshall's court to strike down a challenge by the Maryland legislature that a national bank was unconstitutional. In rejecting the state's right to tax the Bank of the United States in order to protect its local banks, Marshall ruled, "The power to tax is the power to destroy."

Clay's response to the crisis was to endorse the Bank of the United States while pressing for an increase in the tariffs on manufactured goods imported from England. Opponents who supported free trade were quoting Adam Smith, but Clay countered with an argument from Alexander Hamilton that protective taxes would spur industrialization in a country turning from agriculture to manufacturing. Clay's measures were supported by manufacturers and factory workers who wanted protection from Europe's cheaper wages, and he succeeded where Hamilton had failed.

To heal the strains exposed by the Missouri debate, Clay hoped to unify the country through a system of national roads and canals. Into that ambitious vision, he blended his support for the Bank and for protective tariffs and, borrowing a phrase from Hamilton, promoted his policies as "a genuine American System."

As the campaign to succeed President Monroe began, Clay could argue that he had averted the collapse of the Union over slavery and had laid down a blueprint for American prosperity.

His commanding presence in the Congress had led Clay to dismiss his potential rivals. Secretary of War John C. Calhoun of South Carolina might have been a threat, but soon after entering the race he settled instead for a run at the vice presidency. William H. Crawford also could have been a formidable competitor—born in Virginia but transplanted to Georgia. After serving as a U.S. senator, he had gone on to hold the post of secretary of the Treasury under both Madison and Monroe.

And Crawford was backed by Martin Van Buren, a forty-two-year-old New Yorker whose political acumen was highly regarded. The summer before the election, however, Crawford had been felled by a stroke that rendered him speechless and near blind.

That had left only Andrew Jackson of Tennessee. Still venerated for his victory in the Battle of New Orleans nine years earlier, he had since burnished his popular reputation with his adventure in Florida. Voters did not know that John Calhoun had denounced Jackson in cabinet meetings for risking war with Spain and had demanded that he be censured. Nor did they know that Jackson's strongest defense had come in those meetings from his temperamental opposite, Secretary of State Adams.

Steering a characteristically middle course, President Monroe had rejected censure but managed to rein in Jackson without igniting his notorious temper.

When the controversy spilled over to the House, however, Clay took the floor to defend the supremacy of civilian government. He attacked not only Jackson's unauthorized conduct in Florida but also the Indian treaties that Jackson had negotiated after he vanquished the Creek tribe in 1814. Clay charged that the punitive terms Jackson imposed on Creeks had exceeded any humiliation inflicted during "the most haughty period of imperious Rome."

Clay's speech was admired for its rhetorical flourishes but did not persuade the Congress to censure Andrew Jackson for his actions in Florida. To Jackson, however, it did establish Clay as a lifelong enemy. Clay had added to the hostility with his airy dismissal of Jackson's chances of winning the 1824 presidential election: "I cannot believe," Clay said, "that killing two thousand five hundred Englishmen at New Orleans qualifies for the various difficult and complicated duties of the Chief Magistracy."

The election season, however, was proving to be rife with surprises. Jonathan Russell, a Massachusetts congressman who had served with Adams and Clay on the peace delegation in 1814, claimed that Adams had been ready to sell out to the British the rights of Americans over access to the Mississippi River. Among westerners, the river was their lifeline, and Russell's charge was potentially devastating.

Any slur to his reputation aroused Adams, and in this case his rebuttal was so ferocious that it drove Russell to retire from politics. For years afterward, men used the phrase "to Jonathan Russell" as a synonym for destroying a political opponent.

In his fury, Adams also reneged on his earlier vow not to stir up regional prejudices. Now Adams capitalized on the rancor left by the War of 1812 by warning politicians in Massachusetts that if Andrew Jackson won the presidency, New England would be absolutely shut out of his administration.

Adams justified those attacks by claiming that his vision for the country was superior to Jackson's. Like Clay, Adams intended to commit federal money for "internal improvements"—building interstate highways, bridges, and canals—and to boost manufacturing and trade in ways that Jackson was likely to reject. Above all, Adams had come to regard the election as a referendum on his own lifetime of public service. Defeat, he felt, "would be equivalent to a vote of censure by the nation."

As Clay confronted Adams's new aggressiveness, he also found that Crawford's incapacity had not taken him out of the race. Van Buren was able to keep the severity of Crawford's afflictions a tightly held secret while he worked tirelessly to cut into a New York vote that Clay had been counting on.

When the 1824 results were tabulated from state elections across the country, Clay learned that Americans did not share his disdain for Andrew Jackson. The hero of New Orleans won the popular vote with 152,901 votes. Adams followed with 114,023. Although Clay edged out Crawford 47,217 to 46,979, he lost the one tally that mattered most: The Twelfth Amendment to the U.S. Constitution stipulated that if no candidate won a majority in the electoral college, the president would be chosen by the House of Representatives from the three candidates with the highest electoral numbers.

In that tally, Jackson led with 99 electoral votes, and Adams followed with 84. But Clay got only 37 votes, which meant that Crawford's 41 votes assured him the third place on the House ballot. As for the vice presidency, Calhoun was elected easily with 182 votes to a combined 72 votes for his challengers.

Hugely disappointed, Clay thrashed about as he cast blame for his humiliation. He claimed that the power of newspapers along the Atlantic seaboard was responsible. Or the influence of patronage from the Monroe administration. Or the way his friends had been discouraged by a rumor that he had withdrawn from the race, a lie that had circulated too late to be refuted.

But as his recriminations faded, Clay confronted a crucial question: Endorsing which of the candidates would keep his presidential hopes alive?

Immediately, the jockeying for a House majority became intense among the three factions. Even before the national election, Van Buren had made a surreptitious trip to Monticello to ask that Jefferson endorse Crawford. The former president, now eighty-one, reminisced happily about the early days of the republic. He was alert, warm, and witty, but he resisted making a public recommendation for 1824.

Van Buren had returned to New York, where his carefully constructed coalition appeared to be crumbling. Still, as the decision moved to the House, Van Buren thought that Crawford could be the compromise choice in case of a deadlock between Jackson and Adams. To allay concerns about Crawford's health, Van Buren offered assurances that his candidate was "substantially well" and that Clay's support for him was "probable but not certain."

That claim was an indication of how adroitly Clay was parrying Van Buren's overtures. Clay had no intention of endorsing Crawford since he understood very well that even if Van Buren somehow got his man into the White House, Crawford might die there. Then John Calhoun, another Clay nemesis, would become president.

It began to look as though a second military figure from America's recent past was going to play a crucial role in the House election. Stephen Van Rensselaer, a militia general in the War of 1812, had led the attack on Queenston in Canada that killed the popular British commander Isaac Brock. But that battle had ended in a disaster for the Americans. Now, since military honors had eluded him, Van Rensselaer—called the Patroon of New York State—hoped at the age of sixty-one to play a decisive political role. Awed by Van Rensselaer's wealth and social position, Van Buren had courted him assiduously until he considered his vote for Crawford assured.

The maneuvering had extended to the candidates' wives. Louisa Adams and Floride Calhoun were each hostesses to large theater parties, which alarmed the wife of a Crawford supporter, who urged that Susanna Crawford do the same thing "to show our strength." Van Buren agreed and helped to organize a contingent of ten society women, twenty senators, and a collection of other dignitaries to settle in behind Mrs. Crawford in front boxes at the theater.

The gala evening was another sign of Van Buren's rise from a tavernkeeper's son to one of the most powerful men in the Congress. As he was growing up, Martin, a delicate blond child with a winning smile, had attracted the favor of leading Federalists in his village of Kinderhook, New York. But when he finished his law studies and entered politics, he defied his benefactors and allied himself with the more powerful Jeffersonians. By the time Van Buren moved to the state senate in Albany—and, in 1821, to the U.S. Senate at the age of thirty-eight—political rivals were citing examples of his duplicity.

Van Buren, born five days before the treaty that ended the Revolutionary War, had strongly supported the War of 1812 and came to have a special respect for one leading general, Winfield Scott. His esteem had made it a harsher blow when Van Buren's fourth son, named for the general, died in infancy. Van Buren's wife, Hannah, lived only long enough to bear another son. In the five years since her death, Van Buren had relied on his sister for help in raising his four surviving boys.

Stocky, short, and consumed by ambition, Van Buren did not seem inclined to marry again. He took meticulous care with his appearance, however, always stylishly turned out in shoes of Moroccan leather and silk hose that matched the color of his vest.

But no one made the mistake of dismissing Van Buren as a mere dandy. When he predicted that Adams would not have enough votes on the first House ballot, every informal tally backed him up. Jackson's unshakable seven states included his home of Tennessee, Alabama, Mississippi, Calhoun's South Carolina, and, to the north,

Indiana, Pennsylvania, and New Jersey. Because Crawford identified himself with the philosophy of Jefferson and Madison, he had the certain support of Virginia and perhaps of Delaware, North Carolina, and Georgia.

New England's six states seemed solid for Adams, who could also expect to win Maryland, Illinois, and Louisiana. But for the thirteen votes he required, Adams would need New York and the three states controlled by Henry Clay—Ohio, Missouri, and Clay's home state of Kentucky.

Being courted by agents of the other candidates was giving Clay a bittersweet popularity. "I am enjoying, while alive," he said, "the posthumous honors which are usually awarded to the venerated dead." But privately Adams's admiration was limited to Clay's political gifts. He deplored the fact that Clay's "morals, public and private, are loose, but he has all the virtues indispensable to a popular man." As for himself, Adams noted wistfully that he had "no powers of fascination."

Through the intense speculation, Clay's cheeky humor seldom faltered. He foresaw a problem when the Marquis de Lafayette, America's youthful combatant in the fight for independence, toured the United States, since Lafayette's visit would remind the nation of its glorious military history. That, in turn, would recall that Andrew Jackson had fought in the Revolution as a mere boy before he went on to glory in New Orleans.

One night, Clay was attending one of the many banquets honoring Lafayette when he noticed an empty seat between Adams and Jackson. Crossing the floor, he threw himself into it.

"Well, gentlemen," Clay announced, "since you are both so near the chair but neither can occupy it, I will slip in between you and take it myself."

Overhearing the remark, one of Van Buren's friends reported to his wife that everyone had laughed, except Adams and Jackson.

It was at the same dinner that Clay found a chance to whisper to Adams that he wanted to meet with him.

Whenever it was convenient, Adams replied.

"In a few days."

That was the background to the drama on January 9. Earlier in the day, Adams got a note from Clay asking whether he might call on him that evening. It being Sunday, Adams first had two church services to attend. Between those services, Adams spoke with his political allies, who speculated about the House vote but would not predict which way it might go.

Adams found a comfort in religion but, more important, a spur to better behavior. On that day, he noted in his diary that he had preferred the morning sermon with its self-lacerating text from Ecclesiastes: "I said, I will be wise, but it was far from me."

Despite being secretary of state, Adams had accepted the presidency of the American Bible Society because he felt that the nation was threatened by both the permissiveness of the Unitarians and the intolerance of a Calvinist revival movement. Meeting with Jebediah Morse, a prominent evangelical and missionary to Indian tribes, Adams admired his energy but deplored the way Morse's mind had been "trammeled by a vicious religious education."

Henry Clay's visit that evening had been carefully prepared by his friend Congressman Robert Letcher from Kentucky, who sounded out Adams about any lingering hostility to Clay. Both camps remembered the repeated clashes between the two men at the Ghent peace talks of 1814. Part of the discord stemmed from their temperaments. Clay reveled in staying up late, gambling, and drinking with cronies. From his nearby room at their rented quarters, Adams could hear Clay come rattling in at dawn, about the time he was rising for prayers.

But Clay had also been an implacable advocate for the settlers along America's frontier who depended on the Mississippi River for trade and transportation. That was the reason that Adams had viewed Jonathan Russell's accusation about his giving in to the British as an obvious ploy to promote Clay.

Adams assured Letcher that although he still believed Clay had instigated Russell's attack, he was satisfied with the forcefulness of his own rebuttal and felt no more animosity toward anyone. Letcher responded that "the Speaker now entertained only the kindliest feelings toward the Secretary of State."

Those kindly feelings were on display as Clay settled down across from Adams for a three-hour conversation. He complained about the pressure on him from allies of Adams's two opponents. In fact, Clay reported, he had been approached by one of Crawford's friends "in a manner so gross" that it had left him disgusted. Why, even some of Adams's own friends—although they denied being sent by Adams—had made oblique overtures for his support.

Neither Adams nor Clay needed to spell out what the friends had been suggesting—that Clay receive a commitment from Adams that he would be appointed secretary of state.

Clay explained that until recently it had been better not to tip his hand. In his diary, Adams recorded Clay's first wry reason: "To give a decent time for his own funeral solemnities as a candidate." And then, less plausibly, so that his own friends could achieve a neutrality that would leave them free to vote in a way "most conducive to the public interest."

But now, Clay continued, he was prepared to be explicit, which was why he had requested this confidential interview. Adams recorded the lofty language that Clay seemed to think Adams would appreciate: Clay "wished me, as far as I might think proper, to satisfy him with regard to some principles of great public importance, but without any personal considerations for himself."

As to his vote, Clay "had no hesitation in saying that his preference would be for me."

The deal was struck. But, given his temperament, Adams was in no mood to celebrate. Instead, he viewed his impending victory with apprehension. To a longtime friend, Senator Rufus King of New York, Adams bemoaned the prospect of becoming president despite winning only a minority of both the popular and electoral vote. When Jefferson had won in the House over the elder Adams in 1801, he had already received seventy-five electoral votes to sixty-five for Adams.

In that election, Aaron Burr had been the third candidate and forced the House through thirty-six rounds of balloting. But John Quincy Adams worried that winning might expose him "to a far severer trial than defeat" would have done.

Soon after Clay's visit, the Kentucky state legislature passed resolutions instructing Kentucky's delegates in Congress to vote for Jackson. Clay professed to be unperturbed by the defection in his home state and predicted that the congressmen would vote their own judgment. Then he went to work on them. A little more than two weeks before the House would settle the matter, Kentucky's congressional delegation announced that it would cast its ballot for Adams. Clay had carried with him eight of the twelve congressmen. On the same day, Ohio's delegation also announced for Adams.

Across the country, Clay's behavior was met with astonishment. But in Kentucky, the outcry was furious, since in the fall election Adams had not received a single vote in the state. Andrew Jackson's allies denounced the "monstrous union" between Clay and Adams, and Van Buren seemed to grasp its consequences more clearly than Clay did. He warned a Kentucky congressman that if his state actually voted for Adams, "you sign Mr. Clay's political death warrant."

But retribution lay years in the future. For now, Van Buren was working to undo the effect of Clay's decision. Since Adams's hold on Maryland and Louisiana was shaky, they might swing to Crawford if Adams could be stopped on the first ballot. To achieve that deadlock, Van Buren was counting on the vote of Stephen Van Rensselaer. At sixty-one, Van Rensselaer certainly looked decisive—ruddy-cheeked and straight-backed, with vivid blue eyes and a full head of white hair. But the old general was taking his responsibility seriously—too seriously, for Van Buren's taste. He was dithering over his choice, committed to Crawford but attracted by Jackson's military dash.

On January 28, an anonymous letter appeared in a Philadelphia newspaper charging Clay with having bartered the votes he controlled in exchange for Adams's pledge to name him secretary of state. Clay responded with a show of outrage. The man who made the accusation was "a dastard and a liar." Clay went further: If he identified the author he would "apply all the laws which govern and regulate the conduct of men of honor." Translated, that meant a duel, although Clay was not much of a shot.

When suspicion settled on Congressman George Kremer of Pennsylvania, Clay looked slightly absurd, since Kremer was regarded as a buffoon whose chief claim to distinction was his leopard-skin overcoat. For two days, a congressional committee went through the motions of investigating the charge of collusion between Adams and Clay and concluded that Kremer had no evidence. Throughout the uproar, Van Buren remained aloof, urging Crawford's delegates not to get involved.

Adams drew on his years as a diplomat to deflect any suggestion of a corrupt bargain. Asked about the rumors, Adams said merely that "the object nearest to my heart" was to unify the nation, and that would mean inviting western leaders into his cabinet.

The week before the showdown, Clay made it clear that he would be voting against the other candidates rather than for Adams. He and Jackson had been enemies since Clay accused the general of overstepping his authority in Florida, and Jackson had responded with imaginative vituperation. Clay stated his position succinctly: "That I should vote for Mr. Crawford? I cannot. For Gen. Jackson? I will not. I shall pursue the course which my conscience dictates, regardless of all imputations and all consequences."

The vote was set for February 9, one month after Clay and Adams sealed their partnership. The House had agreed that members would take their seats in the same order that the states would cast ballots—north to south along the Atlantic coast, south to north along the Missouri Valley. The sergeant at arms distributed individual ballot boxes to every delegation. Each state would have one vote and appoint its own tellers. They would count the ballots and write the results on two pieces of paper, one to go to Daniel Webster, the other, to guarantee an honest count, to be given to John Randolph. He was considered too erratic to be deceitful.

As the moment approached, it became apparent that Van Rensselaer was not so decisive as his military bearing might suggest.

Clay and Daniel Webster enticed him into the Speaker's chambers and again pressed the case for Adams. Although Van Rensselaer had promised Van Buren he would not vote for Adams, Crawford's supporters saw that Clay's pressure had left him shaken. They sent word to Van Buren to hurry over and shore up Van Rensselaer's resolve.

As fellow New Yorkers, the two men shared the daily intimacy of dining together in a furnished house they rented with other Crawford supporters. Van Buren drew considerable prestige from being seen as the companion of his state's wealthiest man, but he had no way of knowing that the general had lately called on Adams to complain about him. Van Rensselaer was annoyed that Van Buren had blocked the political appointment of his kinsman, Solomon Van Rensselaer, because Solomon was affiliated with Van Buren's rivals in New York. After listening to the general express his misgivings, Adams took the opening to knife Van Buren in a high-minded way:

"I said," Adams recorded that night in his diary, "Mr. Van Buren was a man of great talents and of good principles, but he had suffered them to be too much warped by party spirit."

Adams had added that since Van Buren sometimes followed a wiser and more generous policy he hoped "he would ultimately return to it."

When the ballots were counted, Van Rensselaer of New York had cast the decisive vote. The state gave Adams the thirteen states he needed to win on the first ballot, and Daniel Webster announced the results to the thousand people who had gathered at the Capitol. When Webster's deep and somber voice died away, John Randolph repeated the tally in his reedier and more excitable way. At that point, Adams supporters began to applaud. The Jackson camp started to hiss. As Speaker, Clay ordered the galleries closed and the crowd dispersed.

Remembering that balloting had taken six days in 1800 before Jefferson prevailed over his father, John Quincy Adams expected this vote to be equally protracted, and he had walked as usual to the State

Department to take up pending business. It was midafternoon by the time a jubilant Alexander Everett burst into his office. As a student, Everett had gone to Russia in 1809 to be Adams's clerk in the American embassy. Lately, as an editor, he had been promoting Adams's candidacy more vigorously than Adams thought seemly. Now, Everett announced that Louisiana, Illinois, and Maryland had all defected from Jackson and that Van Rensselaer's vote had carried New York.

In his first act as president-elect, Adams dashed off a quick note to his father. His mother, Abigail, had died in 1818, and at eighty-nine his father was frail and nearly blind. The son agreed with their family friend Rufus King that today's election made amends for the injustice that the elder Adams had suffered a quarter of a century earlier when Jefferson's victory denied him a second term.

Van Buren returned to their house just behind the Capitol to find a contrite Van Rensselaer waiting for him on a sofa. "Well, Mr. Van Buren," he said, "you see that I could not hold out!" To explain betraying Crawford, he concocted the story that he had dropped his head to pray for divine guidance, and when he opened his eyes he "saw on the floor directly below him a ticket bearing the name of John Quincy Adams." Van Rensselaer took it as a sign from heaven that he must not ignore.

Van Buren had already begun to look toward the next election and could not afford to break with the richest man in his state. Rather than challenge the story, he soothed Van Rensselaer's conscience by assuring him that he had done only what he believed was right for the country. Van Buren added that his vote should not affect their compatible life together in Washington.

Andrew Jackson and his Tennessee allies did not take his defeat so philosophically. Jackson's nephew, Andrew Jackson Donelson, was especially bitter. "What a farce!" he wrote. And Jackson himself concluded that the "rights of the people have been bartered for promises of office." To all who came to console him, Jackson asked the same question: How could any man accept the presidency knowing that the people did not want him?

Adams approached the evening of his triumph with considerable apprehension. President Monroe had scheduled a public reception at the White House for February 9, before he could appreciate the date's significance. His wife, Elizabeth, was already greeting guests serenely in a black velvet gown, her hair set off with white ostrich plumes. But the room's attention was focused on the spectacle of Adams and Jackson, who were arriving in public together for the first time since the vote. Other guests moved closer to watch their meeting, but to Adams's relief, Jackson's expression was "altogether placid and courteous."

The general already had on his arm a large, good-looking woman. "How do you do, Mr. Adams?" Jackson said. "I give you my left hand, for the right, as you see, is devoted to the fair. I hope you are very well, sir."

That sort of banter was beyond Adams. He said, "Very well, sir. I hope General Jackson is well."

One man observing their exchange was struck that the more gracious of the two was "the Indian fighter, the stern soldier who had written his country's glory in the blood of the enemy at New Orleans," while Adams, the practiced diplomat, "was stiff, rigid, cold as a statue"—in short, behavior "which repelled all."

The next day, Adams delivered a written acceptance of the presidency to the committee that came to notify him officially of the House balloting. Adams observed that he was the first president to receive a minority of electoral votes and wished he could refuse the office and allow Americans to hold a second election. But since the Constitution did not provide for that alternative, he would enter office "oppressed with the magnitude of the task before me."

As Adams prepared his agenda for the nation, he was confirming Van Buren's fear that he meant to betray the restraint of Jefferson and Madison. The outlines of the new president's policy had been clear even before he spelled them out later in his first annual speech to the Congress. Steeped in the classics, Adams praised "the magnificent splendor" of public works—the roads and aqueducts that the United States must create to match "the imperishable glories of the ancient republics." That meant an ambitious network of highways, bridges, and canals.

To Van Buren, Adams's heresy meant that he would not only centralize power in the federal government but would try to restore Monroe's one-party Era of Good Feelings. Van Buren considered construction projects on the grand scale that Adams envisioned to be the responsibility of the states. At home, New Yorkers had raised their own taxes to build the ambitious Erie Canal, which was soon to open. Pennsylvanians and Virginians had also undertaken the improvements in their states. Why should they be taxed again to build up distant western states with neither the resources nor the initiative to help themselves?

Adams also proposed even more visionary projects: a national university; a naval equivalent of West Point; a federal astronomy plan to build observatories. Adams called them "lighthouses of the skies," a fanciful description that was immediately ridiculed. Although the president sensed that such erudite projects might be unpopular along the nation's rough frontier, he urged rashly that congressmen not be "palsied by the will of our constituents."

Adams's seeming expression of contempt for the voters confirmed to Van Buren that his arrogance would make him dangerous in the White House. He resolved to strengthen a party structure that could resist autocratic policies that Van Buren saw as a throwback to Alexander Hamilton.

For now, however, Adams was trying to pick a cabinet that would further his goal of national unity. He made overtures to his recent opponents, but William Crawford declined to stay on as Treasury secretary, and Adams learned that asking Jackson to replace Calhoun as secretary of war would be taken "in ill part." Selecting his own successor as secretary of state, Adams found logical reasons—reasons that had nothing to do with any "corrupt bargain"—that he could use to justify naming Henry Clay.

To begin with, Clay endorsed Adams's vision of an active federal government. He was experienced in foreign affairs but, as a westerner, would furnish a unique perspective. And Clay desperately wanted the job, to the point of assuring Adams that his appointment would meet with only "trifling" opposition.

An early indication that Clay was wrong came when Adams's friend George Sullivan called on him to say that Vice President Calhoun wanted to see one of his own backers named secretary of state. Sullivan added that if Joel R. Poinsett were passed over, a strong opposition faction, led by Jackson in the Congress, would guarantee that Adams was stripped of all support except from New England.

Adams was outraged enough to threaten his friend with exposing his role in conveying the ultimatum: "I told Sullivan that I would some day call upon him to testify to these facts in a Court of justices."

Appalled, Sullivan exclaimed, "Surely not!"

Adams assured him he was serious. The intent of the message was "to intimidate me, and deter me from the nomination of Mr. Clay." And so, Adams repeated, it was likely that Sullivan would have to repeat publicly what he had just said.

Sullivan said that he would certainly refuse.

Adams said that his refusal "would be as good for me as the answer itself."

With that, Sullivan backtracked hastily. He assured Adams that Calhoun had not asked him to pass along the threat, and the president was mollified enough to drop his bullying tone. He observed that if John Calhoun did intend to make his administration unpopular, "I am at least forewarned."

Calhoun's reaction to Clay's appointment bore out Sullivan's warning. He called it "the most dangerous stab which the liberty of the country has ever received." But he was already looking to the next election. "Principles," he said, "cannot be violated in this country with impunity."

Given his temperament, Jackson's response to Clay's appointment was more volcanic. "So you see," he shouted, "the Judas of the West has closed the contract and will receive the thirty pieces of silver!" And he demanded to know, "Was there ever witness to such a barefaced corruption in any country before?"

The Senate approved all of Adams's other cabinet nominations unanimously but confirmed Clay only by twenty-seven to fourteen, with Andrew Jackson among the opponents. Despite being forewarned, the new president was surprised by the size of the negative vote. At least, Adams said, he could now be sure that hostile votes came from men carrying "the banners of General Jackson."

Adams had often suspected cabals against him but seldom with more justice. After Jackson calmed down, he had written to his former political manager in Tennessee to suggest a newspaper campaign throughout the state to draw public attention to the corruption of the Clay appointment.

Adams entered office opposed to nepotism, but his youngest son, John, needed a job. Already in the lower half of his class at Harvard, John had been expelled for joining a campus protest against the treatment of a popular teacher. When Harvard's president declined to reinstate his son, John Quincy Adams refused to attend the graduation ceremonies and then appointed the young man as his private secretary.

One of the first papers awaiting Adams was a document concerning the Indian tribes of Georgia. Monroe had used his final presidential message to address the issue of tribal lands that had become attractive to white settlers. To remove the Indians "by force, even with a view to their own security and happiness would be revolting to humanity and utterly unjustified," Monroe wrote. But the outgoing president also noted that "between the limits of our present States and Territories and the Rocky Mountains and Mexico there is a vast territory, to which they might be invited with inducements which might be successful."

The Treaty of Indian Springs had just passed the Senate by a vote of thirty-eight to four. It was now up to Adams to judge whether moving the Indians under that treaty should be considered inducement or force.

Major Ridge

2 · Major Ridge (1825)

President Adams already knew the recent tangled history of the Cherokee Nation from his years in the State Department. Now, however, his conscientious nature required that he immerse himself in the background of a people far removed from his own New England upbringing.

Putting the Treaty of Indian Springs into its context meant understanding that it was the sort of pact that Tecumseh, the legendary Shawnee chief, had given his life to resisting. Many Indians had agreed with him that they were hastening their own destruction by selling their territory to the U.S. federal government. By the early 1800s, the Choctaw tribe lived in a swath of land from the Tombigbee River in northeastern Mississippi to the Mississippi River, and the Chickasaws held the land north of them. Creek territory spread from eastern Georgia to central Alabama. The Cherokees claimed the valleys of Georgia, Tennessee, and the Carolinas, ringed by mountain ridges bright with azaleas and rhododendrons.

Shortly before the War of 1812, Tecumseh had gone south to recruit followers among tribes that were already trying to stop further sale of their land. In one case, the Cherokees turned to blood law—a death sentence imposed on any man who sold their communal land without the consent of the full Cherokee Nation.

When a tribe gave that consent, however, radical changes uprooted a way of life that dated to long before Hernando de Soto arrived from Spain in 1540. To adopt the white man's culture required Indians to abandon centuries of hunting and turn instead to cultivating individual farms and to opening private stores.

For Cherokee women who had farmed together on common fields in the center of their village, the new parceling of land into separate plots threatened their shared values and easy hospitality, while their husbands deplored the decline of such traditional male skills as archery. But many Indians accepted the argument that their new life promised greater comfort and—more important—less hostility from white settlers.

For the time being, a worrisome contradiction was ignored: Tribes were being encouraged to become dependent on farming the land even as the federal government was urging them to sell it.

The Cherokees may have signed away their first parcel of land in 1721, when the governor of South Carolina negotiated a trade treaty with chiefs from thirty-seven towns throughout Cherokee country. But change was occurring in other ways. When Cherokee shamans could not protect the tribe against a 1738 smallpox epidemic, the tribe was cut to seventeen thousand, and shamans lost much of their hold over the survivors.

William Fyffe, a white South Carolinian traveling among the tribe in 1761, set down his impressions: The Cherokees were straight-limbed and taller than whites. Fyffe considered them to be amiable enough but indolent after the hunting season had ended. He also noted that the men "have no hair on their chin or lips, and both sexes shave it off their privities."

Fyffe found the Cherokees taciturn in public assemblies, and he heard them mock the Europeans for being so quick to offer an opinion. They paid great deference to the judgment of their elders, but if they got hold of enough rum, they might stay drunk for a week.

As warriors, their strengths were vigilance, hardiness, and a keen sense for tracking their enemies. Going to battle, they marched from the village in their finest attire before accepting their oldest clothes from their squaws—"a blanket and arse clout"—for the fighting itself. Afterward, they returned to the village to mourn the dead and rejoice over their success.

Fyffe passed on rumors from their white adversaries about the way Cherokees treated the men they took prisoner. They did not mistreat them during the march home, he wrote, but once they arrived in their village, their friends "who came out to congratulate them think they show their love by beating & bruising the prisoners."

After that, prisoners were distributed as slaves to the relatives of braves killed in battle. Families that thirsted for more revenge could condemn the prisoner to death at the stake in a scene Fyffe described as more horrid than an auto-da-fé.

But to be fair-minded, Fyffe added that one must consider Europe and the way that poor wretches "should be so barbarously murder'd because they're born Jews."

In the decades before the Revolutionary War, British traders had won the chiefs away from their original French trading partners and persuaded them to back Great Britain against America. During the war itself, a revolutionary soldier in the Smoky Mountains named John Sevier successfully led American forces against the Cherokees and their British allies; Sevier later became Tennessee's first governor.

Two years after the American victory in 1783, the Cherokees concluded a pact with the fledgling United States. Even as they were signing, however, their chiefs protested that three thousand white settlers had already encroached on their land, for which they were receiving no compensation. In place of money, the United States agreed to extend to the Cherokees the protection of the federal government.

Within four years, America's secretary of war was complaining that Southern white homesteaders had disregarded the government promises. George Washington, newly elected as president, reported that five hundred white families were living on land that rightfully belonged to the Cherokees.

Washington said he hoped to civilize the Indians and prepare them for full citizenship; but he wondered whether Indians could ever coexist with the white settlers and land speculators who were already pushing westward. He predicted a clash between the Indians and "a few avaricious men" that could result "in a great deal of bloodshed." And, Washington asked, "For what?"

In 1792, Washington issued a proclamation offering a reward of five hundred dollars for the capture of any of the "lawless and wicked persons" who had recently destroyed a Cherokee town and killed several Indians. He denounced the crime because it "not only violates the rights of humanity, but also endangers the public peace."

Washington's successors considered keeping the peace their highest goal. But they also wanted to be seen as both law-abiding and compassionate. Long before he became president, Thomas Jefferson had tried to allay the misgivings of Europeans about his nation's Indian policy. To one friend, he wrote in 1786, "It may be regarded as certain that not one foot of land will be taken from the Indians without their own consent. The sacredness of their rights is felt in America as much as in Europe."

Fifteen years later, Jefferson's position had changed: Tribes that would not adapt to the white man's ways must be either enticed or driven to move as far west as the Rocky Mountains, and he hatched a plan that confirmed his opponents' view of him as sly and underhanded. "We shall push our trading houses," Jefferson suggested, and watch happily as the most influential chieftains run up large debts. "When these debts get beyond what the individual can pay," Indians will be willing to settle their obligation by ceding lands to the administration in Washington.

"If the United States could be creditor to enough Indians," Jefferson continued, their tribal lands would gradually shrink, and they would either agree to become American citizens or move past the Mississippi River. The trading marts Jefferson envisioned did become a feature of federal Indian policy, but the result was too slow for impatient white settlers.

To speed the process during Jefferson's first term, the state of Georgia tried a more direct approach with the Compact of 1802. Georgia turned over to the federal government its western territory—rich farmland that would become Alabama and Mississippi. In return, the Jefferson administration would pay off the speculators who were occupying that land under charters awarded by corrupt state legislators. The federal government also agreed to buy up all Creek and Cherokee land within the redrawn Georgia state lines. That purchase would take place as soon as reasonable and peaceful terms could be reached with the tribes.

Before signing the Compact on April 26, 1802, Jefferson did not consult with the Indians. And because the treaty's terms were not immediately enforced, their legality went untested.

A Cherokee named simply Ridge found himself torn between endorsing the white man's treaties and enforcing his tribe's blood law. Ridge's grandfather had been a Highland Scot, a trader who returned to Europe and left behind a Cherokee wife and daughter. Raised as a Cherokee in eastern Tennessee, Ridge had laughed in disbelief when he heard that his grandfather had often spoken to God as though he were talking to a personal guardian. Cherokees knew the Great Spirit was nothing like that.

The Europeans who followed William Fyffe to Cherokee country agreed with him that they were an amiable and well-proportioned people. They found Cherokee women, with their olive skin and small hands and feet, remarkably attractive. Records indicated that as far back as 1690, a white Virginia trader named Alexander Dougherty had taken a Cherokee bride.

Europeans commented on the Cherokee habit of not looking directly into the eyes of another person and of speaking so softly they often had to repeat what they had said. To the white man's ear, everyday Cherokee speech could sound like singing. When they got hold of liquor, the men might drink too much, but they forgave one another any offense committed while drunk, except murder.

Unsympathetic white observers regarded one habit as particularly "savage." The Cherokees had no fixed time for meals. They ate only when they were hungry.

Ridge's English name had come from the neighboring mountains. In Cherokee, he was Nun-na-dihi—He Who Slays the Enemy in the Path. Throughout his teens, he had sometimes joined in terrorizing white settlers on their neighboring farms, but by his twenties, he had settled down and courted Sehoya, a good-looking girl of mixed blood often called Susanna Wickett. With Ridge's imposing height and heavy features, he commanded an easy respect within the Cherokee council. His frown could be intimidating, but Susanna saw a softer side.

The couple was married at the council house in Pine Log village, attended by their families and the local shaman. The service was simple. Susanna took Ridge's ceremonial blanket from his hand and clasped it to her own. At that, the town chieftain stepped forward to say, "The blankets joined," and Ridge had taken a wife.

As his hair turned white, Ridge became a dominant voice on the local council, and he could expand his modest holdings. He continued to hunt for animal hides while Susanna worked at a loom sent by the federal government. When the cloth produced by the village women proved profitable, Ridge bought a few slaves so he could harvest even more cotton for their weaving.

Raw cotton had become a prized commodity and one more reason for white settlers to covet Indian land. Farmers were turning their tobacco fields over to the far more lucrative crop with the white flowers that dropped as cotton bolls. In a good year, a five-hundred-pound bale could fetch $145, and Georgia's expanding crop made the state the world's largest cotton producer. Men were calling it, with due respect, "King Cotton."

Susanna gave birth to four children who survived; the third child, Walter, was born weak-minded. At about the time that she gave birth to a son and named him John, another boy was born to Ridge's shy brother—a religious convert who had shortened his surname from Oo-watie to Watie and taken David as his Christian name. David Watie christened his boy "Buck." In 1806, Buck Watie was joined by a brother, called in Cherokee Ta-Ker-Taw-Ker. Since that name translated to "Stand firm," he became Stand Watie.

Ridge and Susanna also had two daughters, Nancy and Sarah, and as their names suggested, Ridge had grown increasingly comfortable in white society. He bought a buggy for his horses and built a smoke house for hams and a cellar for cider.

Then, in 1807, a grasping chief named Doublehead was discovered to be taking bribes and selling off Cherokee land without tribal approval. Ridge already disliked him because of a raid that Doublehead once led against a small white settlement at Cavitts Station, a few miles west of Knoxville. Doublehead had promised to spare the post if the three men living there surrendered. When they did, he went back on his word and ordered the slaughter of everyone, including thirteen women and children. Sickened, Ridge had turned away from the scene. Now he agreed to join a group of young Cherokee leaders who were determined to punish Doublehead for betraying the tribe.

One night as Doublehead was sitting drunk in a tavern, Ridge approached him and blew out the candle on his table. In the darkness, Ridge shot him through the jaw below his ear.

After he had slipped away, Ridge learned that his bullet had not been fatal. With an accomplice, Alexander Saunders, he returned and tracked Doublehead to his hiding place. In the struggle that followed, Saunders drove his tomahawk so far into Doublehead's head that he had to brace his foot against the dying man's chest to pull it out.

Ridge confronted the crowd that had gathered and explained why Doublehead had to die. No one was arrested for the murder.

But the following year, Cherokees became increasingly divided between those who wanted to sell more tribal land and those who insisted on staying on it. Some Indians had been accepting Jefferson's offer to exchange their holdings for land from the Louisiana Purchase, and they were establishing a Cherokee Nation West in what would become Arkansas.

When Ridge's Cherokee council debated whether the entire tribe should join the move, he gave a powerful speech against the migration: "I scorn this movement of a few men to unsettle the nation and trifle with our attachment to the land of our forefathers."

Ridge then joined a delegation that headed for Washington City to lay the matter before Jefferson in the final months of his presidency. Riding through South Carolina and Virginia, they reached the city in time to see slaves constructing the U.S. Capitol.

Receiving them courteously, Jefferson endorsed the idea of separating those chiefs who favored "agriculture and civilization" from those who resisted the change. Tribes that did not want to assimilate should migrate west to the Arkansas River, the president said. That way they could avoid further contact with white people. But Ridge had already shed blood to stop the selling of ancestral land through rogue treaties. Back home again, his strenuous opposition helped to quash sentiment for the move.

Ridge's defense of his Indian heritage did not mean a break with European culture. As an observer, he had joined the nearby Creeks when Tecumseh, the Shawnee chieftain, came south to urge them to spurn the white man's civilization. Give up the plows and the looms, Tecumseh exhorted them, even the use of tables and the adoption of cats as house pets. Become true Indians again and prepare to fight to defend your land.

Observers said that after the speech Ridge faced down Tecumseh and warned him that if he tried to spread his message among the Cherokees, Ridge would kill him.

But many younger Creeks had been impressed by Tecumseh. Called Red Sticks, they began to raid white communities, and in the War of 1812 they took the side of Great Britain in hopes that the British might protect them from the constant encroachment of American settlers.

Ridge remained loyal to the United States. He volunteered his Cherokee warriors to the Tennessee militia led by Andrew Jackson.

At first, the administration of James Madison, Jefferson's successor as president, had declined his offer in order to avoid warfare among the nation's tribes. But as the Creek threat grew, Madison's War Office reversed its policy and welcomed Ridge and his volunteers. Setting off for battle, the Cherokees stuck two white feathers in their headbands to distinguish them from the Creeks they would be fighting.

By the time Ridge joined the war, the army of William Henry Harrison had killed Tecumseh in fighting at the Thames River in Michigan. His dream of tribal unity died with him. Tecumseh was survived by his younger brother, Tenskawatawa, an unstable mystic called the Prophet, but he had already been discredited for predicting an Indian victory before the Shawnee defeat at Tippecanoe. With Tecumseh gone, the Prophet fled to Canada.

Before their first battle, Cherokee recruits gathered at a site called Turkey Town on the Coosa River in upper Alabama to hear an inspirational talk from Colonel Return Jonathan Meigs. Born in Connecticut, Meigs was a longtime federal Indian agent who had aggressively pushed the U.S. policy of acquiring Indian land by any means. Meigs had bribed every chief he found receptive, including Doublehead. Only a few leaders like Ridge rejected his cash.

Cherokees called Meigs "White Eagle" for his thatch of white hair, and they had heard the romantic legend that Meigs's given names had come from his grandmother's call to her suitor after they quarreled and he stomped away: "Return, Jonathan."

The Cherokees gave Meigs credit for rousting white squatters on Indian land and for dealing firmly with James Vann, a wealthy mixed-blood brute who got drunk regularly and threatened his neighbors. Meigs showed the same spirit when the first white Moravian missionaries were granted permission to live within Cherokee territory. The Northerners saw their role as converting Indians and not merely teaching their heathen youths. But Meigs said he would evict them if they did not raise their enlistment of Cherokee students.

In 1809, Meigs had overseen a meticulous census, showing that

12,395 Cherokees lived in Cherokee Nation, along with 314 whites and 535 Negro slaves. Their switch from hunting to farming meant replacing their traditional slaves—Indians from conquered tribes—with black slaves to work their plantations. Missionaries who arrived from New England were often appalled to find Cherokees buying and selling Negro families. But like their white competitors, the chiefs claimed the economy left them no choice.

Besides, they said, slaves preferred life among the Indians to serving white masters.

As Ridge's Cherokee recruits faced their first battle, Colonel Meigs promised food, weapons, and, if necessary, medical treatment. In return, he said, "it will be expected that you will be obedient to every order and regulation" of the federal government. Meigs would permit the Cherokees to take slaves but demanded that they treat their Creek prisoners humanely.

Acting on that policy, Ridge celebrated an early skirmish by sending to his home several Negroes who had been Creek slaves. The men would work in his cotton fields; a young Creek girl would serve in his household.

Rallying at Horseshoe Bend on the Tallapoosa River for the decisive battle of the Creek War, Ridge was joined by John Ross, a young man who considered himself a Cherokee although he was pale-skinned, blue-eyed, and seven-eighths white. Also on hand were David Crockett, a militia volunteer, and Sam Houston, a white youth besotted with the Cherokee way of life. When the battle ended in violent hand-to-hand fighting, Jackson's officers credited Ridge with killing six Creeks.

Soon afterward, Ridge was granted a personal meeting with Jackson, who promoted him on the spot from being an unofficial militia lieutenant. Ridge proudly adopted his new rank as his first name and, for the rest of his life, became Major Ridge.

Despite the triumph, Ridge and his Cherokees returned home to find only desolation. As they rode to battle, Jackson's white militia had swept through the Indian towns, stealing horses, slaughtering cattle, and stealing whatever they could carry off.

In the aftermath of Horseshoe Bend, some Creeks escaped to the south, but otherwise Jackson had crushed their nation and put an end to Indian defiance. To vanquish the holdouts, Jackson risked Washington's censure by pursuing them into Florida, and Major Ridge joined his expedition briefly.

Back in Tennessee, Jackson drafted treaties that were not generous in victory. Over the next months, he used his new prestige to impose pacts that not only confiscated land from Creeks who had fought against him but also seized millions of acres from those Creeks who had remained loyal to the United States. When Colonel Meigs testified to the plundering of Cherokee towns by white militia, Jackson branded the charges "one complete tissue of groundless falsehood."

Jackson's treaty of 1814 claimed half of the Creek Nation for the federal government—23 million acres of valuable cotton land across Georgia and southern Alabama. As a concession, his agreement called for friendly Creeks to be paid for their property, estimated to be worth $195,417.90. By the time John Quincy Adams was sworn in as president, Congress had appropriated $85,000.

Three years after the start of the War of 1812, a peace treaty specifically pardoned the western tribes that had fought for the British. Given that promising development, Ridge returned to Washington as a Cherokee delegate pressing claims for the damage to tribal property. The tribe also instructed him to negotiate a good price for a tract of land that the Madison administration wanted the Cherokees to cede to South Carolina.

Meeting with the chiefs, President Madison offered polite reassurances about the future, but his negotiators' sharp bargaining led the

Cherokees to accept only $25,000 for their losses in the Creek War and another $5,000 for the South Carolina land.

Even that sop infuriated Andrew Jackson. Major Ridge was already marking new boundaries in the disputed territory when Jackson's explosive protests against any modification of his treaties compelled Madison to reopen negotiations.

Ridge boycotted the subsequent meeting with Jackson, but the fifteen chiefs and warriors who attended gave way to Jackson's passion—and his bribes. They signed away a disputed 1.3 million acres south of the Tennessee River for an immediate $5,000, plus $60,000 to be paid over ten years.

Jackson argued that he was giving realistic support to the Indians who had fought at his side. As he pondered their future, Jackson ended a statement to the House of Representatives early in 1818 by saying that either "those sons of the forest should be moralized or exterminated." Jackson knew which choice he preferred: "Humanity would rejoice at the former, but shrink with horror from the latter."

To accomplish that better way, Jackson repeated the proposal of most white politicians before him. He called for a civilizing process that would expose Indian children to the primer and the hoe. "And they will naturally, in time, take hold of the plow; and, as their minds become enlightened and expand, the Bible will be their book, and they will grow in habits of morality and industry, leave the chase to those whose minds are less cultivated, and become useful members of society."

Over the next years, Jackson inveigled more land concessions from the Cherokees and from remnants of the Chickasaw tribe in eastern Tennessee. Throughout a succession of treaties and land sales, Ridge continued to challenge Jackson and his allies but with little success. In 1819, the struggle to maintain their territory caused the Cherokee Council to revoke the citizenship of any Indian who accepted a reservation off their traditional land. It was a harsh penalty, but it did not discourage one band of Cherokees, who severed their ties with the council and settled along the Oconaluftee River in North Carolina.

The next year, the Choctaws of Mississippi balked at giving up five million acres of cotton land along the western border of the state. At a meeting, Jackson treated them to a virtuoso performance. He extolled the Arkansas property they would be getting in return: "A country of tall trees, many water courses, rich lands and high grass abounding in game of all kinds—buffalo, bear, elk, deer, antelope, beaver and turkeys . . ."

Pushmataha, a revered Choctaw chief, had fought with Jackson against the Creeks and again at New Orleans. But he had also seen this promised land. At fifty-six, Pushmataha was three years older than Jackson, although he began by saying that in the general's presence, he "always felt myself a mere boy." Yet he was compelled to report that "the grass is everywhere very short, and for the game there is not plenty, except buffalo and deer." Honey and fruit were rare, and many white men were already living on the land.

Despite that testimony, Jackson carried the day with more promises and finally with the threat that if the Choctaw refused, their nation "will be destroyed." On October 18, 1820, the Treaty of Doak's Stand was signed. In Mississippi, a state for only the past three years, jubilant citizens showed their gratitude by naming their capital Jacksonville.

By the end of his negotiations, Jackson had provided white settlers with some fifty million acres that had recently belonged to the Indians. In the process, he confirmed George Washington's prediction about the avarice of speculators, and Jackson himself proved adept at snapping up potentially valuable land.

In his dealings, Jackson was aided by John Coffee, an able commander at both Horseshoe Bend and New Orleans. Coffee was also Jackson's nephew by marriage, and Jackson contrived to get him an appointment as a government surveyor. Coffee made both of them rich by buying land cheap and splitting the bribes he received from other speculators with clerks in the federal Land Office. In two highly lucrative deals, Jackson bought hundreds of acres with no competitive bidding, and Coffee paid $4.75 an acre when the market price was upward of $40 an acre.

Increasingly disillusioned with the white man's leaders, Major Ridge continued to share their faith in education, and he sent his children and his nephew, Buck, to study with a Moravian missionary couple. But John and Anna Gambold could not convert Ridge himself to Christianity. He retained his belief in the Immortals, those spirits that intervened to help the Cherokees in their darkest hour, and he trusted to the Little People, no higher than his knee, who had their own magical powers.

And yet Brother John and Sister Anna impressed Ridge enough that he confessed to them his feelings of remorse for the murder he had committed. "I've resolved never to do such a thing again," he assured the missionaries. "Unless the Council orders me to rid the world of a bad man, as the case was with Doublehead."

When Ridge hired a white tutor and took his children to study at home, the Gambolds were not entirely sorry to see young John leave. "Because for all his skill for learning," they noted, "he is real *proud to be a savage.*"

Publishing a report from Cherokee country, the *Boston Record* gave its readers a taste of what missionaries were confronting when they went south. The story included dialogue that took place between a Northern clergyman and a Cherokee woman, "very decent in her appearance," who had come to his mission for the first time.

Asked if she had many thoughts about God, the Great Spirit, the woman replied, "I do not think much about him."

Did she regard herself as a sinner? "No."

Where would her spirit be when her body died? "I do not know it would be anywhere."

"In short," the clergyman noted, "she appeared to have thought very little on these most important subjects."

It required a lengthy conversation, he added, "before she said she believed she was a sinner."

Although Major Ridge was impervious to Christian preaching, he wanted his children to have the education that the Gambolds offered. His oldest daughter, Nancy, was gone—married to an Indian, then dying in childbirth. And Ridge's choice as schoolmaster turned out to drink heavily, and he left after three months. To teach John, now fifteen, what he would require to lead the Cherokee Nation, Ridge packed him off to the Foreign Mission School in Cornwall, Connecticut.

Since the Creek War, a remnant of the Creeks had been quarreling with the Cherokees over that perennial sticking point—the selling of tribal land. By the early 1820s, the state of Georgia was demanding that the federal government enforce the agreement of 1802 that eliminated all Indian claims within its state boundaries.

U.S. Chief Justice John Marshall supported the state's argument by ruling in 1823 that the United States had adopted a British law that favored the Georgians. Marshall held that the state owned the territory by "right of discovery." The Indians merely lived on it by a lesser "right of occupancy." Marshall's opinion endorsed the state's claim that Indians were simply Georgia's "dependent tenants."

The setback required the Cherokees to devise a new strategy. They would now be dealing with an Indian agent named Joseph McMinn, who had been appointed after Colonel Meigs caught cold and died earlier in the year, and McMinn was arriving to negotiate a new treaty.

The Cherokees' final judgment on Meigs had been tempered by a proposal he had once floated for resolving the constant tension between Indians and whites. The Cherokees "should begin to fight their own battles of life," Meigs wrote, and give up the government support that only made them more dependent. He estimated that the tribe possessed ten million acres of land in Georgia, North Carolina, and Tennessee. Since their population numbered about two thousand families, they could flourish on 640 acres per family.

Because that distribution would require only 1,280,000 acres, it would leave 8 million acres to be sold. The proceeds could be spent on housing, fencing, and clearing land to make individual properties profitable. At that point, the Cherokees "should be vested with the rights, privileges and immunities of citizens" of the three states in which they lived.

Meigs's proposal was never considered seriously in Washington.

Joseph McMinn was a different sort of agent. As governor of Tennessee, he had joined with Jackson in imposing punitive treaties after the Creek War. He had regularly inflamed white settlers with reports of threats against his own life and once succeeded in forcing the government to send troops to intimidate a Cherokee Council meeting. Now McMinn could expect to be supported in these latest negotiations by officials from Georgia and by U.S. commissioners from Washington.

The session began amicably until the Georgians announced that they intended to enforce the commitments from two decades earlier. At that, Major Ridge and his chiefs held firm against any concessions. The Georgians coaxed and threatened, but even with their offer of cash bribes they did not prevail.

The stalemate was broken only when General William McIntosh appeared at the bargaining table. Half of McIntosh's ancestors were Creek, but on his mother's side he was a cousin of Georgia's governor George Michael Troup. McIntosh had fought along with Jackson against the dissident members of his tribe and had gone on to win his high rank by fighting the Seminoles in Florida. Despite his Indian ancestry, McIntosh was committed to the U.S. position on the new treaty.

Moving among the adamant Cherokees, McIntosh warned them that the white man's lust for Indian lands was insatiable. "By and by, he will take them and the little band of people, poor and despised, will be left to wander without homes and be beaten like dogs," McIntosh predicted. Better to sell now, move to new territory, "and learn to live like the white man."

When that argument was not persuasive, McIntosh reverted to the seduction of cash. On October, 21, 1823, he dictated a letter that his son wrote for him, promising two thousand dollars to young John Ross, as an emerging Cherokee leader. McIntosh said he could offer the same amount to the Cherokee Council clerk. A third man, who had served for many years as Colonel Meigs's interpreter, could expect three thousand.

Nor was that all. Any friend whom Ross could convert to the Georgians' position "shall receive the same amount." Georgia's agents had set aside twelve thousand dollars for bribes, and Ross could divide the rest among his friends. McIntosh assured Ross that "nobody shall know it."

Ross was amazed by the brazenness of McIntosh's approach. He asked Major Ridge and another respected Cherokee to confirm with McIntosh that the U.S. commissioners knew of the offer. McIntosh not only assured Ridge on that point but boasted of money he had already pocketed from previous treaties.

Ridge and the others agreed that the entire council must hear of McIntosh's corruption. He enjoyed high standing among the Creeks, but after they had exposed him even the venerable chief called Pathfinder—who outranked them all—would not rise in his defense.

The Cherokees invited McIntosh to a joint meeting of the two tribes. When he showed up, they ushered him in with the usual courtesy, but once they were seated, John Ross brandished McIntosh's letter. He said it would speak for itself and that "the author has mistaken my character and my sense of honor."

The council clerk read the letter in English and translated its meaning. After he finished, Pathfinder rose in the silence and asked sadly for McIntosh's response. When McIntosh stumbled over his explanation, Pathfinder said, "Set him aside."

Major Ridge then recounted the history of his military campaigns with McIntosh. But now, he concluded, "I cast him behind my back." Ridge added that he did not consider the entire Creek tribe disgraced by McIntosh's actions.

With emotions running high, the meeting broke up, and McIntosh rode off furiously. One of the U.S. commissioners objected to the way the Cherokees had treated the Creek chief. He warned that his federal delegation might not be coming back since the U.S. president would "have to learn his children better manners."

Had McIntosh understood John Ross's character, he would not have tried to compromise his loyalty to the tribe. His family traced their bloodline to a Scot, William Shorey, and his full-blooded Cherokee wife, Ghigooie. Shorey had first come to America in the mid-1700s and become fluent in the Cherokee language. He died in 1762, on a return voyage from England, where he had served as interpreter for a Cherokee delegation in London. He left behind a daughter—John Ross's grandmother—who married a Highland Scot named John McDonald.

A slick operator, McDonald played the British, Americans, and Spaniards against one another as he built a booming trade on Cherokee land near what became Chattanooga. His daughter Mollie married Daniel Ross and bore him nine children; John was the third child and oldest son.

Like the young Sam Houston, who preferred Indian society to living with his white family, John Ross became entirely assimilated into Cherokee life. He never forgot his humiliation during a green corn dance when his mother dressed him as a little white gentleman. The next day, he insisted on wearing an Indian outfit.

But Ross's father imported a white schoolmaster for the education of John and his brother, Lewis, and when they were old enough, he shipped them to an academy in Kingston, Tennessee. On graduating, John and Lewis Ross joined a son of R. J. Meigs in opening their own trading post. John strengthened his ties with the tribe by marrying Quatie, a full-blooded Cherokee.

Although Ross had fought for Jackson at Horseshoe Bend, he had come to see the wisdom in Tecumseh's attempt to unite tribes from across the country. Joining with other men of mixed blood, Ross founded a select group within the Cherokee Council called the National Committee and in 1819 became its president.

Ross's alliance with Major Ridge—and, in time, with Ridge's son and nephew—seemed unshakable.

The break with McIntosh had alerted other Cherokees to the need for a fresh diplomatic mission to Washington. On January 5, 1824, John Calhoun, President Monroe's secretary of war, escorted Ridge and the other delegates into the whitewashed executive mansion to meet with Monroe and Secretary of State John Quincy Adams. Dry and precise in his own language, Adams was struck by Major Ridge's florid oratory and his frequent references to the Great Spirit.

When the ceremonial visit ended, Calhoun led the Indians back to his office for the negotiations he intended to oversee. Along with his reputation for brilliance, Calhoun was known for imposing his will on fellow politicians. He had joined with Henry Clay in 1812 as one of the congressional War Hawks who pumped up support for a second war with Great Britain. But now, as he explored the position of the Cherokees, he found that they matched him in determination. They would give up no more land.

"Sir," the Indian delegation wrote to Calhoun in English, "we beg leave to remind you that the Cherokees are not foreigners but the original inhabitants of the United States." They assured Calhoun that neither the offer of twice as much territory west of the Mississippi nor all of the money in the U.S. Treasury would induce them to sell their native land.

Calhoun found himself caught between the unyielding chiefs and Georgia's indignant representatives, who had objected even to Calhoun's referring to the Cherokee delegates as "gentlemen." Addressing the Georgia legislature, Governor Troup had attacked the Cherokee Council as "an independent government of a semibarbarous people" and predicted open warfare if the current situation, "a state of things so unnatural and fruitful of evil," were allowed to continue.

In a letter to President Monroe, Georgia's officials underlined the governor's threat: The federal government must teach the Indians, "these misguided men," that there was "no alternative between their removal beyond the limits of the State of Georgia and their extinction."

To Secretary Adams, that intemperate language fell just short of accusing the United States of fraud and of blaming Calhoun for the Cherokees' obstinacy. But Major Ridge took the bombast in stride: "It is a very hot talk—I suppose it was intended for the people at home."

In the White House, Monroe held firm against the Georgians' onslaught. Reviewing the history of the last quarter-century, he concluded that the Indians' title to land was not affected by whatever Georgia might claim and that the United States had no obligation to remove the Indians by force. But Monroe also shared the sentiments of the presidents who preceded him—the tribes should move west voluntarily.

Georgians were suggesting that white men had written the Cherokee statements for them, but when the Indians restated their position and appealed to the fairness of the American people, Adams was impressed by their command of English. "They write their own state papers," he observed, "and reason as logically as most white diplomats."

Adams also noted that the Indians' clothes and manners compared favorably with those of anyone in Washington. "They dress like ourselves," he wrote in his diary, except for one "young and very handsome man" who always wore an ornamental scarf. In a gesture of hospitality, Louisa Adams invited the Cherokees to her Tuesday evening receptions, and they were asked to White House soirees.

But despite the Indians' social success, Congress voted funds for sending another commission to Georgia to explore further ways of obtaining the disputed land. Calhoun was feeling swamped by the time-consuming controversy and began to look for bureaucratic relief.

White-haired and affable, Thomas Loraine McKenney had once been superintendent of Indian trade and had envisioned a day when Indians and white men could live in peace. But first, he had written, his countrymen must change their preconceptions. That would mean "Indians be looked upon as human beings, having bodies and souls like ours."

To John Jacob Astor—reputed to be the richest man in America—McKenney's approach was heresy. He particularly resented

McKenney's support for frontier factories that would lessen a tribe's dependence on Astor's American Fur Company.

Astor had an ally in Missouri senator Thomas Hart Benton, who denounced McKenney for fraud and mismanagement. In 1822, Congress abolished McKenney's job, clearing the way for Astor's fur company to dominate western trade. Without a salary, McKenney was financially strapped during the time he campaigned for Calhoun in the 1824 elections. In return, Calhoun used his position as secretary of war to open a new Bureau of Indian Affairs and appointed McKenney to head it. The bureau had a staff of two clerks and a messenger.

In an effort to persuade official Washington to see the chieftains as he did, McKenney commissioned a leading New England artist to produce portraits of them in full tribal regalia whenever they visited the capital. To pay for each painting, McKennedy scraped together the twenty-dollar commission.

At home, the tribes found that they had not seen the last of General McIntosh. Although the Creeks had stripped him of all authority, he met secretly with the U.S. commissioners on February 12, 1825, at Indian Springs, Georgia. During that meeting, McIntosh accepted a lavish bribe of land on the Chattahoochee river from U.S. Commissioners Duncan G. Campbell and James Meriwether. In return, McIntosh convinced a few Indians still loyal to him to join in signing away the remaining Creek land in Georgia, along with several million acres in Alabama. McIntosh's allies represented only eight of the forty-six towns covered by the treaty.

The pact at Indian Springs also granted the fervent wish of white Georgians by compelling the Creeks to move west of the Mississippi.

McIntosh did not sign blindly. A fellow chief said to him, "My friend, you are about to sell your country. I now warn you of your danger."

McIntosh reported the chief's threat to the federal commissioners. He reminded them that his tribe's blood law could mean that he might pay for his signature with his life.

John Quincy Adams

3 · John Quincy Adams (1825–27)

President Adams first suspected that the Treaty of Indian Springs was fraudulent because of complaints from Indian Agent Colonel John Crowell, who pointed out that General McIntosh was not authorized to deal on behalf of the Creeks. Crowell also noted that Campbell and Meriwether, who claimed to have negotiated with the full Creek Council, were both Georgians.

The treaty's terms were simple: "The Creek nation" would surrender all of its land in Georgia in return for equal acreage west of the Mississippi, plus a bonus of $400,000 and certain annuities. The agreement went on to reward the citizens of Georgia beyond that gift of Indian land: The U.S. Congress would pay $109,000 to reimburse them for the loss of ninety-two slaves who had escaped to Florida.

The treaty gave the Creeks a year and a half to evacuate and stipulated that no survey of their land would be allowed before September 1, 1826. A provision also promised that the federal government would protect "against the encroachments, hostilities and impositions of the whites."

Despite Crowell's objections, the treaty awaiting Adams's signature had been approved overwhelmingly by the U.S. Senate after a minimum of discussion.

In Georgia, however, his white constituents were pressing Governor Troup not to wait eighteen months to enforce the treaty. Troup shared both their impatience and their antagonism to the federal government. His dedication to the cause of states' rights harked back to his earliest days in politics.

Born in 1780, Troup had been raised in Savannah before being sent north to a preparatory school and then to Princeton when it was called the College of New Jersey. Short but husky, Troup was a striking figure with his red hair and intense blue eyes. Upon graduation in 1797, Troup adopted an eye-catching style of dress—blue coat with brass buttons, vest, and a fur cap. He wore summer clothes on freezing days and a cloak at the height of summer.

Throughout the War of 1812, Troup had represented Georgia, first in the House, then in the Senate. His commitment to the supremacy of state government brought him to the attention of William Crawford, who selected him to run for governor. Troup lost twice before winning by a narrow margin in an election that was seen as a victory for Georgia's plantation owners over its subsistence farmers.

When Lafayette's American tour took him to the banks of the Savannah River, Governor Troup treated him to a proud recounting of his state's progress: "Welcome, Lafayette!" Troup cried. "Tis little more than ninety years since the founder of this state first set foot on the banks on which you stand. Today, some 400,000 people open their arms and hearts to receive you."

Troup believed that the North American continent rightfully belonged to its white settlers, and he backed the construction of new canals and roads, along with an expansion in public education. When Troup urged his cousin, General McIntosh, to undertake an immediate survey of Creek land, McIntosh was ready to oblige.

But on the morning of April 30, 1825, two hundred Creek men stole up to the McIntosh plantation on the banks of the Chattahoochee and spread kindling around its buildings. They ignited bonfires, and when smoke drove McIntosh's wives and his children outside, they were allowed to escape. An older son called Chillie dived out a window and made it to safety in the river.

Through a second-story window, the Creeks caught sight of McIntosh brandishing a rifle. As he came down the stairs, they fired a round of shots that dropped him to his knees. But they were not content to watch him burn to death inside his house.

Several Creeks ran past the flames to pull out his body. Bleeding profusely, McIntosh raised himself on an arm and was glaring at them when a Creek stabbed him in the heart with a long knife. Even though McIntosh was clearly dead, other Creeks shot him in the head more than fifty times.

They found McIntosh's chief lieutenant in a second building, killed him, and destroyed the horses and cattle. McIntosh's wives asked for a suit for burying him, but his executioners insisted he be thrown into his grave naked.

When the Cherokees heard about the Creeks' vengeance, McIntosh went unmourned. A newspaper quoted one of John Ridge's young friends as saying that the general's death had given the Cherokees universal satisfaction: "I say *satisfaction*, the same that is felt when a dangerous rattlesnake is killed."

Chillie McIntosh was determined, however, to see his father avenged. Two weeks after the murder, he was in President Adams's office, presenting a letter from Governor Troup that blamed the federal government for not protecting McIntosh. Troup accused John Crowell of inciting the Creeks to violence and demanded that he be fired.

The governor couched his letter in extravagant language that was alien to Adams, and he found Troup's vow of revenge revealing "a spirit as ferocious as ever inspired by a Creek Indian." When Adams read Troup's prediction that McIntosh's death would set off a border war between whites and Creeks, the president dismissed the governor as a madman.

At the same time, Adams assured Chillie McIntosh that he was deeply depressed by his father's death. He advised the young man to consult with James Barbour, the man Adams had appointed to replace Calhoun as secretary of war. In all, Troup's letter had the opposite effect from what the governor intended. Adams did dispatch an army officer, Major Timothy P. Andrews, to Georgia to weigh the charges against Crowell, but he had become even more dubious about the Treaty of Indian Springs.

John Quincy Adams brought to his deliberations no particular sympathy for Indian culture. His frontier critics often pointed out that his character had been formed by New England and parents devoted to classical literature and the Bible. Entering adolescence, John had traveled with his father to Paris and gone on, at fourteen, to St. Petersburg as a secretary to America's representative in Russia. When he did return home, he had gravitated to Harvard—as a student and later as a professor.

But if Adams's cerebral nature left him unmoved by Indian pageantry and lore, he prided himself as president on obliging any chief who requested an audience. He had decided that receiving them made better use of his time than the hours he wasted with men seeking government jobs.

Now evidence was convincing Adams that the treaty he had signed was illegal. If so, the only honorable course was to revoke it. Then his government must find a way to protect Indian rights until a more satisfactory treaty could be drafted. Adams and Barbour sent that explicit instruction to the army commander in Georgia, General Edmund Pendleton Gaines. The general was another officer who had fought beside Jackson, this time in Florida, and he was reported to harbor a strong aversion to all Indians. But Gaines also had a reputation for being fair.

Adams directed the general to explore the Creeks' version of the controversy and keep the peace until a compromise could be reached. Adams was beginning to accept Troup's warning that the slaying of McIntosh could prove "the signal for a ferocious Indian war, bursting upon us like a thunderbolt."

On May 18, 1825, Adams met with Secretary Barbour, who began by reporting that Barbour's father had just died at the age of ninety. All the same, Barbour said, he had come into his office because of important developments in Georgia: John Crowell was reporting that Little Prince, a ranking Creek chieftain, had guaranteed that McIntosh's murder would not lead to hostilities against the whites. That reassurance led Adams to cut back General Gaines's authority and limit him to policing Georgia's frontier. For now, Adams and Barbour agreed not to answer the insulting letters that Governor Troup kept sending to Washington.

Another six weeks had passed when the Adams administration learned that Troup might be ready to carve up Creek lands. Countermanding the Georgia governor, Adams was careful to avoid seeming bellicose. Rather than have General Gaines's aide-de-camp hand Troup the president's cease-and-desist order, Adams considered it less confrontational to send the order by regular mail and let the local postmaster deliver it.

One method for disposing of the Creek land had not been challenged. Starting in 1805, Georgians had adopted a lottery system for assigning property, an attempt to end the corruption that had culminated in the Yazoo Land Fraud of the 1790s. Instead of backroom deals, land would be distributed by chance. Georgia became the only state to employ a large-scale lottery system, and Georgians were generally pleased with the fairness that resulted. After Jackson crushed the Creeks, he demanded that their land be added to the lotteries of 1820 and 1821.

Following the lottery of June 1827, however, the Creeks would have no more land to allocate. By that time, the size of a lot was 202½ acres, and the list of those qualified to draw for one was lengthy: Bachelors from age eighteen with a three-year residence in Georgia got a single draw, along with widows, male and female idiots, and lunatics. Married men and their wives got two draws. Deserters, shirkers of military service, and previous winners were excluded—as were Indians, although the official rules did not need to say so.

A lucky winner like a farmer named Jesse Carter could move immediately onto Creek territory west of the Flint River in Talbot County. The Carters were from old English stock with roots in America that dated back to Thomas Carter's arrival as a colonist in Virginia in 1637. In the mid-1780s, Jesse's parents had taken him and his older brother, James, from eastern North Carolina to Georgia, where both brothers prospered. They amassed a few hundred acres of land and, more valuably, a small number of slaves. As James was turning to cotton, however, Jesse was ready to move south, away from their father's holdings in McDuffie County, to make his home on his new Creek land. Among lottery winners like Carter, a ditty summed up their aspirations:

All I want in this creation
Is a pretty little wife and a big plantation.

And these days, as Georgians turned their eyes to Indian land, they were adding a line:

Way up yonder in the Cherokee Nation.

Divided and embittered by McIntosh's betrayal, Creek elders recognized that they needed experienced negotiators to present their strongest case to General Gaines. They settled on two young Cherokees admired for their education and their fluent command of English—John Ridge and David Vann. They would travel with the Creek leader, Opothle Yoholo, and prepare his negotiating position. The chief—whose name could be translated into English as Good Shouting Child—had fought as a teenager against Jackson in the Creek War.

Major Ridge had encouraged the Creeks to choose his son. He was pleased with John and the education he had received in Cornwall, Connecticut. At first, the presence of several young Cherokees at the Cornwall school had unsettled the local townspeople. But after they had inspected them at a public ceremony, the consensus was that "the Indian pupils appeared so genteel and graceful on the stage that the white pupils appeared uncouth beside them."

Long-faced and serious, with a crest of carefully tended black hair, John Ridge had become a student leader at the school until a lymphatic condition in one hip required him to leave the dormitory and board with a local family. There, John fell violently in love with the red-haired, fourteen-year-old daughter of the house, Sarah Bird Northrup. Like his late sister, the girl was called "Sally," and John had impressed her as well. When Sally's mother learned that the girl returned young Ridge's affections, however, she sent her to her grandparents in New Haven with a letter directing them to "introduce her to other gentlemen and try every way to get her mind off John Ridge." Sally retaliated with a hunger strike. After three weeks, her grandparents sent her home.

Not all resistance to the match came from Sally's family. Major

John Ridge

Ridge had in mind for John a Cherokee chieftain's daughter, and John's mother asked a Christian missionary to help her write a letter to deny the boy permission to marry Sally Northrup. The missionary agreed, pointing out that taking a white-skinned New England wife would make John Ridge less effective as a tribal leader since she "would be apt to feel above the common Cherokees."

But John's pleas were so compelling that his parents asked the missionary to draft a second letter giving their consent. By then, Sally's mother had found new reasons to object: Sally was too young, and John was ailing and hobbling on crutches. She would give her permission only if he recovered his full health. The young couple agreed to separate for two years.

At home on the Ridge plantation in 1822, John gained strength and renewed his ties with the Gambolds. But when he visited their school, he was displeased to find that his mother, along with many of the mission's students, had become Christian. John considered their conversion one more way that Indians were sacrificing their culture.

Yet, like his father, John embraced the value of education and ridiculed the fantasy of noble savages happiest in the wilds. Speaking to raise money for the mission school, John drew a bleak picture of life for an Indian "who walks solitary in the mountains, exposed to cold and hunger, or the attacks of wild beasts" and assured his audience that such a tribesman did not enjoy the contentment of "the poorest peasant in England."

John concluded his speech by claiming that only his listeners' charity could save the Indian from extinction. They responded by contributing two hundred dollars.

When John Ridge returned to Cornwall to claim Sally in December 1823, he still limped slightly, but his health was no longer a deterrent to their marriage. Now that the wedding was moving forward, however, the townspeople had become appalled, even though they could find no fault with John's prospects. When Major Ridge came to visit the Cornwall school, he arrived in a coat trimmed with gold lace and riding in "the most splendid carriage that had ever entered the town."

They objected instead to a white woman marrying an Indian, even one as light-skinned and literate as her fiancé. One young Cornwall woman ridiculed the bride-to-be in a series of satirical quatrains for expecting to lead an opulent life as queen of the Cherokees:

She would be disappointed of her home
To find a little, small wigwam,
And nothing allowed her for a bed,
But a dirty blanket, it is said.

After the wedding ceremony on January 27, 1824, the newlyweds were advised to slip out of town for fear of being mobbed. Hostile crowds jeered at the couple in every town they passed through on their way home, and a local newspaper denounced the disgrace of a girl "who has thus made herself a *squaw*."

With pressure mounting in the town, the Foreign Mission School issued a statement condemning mixed marriages, which complicated the courtship of John Ridge's cousin Buck Watie. His family was less prosperous than the Ridges; there would be no money to send his younger brother, Stand Watie, to Cornwall; and Buck himself had been able to attend only by changing his name.

The change had occurred while Buck was traveling north with several other Cherokee youths and members of an interdenominational missionary group called the American Board of Commissioners for Foreign Missions. Young men like Buck, presentable and speaking English, could expect to find hospitality in the homes of white sympathizers, while the prestige of the adults in the party, most of them Congregationalists, explained the dinner invitations they received from former presidents Jefferson and Madison.

Arriving in Burlington, New Jersey, Buck became the house guest of a distinguished seventy-eight-year-old public servant, Dr. Elias Boudinot. A member of the American Board, Boudinot had once presided over the Continental Congress before serving as director of the U.S. Mint for America's first three presidents. Childless, he was impressed with the fifteen-year-old Cherokee and offered to put him through school if Buck would agree to adopt the Boudinot name.

That was how Buck Watie had arrived at Cornwall as Elias Boudinot. Since the school encouraged Indian students to retain their heritage, the headmaster also entered Elias on the rolls under his Cherokee name of Kuh-le-ga-nah.

The young man found the transition to Northern life difficult. He wrote to assure the Gambolds that he was clinging to the Christian faith they had instilled in him but that he was painfully homesick. His cure came when he met Harriet Gold, the daughter of a white colonel who was a deacon in the Cornwall church.

The youngest of fourteen children, Harriet did not lack for suitors; even her brother-in-law, the Reverend Herman Vaill, doted on her in a decorous way. As an official at the Foreign Mission School, Vaill had learned from graffiti on a back pew that his sermons provoked a mixed

Elias Boudinot

Harriet Gold Boudinot

response: "The eloquence of Herman Vaill," one began, "would make the stoutest sinner quail." That praise had provoked a rebuttal: "The hissing goose has far more sense, than Vaill with all his eloquence."

The clergyman's style was on display in the note of mock sympathy he wrote to his sister-in-law, concluding with a play on her last name of Gold: "Poor Harriet, I am so sorry that you are so attractive, that every old bachelor who owns land near you & every old widower that comes along in search of minerals, should fix their eyes on you."

Like John Ridge, Elias had to drop out of school because of his health. He returned to the Cherokee Nation but wrote regularly to Harriet, and after two years she had made up her mind to marry him. In appearance, they seemed well matched, the same thin, tapering faces, alert eyes, and determined lips. Elias wore his long hair swept back; Harriet's hair, equally dark, set off her pale complexion. True, they were young—Elias twenty-one, Harriet nineteen. But Harriet's greatest apprehension came from anticipating the reaction of her twenty-three-year-old brother, Stephen.

To inform Stephen of her engagement, Harriet handed him a letter, slipped from the room, locked the door behind her, and told their mother not to let her brother out until he had quieted down.

When Stephen finished her letter, he began to scream, "Harriet! Harriet!"

She had gone upstairs to her own room. She refused to come out until his cries subsided and he promised to behave. But a few days later, Stephen Gold joined friends and neighbors on the village green to light a fire that burned his sister and Boudinot in effigy. At the same time, he conveyed the dire news to Vaill and other family members: "The dye is cast, Harriet is gone, we have reason to <u>fear</u>. Yes." She had announced "that she was engaged to that Indian E. and that she is determined to marry him. O!! dear!!! . . . Words cannot, no, let imagination <u>only express</u> the feelings of my heart."

Two weeks later, Harriet wrote her own anguished letter to Vaill and her sister, who had also denounced her engagement. She recounted how she had watched Stephen ignite her picture and then moved out of their house because she was told it was unsafe to stay. At church, she had been forced to give up her customary seat in the choir. Many friends had dropped her, but "the few friends I have are dearer to me than ever."

Harriet's spirit was unbroken: "I feel as though I had wronged no one. I have done nothing but what I had a perfect & lawful right to do."

The controversy spread beyond Cornwall. Another of Harriet's brothers-in-law, General Daniel Brinsmade, weighed in from Washington, D.C., hoping that the marriage could be forbidden. The husband of yet another sister, the Reverend Cornelius Everest, charged that Harriet was seeking only to "gratify" her "animal feelings."

Through it all, Harriet's mother stood by her and, after initial resistance, her father lent his wholehearted support. Nine months after the scandal broke, Elias and Harriet married in her parents' home at 2 p.m. on March 28, 1826. Stephen Gold still opposed marriage between Indians and whites, but his affection for his sister had overcome that sentiment, and they had reconciled. On the afternoon of the wedding, however, he went to work at his job in the sawmill to avoid the ceremony.

The marriages of Sally and Harriet endured; their school did not. The Reverend Vaill had proved prophetic when he pleaded with Harriet to consider the harm she was doing to the mission school, and the Reverend Everest had lamented, "Sad was the day when the mission school was planted in Cornwall." With this second marriage outraging the town, support for the Foreign Mission School dried up, and it closed its doors.

When Major Ridge established the pay for the young Cherokees who would be lobbying in Washington, he was openhanded for himself and his family. At a time when missionary teachers made less than $500 a year, he recommended a flat payment of $15,000 each for his son and the round-faced and curly-haired David Vann, who alternated between wearing tribal regalia and the white man's suits. For his own role, Major Ridge expected $10,000. Convinced of the value of his ties to Andrew Jackson, he wrote to remind Jackson of the battles they had shared: "When first we met we were taking the red path," Ridge began, "we waded in blood until the murders of our women and children had ceased." But Ridge went on to describe his tribe's feeling for "our great father, the president," expressing a greater regard for John Quincy Adams than Jackson was likely to feel.

The Creeks protested that Ridge's fees were too high. He reminded them of the amount of land at stake. Since the Creeks had no men who spoke English in their own ranks, they yielded. Young Ridge and Vann were instructed to prepare remarks for Opothle Yoholo's first meeting with General Gaines.

The speech they wrote struck a bold note. Historians later would point out that Ridge and Vann had expressed an early American version of passive resistance twenty-four years before Henry Thoreau's essay on civil disobedience.

The eloquence of their pledge moved even Gaines, who reported to Washington that they "in the strongest terms deliberately declared that they will not raise an arm against the United States, even should an army come to take from them the whole of their country—that they will make no sort of resistance, but will sit down quietly and be put to death, where the bones of their ancestors are deposited."

By their acceptance of death, the statement continued, the world would know that their tribesmen "so loved their country that they were willing to die in it rather than sell it or leave it."

Won over to the Creeks' position, Gaines hoped to work with them in reaching terms that would mollify the Georgians. But before the Creeks would agree to a new treaty, they wanted to meet with Gaines's superiors in Washington. The general assured them that President Adams would not deal on Creek affairs with two Cherokees. As a compromise, Ridge and Vann joined the delegation as secretaries.

To reach Washington, the fifteen Creeks and two Cherokees had to travel through the town of Milledgeville, then Georgia's capital, but they declined to meet there with the state's white officials. Sailing on to the nation's capital, they put up at the Indian Queen Hotel with its portrait of Pocahontas over the entryway. The hotel was especially appealing because, at no extra charge, the staff set out decanters of whiskey and brandy with the meals. Representatives from the McIntosh faction of Creeks had come to press their case for reparations, but they were staying at Tennison's Hotel.

On November 30, Opothle Yoholo and his men met with Secretary of War Barbour, who reminded them of the terms they had tentatively reached with General Gaines. But now the chief resisted signing that earlier agreement. "The subject is embarrassing," he said cryptically. "Our nation expects us to act under a clear sky," but clouds were obscuring their decision. The Creeks would ponder further and send their answer.

At the hotel, John Ridge wrote a statement in English and translated it for the chiefs, who signed with their marks. The Creeks would not exchange their land for new territories, but they would sell a remnant of their property east of the Chattahoochee River. That would set the boundary between their land and the state of Georgia as the river's east bank at the high-water mark.

The Creeks presented those terms as inflexible. "We may as well be annihilated at once as to cede any portion of the land west of the river."

When Barbour protested that the Georgians were demanding all of the land within their state lines, the Creeks replied that they did not understand white man's lines, only the natural boundaries of a river. Barbour and his aides found Opothle Yoholo steadfast and dignified, but when the chief asked for a meeting with President Adams, his request was denied.

In moving to the White House, Adams had hoped to keep his days routine and orderly. He got up every morning at five o'clock, read two chapters from the Bible, and then a scholarly commentary on them. When weather permitted, he went to the Potomac for a bracing swim and returned to read the newspapers and documents from government departments. He tried to use the time for writing as well, but chided himself for never accomplishing enough.

From 9 to 10 a.m., Adams ate breakfast before receiving a variety of visitors. One morning, Samuel Pooley, a New Yorker who made mathematical instruments, showed up with a box of miniature knives, forks, razors, and scissors. Adams explained that he made it a rule not to accept gifts. But he could not resist Pooley's ingenuity and made an exception for the tiny hardware. Another day, Henry Clay brought a constituent's letter that scolded Adams for the level of his diplomatic appointments. "The whole science of diplomacy consists in giving dinners," the writer complained, and the administration was failing in that respect.

The parade of callers—men seeking appointments or charitable donations or merely curious to meet the president—continued until between 4 and 5 p.m., with cabinet officers presenting themselves from time to time.

Adams reserved the hour from 5 to 6 p.m. for a walk of three to four miles. He dined afterward until 7 p.m. and then, by candlelight, sat at his desk until 11 p.m., signing land grants and patents and trying to catch up on his diary. Early into his term, Adams lamented that he was not making better use of his time.

"There is much to correct and reform," he reminded himself, "and the precept of diligence is always timely."

Of late, the president's workdays were increasingly devoted to the Indian problem. On December 22, 1825, the entire four afternoon hours with his cabinet were taken up with trying to find a solution to the discord in Georgia.

Barbour was now suggesting that all tribes be incorporated within the Union. That would end the need for individual treaties.

Adams asked whether it would not take the constitutional power of Congress to make such a change. Barbour agreed, but he maintained that soon there would be no other choice.

Henry Clay dismissed Barbour's idea as impractical since, Clay said, it was impossible to civilize Indians. One might succeed with half-breeds and others of mixed blood, but there never was a full-blooded

Indian who took to civilization. It was not in their nature. They were headed to extinction and would be gone within fifty years.

Clay went further: He would never agree to inhuman treatment of the tribes, but since they were inferior to Anglo-Saxons, "their disappearance from the human family will be no great loss to the world."

Adams noticed Barbour's shocked response. That evening, he confessed to his diary that, as he mulled over Clay's pessimistic views, "I fear there is too much foundation" for them.

Overnight, Barbour also wrestled with Clay's arguments. In the morning, he was visited by an agitated Senator Howell Cobb of Georgia, who warned him that if Adams invalidated the Treaty of Indian Springs, Georgia would be driven to side with Andrew Jackson in the Senate.

Relaying that threat to the president, Barbour asked: If that is the situation in Georgia, and if Mr. Clay's ideas yesterday were correct and the Indians face inevitable destruction, why quarrel with our friends on the Indians' behalf? Why not yield to the Georgians at once?

Adams responded in his loftiest manner. What Mr. Clay had observed yesterday was a theory, he said, not a plan of action. "We ought not to yield to Georgia because we could not do so without gross injustice."

As for the threat of political retaliation, the president said that he felt "little concern or care for that." He had no more confidence in one faction in the Senate than in the other.

The impasse continued for another three weeks. Adams brought in Colonel McKenney from the Indian Office and Lewis Cass, governor of the Michigan Territory, who had negotiated adroitly with the Indians of his region. As every white official hammered repeatedly at the Creek delegates, even some of their local allies were advising them to yield.

On January 17, 1826, the Creeks left Barbour's War Office convinced that they had failed. Opothle Yoholo, not yet thirty years old, was despondent and unwilling to return home disgraced. He went back to his room at the Indian Queen and tried to kill himself.

The chief's desperation spurred McKenney to make one last effort to salvage the negotiations. That evening, he wrote a personal letter to John Ridge imploring him to persuade the Creeks to compromise.

The day's drama had subdued them all. Opothle Yoholo joined with the other Creeks in agreeing to move their boundary west and set the line at a different branch of the Chattahoochee.

The next morning, President Adams received a new draft of the Creek treaty and decided that since the tribe could be pressed no further, Barbour should agree to its terms. The first article of the new agreement voided McIntosh's treaty, but Adams wanted provision made for those Creeks from the McIntosh faction.

The final terms left the Creeks with almost no territory within the state outlines of Georgia. The treaty paid the tribe $217,000 in cash, with a perpetual yearly annuity of $20,000 in return for leaving the disputed land by the following January 1. The Creeks also agreed to abide by the findings of a War Office special agent who would determine how much they owed McIntosh's supporters. Those families would be moved west by the U.S. government and paid up to $100,000, depending on the size of the migration.

Since the issue had provoked such fury, diplomatic maneuvering in the Congress would be essential. Adams wondered whether Governor Troup's intemperate letters should be included when the administration sent the treaty to the Senate for approval. Barbour thought not. They would only stir up more anger. But as a former House Speaker, Clay thought all relevant documents must be forwarded with the treaty. He agreed, though, to withhold the letters until the Senate had safely consented to ratification. Adams thought the delay would prevent the "excitement or debate" that reading the letters now might provoke.

Clay observed that the new terms were far less favorable to the United States than the Treaty of Indian Springs, but Adams had invested his prestige in this new pact—called the Treaty of Washington—and he disagreed.

On February 7, 1826, the Adams administration sent a letter outlining the new provisions to the House Committee on Indian Affairs. It was clear that Barbour had given up any idea of incorporating the Indians and their land into the states where they were living. Instead, the tribes should be melded into a single Indian government and sent to oversee one vast territory west of the Mississippi. Reading Barbour's proposal, Adams found it "full of benevolence and humanity" and observed that its critics could not come up with anything better.

Colonel McKenney fretted over the way the $217,000 cash payment would be allotted. He preferred that the U.S. government pay only the lump sum and leave its distribution to the Creeks themselves. But because he was keenly aware of the accusations against McIntosh, he was disturbed when John Ridge admitted that so far only Opothle Yoholo and one other Creek leader had signed off on the individual payments. Ridge could provide no more than a list of other chiefs who would share in the money—from $5,000 to $10,000 each—after Vann, Major Ridge, and he had received their promised $40,000.

McKenney shared his misgivings with Barbour, who called the Creeks to his office without their Cherokee secretaries. He demanded, and received, assurances that the Creek Great Council Fire would be asked to approve the way the money would be divided.

In the Congress, however, where the Georgians and their allies resented bitterly any change in the Treaty of Indian Springs, a rancorous debate challenged the behavior of the Creek delegates and particularly of its two young Cherokee aides. Accusations of fraud and bad faith against John Ridge and David Vann were finally rebutted by Senator Littleton W. Tazewell of Virginia.

Portraying himself as a disinterested observer, Tazewell made the point publicly that Clay had made in private—"these two Cherokee boys sent here had completed a treaty on better terms for the Creeks, and worse terms for the United States, than all the diplomatic functionaries" Washington could muster.

Tazewell offered a commonsense solution: "We have nothing to do with that affair except to place the money in the hands of the Creek nation, and let them distribute it according to what they consider justice on their part toward the Cherokees."

John Ridge stayed behind in Washington to attend to final details and to have his portrait painted by Charles Bird King of Rhode Island, the artist McKenney commissioned to paint chieftains visiting Washington. King posed John Ridge in a fashionable waistcoat, holding a quill pen and focusing his deep-set eyes on the middle distance.

Ridge's eventual homecoming was something less than a triumph, however. The Indian Office had bestowed its largest medallion on Opothle Yoholo, with other decorations for ranking chiefs who had not made the trip to Washington. But the Creek Council was not mollified. Meeting near Fort Mitchell in eastern Alabama on June 16, 1826, council members wrangled over the distribution of federal money until finally they upheld the terms recommended by Opothle Yoholo. With two exceptions: The payments to John Ridge and David Vann were cut from $15,000 apiece to $5,000, although Major Ridge got his full $10,000.

His duty done, John Ridge returned to the Cherokees and found that his own tribe was also trying to resolve the prevailing tensions in Georgia, but in its own way. The Cherokees were determined to become the sort of neighbors that white Georgians could accept.

Sequoyah

4 · Sequoyah (1828)

When a young Dutchman, Nathaniel Gist, first began trading among the Cherokees, he seemed to have found an earthly paradise. From boyhood, Gist had been considered lazy. He refused to work with his hands, and his brain was equally idle. Coming to America, he spoke very few words of English and none at all of the Cherokee language. Many traders lived with two or three squaws, but a single woman suited Gist's indolence.

The bride he chose shared the Cherokee women's pride in their capacity for hard work. Gist's wife reveled in his sloth, which left her free to clear the land, cultivate crops, and butcher game from the tribal hunt. She tended to their home, a comfortable wigwam thirty or forty feet in diameter and covered with willow branches. She sewed their clothes from animal skins, chopped wood, and fetched water, all the while going about her chores with a happy heart since she was behaving as a good wife should. For a Cherokee woman, the unforgivable insult was any gossip that her husband had been seen "making a squaw of himself" by carrying firewood to their wigwam.

Despite the idyll he had found, Gist was a wanderer. One night in 1770, he packed up his few belongings and disappeared, leaving his pregnant wife behind. Following Cherokee custom, she went to a glade far from home and gave birth to a son. She called the infant by the cryptic name of Se-quo-yah—"He guessed it."

For the next ten months, she toted the child everywhere on a board strapped to her back. Cherokee mothers had developed an effective way of keeping a child quiet and obedient. If he cried, they pinched his nostrils shut until he felt smothered, and they let go only after he had calmed down. As Sequoyah grew older, he received no schooling but showed promise as a hunter and fur trader. By the time white settlers infiltrated Cherokee country, he was past thirty. From them, he learned the skills of a silversmith, but he was more impressed with their ability to make marks on paper that held a meaning for other men.

During the War of 1812, Sequoyah fought under Andrew Jackson in defeating the British-led Creeks at Horseshoe Bend. White comrades called him George Gist—or sometimes George Guess—while Sequoyah watched them use their "talking leaves" to send messages to families far away. Rather than learn to read or write English, he began to develop his own system that would allow Cherokees to communicate in writing.

When he was crippled in a hunting accident, Sequoyah was reduced to a sedentary life and began to drink heavily. But he could also spend hours pursuing his attempt to put speech on paper. He started by drawing pictures to symbolize a word, and before long he had amassed hundreds of them. By 1821, however, he had found that to illustrate a single verb could take an unwieldy number of his pictographs and looked for a simpler method.

His elders regarded Sequoyah—with his shattered leg and his constant puffing on a long-stemmed pipe—as a harmless eccentric since their tradition guaranteed that he could never duplicate the white man's writing: When the Great Spirit first created a red child and a white one, He gave the red boy a book and the white boy a bow and arrow. But the white boy stole the book, leaving behind only the bow and arrow. From that time on, Indians were destined to hunt but never to read.

And yet Sequoyah persevered. His wife agreed with their neighbors that he must be crazy and burned whatever of his manuscripts she could find. When a friend told him that he was making a fool of himself, Sequoyah tried to explain his obsession: "What I have done, I have done from myself," he said. His neighbors "did not cause me to begin and they shall not cause me to give up, and so I shall go on, and you may tell our people."

Sequoyah set off in another direction. Counting the number of individual sounds in the Cherokee language, he concluded that there were eighty-six and devised a character to represent each of them.

By combining those syllables, he could reproduce different words into a "syllabary." Instead of the cumbersome pictures, he chose symbols from a Noah Webster blue-backed speller he had acquired. He adapted some characters from the Greek, others from Roman script, even though the ancient languages were meaningless to him.

To win over skeptics, Sequoyah brought together six neighbors and announced, "Now I can write a book." He asked each of them to make a speech. As the man spoke, Sequoyah made marks on tree bark with pokeberry juice. When the man finished, Sequoyah read back to him what he had just said. Hearing their words repeated accurately amazed and convinced them.

Sequoyah drew up a chart, with one character for the sound of s,

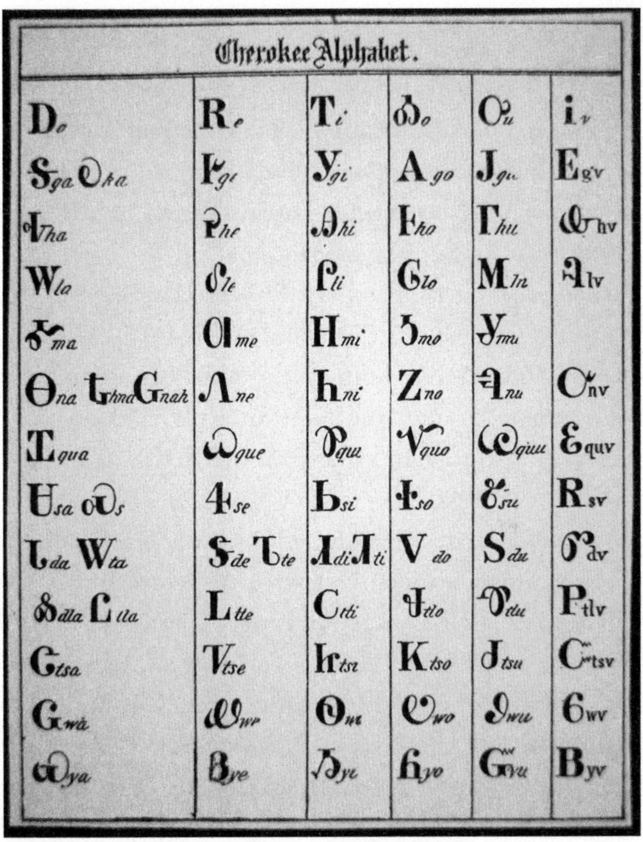

The Cherokee Alphabet

which could be combined with other syllables. He found that a Cherokee could learn his symbols in only one week. After that, to form words simply meant arranging them in the order of their sounds.

He taught the system to his six-year-old daughter, A-yo-ka, and a group of her friends. Taking the children to a Cherokee National Council meeting, he asked them to transcribe messages that he dictated to them separately. Then he collected the results, shuffled them, and passed them out to different children. When they read them back perfectly, the dazzled council adopted Sequoyah's syllabary for use by the entire Cherokee Nation.

His own first composition described the boundary lines between Georgia, Tennessee, and the Cherokee territory. At a court hearing in Catonga, he read his statement from a page of his markings and won over another skeptical audience.

Throughout the early 1820s, Sequoyah's method spread from the eastern Cherokees to those western members of the tribe who were already living in Arkansas. People quickly agreed that Sequoyah had mastered the art of "talking at a distance."

He next focused on problems in Cherokee arithmetic. The tribe could imagine what they called "mental numbers" up to one hundred. Sequoyah devised instead a written method based on the decimal system to allow them to add, subtract, multiply, and divide, but the council rejected his proposal in favor of the Arabic numerals already widely used.

Sequoyah found that he preferred the simpler life in Arkansas and moved there to continue his studies. Becoming one of the group called Old Settlers, he supported himself with his ornamental silver work. In 1825, the Cherokee legislative council voted twenty dollars to strike a silver medal honoring his ingenuity.

Three years later, when the Old Settlers traded their Arkansas land for some 14 million acres in northern Oklahoma, their treaty awarded five hundred dollars to George Guess for "the great benefits he has conferred upon the Cherokee people."

That admiration was shared by white observers. Albert Gallatin, who had served with Henry Clay and John Quincy Adams in negotiating an end to the War of 1812, was shown a copy of Sequoyah's early work. At first, Gallatin was incredulous that the bountiful Cherokee language could be reduced to so few syllables. Then he decided that Sequoyah should have taken one more step and cut back his consonants to sixteen. On reflection, however, Gallatin found Sequoyah's invention superior to the English alphabet: "You must learn and remember eighty-five letters instead of twenty-five," Gallatin wrote. "But this once accomplished, the education of the pupil is completed; he can read, he is perfect in his orthography without making it the subject of distinct study. The boy learns in a few weeks that which occupied two years of the time of our boys."

As Sequoyah was changing Cherokee history, Major Ridge was drawing ever closer to the white community. Because tribal law prohibited anyone who was not a Cherokee citizen from doing business within the Cherokee Nation, Ridge had taken as his partner an ambitious young white man named George Lavender, who made a great success of their trading post. They dealt in staples but also in luxury goods—calico and silks—from the town of Augusta. Besides that income, Ridge took in twelve hundred dollars a year from his ferry, carrying wagons and their teams on a flat-bottomed boat across the Oostanaula River. Ridge devoted those profits to expanding an estate in which his son took great pride. John thought that his father's gracious two-story house "would look well even in New England," and white observers agreed that Major Ridge's home "resembled in no respect the wigwam of an Indian."

An inventory of the plantation's nearly three hundred cleared acres listed 1,141 peach trees, 418 apple trees, as well as quince, cherry, and plum. Ridge's main cash crop was corn, but he also grew tobacco and cotton harvested by his thirty slaves.

Despite being only one-eighth Cherokee, John Ross had taken Major Ridge as his model. His plantation with its nineteen slaves also provided a prosperous living, and Ross's brother Lewis did equally well with his stores, a mill, and three ferryboats.

The Ross brothers shared Ridge's ardor for learning. They were striving to live up to a description by Colonel McKenney from the Office of Indian Affairs: "The Cherokees on this side of the Mississippi," McKenney wrote, "are in advance of all other tribes. They may be considered a civilized people."

For Ridge, Ross, and their fellow leaders, the capping achievements would be a Cherokee constitution and a Cherokee newspaper. In Elias Boudinot, they had a logical candidate to edit their paper, except for one blemish on his record. On a Sunday, while he was wooing Harriet Gold by mail, Boudinot had alienated the territory's missionaries by taking part in a Cherokee ceremony called the ball-play.

The event was surprisingly violent for a peaceable people. Two teams tried to put a ball through two poles twelve times without touching it with their hands. Instead, they tossed the ball between rackets with pockets woven from deer sinew. Each team member faced an opponent directly. Should a player fail to catch the ball, the teams could gouge and bite as they scrambled for possession. During the hours of play, a man was often knocked unconscious, which retired his opponent from the field.

Tripping and choking were also allowed. While twenty men might begin the game, only a few survivors finished it, always bloody and bruised.

Missionaries considered the sport vicious and deplored even more strenuously the lascivious dances that followed. Boudinot knew he would be censured for participating. But he was angry about the anonymous death threats he had been receiving from Northern whites opposed to his courtship. Without apology, he defied his former teachers and joined in the undulations of the dance.

Once Boudinot had taken a wife, his rebellion ended. To raise money for a newspaper, he embarked on a speaking tour and made an early stop in Charleston, where white congregations had been generous in the past.

Boudinot launched his oration by acknowledging the prejudice that his audience might harbor. "To those who are unacquainted with the manners, habits and improvements of the aborigines of this country, the term Indian is pregnant with ideas the most repelling and degrading."

Then Boudinot flaunted his credentials dramatically: "You here behold an Indian!" he cried. "My kindred are Indians, and my fathers are sleeping in the wilderness grove—they, too, were Indians!"

Yet he was of a different breed. "I am not as my fathers were—broader means and nobler influences have fallen upon me." The achievements of his generation should end any doubts about whether Indians could be civilized.

He added, "It needs only that the world should know what we have done in the last few years to foresee what yet we may do with the assistance of our white brothers, and that common Parent of us all."

Boudinot cited specifics—the number of Cherokee cattle, spinning wheels, blacksmith shops, schools. He also granted that some of his tribesmen would gladly stop farming and go back to hunting if their plains were not depleted of game. "But these are individual failings," he assured his audience, "and ought to be passed over."

Now history was weighing the fate of all Indians. "Must they perish? Must they all, like the unfortunate Creeks (victims of the unchristian policies of certain persons), go down in sorrow to their graves?"

Although Boudinot included a tactful endorsement of the value of the missions in the territory, he said that the Cherokees' future progress had to depend on their establishing their own institutions, including a seminary and a printing press. "For those purposes, your aid and patronage are now solicited."

His appeal did not generate much money from any one congregation. By the time he returned to the Cherokee Nation, Boudinot had raised about six hundred dollars. But when his talk was printed as a sixteen-page pamphlet by the First Presbyterian Church in Philadelphia, his eloquence shook loose larger contributions.

The Cherokee national council was convinced of the need for a newspaper and appropriated the funds. At the beginning, however, the project would depend on the enterprise of Samuel Worcester, an energetic Vermont missionary sent south by the American Board of Commissioners for Foreign Missions.

Son of a village parson, Worcester had graduated from Andover Theological Seminary in Massachusetts, expecting to preach the gospel in India, Palestine, or possibly the Sandwich Islands. At the age of twenty-seven, he learned that his elders had scaled back those youthful dreams. He would be going to convert the Cherokees of Georgia.

In August 1825, Worcester and his wife set off, taking along feather beds and fine linen to ease their entry into frontier life. Samuel's wife had been born Ann Orr, and it testified to both his Yankee humor and his appreciation of grammar that he joked to people that he had married "an indefinite article and a disjunctive conjunction."

After six weeks, the couple reached the Brainerd mission. Built in 1817, it had become an outpost for New Englanders. Dr. Samuel Worcester, a founder of the American Board of Missionaries and the uncle for whom Samuel was named, had visited Brainerd and, when he died there, had been buried in its cemetery.

The American Board had spelled out goals for Samuel and Ann Worcester: "To make the whole tribe English in their language, civilized in their habits and Christian in their religion." But missionaries already working with the tribe had modified that first goal; they found that the Indians had to be reached in their native tongue. Worcester immediately set out to learn to write the language Sequoyah had devised. When he became sufficiently fluent, he intended to translate the New Testament into Cherokee.

While at Brainerd, Ann Worcester gave birth to their first child. The Cherokees had bestowed on Samuel a name that translated as the Messenger. Now, in their own slang, they inquired whether the Messenger's child was "a bow" or "a meal-sifter." The child was the latter—a girl—and Cherokee women had ample advice for the young mother.

Ann Worcester thanked them politely but did not give her daughter liquid from brewed cockleburs so that facts might stick in her memory. Nor did she feed her the heart of a *huhu*—a mockingbird—to help her learn more quickly.

By the time the Cherokees were ready to publish their newspaper, Worcester had become a trusted ally, and the tribe's leaders asked him to contact the American Board in Boston to buy their press. The press that Worcester selected was a simple iron machine that weighed a thousand pounds but could be easily set up and was unlikely to break down. Casting typefaces, however, would require ingenuity, since few Northern craftsmen had ever seen Sequoyah's alphabet.

The press, boxes of type, and office furniture were shipped by steamboat from Boston to Augusta and hauled by wagon over rough Georgia roads to the raw Cherokee capital in Conasauga Valley called New Echota. The press arrived on February 1, 1828, but because no printing paper had been sent, publication was held up until bundles could be transported from Knoxville.

The council had voted to call the weekly the *Cherokee Phoenix* and print it partly in English, partly in Sequoyah's characters. Boudinot had chosen the name because he believed that his tribe, like the fabulous bird, had to be born again from the ashes of its past. On the masthead, he proposed to print, "I will arise."

To work with the newspaper, Samuel Worcester moved his family from Brainerd to New Echota and joined Elias and Harriet Boudinot. The couples built two-story houses on acre lots that had been laid out at the center of the new capital. They caulked chinks in the log walls with red mud and used clay from a nearby riverbed to whitewash the interior.

When Harriet delivered another blond child, her parents made the forty-seven-day trip to visit their grandchildren. The Golds found their daughter "well furnished with the comforts of life," including clothes and groceries imported from Boston and Augusta. Harriet's father was impressed that she always had on hand two—even three—barrels of flour.

Worcester wrote a prospectus promising that the newspaper would cover the nation's laws and public documents as well as include articles on Cherokee manners and customs. It would promote literature, civilization, and religion, and would print "the principal news of the day."

But in a letter to his brother-in-law, the Reverend Vaill, Boudinot described the project more modestly. He did not expect to rival other newspapers, Boudinot wrote, by "exhibiting to the public learning, talents and information, for those we do not profess to possess." His object was simpler and required "no great attainments." The paper would be published only "for the benefit of the Cherokees, who, you know, are uninformed."

Subscribers who could read only Cherokee would get the paper free. Those who knew English were offered a sliding scale—$2.50 a year if they paid in advance, a dollar more if they waited a year to pay. A white printer was hired. He moved to New Echota and spent the next four weeks learning Cherokee. On February 21, 1828, the first number appeared of Tsa-La-Ge-Tsi-Le-Hi-Sa-Ni-Hi—the *Cherokee Phoenix.*

That issue ran to five columns on each of its four pages, with the Lord's Prayer printed in both languages. The editor explained that, because translation was a slow process, early issues would include only three columns each week in Cherokee. Worcester contributed an essay praising Sequoyah's alphabet, and Boudinot's first editorial denounced whites for coveting Cherokee land.

But Boudinot held to the pledge that had impressed General Gaines. The Cherokees "would not return any abuse from Georgians," he promised, "for we have been taught to believe that a soft answer turneth away wrath, but grievous words stir up anger."

As further proof of the Cherokees' determination to live like their white neighbors, Boudinot printed sections of a new Cherokee constitution. Major Ridge and his protégé, John Ross, had produced a document with echoes of its U.S. counterpart, but with a more overtly religious tone: "We, the Representatives of the people of the Cherokee Nation, in Convention assembled, in order to establish justice, ensure

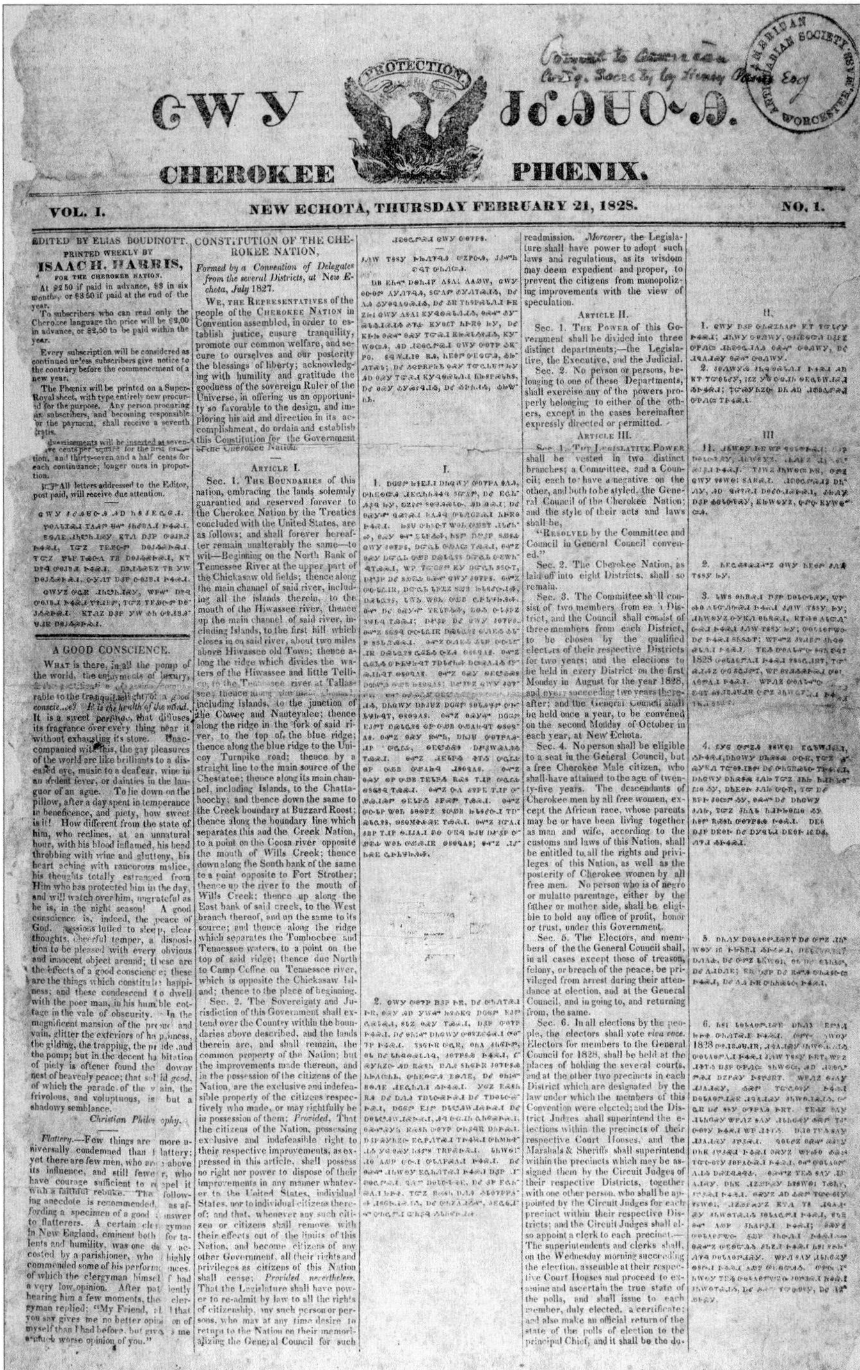

CHEROKEE PHŒNIX.

VOL. I. NEW ECHOTA, THURSDAY FEBRUARY 21, 1828. NO. 1.

EDITED BY ELIAS BOUDINOTT.
PRINTED WEEKLY BY
ISAAC H. HARRIS,
FOR THE CHEROKEE NATION.

At $2 50 if paid in advance, $3 in six months, or $3 50 if paid at the end of the year.

To subscribers who can read only the Cherokee language the price will be $2,00 in advance, or $2,50 to be paid within the year.

Every subscription will be considered as continued unless subscribers give notice to the contrary before the commencement of a new year.

The Phœnix will be printed on a Super-Royal sheet, with type entirely new procured for the purpose. Any person procuring six subscribers, and becoming responsible for the payment, shall receive a seventh gratis.

Advertisements will be inserted at seventy-five cents per square for the first insertion, and thirty-seven and a half cents for each continuance; longer ones in proportion.

☞ All letters addressed to the Editor, post paid, will receive due attention.

A GOOD CONSCIENCE.

What is there, in all the pomp of the world, the enjoyments of luxury, [illegible] comparable to the tranquil delight of a *good conscience? It is the health of the mind.* It is a sweet perfume, that diffuses its fragrance over every thing near it without exhausting its store. Unaccompanied with this, the gay pleasures of the world are like brilliants to a diseased eye, music to a deaf ear, wine in an ardent fever, or dainties in the languor of an ague. To lie down on the pillow, after a day spent in temperance in beneficence, and piety, how sweet is it! How different from the state of him, who reclines, at an unnatural hour, with his blood inflamed, his head throbbing with wine and gluttony, his heart aching with rancorous malice, his thoughts totally estranged from Him who has protected him in the day, and will watch over him, ungrateful as he is, in the night season! A good conscience is, indeed, the peace of God. Passions lulled to sleep, clear thoughts, cheerful temper, a disposition to be pleased with every obvious and innocent object around; these are the effects of a good conscience; these are the things which constitute happiness; and these condescend to dwell with the poor man, in his humble cottage in the vale of obscurity. In the magnificent mansion of the proud and vain, glitter the exteriors of happiness, the gilding, the trapping, the pride, and the pomp; but in the decent habitation of piety is oftener found the downy nest of heavenly peace; that solid *good*, of which the parade of the vain, the frivolous, and voluptuous, is but a shadowy semblance.

Christian Philosophy.

Flattery.—Few things are more universally condemned than flattery; yet there are few men, who are above its influence, and still fewer, who have courage sufficient to repel it with a faithful rebuke. The following anecdote is recommended, as affording a specimen of a good answer to flatterers. A certain clergyman in New England, eminent both for talents and humility, was one day accosted by a parishioner, who highly commended some of his performances, of which the clergyman himself had a very low opinion. After patiently hearing him a few moments, the clergyman replied; "My Friend, all that you say gives me no better opinion of myself than I had before, but gives me a much worse opinion of you."

CONSTITUTION OF THE CHEROKEE NATION,

Formed by a Convention of Delegates from the several Districts, at New Echota, July 1827.

We, the Representatives of the people of the Cherokee Nation in Convention assembled, in order to establish justice, ensure tranquility, promote our common welfare, and secure to ourselves and our posterity the blessings of liberty; acknowledging with humility and gratitude the goodness of the sovereign Ruler of the Universe, in offering us an opportunity so favorable to the design, and imploring his aid and direction in its accomplishment, do ordain and establish this Constitution for the Government of the Cherokee Nation.

Article I.

Sec. 1. The Boundaries of this nation, embracing the lands solemnly guarantied and reserved forever to the Cherokee Nation by the Treaties concluded with the United States, are as follows; and shall forever hereafter remain unalterably the same—to wit—Beginning on the North Bank of Tennessee River at the upper part of the Chickasaw old fields; thence along the main channel of said river, including all the islands therein, to the mouth of the Hiwassee river, thence up the main channel of said river, including Islands, to the first hill which closes in on said river, about two miles above Hiwassee old Town; thence along the ridge which divides the waters of the Hiwassee and little Tellico, to the Tennessee river at Tallassee; thence along the main channel, including Islands, to the junction of the Cowee and Nanteyalee; thence along the ridge in the fork of said river, to the top of the blue ridge; thence along the blue ridge to the Unicoy Turnpike road; thence by a straight line to the main source of the Chestatee; thence along its main channel, including Islands, to the Chattahoochy; and thence down the same to the Creek boundary at Buzzard Roost; thence along the boundary line which separates this and the Creek Nation, to a point on the Coosa river opposite the mouth of Wills Creek; thence down along the South bank of the same to a point opposite to Fort Strother; thence up the river to the mouth of Wills Creek; thence up along the East bank of said creek, to the West branch thereof, and up the same to its source; and thence along the ridge which separates the Tombecbee and Tennessee waters, to a point on the top of said ridge; thence due North to Camp Coffee on Tennessee river, which is opposite the Chickasaw Island; thence to the place of beginning.

Sec. 2. The Sovereignty and Jurisdiction of this Government shall extend over the Country within the boundaries above described, and the lands therein are, and shall remain, the common property of the Nation; but the improvements made thereon, and in the possession of the citizens of the Nation, are the exclusive and indefeasible property of the citizens respectively who made, or may rightfully be in possession of them; *Provided*, That the citizens of the Nation, possessing exclusive and indefeasible right to their respective improvements, as expressed in this article, shall possess no right nor power to dispose of their improvements in any manner whatever to the United States, individual States, nor to individual citizens thereof; and that, whenever any such citizen or citizens shall remove with their effects out of the limits of this Nation, and become citizens of any other Government, all their rights and privileges as citizens of this Nation shall cease; *Provided nevertheless*, That the Legislature shall have power to re-admit by law to all the rights of citizenship, any such person or persons, who may at any time desire to return to the Nation on their memorializing the General Council for such readmission. *Moreover*, the Legislature shall have power to adopt such laws and regulations, as its wisdom may deem expedient and proper, to prevent the citizens from monopolizing improvements with the view of speculation.

Article II.

Sec. 1. The Power of this Government shall be divided into three distinct departments;—the Legislative, the Executive, and the Judicial.

Sec. 2. No person or persons, belonging to one of these Departments, shall exercise any of the powers properly belonging to either of the others, except in the cases hereinafter expressly directed or permitted.

Article III.

Sec. 1. The Legislative Power shall be vested in two distinct branches; a Committee, and a Council; each to have a negative on the other, and both to be styled, the General Council of the Cherokee Nation; and the style of their acts and laws shall be,

"Resolved by the Committee and Council in General Council convened."

Sec. 2. The Cherokee Nation, as laid off into eight Districts, shall so remain.

Sec. 3. The Committee shall consist of two members from each District, and the Council shall consist of three members from each District, to be chosen by the qualified electors of their respective Districts for two years; and the elections to be held in every District on the first Monday in August for the year 1828, and every succeeding two years thereafter; and the General Council shall be held once a year, to be convened on the second Monday of October in each year, at New Echota.

Sec. 4. No person shall be eligible to a seat in the General Council, but a free Cherokee Male citizen, who shall have attained to the age of twenty-five years. The descendants of Cherokee men by all free women, except the African race, whose parents may be or have been living together as man and wife, according to the customs and laws of this Nation, shall be entitled to all the rights and privileges of this Nation, as well as the posterity of Cherokee women by all free men. No person who is of negro or mulatto parentage, either by the father or mother side, shall be eligible to hold any office of profit, honor or trust, under this Government.

Sec. 5. The Electors, and members of the the General Council shall, in all cases except those of treason, felony, or breach of the peace, be privileged from arrest during their attendance at election, and at the General Council, and in going to, and returning from, the same.

Sec. 6. In all elections by the people, the electors shall vote *viva voce.* Electors for members to the General Council for 1828, shall be held at the places of holding the several courts, and at the other two precincts in each District which are designated by the law under which the members of this Convention were elected; and the District Judges shall superintend the elections within the precincts of their respective Court Houses, and the Marshals & Sheriffs shall superintend within the precincts which may be assigned them by the Circuit Judges of their respective Districts, together with one other person, who shall be appointed by the Circuit Judges for each precinct within their respective Districts; and the Circuit Judges shall also appoint a clerk to each precinct.—The superintendents and clerks shall, on the Wednesday morning succeeding the election, assemble at their respective Court Houses and proceed to examine and ascertain the true state of the polls, and shall issue to each member, duly elected, a certificate; and also make an official return of the state of the polls of election to the principal Chief, and it shall be the du-

The Cherokee Phoenix

tranquility, promote our common welfare, and secure to ourselves and our posterity the blessings of liberty, acknowledging with humility and gratitude the goodness of the sovereign Ruler of the Universe, in offering us an opportunity so favorable to the design, and imploring His aid and direction in its accomplishment, do ordain and establish this Constitution for the Government of the Cherokee Nation."

Like its model, the Cherokee constitution divided tribal power into three branches—legislative, executive, and judicial. It spelled out terms of citizenship for Cherokee descendants but specified that "no person who is of negro or mulatto parentage, either by the father or the mother, shall be eligible to hold any office of profit, honor, or trust under this Government."

Other provisions protected citizens in their houses from unreasonable search and seizure, guaranteed trial by jury, and protected against the double jeopardy of being tried twice for the same offense.

Missionaries were barred from holding tribal office—ostensibly to guarantee that they not be diverted from their service to God. But Boudinot expected their religious influence to continue and saw the constitution as merely recognizing changes that had long been evolving, including the abolition of polygamy. Boudinot assured readers that "female chastity and honor are protected by law" and that the "Sabbath is respected by the council during session."

In a coda, the ratifying committee agreed that all Cherokee who chose to migrate to Arkansas must immediately dispose of any possessions in Georgia and pay a levy of $150. They would also forfeit citizenship in the Cherokee Nation.

The idea of a written constitution drafted by the tribe's wealthiest members troubled some older chiefs, who already resented the influence of the white missionaries. Led by a sixty-eight-year-old traditionalist named White Path, they claimed to speak for the legion of full-blooded Cherokees who led lives of far less abundance than those of mixed-race families like the Ridges and the Rosses.

At a protest meeting, hundreds of Cherokees opened the proceedings by worshipping with shamans and dancing to the ancient rhythms before they turned to debating the new constitution. They passed one resolution closing the Christian missions and another canceling any new law passed in recent years. When Major Ridge got word about speeches that were inflaming the old chiefs, he urged his younger colleagues to appear before their critics and explain the value of the constitution.

But John Ross believed that the rebellion had no effective leaders. He expected the protests to die away and, after three months, he was proved right. The attempt had failed to stir popular resentment against the wealthy families of mixed white and Cherokee blood. As Ross had predicted, poor Indians, who seldom participated in Cherokee politics, seemed content to scrape by in their two-room log cabins on their ten-acre farms so long as the tribe's common territory was protected.

The authorized council then met on July 26, 1827, and adopted the constitution. John Ross was overwhelmingly elected as the Cherokees' principal chief and John Ridge as council clerk. They won their posts in part because rival candidates were accused of contacting federal agents to ask how much Washington would pay them to leave for Arkansas.

The resentment against those men was a reminder that President Adams had not quelled the debate over removing Indians from their land. Despite Cherokee prosperity and a constitution that declared the tribe "sovereign and independent," demand was growing among their Georgia neighbors to possess the Cherokee Nation.

John C. Calhoun

5 · John C. Calhoun (1828)

John Caldwell Calhoun might be serving as John Quincy Adams's vice president, but he did not consider himself obliged to support the president. As Monroe's former secretary of war, Calhoun's own political stature was imposing. He had received as many votes in the Electoral College for his position as the combined total of Adams and Jackson for theirs. And Calhoun represented an emerging political trend. As the seventh vice president in American history, he was the first man—president or vice president—who had not come from Virginia, Massachusetts, or New York.

Although Calhoun's Scotch-Irish grandfather had arrived in Philadelphia in 1735, he had gone south twenty years later, and Calhoun was born in South Carolina on March 18, 1782. After graduating from Yale in 1804, Calhoun studied law and served in the South Carolina General Assembly before going on to three terms in the U.S. House of Representatives. There, as a War Hawk in the months leading up to the War of 1812, Calhoun had joined forces with Henry Clay in pressing President Madison to stand up to Great Britain.

Lacking Clay's charm, Calhoun had to win over audiences with the chilling force of his logic. A neighbor who avoided his company explained forthrightly, "I hate a man who makes me feel my own inferiority." Even an admiring hostess summed up Calhoun as "the cast iron man, who looks as though he had never been born and never could be extinguished." All the same, he had courted and married Floride Bonneau, a distant cousin, and fathered seven children.

Calhoun had considered running for president the last time before deciding on the less-contested post of vice president. Now his strategy was evolving for another attempt at the presidency, but the hurdles remained substantial. From his years as secretary of war, his Indian policy of gradually integrating Georgia's Cherokees into white society had alienated Governor Troup and the remnants of the Crawford political machine. To improve his odds, Calhoun was supporting a constitutional amendment to do away with the Electoral College. He had already demonstrated his appeal if elections for president and vice president could be decided by the popular vote.

But another potential obstacle arose when Calhoun heard rumors that Martin Van Buren was forging an alliance with Andrew Jackson. The combination of New York and the frontier could make Jackson hard to beat in 1828. Even if the stories were true, however, Jackson had promised to be a one-term president. In 1832, Calhoun would be only fifty.

Since Adams was certain to seek a second term, and since Clay had anointed himself as Adams's heir, Calhoun could best secure his future Southern support by opposing Adams on domestic issues. He would do it in the name of states' rights.

That was his plan. Yet Calhoun's first chance for a break with the administration came over foreign policy. Simón Bolívar, El Libertador of Colombia, was discouraging Northern intervention in Latin America. He had enlisted Mexico to join him in hosting a conference in Panama and initially had resisted inviting the United States. When he relented, Adams announced in his first message to Congress that he had accepted the invitation, and the American public seemed to welcome closer ties with the Southern Hemisphere. Adams's opponents claimed, however, that the nation risked becoming dangerously entangled.

In his farewell address, George Washington had warned against permanent alliances. Now, from the Hermitage, Andrew Jackson's estate outside Nashville, Jackson repeated that warning in apocalyptic language:

"The moment we engage in confederations or alliances with any nation, we may from that time date the downfall of our republic."

For Calhoun, there was another, less high-minded objection: Countries like Haiti might very well send former slaves as delegates. As a boy, Calhoun often boasted about his family's owning thirty slaves, even though his father had tried to instill in the boy a sense of responsibility. Patrick Calhoun had always spoken of "my family black and white."

John Calhoun's wife rejected her father-in-law's sentiment. Floride Calhoun preferred white servants and felt she had valid reasons: When she was six years old, slaves on her family's plantation had tried to poison her father. The plot was discovered, and one young slave was hanged. Three others were whipped, branded, and had their ears cropped.

Now John Calhoun wrote, "We must send and receive ministers, and what would be our social relations to a Black minister in Washington? Must he be received or excluded from our dinners, our dances and our parties, and must his daughters and sons participate in the society of our daughters and sons?"

Calhoun concluded, "Small as these considerations appear to be they involve the peace and perhaps the union of the nation."

During debate over the Panama conference, John Randolph took the floor for vituperative attacks on the Adams administration. Randolph was newly elected as senator from Virginia after stormy years in the House, and hearing of his tirades, Adams was furious that Calhoun let Randolph "drink himself drunk with bottled porter" and indulge in "raving balderdash."

To enliven his insults, Randolph drew on the novel *Tom Jones* by his favorite author and described Adams and Clay as "the coalition of Blifil and Black George"—Henry Fielding's fictional hypocrite and his rascally gamekeeper. To underscore the point, Randolph added that it was a union of "the Puritan and the blackleg." His audience might not have read Fielding, but everyone knew that a blackleg was a man who cheated at cards. Clay felt compelled to demand a duel.

His challenge came not long after Clay had suffered, within one month, the loss of two of his six daughters to yellow fever. His wife, Lucretia, was still grieving on the night before the duel when her cousin, Senator Thomas Hart Benton of Missouri, came to call.

The next day, Benton went to Randolph to describe the scene of mourning at Clay's house and to remind Randolph that he might soon be adding to Lucretia's misery. Randolph replied that Benton's intervention was unnecessary. It was against his principles, Randolph said, to "make a widow and orphans."

Yet on Saturday, April 8, 1826, the two men went through the travesty of firing wide and high. In the heat of the moment, however, Clay put a bullet through Randolph's white flannel overcoat. With that, Randolph threw down his pistol and approached Clay for a handshake.

"You owe me a coat, Mr. Clay," he said.

Relieved, Clay shook his hand warmly. "I am glad the debt is no greater."

Within two days, Clay and Randolph had exchanged cards before resuming their customary antagonism.

Van Buren had also seized on the proposed Panama conference as an issue that could ramp up hostility to Adams. He contended that the president should not accept a foreign invitation without congressional approval and was pleased when Calhoun indicated that he was prepared to join in what Van Buren termed a "general agreement of action between us."

In the past, the Monroe presidency often had seemed to embody George Washington's dream of a government without factions, but to Van Buren that vision was a nightmare. He considered tranquility an invitation to corruption and, inevitably, to tyranny. He wanted to revitalize the two-party system, and by late 1826, he believed he would achieve his goal by aligning himself with Jackson in upholding Jeffersonian principles and resisting Alexander Hamilton's vision of a powerful central government.

If Van Buren prevailed, the clash between two philosophies of government that had distressed Washington would be played out again three decades later.

The Panama conference seemed scuttled when members of the Senate Foreign Relations Committee resisted sending delegates, but the House and then the full Senate appropriated the necessary funds. To send along with the delegation, Clay prepared an eighteen-thousand-word document that outlined a policy of "good neighborhood." He upheld America's strict neutrality and urged the countries of the Southern Hemisphere to avoid European wars and resist colonization. Clay also floated a novel idea—forming an international coalition to fund the building of a canal through Panama's isthmus.

Fate and bad timing conspired to doom Clay's blueprint for the hemisphere. One commissioner died of a tropical fever before the convention began, and the other U.S. representatives arrived just as a follow-up session was concluding in Tucubaya, Mexico.

Van Buren could hobble the Adams administration, but he faced his own difficulties in cementing a coalition for the 1828 election. The previous year—to please sheep raisers in the North—he had supported higher tariffs on raw wool. That position risked alienating Southerners who would have to pay more for wool for their textile plants. With his customary deftness, however, Van Buren had emerged unscathed for the moment.

As Van Buren expanded his coalition, Adams was forced to recognize that leadership was slipping from his grasp. He was particularly annoyed by congressmen who reviled him in private but then showed up at White House dinners "always ready to introduce their friends to the President, to partake of his hospitality, and to recommend candidates for every vacant appointment."

Simply discrediting Adams, however, could not paper over the continuing disagreement about tariffs. Southerners complained that they sold their cotton on the open market, but were forced to buy manufactured goods protected by the U.S. government. Rather than sympathizing, Northern manufacturers held a convention in August 1827 to demand an increase in tariffs that would boost the high prices Southerners already paid.

Catering to the South, Van Buren and his bloc threw together the tariff bill of 1828, which favored farmers over New England manufacturing. Clay suspected that Van Buren's forces were not, in fact, backing their own proposal. He thought they wanted New England congressmen to kill the bill in order to reinforce Southern support for Jackson. Hoping to thwart them, Clay lobbied for the legislation's passage.

After enough compromises made the bill palatable to the North, Southerners took to calling it "the Tariff of Abominations." When it passed and Adams signed it, Van Buren's Southern allies were as outraged as he had expected. But there was an ominous side effect: John Calhoun returned home to South Carolina to write a manifesto upholding the right of any state to nullify a federal law that violated its constitutional rights.

Georgia's Cherokees had little interest in the intricate political games being played in Washington, except to deplore the growing support of white voters for Andrew Jackson. The chiefs saw Jackson's attitude toward them as, at best, conflicted. They maintained a forlorn hope that his expressed concern for his Indian allies from the Battle of Horseshoe Bend might temper his loyalty to his white militia.

President Adams had sent three army generals to learn whether the change in Cherokee leadership had softened opposition to the sale of tribal land. General John Cocke saw reason for optimism in the warm greeting he received from Major Ridge as an ally from the Creek War. Ridge also smoothly accepted a hundred-dollar "present" from Cocke. But citing their new constitution, Major Ridge and John Ross declined to meet further with the commissioners.

Because Georgia had never accepted Adams's Treaty of Washington, Governor Troup had sent out surveyors on September 1, 1826, the date fixed by the Treaty of Indian Springs, to begin identifying Creek and Cherokee lands for sale. When Creeks arrested the surveyors, Troup sent in soldiers to free them. He maintained that "Georgia is sovereign on her own soil."

Within the cabinet, Clay was the strongest advocate of dispatching federal troops to protect Indian rights, but Adams had lost heart for confrontation. He agreed that Clay was right in theory but doubted whether his administration could prevail. The president compromised with a threat that he had no intention of enforcing. Troup called Adams's bluff with deliberately insulting language.

"From the first decisive act of hostility" by the Adams administration, Troup wrote, "you will be considered and treated as a public enemy." In addition, the president and his cabinet would be seen as "the unblushing allies of the savages whose cause you have adopted."

Since the House and Senate seemed intent on frustrating him, Adams retaliated by turning the problem over to them. Yes, Adams said, he had a duty to enforce the law. But since the result could be civil war, he was submitting the question "to the wisdom of the Congress."

The House upheld Adams's Treaty of Washington in theory. With less enthusiasm, senators also approved Adams's actions but showed more concern for the state's rights of the Georgians. On November 13, 1827, the demoralized Creeks signed over their small remnant of territory within the state for a sum running to forty-three thousand dollars.

The experience contributed to Adams's disillusionment with the limits of his office. Despite the talk of benevolence and humanity, he lamented to his diary, "none of that benevolence is felt when the rights of the Indian comes in collision with the interest of the white man."

Adams's observation was a variation on a theme Thomas Jefferson had sounded as the Revolutionary War was ending. At that time, Jefferson had privately admitted the immorality of slavery and concluded, "Indeed, I tremble for my country when I reflect that God is just."

Nearly fifty years later, John Quincy Adams had come to believe that his countrymen had done more injuries to the Indians than all of the European colonists, soldiers, and traders combined. In language drier but equally heartfelt, his conclusion echoed Jefferson's: "They are crying sins for which we are answerable before a higher jurisdiction."

In December 1827, Georgia launched a legislative skirmish against the Cherokees by giving its state courts jurisdiction over the tribe in counties bordering the Cherokee Nation. The state legislature met yearly in November and December, and if no removal treaty was signed by 1828, Georgia threatened to extend its authority over the entire Cherokee territory. Legislators claimed the right to compel obedience to state laws "from all descriptions of people, be they white, red or black, who may reside within her limits."

Georgia's senators decided that the new Cherokee constitution was "inconsistent" with their state's rights and claimed not to be restricted by earlier agreements that Cherokee land must be obtained only peaceably. Instead, the Senate ruled that land could be taken on any terms recommended by the state's general assembly—although Georgia "would not attempt to improve her rights by violence until all other means of redress failed."

When George Troup declined to seek a second term that year, his party nominated John Forsyth. Like Troup, Forsyth was a Princeton graduate. A handsome, highly gregarious congressman and former U.S. minister to Spain, he had been accepting federal positions in Washington to please his wife, who detested Georgia's muggy heat. But coming back home, Forsyth was swept into the governorship when his opponent died just before the election. Although his words were genteel where Troup's had been bombastic, the new governor seemed committed to the same implacable policy.

The presidential candidates in 1828 were separated by significant differences on the issues, but lingering bitterness from the Adams-Clay bargain guaranteed that the campaign would be intensely personal. Adams understood that his cabinet officers would soon find excuses to leave his administration, and in his diary he exonerated them for looking for "a harbor from the storm." James Barbour wanted to give up the War Department to become minister to Great Britain, a post also sought by Daniel Webster of New Hampshire. Even Clay was talking about resigning because of poor health. Adams sympathized with the "load of obloquy, slander and persecution that had been heaped" on Clay and believed he "must go home and die or get better."

In the end, however, Clay would not risk the political impact of his resignation, and he stayed on to oversee Adams's reelection strategy.

Finessing the tradition against personal campaigning by presidential candidates, Andrew Jackson accepted an invitation from the Louisiana legislature to return to New Orleans for a belated victory celebration. Jackson found the recognition gratifying since many of those same men had been outraged by his high-handed conduct during the War of 1812 and had pointedly refused to thank him for saving their city.

The roistering in New Orleans lasted four days, longer than the battle itself. President Adams glanced through the extended coverage by newspapers from across the country and sneered that any man would "exhibit himself in pompous pageantry."

Adams demonstrated more seemly behavior when his ride home to Massachusetts called for him to stop for the night in Maryland. Competing rallies were under way for Jackson and himself in Baltimore, and Adams noted disdainfully, "A stranger would think that the people of the United States have no other occupation than electioneering."

When he reached Philadelphia, Adams could not avoid his well-wishers, who clamored for a speech. He could, though, deny them an effective one. Addressing the crowd from the porch of his hotel,

Adams held himself to eighteen words: "Fellow citizens, I thank you for this kind and friendly reception, and wish you all a good night."

Adams devised other ways to resist political expediency. By now, Calhoun was too estranged to serve again as his vice presidential candidate, and Adams flatly rejected advice that he entice the partially recovered William Crawford to replace Calhoun on the ticket. Adams appreciated the value of having a Georgian as his running mate, but he considered Crawford "like one of Milton's fallen angels." Except, Adams added, that Milton's creatures were at least loyal to one another, while Crawford had displayed "treachery of the deepest dye."

For vice president, Adams turned instead to his secretary of the Treasury, Richard Rush, a Philadelphian said to be more popular than Adams in the Middle States.

By now, members of the president's own administration could express open hostility to his policies, knowing they would pay no price for disloyalty. Adams had made it clear that he would reappoint each of them unless they were charged with "official or moral misconduct."

That blanket protection extended to Postmaster General John McLean, who was accused by Clay and Barbour of using his patronage to lobby against the administration. But when Adams demanded proof of malfeasance, neither man could supply specific examples, and McLean stayed on.

Adams was being subjected to scathing attacks by the opposition newspapers he called "peddlers of filth." One paper accused the president of polluting the White House by bringing in—admittedly, at his own expense—a billiard table. When Isaac Hill, editor of the *New Hampshire Patriot*, claimed that Adams had procured women in St. Petersburg for Czar Alexander, Hill's information came from the same Jonathan Russell who had tried to besmirch Adams during the last election. Now Russell claimed that Adams had attempted to influence the czar's policies by offering him a beautiful girl.

In his diary, Adams had long ago disposed of the kernel of fact behind the libel: A Boston housemaid had accompanied the Adamses to Russia. Writing home, the girl had referred to the czar's "amours and gallantries." Censors had opened her letter and sent it to Alexander, who laughed and showed it to his wife. When the maid later took young Charles Francis Adams to the palace, the royal couple chatted with the child for several minutes and met the Boston girl whose gossip had amused them.

"It is from that trivial incident," Adams complained in his diary, "that the base imputation has been trumped up."

From then on, antagonistic newspapers felt free to call Adams a pimp. The abuse echoed what had been heaped on his father during the 1800 election, but then friends of the elder Adams could punish attackers under the short-lived Alien and Sedition laws. These days, editors could assail this President Adams with impunity for his "kingly pomp," his habit of taking early morning swims, and, improbably, his sexual appetites.

Adams despaired at the effect the attacks would have on his future reputation. He lost the energy to keep up his previously crowded calendar and instead spent hours in his garden. Then he gave up even that pastime and sat at sundown each evening, condemning himself for his "torpid inaction."

Clay was trying to build a grassroots political organization called the National Republicans to challenge the expanding Jackson coalition. Allies urged him to admit that Adams was so unpopular that he was doomed to lose, and Clay should launch his own campaign for 1828. But Clay vowed to stick by Adams: "We are both guilty or innocent of the calumnies that have been propagated against both," he said, although he acknowledged that the accusations coming out of Kentucky were directed chiefly at him.

Hoping to counter the lingering charge of a corrupt bargain, Clay published late in 1827 a thirty-page pamphlet with a title that summed up its thrust: *"An Address of Henry Clay to the Public, Containing Certain Testimony in Refutation of the Charges against Him, Made by Gen. Andrew Jackson, Touching the Last Presidential Election."* In it, Clay included affidavits from Kentucky's representatives swearing that they had not voted for Adams because of undue pressure from Clay.

Adams did not try to dissuade Clay from circulating a document that was certain to keep the controversy alive. But he believed that "suspicion has been kindled into popular delusion" and that "General Jackson will therefore be elected." Adams's sole consolation was that, in time, "the electorate will find Jackson incompetent."

While white politicians were campaigning nationally, John Ross was absorbed with the parochial concern of staving off intrusions onto Cherokee Nation. Writing to one federal agent, Hugh Montgomery, Ross wanted to quiet what he termed the "clamour" in Georgia set off by the Cherokee constitution.

All the same, Ross resisted Secretary Barbour's request that the tribe give up a strip of its land for the seemingly benign purpose of building a canal to join rivers in Tennessee with those in Alabama. Ross warned that "the Cherokee nation objects to making further cession of lands to the United States, for any purpose whatsoever." The resulting canal might be only a narrow strip but it would be "in the heart of the nation" and would lead to "much embarrassment and litigation." As an alternative, Ross promised better roads.

With the presidential campaign exposing the biases of the nation's press, Ross and William Hicks spoke in their annual message of October 1828 for continued support for their own newspaper. They described the *Cherokee Phoenix* as a "powerful auxiliary in asserting and supporting our political rights." But except for restrictions against libel or inappropriate religious commentary, "the liberty of the press should be as free as the breeze that glides upon the surface."

They also addressed head-on the accusations circulated by white Georgians that "na-bobs" and Cherokees "*ruling* with an *'Iron rod'* were grinding down into dust the wretched and abject mass of our citizens." Ross and Hicks called on the tribe to reject those appeals to class hatred and continue instead on "the path of rectitude"—which meant selling no more Cherokee land.

As voting neared, Martin Van Buren had reason for confidence in his thriving "Jacksonian Democrats." Van Buren had been overwhelmingly elected to a second Senate term even before the unexpected death of his rival, Governor De Witt Clinton, left him in still greater command of New York politics.

For years, Van Buren had been waging a struggle for preeminence in New York among the factions that called themselves Republicans. His group from Tammany Hall was labeled the Bucktails for adorning their hats at political rallies with deer tails. Those Bucktails admitted that Clinton had brought off a solid achievement in pushing through funds for the Erie Canal. But they wanted to extend the vote to more farmers and city workers, and they regarded Clinton—although he might call himself a Jeffersonian Republican—as an aristocratic Federalist.

With Clinton gone from the scene, Van Buren considered his future and concluded that in 1824 he had concentrated on national campaigning at the expense of his New York base. He resolved not to repeat that mistake. Already he saw one potential threat in upstate New York from a growing anti-Masonic mood that might work to Adams's advantage.

The movement had begun after four Masons kidnapped—and presumably murdered—a stonemason named William Morgan for publishing secrets from the Masonic Lodge. Neither Van Buren nor President Adams were Masons, but Jackson was a prominent member—like George Washington and Benjamin Franklin before him. So, providentially, was Henry Clay. Van Buren hoped to neutralize Jackson's damning membership by identifying Clay with the society.

More crucial than tactics, however, was whether Van Buren should listen to friends and run to replace De Witt Clinton as governor. To weigh the political odds, he subjected himself to sweltering heat, rutted roads, and clouds of mosquitoes to make a lengthy canvass of upstate New York.

Van Buren did not dress down for his rural audiences. One Presbyterian churchgoer in Rochester marveled at the sight of him wearing "an elegant snuff-colored broadcloth coat, with velvet collar to match." It was set off by an orange silk cravat tipped with lace, yellow kid gloves, and a broad-brimmed beaver hat worthy of a Quaker.

His tour convinced Van Buren to seek the governorship while also keeping a firm hand on Jackson's presidential campaign. He did not expect to serve long as governor. A victorious Jackson was sure to offer him a cabinet post, and to guarantee that victory, Van Buren took time to dictate to editors how their newspapers should portray the hero of New Orleans. He stressed that the election represented a revival of Jeffersonian idealism, that it pitted Jackson's old-fashioned virtues against the power-hungry aristocracy exemplified by John Quincy Adams.

Calling the president of the United States a pimp might seem to be the low point of a political campaign, but worse was to come.

Attempting to match Van Buren's national network of friendly newspapers, Clay called on Daniel Webster to raise money for those editors who supported Adams and Clay's American System. One sympathizer, John Binns in Philadelphia, printed a leaflet with a black border titled *Some Accounts of Some of the Bloody Deeds of GENERAL JACKSON.* Binns's "Coffin Handbill" showed six coffins labeled with the names of militiamen whose death sentences Jackson had once approved.

Jackson protested that they were men who had mutinied and deserted before the Battle of New Orleans. One of them had been pardoned, he said, the others shot "for crimes of the deepest dye, perilous to the country." But the accusation also dredged up the case of hapless John Woods, a young militia recruit sentenced to death during the Creek War. Woods's offense was a trivial insubordination, but it had come when Jackson was facing an uprising of disgruntled militia. To enforce discipline, he had made an example of Woods, but, then and later, he had seemed to regret the boy's execution.

Joining in the attacks on Jackson, the editor of the *Cincinnati Gazette*, Charles Hammond, printed a list of fourteen indications of intemperate misconduct that should disqualify Jackson for high office. Daniel Webster's successful fund-raising allowed Clay to subsidize Hammond's paper by presenting him with a collection of typefaces worth five or six hundred dollars.

To refute the Coffin Handbill, Jackson's friends in Nashville banded together—opponents called them "the White-washing Committee"—and responded to the handbill with a sly satire: "COOL AND DELIBERATE MURDER," read their headline. "Jackson coolly and deliberately put to death upwards of fifteen hundred British troops on the 8th of January, 1815, on the plains below New Orleans for no other offense than they wished to sup in the city that night."

During America's brief history, politicians' wives had been spared even in the hardest-fought campaigns. Now, with the Adams supporters spreading salacious stories about Rachel Jackson, an editor named Duff Green struck back. The impecunious proprietor of a St. Louis newspaper, Green had come to Washington to acquire the *United States Telegraph*. He hoped to land lucrative government printing contracts once Jackson was elected.

To achieve that goal, Green printed the implausible suggestion that John Quincy and Louisa Adams had not waited for their wedding night to consummate their love. Upon publication, Green wrote proudly to Jackson: "Let Mrs. Jackson rejoice. Her vindication is now complete."

Instead of thanks, Green got the back of Jackson's hand: "I never war against females," Jackson wrote, "and it is only the base and cowardly that do."

Jackson was convinced that Henry Clay was just that base and cowardly. He blamed Clay for a barrage of stories about Rachel Jackson that sank below any speculation about Louisa Adams's deflowering.

Rumors about the Jacksons dated to a time in Nashville when Andrew was a young lawyer renting a room from Rachel's mother. Jackson had been drawn to Rachel Donelson Robards, whose husband was a womanizing brute both madly jealous and himself blatantly unfaithful. Rachel was no vamp, merely a plump and playful girl who enjoyed the lusty frontier dances. But Lewis Robards tormented his wife with accusations of infidelity until Rachel fled to Natchez with Jackson at her side.

Robards pursued them furiously through the legislature and the courts. After a hasty divorce, Jackson and Rachel thought they had been married, but Robards challenged the divorce's legality, and the marriage had to be repeated. Throughout the years afterward, the union of Jackson and Rachel was widely celebrated for its mutual affection. "The General always treated her as if she were his pride and glory," one army officer's daughter observed, "and words can faintly describe her devotion to him."

But Charles Hammond had seized upon the messiness of Rachel's earlier status to denounce Jackson for inducing another man's wife to desert her lawful husband. In an editorial, Hammond put the question starkly: "Ought a convicted adulteress and her paramour husband be placed in the highest offices of this free and christian land?"

Until that point, Hammond had merely embroidered on the known facts, and Clay continued to praise him as the most effective journalist supporting the president. Then Hammond veered into fiction: "General Jackson's mother was a COMMON PROSTITUTE," Hammond began another editorial, "brought to this country by the British soldiers! She afterwards married a MULATTO MAN, with whom she had several children, of which number GENERAL JACKSON IS ONE." In case readers missed that revelation, Hammond added three exclamation points.

Reading the allegations against Rachel, Jackson had longed to horsewhip their authors. To John Coffee, he wrote, "How hard it is to keep a cowhide from these villains." But it was the attack on his mother, a widow who had raised him until she died when he was fourteen, that brought Jackson to tears. He expressed his bitterness to a friend that "my pious mother, nearly fifty years in the tomb, and who, from her cradle to her death, had not a speck upon her character, has been dragged forth." Jackson could only try to keep on shielding his wife, whose health these days seemed increasingly fragile.

Rachel Jackson was already dreading the prospect of life in Washington, sure that her plain and rustic ways would be mocked there. That same officer's daughter who praised Rachel's devotion also described the mistress of the Hermitage as "a stout little old woman, whom you might easily mistake for the General's washerwoman."

Throughout Tennessee, she was "Aunt Rachel," known for her good heart and abiding faith. But her favorite dances were the thumping reels of the frontier, and she knew that fashionable ladies did not share her habit of smoking a pipe after dinner. When she permitted herself a rare lamentation, Rachel Jackson would sigh and say that she "had rather be a doorkeeper in the house of God than to live in that palace in Washington."

To add to her cares, Rachel's adopted son, Lyncoya, took seriously ill in the spring of 1828. Jackson had come upon the Indian child after his defeat of the Creeks at Tallushatchee left the boy an orphan. A white colonel's daughter had first taken charge of the child and named him before Lyncoya was sent to the Hermitage with a Creek slave as his nurse. Jackson intended him as a playmate for his adopted son, the nephew named Andrew, Jr., and a second Indian child whom the Jacksons called Theodore.

The boy surprised the Jacksons when, at age five, he could already make an Indian bow despite having no contact with his former tribe. The family also observed that Lyncoya enjoyed painting his face and jumping out from behind trees to scare his schoolmates. As Lyncoya was growing up, Jackson had hoped he would be accepted at West Point, but the boy was sent instead to Nashville as a saddle maker's apprentice. When he developed lung trouble, he returned to the Hermitage, where, despite Rachel's nursing, he died at the age of sixteen.

Rachel continued to give public support to her husband's ambitions, but what she managed to hear of the campaign rumors could bring her to tears. Jackson sensed the toll on her health: "The persecution she has suffered," he wrote, "has endeared her to me more if possible than ever."

Rachel's own lungs seemed as damaged as Lyncoya's had been. She spoke of heart palpitations, and she wheezed as she moved laboriously from room to room.

At least one newspaper was ignoring the sordid presidential campaign. The focus of the *Cherokee Phoenix* remained resolutely local, concentrating its wary attention on Georgia's governor, who had decreed, "To the Cherokees within the State, we owe protection and to us they owe obedience."

At one point, Elias Boudinot tendered his resignation after he could not persuade the Cherokee Council to vote enough money for him to hire an assistant. But he recognized the importance of his creation and, although he complained about being overworked, he carried on as editor. At home, Boudinot could depend on the support of his wife and children—Mary, Eleanor, and William Penn. The boy had not been named for the Quaker colonist but for Boudinot's friend Jeremiah Evarts, who was signing that alias to the pro-Cherokee letters he published in Boston.

The *Phoenix* was on guard when Georgians returned to the argument that the mass of Cherokees wanted to move west but were being prevented by an elite within the Cherokee Nation. The paper quoted a Georgia state senator named Wofford: "The majority of these Indians do not wish to remain where they are. But they are kept there by cunning white men, and half-breeds, for their own purposes. It is not in the interest of the Indians to stay there, and if they were not restrained, they would not remain one year in the territory."

Boudinot labeled it a "bare-faced falsehood," but he knew how persuasive that explanation might sound to Andrew Jackson with his commitment to the common man. Samuel Worcester weighed in against a Georgia newspaper's accusation that a "northern missionary" was dictating the policies of the *Phoenix.* Worcester asked that the hostile editor run his disclaimer that he had never "given or initiated my opinion to the editor of the *Phoenix*, in regard to the insertion or rejection of any communication in that paper."

By now, Boudinot was editing his journal with an eye toward sympathetic subscribers in the North who might raise a public outcry against the Georgians. In that spirit, Boudinot printed the final report from Adams's secretary of war. Although it denied that the Cherokees were an independent nation, it also rejected Georgia's view that the tribe was "mere tenants at will, subject, like the buffalo of the prairies, to be hunted from their country whenever it may suit our interest or convenience to take possession of it."

John Quincy Adams had been, at best, an ineffectual guardian of the Cherokees, but he had not been their enemy.

With sentiment running strongly against Adams, his campaign attempted to exploit a rift that had opened between Jackson and James Monroe. A Tennessee editor claimed that Monroe, as secretary of war, had not supported Jackson fourteen years earlier at New Orleans. Monroe defended his actions but in a way that ruffled Jackson, and Adams supporters seized on the controversy to ask both Monroe and James Madison to back their ticket in Virginia.

Both men refused. Monroe explained that men who had held the office of president "should abstain after their retirement from becoming partisans in subsequent elections to the office."

But dredging up that dispute from bygone days had disturbing repercussions for John Calhoun. In recent years, Jackson had come to regard Calhoun as a loyal ally and was pleased to run with him as his vice presidential candidate. Then Sam Houston, now one of Jackson's aides, got hold of a letter from President Monroe that made it clear Calhoun had urged cabinet members to censure Jackson for his rash actions in Florida. At the time, Secretary of State Adams had been the one to defend Jackson. But by 1828, that hardly mattered. Reading of Calhoun's duplicity set off one of Jackson's rages:

"It smelled so much of deception," Jackson said, "that my hair stood on end for one hour."

Monroe could patch things over with Jackson, but Jackson remained cool to Calhoun, even though they were now linked on the same ticket. They might both be dedicated to unseating Adams, but the tariff debate had revealed a fundamental difference: Jackson remained dedicated to preserving the Union. Calhoun upheld the Union in theory even as he was devising a rationale for its dissolution.

After the months of scurrility, votes were finally cast in Pennsylvania and Ohio during the two weeks starting on October 31. The last ballots came in from Tennessee on November 14, and the electoral vote reflected the country's division—83 for Adams, 178 for Jackson.

The president carried all of New England, except for one renegade district in Maine. He took New Jersey and Delaware, and another six votes in Maryland to Jackson's five. In New York, only Van Buren's presence on the ticket had saved the state for Jackson. As Van Buren was winning the governorship by 30,000 votes, Jackson's majority was a mere 5,000.

The popular vote was not entirely a rout, although Adams lost to Jackson 508,064 to 647,276. The president's respectable showing was due to large majorities in New England and New York.

But throughout all of Tennessee, Adams and Rush got fewer than three hundred votes. In one village, Jackson's supporters had hoped to cast a unanimous vote for him and chased into the woods two men who voted for Adams. Had the men not escaped, their pursuers intended to tar and feather them.

Late in November, after his home state of Kentucky had gone solidly for Jackson, Clay stated the obvious to Daniel Webster: "We are beaten." Clay did not want to dwell on the reasons. He preferred to remember that their party still had the superior policies while the opposition had only the presidency.

At a dinner in his honor before he left Washington, Clay could not resist a few jabs at Jackson. Rather than utter his name, Clay called him "that citizen." He "has done me much injustice—wanton, unprovoked and unatoned injustice." In an attempt at magnanimity, Clay went on, "But my relations to that citizen by a recent event are now changed. He is the Chief Magistrate of my country."

Clay concluded that if that man's own conscience and his God could forgive him, "suppressing, as far as I can, a sense of personal wrong," Clay, too, would be "willing even to forgive him" and hope that he would uphold the country's free institutions and increase the nation's happiness.

Once again, an election had thwarted Clay's dream of the presidency, but he turned away sympathy and reminded supporters that after an election "patriotism and religion both unite in enjoining submission and resignation."

As for Adams, the sweep of his loss depressed him. He began the New Year by writing on January 1, 1829, that he took "comfort and consolation" from the Bible's first psalm, which promised blessings for the righteous man. Twenty-eight years earlier, his father had trumped up an excuse to avoid watching Thomas Jefferson be sworn in as his successor. Now John Quincy resolved not to attend the inauguration of a man who had spent four years undercutting and reviling him.

For the nation's politicians, the months between Jackson's election and his inauguration were given over to intense jockeying for power. From New York, Van Buren solicited Washington news from an ally by joking that "you might as well turn the current of the Niagara with a lady's fan as to prevent scheming and intrigue."

As he waited during the first week of January 1829 for the invitation to join Jackson's cabinet, Van Buren delivered his inaugural address as governor. He called for a program to house the growing number of young criminals being bred in New York City slums and urged a curb on election excesses—presumably including those by his own party. He persuaded the legislature to forbid the entertaining of voters, and he also addressed a banking problem that was certain to occupy the Jackson administration. Van Buren recommended a plan to let the forty state banks band together for protection against catastrophic losses.

In Kinderhook, Van Buren had grown up in cramped family quarters, and he reveled now in the chance to buy a three-story brick mansion in Albany called Stevenson House, a few blocks from the capitol building. Since he did not intend to live there long, he took care to choose a house that could be easily rented.

Van Buren might have been disconcerted had he known that at the Hermitage the president-elect was drawing up a list of rules for his administration. To avoid any echo of the Adams-Clay deal that Jackson had been denouncing for the past four years, he intended to stipulate that no member of his cabinet should succeed him in the White House.

From their home states, Van Buren and Calhoun eyed each other warily. One neutral Massachusetts congressman noted that Calhoun "has been working South Carolina into a frenzy on the tariff question for the purpose of re-popularizing himself in the Southern Crawford states, and making it impossible for Van B. to get any strength there."

On his plantation, Calhoun distracted himself from politics with his four sons and two daughters. He had secured an appointment to West Point for seventeen-year-old Andrew, but the boy decided against a military career and switched to Yale. His father accepted the change but worried about the fiber of Andrew's fellow students. As Calhoun wrote to one of his former professors, "I would deem an idle and immoral room mate a great misfortune."

Otherwise, Calhoun assured his correspondents that "we are quiet here, and will remain so till the President elect arrives, when, I suppose, the formation of his cabinet will lead to some excitement."

Since Jackson had not announced his rule about succeeding him, the obvious prize once again would be secretary of state. As vice president, Calhoun was ineligible and was troubled by signs that Van Buren did not intend to fill out his term as governor and would be heading back to Washington. Everyone was taking Jackson at his word that he would serve a single term, and Duff Green was already suggesting in his *Telegraph* that Calhoun was the best man to succeed him.

But Jackson was about to be distracted by a crisis more urgent to him than filling his cabinet posts, coping with tariffs, or dealing with the obdurate Cherokees.

Andrew Jackson

6 · Andrew Jackson (1829)

WITH THE ELECTION decided, the president-elect asked Andrew Jackson Donelson—Rachel's nephew and his namesake—to go with him to Washington as his secretary. Donelson, about to turn thirty, had been raised as Jackson's ward at the Hermitage. His uncle had arranged his appointment to West Point, had taken him as an aide on the Florida skirmishes, and had underwritten his law studies. In 1824, Donelson had married his cousin, Emily Donelson, who was twenty-one and would serve as Rachel's companion.

The new First Lady sounded resigned about the future: "Well, for Mr. Jackson's sake, I am glad. For my own part, I never wished it."

A family member, mocking the patois of slaves at the Hermitage, portrayed them as more enthusiastic than Rachel about the move: "Mistus and Marster done elected President, and gwine lib in de White House."

If Rachel had winced at the prospect of life in Washington, a fresh reason now presented itself. Unaware that Nashville's matrons had gathered in secret to sew a wardrobe suitable to her new position, Rachel had gone to town to buy dresses since, even at his most affectionate, Jackson had sometimes reminded her of the figure she must cut as his wife.

Walking between shops soon tired her, and Rachel went to rest in the private office of a relative in town. But he happened to be a newspaper editor. On his desk was one of the leaflets prepared by the Jackson camp to counter charges from the opposition.

For the first time, Rachel realized the extent of the personal campaign waged against her. Sobbing hysterically, she crouched in a corner and sank to the floor. When her friends came to collect her, they found her still there, shaken and weeping. But Rachel was determined not to distress her husband, and during the twelve-mile carriage ride back to the Hermitage she composed herself. Once there, however, her efforts to appear blithe were so transparent that Jackson soon pried out the truth.

When Rachel's depressed mood persisted, Emily Donelson's mother grew alarmed and urged her simply to dismiss the malicious gossip. No, Rachel replied, "I'll never forget it." She said she appreciated the care her family had taken to spare her but "it seemed as though a veil had been lifted" and she was forced to see herself "as others see me, a poor old woman."

Rachel announced that she would not be going to Washington. Instead, as she had done many times during her husband's military excursions and service in Congress, she would stay on at the Hermitage.

Her decision was never tested. Rachel began to withdraw into herself, and on December 18, 1828, she had a heart attack and died four days later. Jackson spent the night sitting next to her body, his face in his hands.

In Cherokee country, even the children understood that a new assault on their land might be coming. The teacher in a missionary school told her class that they must get a good education quickly because they could soon be removed to a place where there were no schools. A teenage girl reported that the younger children rebelled against that warning. One boy protested, "They have got more land than they use. What do they want to get ours for?" And another said, "If the white people want more land, let them go back to the country they came from."

John Ross shared the apprehension. He led a delegation to Washington early in January 1829 to urge replacing Hugh Montgomery, the federal agent whom Ross considered hostile. Although Montgomery had failed to negotiate the settlement that Adams sought, he was having some success in persuading Cherokees to move west voluntarily. But other Cherokees resented Montgomery because he had refused to move to New Echota. He complained that too few of its residents observed the Sabbath and that too many drunks lived there.

Ross's delegates also accused Montgomery of violating both U.S. and tribal laws by allowing white men to live within the Cherokee Nation and by declining to prosecute other white intruders. Ross brought supporting statements from Thomas McKenney, the Indian Affairs commissioner, but his request for a new agent was denied.

With Washington in turmoil from the recent election, Ross made no progress on other fronts, and he prepared to leave for home soon after Andrew Jackson was inaugurated.

Rachel Jackson had been dead barely a month when her widower had to launch his triumphant march to claim the presidency. Traveling with the Donelsons and a party of friends, Jackson took a steamboat down the Cumberland River to the Ohio and then up the river to Cincinnati. A huge crowd turned out to cheer his progress, and he received another ovation when he disembarked in Pittsburgh.

Spectators saw a subdued Jackson dressed in deep mourning. His rigid posture and coxcomb of white hair gave him a look of severity and age beyond his sixty-one years. Men closest to him had observed a change that they attributed to losing Rachel; the casual oaths with which he had peppered his speech were largely gone. In putting down a mutiny among his militia, Jackson's prodigious gift for swearing had been invaluable in cowing the rebels. But grief seemed to have purged his vocabulary.

After three weeks of traveling, Jackson reached the capital. During his overland route along Cumberland Road, supporters ignored his stated wish that his mourning be respected and swarmed around his entourage, begging for a handshake, a touch. Daniel Webster's brother reported on the phenomenon. "The people always supported Mr. Adams' cause from a cold sense of duty," Ezekiel Webster wrote, "and not from any liking of the man." If their party had nominated a more popular man, either Clay or indeed "any man who we are not compelled by our natures, instincts and fixed fate to dislike, the result would have been different."

Perhaps not. There was only one Hero of New Orleans, and Van Buren's strategy had been to hail Andrew Jackson as the nation's savior against an entrenched and corrupt elite. Although they had both won fame on the battlefield, Jackson's differences with George Washington were pronounced. At the age of twenty, Washington had inherited substantial property upon the death of an older brother. Born thirty-five years after Washington, Jackson had been left an impoverished orphan at the age of fourteen. While Washington grew up seeking approval from the landed gentry, Jackson wanted to strip them of their inherited privilege.

Jackson had become the first man since Washington to reach the presidency without a college education. Washington had worked in his youth as an apprentice surveyor; Jackson completed the informal studies to become a lawyer.

As a military commander in his early twenties, Washington had committed a series of blunders during his first battle in the French and Indian War. But with luck and by learning from his mistakes, he led his new nation to independence.

Jackson's service in uniform was briefer but epic in its own way. The improbable scale of his victory over the British in the Battle of New Orleans at the age of forty-eight captured the imagination of the world and left him lionized by his countrymen.

But Jackson was not venerated in the way of Washington. His manners, although marked by a natural courtliness, had never lost their trace of the backwoods. And from his diligent study of the ways of society, Washington could rein in the same sort of explosive temper that Jackson freely indulged.

In marriage, both men found congenial wives. After his first love rejected him, Washington had courted a wealthy widow, Martha Custis, and achieved tranquility with her. Jackson ran off with another man's wife and clung to her until her death.

As for their dealings with America's Indians, Washington owed his first victory to the native warriors of the French and Indian War. Jackson also drew on friendly tribes for support, but his first great victory had come at Horseshoe Bend with the slaughter of the Creeks.

Washington entered the presidency at the age of fifty-seven, dedicated to bringing the nation together. Four decades later, Jackson was reaching the presidency two weeks before his sixty-second birthday and with an expanding United States clamoring for partisan leadership. There could be only one father of his country, but Andrew Jackson was temperamentally suited to becoming America's stern uncle.

Jackson checked into a large suite at the National Hotel—promptly labeled "the Wigwam"—and tried to receive every visitor until the demand grew too great and he became available only to his political cronies and to officials like Calhoun.

Jackson sounded out his allies about naming Van Buren his secretary of state, and finding no opposition, offered him the job in mid-February. Writing to Albany, Jackson said that he needed Van Buren's "intelligence & sound judgment" and urged him to come to Washington as soon as possible.

Several in Van Buren's inner circle argued against his accepting the call. They claimed he could be more valuable by staying in Albany and building up a Northern party than by taking a subordinate position with a Southerner. But Van Buren was reversing himself again. Since the defeat of Crawford, he had devoted much of the past four years to state politics. Now was the time to forge a stronger bond between the geographical wings of his party. Then, too, the State Department offered a more reliable path to the presidency than anything Albany could promise. Within a week he accepted Jackson's invitation. Van Buren's ally in Washington, James A. Hamilton, the third son of Alexander Hamilton, would fill the position at State temporarily while Van Buren wound up his affairs in New York.

Despite Jackson's professed need of him, the new president was cavalier in rejecting his recommendations for other cabinet posts. Edward

Livingston, a former New York City mayor who had left the North tainted by financial scandal, had become a trusted Jackson aide during the Battle of New Orleans. Jackson told him he could have any cabinet job he wanted except secretary of state. Since State was the only position that tempted him, Livingston decided to remain in Louisiana and let friends angle for his being appointed minister to France.

As a young congressman, Louis McLane had been one of those men who shared quarters with Van Buren in Georgetown. But when Van Buren recommended McLane as secretary of the Treasury, a job considered second in importance only to his own, Jackson appointed instead Samuel Ingham of Pennsylvania. Ingham had supported Crawford in 1824 before swinging to Jackson in the last election and proving his new loyalty with attacks throughout his state on the unholy Adams-Clay bargain.

John McLean, a fifth column in Adams's administration, welcomed a nomination to the U.S. Supreme Court. His replacement as postmaster general was William Barry, a Kentuckian who had broken off a long friendship with Clay because of the rumored deal with Adams.

In many ways, John Henry Eaton's appointment was as inevitable as Van Buren's. Born in North Carolina but moving to Tennessee in his early twenties, Eaton was one of Jackson's closest friends and a fund of stories, humorous but always decorous. Eaton had written an admiring Jackson biography and had managed his Senate campaign in 1822, and Eaton's first wife had been one of Jackson's wards. Since her death, Eaton had become linked in public with a young widow, Margaret Timberlake.

Margaret O'Neale had first met Andrew Jackson early in 1819, when Jackson came to Washington to defend himself against charges that he had overstepped his authority by his conduct in Florida. During his short stay in town, he had taken most meals with the O'Neale family at the popular Franklin House and had come to enjoy the company of their pert nineteen-year-old daughter. Margaret liked to think that she and Jackson shared the same temperament—passionate in both their loves and hates. After their evenings of spirited conversations, Jackson paid her his highest compliment: "Young lady, you remind me of my wife."

Margaret's father ran Franklin House, which was between the White House and Georgetown. Much later, when Margaret was scorned for being merely a tavernkeeper's daughter, she embraced that description defiantly. But she preferred to think of the Franklin as "a first-class boarding house for first-class people."

Extremely pretty, Margaret had grown up as the pet of her father's distinguished boarders, and Dolley Madison once presented the girl with a prize for dancing the gavotte. When Jackson returned to stay at Franklin House four years later as a freshman senator from Tennessee, he had written home to Rachel to praise Margaret's talent at the piano and the way on Sunday evenings that she "entertains her pious mother with sacred music to which we are invited."

For her part, Margaret appreciated Senator Jackson's innate delicacy. He would never simply hand her mother the money he owed her. Instead, he would enclose the bills in an envelope and add a note of appreciation. As for Rachel, when Margaret met her, she found Jackson's wife extremely good-hearted and kind—as everyone did—but also large, portly, and "a woman of uncultivated manners."

With adolescence, Margaret displayed a marked susceptibility to good-looking men. She flirted merrily with the army's adjutant general before deciding he was too old to be a serious candidate for marriage. Next she tried to elope with a dashing aide to General Winfield Scott, since she was giddy enough at fifteen to think that "an elopement was the crowning grace of a girl's life." Her father foiled that attempt and shipped her off to a New York boarding school, where Governor De Witt Clinton was more than willing to keep an eye on his friend's spirited daughter.

Begging to come home, Margaret promised to end her romantic escapades. But standing at the window one day, she called, "Come here, Mother. Here is my husband riding on horseback."

Mrs. O'Neale said the girl was being ridiculous, but after going to take a look, she admitted, "He *is* a handsome fellow."

Margaret Eaton

John Henry Eaton

John B. Timberlake, a purser in the U.S. Navy, had seen Margaret at the same moment, and he inveigled an invitation to dinner. Before the next weekend was out, they were engaged.

Margaret was elated to have the chaplain of the U.S. Senate conduct her wedding ceremony. President Monroe's secretary of the navy and Dolley Madison were among the guests, along with, as the bride would recall, "all the best families in the neighborhood."

Timberlake, however, proved to be a poor provider. He ran through the money that Margaret's father had given him to open a store and then added debts that totaled another fifteen thousand dollars. To support his family, he returned to sea, shipping out with Oliver Perry's brother, Matthew, and sending home twenty-five dollars in gold and baskets of fruit from his Southern ports of call. During a period when Timberlake was back in Washington, John Eaton arrived as a senator and moved into Franklin House. To hear Margaret tell it, Major Eaton became a close friend of her amiable if improvident young husband and had once bailed Timberlake out of another serious financial crisis.

It could seem natural, then, that when Timberlake went back to sea, Eaton would take Margaret—now the mother of a son who was destined to die in his sixth month—for rides in his carriage and would try, in other avuncular ways, to divert the restless young woman.

Between his travels, Timberlake returned to Washington, where a daughter was born. As he left in 1828 for what would prove to be the last time, Margaret was pregnant again but expected him home for the birth. While his ship was sailing the Mediterranean, however, Timberlake died in his bunk at Port Mahon in the Balearic Islands. The ship's log listed the cause of death as pulmonary disease. Death at sea was an occupational hazard; soon after she lost her husband, Margaret's two brothers, both West Point graduates, died of a fever contracted in Havana.

All the same, rumors spread in Washington that Timberlake had cut his throat because of Margaret's affair with John Eaton.

Margaret withdrew from society for one year of mourning. After she emerged, Major Eaton was often seen at her side whenever he could spare time from Jackson's presidential campaign.

Eaton intended to propose to the widow, now twenty-eight, although he had heard the salacious stories about their conduct before Timberlake's death. Troubled, he wrote to Jackson, who considered Eaton like a son.

Eaton said he was prepared to save Margaret from the slanders of "a gossiping world." Jackson still seethed from the abuse heaped on his own wife. To Eaton's implicit request for permission, he responded from the heart: "If you love Margaret Timberlake, go and marry her at once and shut their mouths."

That the widow Timberlake would accept Eaton was never in doubt. Margaret thought he represented "a great match for any girl in America." She found him handsome; at thirty-eight, he had lost his wife but kept his hair. And he was still rich, even after returning her dowry to his first wife's family. Margaret expected blithely that because "most of the belles in Washington were setting their caps for him," she would become the object of their jealousy. They were wed on January 1, 1829.

By the time Jackson completed his cabinet, his appointees shared two qualities—they were hostile to Henry Clay and they were considered second-rate. Navy Secretary John Branch and Attorney General John McPherson Berrien had both voted against confirming Clay as secretary of state. Although other nominees were known to be loyal to Calhoun, Jackson refused to name anyone from South Carolina who might share Calhoun's views on states' rights and nullification. "They are fine fellows," Jackson said, "but their zeal got the best of their discretion." He showed his lingering resentment over past snubs by shutting out Virginias from consideration. Their state had already held its share of high offices, Jackson said.

Official Washington commented harshly on the cabinet's lack of distinction. Except for Van Buren, the appointments were summed up in a popular catchphrase—"the millenium of the minnows." Britain's minister reported to London that the list had been met by "a general expression of disappointment."

Jackson was pleased to have surrounded himself with such affable men, however, and claimed his cabinet was "one of the strongest" in the nation's forty-year history. Yet even a newspaperman friendly to Jackson now questioned the campaign slogan of "Jackson and Reform." He said reform seemed to mean merely substituting Adams's placeholders with mediocrities loyal to Jackson.

Van Buren gave no sign that he was dismayed to be serving with men without his ability or prestige. Their lack of distinction would make it easier to counter whatever influence Calhoun might try to exercise through his friends.

The day of the inauguration on March 4, 1829, dawned sunny and pleasantly warm. To profit from the massive influx of tourists, boarding houses had tripled their rates, and visitors were sleeping on tavern floors or outdoors in the pastures around Georgetown.

Daniel Webster said he had never seen such a crowd and noted wonderingly, "Persons have come five hundred miles to see General Jackson, and they really seem to think that the country is rescued from some dreadful danger!" As a friend of the Adams administration, Webster was reminded less of voters celebrating a return to the "people's government" than of barbarians sacking ancient Rome.

Fifteen years earlier, Francis Scott Key's stanzas had celebrated America's survival at Fort McHenry, and today Key's view of the throbbing mass of humanity was different from Webster's. "It is beautiful!" Key exclaimed. "It is sublime!"

At 11 a.m., Jackson stepped out from his hotel, surrounded by the cadre of veterans from the Revolutionary War that would escort him to the Capitol. Behind them came troops from the Battle of New Orleans, now fourteen years older. Bareheaded and dressed simply in black, Jackson towered over his guardians, waving and nodding to the cheers and cries of good luck.

Once inside the Capitol, Jackson joined the assembled officials to witness Calhoun being sworn in as vice president. A chair set out for Adams remained empty. At noon, Jackson filed with the others to the East Portico, where women from the official party were occupying a row of sofas. At the sight of Jackson, they saluted by waving their handkerchiefs.

When he reached the building's steps, thousands of men removed their hats in tribute. The Marine band struck up "The President's March," while an artillery company launched a twenty-four-gun salute. As the music faded, Jackson faced the crowd silently for a moment and then made a low bow to the people who had brought him so far.

Spilling across the south side of the Capitol lawn, his audience strained to hear Jackson begin his address with a close paraphrase from Jefferson's first inaugural. Although Jackson had been hailed as Jefferson's heir, the two men had never been close. Jefferson found Jackson somewhat vulgar and ill-educated; Jackson regarded Jefferson as one more of the aristocratic Virginians who despised him. He saw

Jefferson as a man unproved in battle but endowed at birth with the standing that Jackson had fought a lifetime to achieve. What united them was their hostility to Northern bankers and speculators and the danger those men posed to the country.

Jackson's address lasted a scant ten minutes. Perhaps intentionally, his remarks on the issues of the day were vague. He made no mention of slavery since it had played no part in the campaign, and only the *New York American* had condemned Jackson for owning slaves. Instead, the divisive national issue of the day was the tariff, and Jackson's remarks trod cautiously: The Constitution required "that the great interests of agriculture, commerce and manufacturers, should be equally favored." Exceptions should be allowed only if a specific product was essential to preserving America's independence.

As for the construction projects and other national improvements that Adams had promoted, Jackson acknowledged their importance, but he insisted that they must conform to the Constitution.

Arguing that standing armies were dangerous to freedom, Jackson pledged not to enlarge the military services. Then, in a gesture to critics who had deplored his own high-handed behavior in uniform, Jackson said he would not "disregard that salutary lesson of political experience which teaches that the military should be subordinate to the civil power."

For the Cherokees waiting for clues to Jackson's Indian policy, the new president offered one highly qualified guarantee: "It will be my sincere and constant desire to observe toward the Indian tribes within our limits a just and liberal policy, and to give that humane and considerate attention to their rights and their wants which is consistent with the habits of our Government and the feelings of our people."

In his closing moments, Jackson finally gave the crowd an echo of the partisanship from the last election. He would undertake "the task of *reform*," he promised, stressing the word. Reform was vital because of abuses that had placed "power in unfaithful or incompetent hands."

Jackson concluded with a nod to "the goodness of that Power whose providence mercifully protected our national infancy." With the speech concluded, U.S. Chief Justice John Marshall prepared to administer the oath of office. Jackson was handed a Bible, which he pressed to his lips before setting it aside to shake hands with the chief justice.

Then it was off to the White House and a reception unmatched before or since.

As Jackson came down from the Capitol, a vast wave of men rushed to shake his hand. Although he towered over his countrymen, age and wounds from a lifetime of dueling had left him vulnerable to the crowds that hemmed him in on all sides. When at last a path was cleared, Jackson mounted a white horse waiting to carry him to his new home. The vast throng followed on foot and in wagons, carriages, and the carts used on other days to haul wood and vegetables.

When Jackson reached the White House, he found the lawn dense with more well-wishers. He was able to slip inside, but the crush made it impossible for his friends to join him. The lower floor was packed with a motley crowd of men and women whose appearance scandalized Associate Supreme Court Justice Joseph Story. "All sorts of people," Story complained to his wife back in Boston, "from the highest and most polished, down to the most vulgar and gross in the nation."

It was the class of citizens that the nation's founders had feared and tried to insulate their new republic against, the sort of men who had destroyed the house of the Massachusetts governor in the days when he was appointed by the British king. Even the language of Joseph Story's letter harked back to that revolutionary era. "The reign of King Mob seemed triumphant," he wrote. "I was glad to escape from the scene as soon as possible."

Very soon, a getaway had to be arranged for the guest of honor. Trying to reach Jackson, one journalist jumped through the window of an adjoining room, then watched as a cohort of the new president's friends barricaded him behind their bodies and pressed through the clamoring masses to safety. Jackson went gratefully to rooms at a nearby hotel. It was already 4 p.m., but for his uninvited guests, the afternoon had just begun.

Servants had mixed barrelsful of orange punch. When they tried to bring them out, a new surge of people knocked over their pails and broke the serving glasses. James Hamilton, Jr., of South Carolina, surveyed the scene with grim humor. He described the mob as "spirits black, yellow and grey" who assaulted the mansion "in one uninterrupted stream of mud and filth, among the throngs many fit subjects for the penitentiary." Hamilton, who detested the views of William Wilberforce, a prominent British opponent of slavery, delighted in imagining his reaction: "It would have done Mr. Wilberforce good to have seen a stout black wench eating a jelly with a gold spoon on the lawn of the President's House."

As dusk approached, boys were still larking in the halls and leaping on damask chairs with their muddy boots. The celebration might have gone on to midnight if waiters had not cleared the mansion by carrying tubs of punch to the grass outside.

While Jackson's supporters reveled in a style befitting the first frontier president, the last president linked directly to the nation's creators continued his melancholy ride home to Massachusetts. John Quincy Adams was preparing to devote the rest of his life to salvaging the thing dearest to him and "defend and vindicate my own reputation."

Returning to Congress in 1827 after a three-year hiatus from politics, Wilson Lumpkin of Georgia had worked tirelessly behind the scenes to rid his state of the Cherokees. Like many Virginians, his family had moved to the frontier when Lumpkin was an infant, and he grew up in the Georgia piedmont that would become Oglethorpe County. A bookish young man, Lumpkin left farming to study law and became absorbed with the relationship of Indians to his state. He had been serving in the Georgia legislature after the first Creek treaty when President Monroe appointed him as federal commissioner to set the treaty's official boundaries.

Lumpkin's other compelling interest was transportation. Named to his state's new board of public works, he produced a study of the terrain for a rail line from Milledgeville to Chattanooga that convinced him even further that the presence of the Cherokees hindered Georgia's development.

Lumpkin's first wife had died in 1819 after nineteen years of marriage. A widower with five children, he married again two years later and started a new family. Most recently, as a member of the House Committee on Indian Affairs he had been arguing strenuously that evacuating the Indians would be for their own good, that placing them under federal control far away from Georgia would give them a home where (Lumpkin's audience might detect sarcasm) "the missionary efforts of all pious and good men—Churches, Christian Associations—might have a permanent field of labor, to carry out their good designs of Christianizing and civilizing a most interesting heathen people."

Lumpkin made no apology about taking the lead in Congress for removal. He deliberately kept silent on other matters to avoid offending House colleagues whose votes he would need for his cause, which he preferred to call "Indian reform."

In the 1824 election, Lumpkin had supported Jackson over William Crawford and felt vindicated to see his state swing to Jackson four years later. "I was now applauded," he said, "for what I had then been condemned." Although Lumpkin fully expected Jackson's support for removal, he delayed in introducing his legislation because the congressional short session ended on March 4, 1829.

Lumpkin fretted over the delay because "Northern fanatics, male and female, had gone to work and gotten up thousands of petitions, signed by more than a million, of men, women and children, protesting against the removal of the poor, dear Indians, from the states where they were located to West of the Mississippi."

In his *Phoenix*, Elias Boudinot was regularly reprinting Northern editorials that supported the Cherokee position. The *Connecticut Journal* suggested that if Georgia forced out its Indians, what would stop New York State from dispossessing Red Jacket and his tribe of

Senecas? "It is quite idle, at this time, to talk of coercion," the *Journal*'s editor wrote. Giving Indians a fair chance to better themselves on their own territory "would seem to be the part of wisdom, of mercy and of justice."

A Vermont newspaper printed a stirring address given by Justice Story in Salem, Massachusetts, that took up the Indian cause extravagantly: "Braver men never lived," Story declaimed. "Truer men never drew a bow. They had courage and fortitude, and sagacity, and perseverance beyond most of the human race." And yet, he concluded sadly, "the winds of the Atlantic fan not a single region which they may now call their own."

As a small consolation for his people's losses, Boudinot ran a summary of an argument from London that America's Indians were "in all probability the descendants of the lost Ten Tribes of Israel."

Wilson Lumpkin found the onslaught from Northerners the more galling because they "often denounced my own beloved Georgia as the headquarters of all that was vile and wicked." Not only was the state condemned for its dealings with the Cherokees, but the indictments were capped by attacks on Georgians for owning slaves. If Northerners were allowed to dictate a state's Indian policy, abolition could become their next crusade.

At the Hermitage, Jackson had shown that he valued the outward signs of gracious living. Although Rachel was no longer by his side, he focused attention on the White House and, with Congress inclined to be generous, spent ten thousand dollars to repair the damage wreaked by his supporters on the East Room. Four sofas and twenty-four armchairs required replacing or recovering. Jackson and his family added a carpet imported from Brussels, along with marble-topped tables and three cut-glass chandeliers.

Jackson also undertook construction of a north portico, which had not been built to Benjamin Latrobe's original design after the British burned the mansion. To set off the first formal garden, Jackson personally planted magnolia trees in his wife's memory.

Meanwhile, his allies were interpreting Jackson's pledge to reform the bureaucracy in different ways. Did it mean replacing incompetents? But, as Representative Edward Everett pointed out, Adams had committed political suicide by retaining unfriendly officials simply because they were effective in their jobs. Congressman William L. Marcy, one of Van Buren's closest allies, gave the game away by admitting what his party's true philosophy was: "To the victor belong the spoils of the enemy."

Jackson preferred to see himself as a reformer. He referred often to the "Augean stables" he had found and likened himself to Hercules, who had to cleanse the filth of three thousand oxen. Another favorite image was that of "rats" who had been misappropriating public funds.

But Colonel McKenney soon learned that disloyalty was even more damning than fiddles with government money. Major Eaton showed up at the Indian Affairs office to ask McKenney whether he had been to call on the new president.

When McKenney said he had not, Eaton told him to make an appointment immediately, hinting that Jackson had heard negative reports about him. Taking the advice, McKenney found that Jackson acknowledged being disturbed about rumors he had heard.

"You know, Colonel McKenney," Jackson began in a placating tone, "I am a candid man—"

McKenney was too aggrieved to be deferential. "I beg pardon, sir," he cut in, "but I am not here to question that, but to hear charges, which it appears have been made to you, affecting my character either as an officer of the government or a man."

Pressed for specifics, Jackson said he had heard that McKenney had contributed to the abuse against Rachel Jackson and had misused his government franking privilege to distribute the Coffin Handbills.

In responding, McKenney made the sort of dramatic gesture typical of Jackson himself. He threw up his hand as though taking an oath to heaven and began, "I solemnly swear—"

This time, it was the president who interrupted. "You are making quite a serious affair of it."

"It is, sir, what I mean to do." McKenney proceeded to refute each charge in elaborate detail. Jackson watched him steadily through his recitation and then said, "Colonel McKenney, I believe every word you have said, and am satisfied that those who communicated to me those allegations were mistaken."

Not mollified, McKenney insisted on knowing the names of his accusers so that he could confront them in Jackson's presence.

"No, no, sir," the president said. "I am satisfied. Why push the matter further?" He stood up and took McKenney by the arm. "Come, sir, come down and allow me to introduce you to my family."

McKenney permitted himself to be led to the family quarters and take a glass of wine with the Donelsons.

But the affair was not ended. Beneath the surface was the continuing battle over the lucrative Indian trading posts. George Washington had originally set up the posts to protect Indians "from scoundrels in the fur trade; and from confrontation with the white man's civilization." McKenney's office had inherited their oversight from the War Department and had been diligent about enforcing their regulations, including a prohibition against the selling of whiskey.

Most posts had opened in the northern Midwest on land that became Wisconsin and Illinois. John Jacob Astor had already amassed a fortune by bartering for furs, but his profits would soar if the federal trading posts were abolished and he could enjoy a monopoly throughout the northern Indian territory.

For two decades, Astor's exploitation of the Indians had troubled McKenney. He complained that Astor's agents dominated the tribes by supplying contraband liquor and by opposing the creation of factories that would give the tribes an income that did not depend solely on trapping pelts.

As a result, from the days even before the War of 1812, McKenney had proved a formidable irritant to Astor. Missouri's Senator Thomas Hart Benton had long been promoting Astor's interests by harassing McKenney at public hearings, but McKenney's careful bookkeeping had deflected the attacks.

Congressmen continued to question certain expenditures by the Bureau of Indian Affairs, however, including the three thousand dollars McKenney had spent on paintings of various chiefs—"those savages," in the words of one critic. And admittedly, when Indian delegates came to Washington, McKenney picked up the tab for their oysters and gin, generosity that made him a tempting target.

All the same, his face-down with Jackson had not prepared McKenney for the arrival of a young man who looked around his office and then asked about the portraits on his wall. McKenney described the treaties he had negotiated with each chief.

His caller seemed to find the recitation distasteful. "Well, then," he said, "the office will not suit me."

"What office?" McKenney asked.

"This," the man replied. "General Jackson told me this morning it was at my service. But before seeing the secretary of war, I thought I would come and have a little chat with you first."

McKenney rose from his chair. "Take it, my dear sir, take it. The sword of Damocles has been hanging over my head long enough."

"No, it is not the sort of place for me. I prefer an auditor's office, where forms are established."

After that episode, McKenney held on to the post somewhat longer only because Eaton convinced Jackson that the job required considerable expertise. The insult was repeated, however, when Jackson seemed ready to appoint a Georgia congressman to head Indian Affairs. Once again, Eaton saved McKenney's job, even though Eaton himself was firing competent and experienced workers in his own department to make room for political cronies. The Jackson administration—operating on Congressman Marcy's principle—had launched the spoils system.

Aware of McKenney's eagerness to hold on to his position, Jackson found a shrewd way to make use of him for the battles to come. Because McKenney had achieved a reputation as a fair-minded friend of the tribes, Jackson delegated him to counter the resistance against removal that Jeremiah Evarts—writing as "William Penn"—was generating among the Northern clergy.

Since McKenney agreed that removal was inevitable, he began his campaign by calling on Van Buren's longtime ally, Stephen Van Rensselaer, who was president of the Missionary Society of the Dutch Reformed Church. McKenney put the issue to him starkly and urgently: The Indians "must remove, or perish!"

After that successful interview, McKenney ignored his own uncertain health and pushed the matter forcefully. With Van Rensselaer's church as his base, he organized the New York Board for the Emigration, Preservation and Improvement of the Aborigines in America. To finance the new organization, McKenney tapped into the congressional appropriation meant for civilizing the Indians, and he drew on his office's federal funds to print two thousand copies of a bulky propaganda pamphlet.

McKenney's New York board expanded beyond its Dutch constituents until it took in Episcopalian and Presbyterian churches. Traveling to speak on behalf of removal, McKenney was so low-key and persuasive that one listener wrote that his address reflected "humanity and justice."

In Washington, Van Buren was playing by the new patronage rules, even though they offended his political instincts. He spelled out his misgivings to a bumptious young man named Clark, a disciple of the Van Buren faction in New York, who had arrived with a letter of introduction.

With Clark looking on, Van Buren summoned to his office a financial clerk appointed by the Adams administration.

"Mr. Jones," Van Buren began when the clerk appeared, "I beg to make you acquainted with Mr. Clark of New York. The government, Mr. Jones, has no further occasion for your services in the department. Mr. Clark is appointed your successor. Have the goodness to take him to your room, and give him what information he requires respecting his duties."

Stunned, Jones left Van Buren without a word. Back in his office, he spoke in a shaken voice: "Excuse me a moment, Mr. Clark, this is rather sudden. I will rejoin you in a moment."

It took ten minutes for Jones to compose himself. As Clark waited, he pitied the fellow and reflected that Jones had both a fine reputation and a young family to support. Clark resolved that he would never "dismiss a scullion from my kitchen" so abruptly. But he was glad for the appointment.

When Clark rejoined Van Buren, the secretary of state assured him that he hated patronage and would have preferred an assignment without it. His reasoning was entirely practical: "No matter how you dispense it, you make enemies. The man you remove is your enemy. His friends are offended. The man you appoint is not likely to be satisfied, and all the unsuccessful applicants feel themselves injured."

Clark's response indicated that he had learned his first lesson in Washington survival: "I am the exception to your remark, Mr. Van Buren, for I am perfectly satisfied with my place."

Friends and enemies understood that when Andrew Jackson focused his attention on a subject, he was impossible to deflect. Soon he was personally inspecting all federal contracts and expenditures, and purging about 10 percent of the federal payroll. One opponent compared his actions to France's Reign of Terror. Jackson's suspicions were confirmed when an accountant from the Adams years fled Washington after an audit revealed that he had helped himself to $7,000. Examining the books at the Treasury showed that in that department alone half a million dollars had disappeared. Missing amounts elsewhere ranged between $10,000 and $12,000.

Besides exposing embezzlement, Jackson was crusading against an entrenched elite. In his journal, he emphasized that public office was a privilege, not a "vested right," and certainly not a sinecure to be passed along to one's children. Looking ahead to his first message to Congress in December 1829, the new president intended to call for limiting all government appointments to four years.

Although Jackson was determined to end the standoff between the Cherokee Nation and the state of Georgia, he intended to wait for Congress to reconvene. Like Lumpkin, Jackson was aware of Northern resistance to his policy and wanted a congressional mandate before he acted.

Meanwhile, the president directed Eaton as his new secretary of war to send two men—the governor of Tennessee, William Carroll, and Jackson's kinsman John Coffee—to urge once again that the tribe move west. Eaton suggested that the emissaries should not waste their time with a general assembly of Cherokees but seek out instead the most influential chiefs for private talks.

In mid-August 1829, Carroll consulted with Agent Montgomery and invited John Ross and several other leaders for a bargaining session. But by the time Coffee arrived to join the negotiations, Carroll had met with the Cherokees a dozen times and had their answer: They would not budge. They were sure that when Congress resumed, its members would side with them against the Georgians.

Rather than appearing conciliatory, the Georgia legislature responded with a deliberate provocation. This time, it was new legislation aimed at blacks. Throughout the country, the controversy over slavery had been simmering long before Clay's Missouri compromises. Congress had outlawed the African slave trade in 1808, but New York State had freed its last slaves only on July 4, 1827.

Now Georgia voted to subject any ship carrying black passengers into a Georgia port to a forty-day quarantine. Even free blacks who came ashore during the quarantine could be imprisoned until their ship sailed; a similar law in South Carolina applied only to black sailors, but Georgia included all passengers and employees. In London, the Foreign Office considered protesting the indignity to its black citizens but recognized that the Jackson administration was likely to side with the Georgians and decided against it.

The federal government's obvious shift in sympathies was also prompting bolder intrusions by white Georgians onto Cherokee land. When John Ross appealed to Agent Montgomery, he learned that, whatever President Adams had seemed to promise, the Jackson administration would not use military force to defend his tribe. To Ross's fury, Montgomery argued that the federal government could not remove the intruders because title to the land was uncertain.

Given that stalemate, Major Ridge rode out to rally the Cherokee Nation, and Ross and his allies issued a statement that ignored the ambiguities of previous U.S. policy. It urged the tribe to "walk in the straight-forward path of the impartial recommendations of Washington, Jefferson, Madison, and Monroe," which was "best calculated to promote our happiness."

Not every threat to the leadership of Ross and Ridge came from beyond their borders. Ever since the debate over the Cherokee constitution, men who lost that argument had resented their diminished role in tribal affairs. One of them, William Hicks, had remained a tribal counselor and had gone with John Ross to Washington. But since his return, Hicks seemed disoriented and erratic, skulking about to avoid his neighbors and finally holing up in his house. He muttered against the men who had supplanted him and refused a request from council members at New Echota to appear before them.

Alexander McCoy also had been punished for asking federal agents to assess his holdings within the Cherokee boundaries. Branded "disloyalty," his request had led to John Ridge's replacing him on the national council. Now, as pressures mounted from Washington, the current Cherokee leadership decided to strengthen their ancient blood oath by putting it in writing. The idea was publicly endorsed by Womankiller, a chief more than eighty years old. John Ridge took down the venerable chief's speech to publish in the *Cherokee Phoenix*.

Invoking his age, Womankiller said, "When I sleep in forgetfulness, I hope my bones will not be deserted by you." He added that he had heard that the U.S. government planned to break its treaties and trample on the Cherokee national council.

"It may be so, but it shall not be with our consent, or by the misconduct of our people." He said that the tribe was linked to the United States "by a golden chain of friendship, made when our friendship was worth a price, and if they act the tyrant and kill us for our lands, we shall, in a state of unoffending innocence, sleep with thousands of our departed people."

With Congress preparing to act, John Ridge and other council members felt a sense of urgency. Their bill passed the council late in October 1828—verbose and legalistic but its intent unmistakable. Any persons who disposed of Cherokee land without permission from the Nation's authorities were declared to be outlaws, and any Cherokee citizen could kill them. The killing could be "in any manner most convenient," and the killers were not to be held accountable.

The Ridges, father and son, expected that by reinforcing that tradition in writing, they were dissuading Alexander McCoy and any other Cherokees who might be tempted by federal blandishments.

At an earlier time, the discovery of great wealth beneath Cherokee land might have been a blessing for the tribe. But coming as Andrew Jackson was poised to assume the presidency, it seemed more like a curse.

On October 27, 1828, a white Georgian named Benjamin Parks was celebrating his thirty-first birthday by tracking deer along a path in the northern part of the state. Parks was hobbling from a new pair of boots he was breaking in, but what he saw on the ground made him forget his sore feet.

He immediately sought out the owner of the property, a preacher named Robert O'Barr, and negotiated a forty-year lease. O'Barr had paid only one hundred dollars for the property and was amused when Parks offered him one-fourth of any profit, in the improbable event that veins of North Carolina gold ran into Georgia.

Parks recruited a partner and led him back to the spot near the Chestatee River where he had found a glittering stone. Together, they shoveled dirt into a pan and discovered that it was laden with gold. For Parks, "It was more than my eyes could believe."

The sensational news soon reached the Reverend O'Barr, who confronted Parks and demanded to buy back his lease. When Parks refused, the clergyman stomped away, shouting, "You will suffer for this yet!"

By the time O'Barr returned with his family two weeks later, Parks had already hired a crew to extract the gold, and he announced that he would not relinquish his lease for ten times what he had paid. At that, O'Barr's mother began throwing rocks at Parks's men. The shoving match that followed ended inconclusively.

Meanwhile, Georgia newspapers were reporting on the riches to be plucked from the earth. Prospectors—by one estimate, ten thousand of them—poured into Cherokee territory. Parks recalled that they were "acting more like crazy men than anything else." A Georgia judge described them as "thieves, gamblers and murderers," although their number also included two Georgia militia colonels, two candidates for the state legislature, and two Christian ministers. The editor of the *Georgia Journal* pronounced it a sad day for the state of Georgia when gold was discovered.

The Cherokee leadership agreed. The *Phoenix* quoted a hostile editorial that had fueled the madness by speculating that the tribe's land held more than a hundred million dollars in gold. When John Calhoun later bought the O'Barr property at a bargain price, he was rumored to have made more than two thousand dollars in the first month.

What was certain, as the boom continued, was that the U.S. Mint in Philadelphia had taken in more than half a million dollars in gold from Georgia. For the average miner, however, the rewards were less princely. Men arrived with a shovel and a pan, lured by stories of clearing thirty dollars a day, and found themselves lucky to make five.

That rush of prospectors onto Cherokee territory was described—not only by the Cherokees—as the "Great Intrusion." Since Georgia was not scheduled to take over the land until June 1830, its ownership remained in a legal limbo. But that nicety did not stop white marauders from storming the Cherokee Nation, carrying off not only its gold but also its livestock and household goods. The *Phoenix* reported instances of white prospectors' shooting Cherokee horses and cattle for the sport of it.

Benjamin Parks, who had set off this Gold Rush of '29, was saddened by what he witnessed. Parks had once hoped to marry a Cherokee girl—"as pretty a woman as I ever saw"—and though the couple could not surmount the prejudice that the Boudinots and Ridges had faced in the North, Parks felt fondly toward his Cherokee neighbors. "We always treated them right," he recalled of the days before the gold rush, "and they did the same by us."

When Jackson had completed naming his cabinet, a recent American tradition required that he give a dinner in honor of his nominees. Jackson was forced to ignore that bit of protocol, however, because of a scandal that was testing the survival of his administration.

The distraction was not wholly unforeseen. In the days when she was Mrs. Timberlake, Margaret had been assaulted in her father's parlor by Captain Richard Call, who had served with Jackson in Florida. Margaret had to fight him off with fire tongs and complained to Jackson about the incident. Writing to Rachel, Jackson said he had given Call "a *severe lecture*," and from that time on, Margaret refused to appear whenever Call was present. He retaliated by impugning Margaret's virtue around town.

But she had not learned just how widespread the rumors about her had become until her father took a stagecoach to Baltimore and overheard strangers laughing about his daughter and Eaton. For the remainder of the trip, William O'Neale bit his tongue, but silence was not Margaret's style. When a young Jackson relative inadvertently referred to a new rumor—that while married to Timberlake she had suffered a miscarriage with Eaton's child—Margaret rode immediately to the White House.

The president refused to discuss the matter. "Margaret Eaton," Jackson told her fondly, "go home and cook your bacon and greens and eat your dinner in peace."

She replied that she did not keep such frontier victuals in her kitchen. "I have got canvas-back ducks," she said. "But I won't be put off this way. You must tell me all this thing about me."

Margaret detected a glint in Jackson's eye. "Margaret, it is all politics. Perhaps they think that already I am beginning to think of a second term."

Jackson had come to believe that Calhoun was behind the attempt to discredit Eaton through Margaret, in order to clear the way for Calhoun's own run for the presidency in 1832. That theory cast Floride Calhoun as the ringleader of the Washington matrons who were closing ranks against Margaret.

Jackson put his hand on her shoulder. "If I had not believed that you had been a perfectly true and faithful daughter and wife and mother, having known you in all these relations, I never would have recommended you as a wife to Major Eaton—one of the truest and best men I ever knew."

When the glow from those words faded, Margaret was still outraged. She bridled when her exasperated husband gave her the same advice. "Just leave the whole matter to me," Eaton told her. "I can fight your battles and my own."

Unappeased, Margaret traced the rumor to a Philadelphia clergyman named Ezra Stiles Ely and arranged a trip there with her parents, ostensibly to buy furniture. Instead, she showed up on Ely's doorstep. Alarmed by her intensity, he refused to tell her the source of his information.

She settled into a chair and vowed not to move until he revealed the name. At that, the Reverend Ely said the story had come from another Presbyterian clergyman, John Campbell, minister of the church Jackson attended in the capital.

Returning to Washington, Margaret enlisted her husband and together they paid a stormy visit to the Reverend Campbell. Later that evening, the clergyman requested a private meeting with Jackson at the White House. In the president's study, Campbell said he had heard the story from a doctor, Elijah Craven, who was dead and safe from Margaret Eaton's wrath.

Dr. Craven claimed that he had once been summoned to treat Margaret after a minor accident in which Eaton's carriage had overturned and his companion—still Margaret Timberlake at the time—had been slightly shaken. Craven claimed that when he entered her room, Margaret and an older woman had laughed heartily, and Margaret said, "You ought to have been here a little sooner, and you would have seen a little John H. Eaton."

Craven quoted the other woman, whom he took to be Margaret's mother, as saying, "Yes, Dr. Craven, you lost a good fee, for Major Eaton would have paid you well."

The president heard out the clergyman, noting Campbell's nervousness. Then Jackson asked when the episode was alleged to have taken place.

Campbell said he was positive it was in 1821.

The next day, Jackson showed up at the Eaton house and repeated Campbell's secondhand story. Margaret sent for her husband's account books that showed Timberlake having been in Washington for all of 1821 and the first month of 1822.

Jackson was pleased with his detective work, but when he confronted Campbell and suggested that he would now want to apologize, the clergyman said no, Jackson must have misheard him. The date of the event had been 1822. And he claimed that Craven's widow had other unfavorable information about Mrs. Eaton, but the old woman was so distressed at being involved that she was leaving Washington for an undisclosed location in New England.

Margaret O'Neale had always understood that in rejecting the prim behavior that society expected from women, she could be considered shocking. Given her passion for riding, she might jump on anyone's horse and ride off at full gallop. To be outrageous, she sometimes wore one red shoe and one black one. She considered those eccentricities her "little fooleries."

But beneath her frivolous manner, Margaret was conventionally respectable. She even resented that strangers were now speaking of her as "Peg" or "Peggy." As she was growing up, her mother occasionally had called her "Madge," but friends like Jackson invariably addressed her as "Margaret."

Mortified and deeply offended by the rumor of an illegitimate miscarriage, she had as her champion the president of the United States. John Campbell had become enough alarmed by Jackson's fury to hire Francis Scott Key to call at the White House and sue for peace. Never, Jackson replied. Not until Campbell admitted that he had lied and apologized for the slander—preferably from his pulpit and in front of his entire congregation. When Campbell refused, Jackson gathered all of his cabinet members, except for Eaton, on September 10 and made a heated defense of Margaret's virtue. Then he summoned Reverend Ely into the room and demanded that he make a statement.

Ely had already discredited himself further in a letter to Jackson that claimed Rachel Jackson had shared the prevailing low opinion of Margaret. Since Jackson knew that was untrue, it was one more proof to him that Margaret's accusers were liars.

In his response on this day, however, Jackson blamed the attacks less on Calhoun than on "the great exertions made by Clay & his partisans, here & elsewhere to destroy the character of Mrs. Eaton by the foulest and basest means, so that a deep & lasting wrong might be inflicted on her husband."

Jackson also indicted the atmosphere in Washington: "We know, here, that none are spared. Even Mrs. Madison was assailed by these fiends in human shape."

Jackson had been consoling the victim with a similar observation: "I tell you, Margaret, I had rather have live vermin on my back than the tongue of one of these Washington women."

In front of the cabinet, Ely granted that he had no evidence that Major Eaton had been guilty of dishonorable conduct.

Jackson prompted, "Nor Mrs. Eaton, either."

Ely balked. "On that point, I would rather not give an opinion."

Jackson shouted, "She is as chaste as a virgin!"

Campbell was led in next. He announced that he would testify in a court of law but not at the White House and left the room.

At that, Jackson proclaimed, "Mrs. Eaton is vindicated! She is honorable and chaste!"

The president had vowed never to speak again to the Reverend Campbell, but that did not deter Margaret. Seeking him out, she said, "If you told Dr. Ely what he says you told him, you are capable of any deception, any falsehood."

Later, she recalled, with considerable satisfaction, "I did not mince words. To this day, my language is blunt and sharp Saxon rather than round and soft Latin."

Like Clay's denials of a political deal with John Quincy Adams, the furious energies of Jackson and Margaret Eaton only spread the rumors further. Margaret noted with regret that Dr. Craven, the story's creator, was beyond her reach: He had "lied about me years before and was gone to the grave, out of which I could not drag him to make him take the lie back."

After the fiasco at the White House, cabinet officers were torn between standing by their wives and their sense of duty to the president. Jackson sent Colonel Richard M. Johnson of Kentucky—the Indian fighter who claimed to have killed Tecumseh—to deliver an ultimatum to three cabinet members. Navy Secretary John Branch, Attorney General John Berrien, and Treasury Secretary Samuel Ingham were to be told that if their wives did not leave a calling card at the Eaton residence, Jackson would demand their resignation.

As an emissary, Colonel Johnson was himself compromised. He lived openly with Julia Chinn, a mulatto slave he had inherited from his father. Johnson had seen to it that the education of their lovely daughters, Imogene and Adaline, matched that of any young white woman, and he hoped to introduce them to Kentucky society. But when he brought one daughter to a Fourth of July barbecue, Kentuckians had demanded that she wait in his carriage while Johnson delivered his oration.

Johnson's overtures on Margaret Eaton's behalf were equally futile. Secretary Berrien rejected Jackson's authority to force him or his family to do anything at all in the social realm. The two other secretaries backed him up, and Jackson did not make good on his threat.

Widowers like Van Buren faced no conflict in loyalty, and he was thankful that he had not yet come to Washington during the feud's early stages. When a friend tried to fill him in about the scandal, Van Buren replied sternly that he intended to treat all of his fellow cabinet officers and their families with equal courtesy, a statement of impartiality that soon got back to the president.

As for John Eaton, Van Buren knew that Jackson had admired Eaton's mother as a highly respected Tennessee widow and that her son had ingratiated himself with the president. Van Buren, however, found Eaton "a man of moderate intellectual capacities" although kindly enough and properly unobtrusive.

But whenever the president was within earshot, Van Buren would praise Margaret's intelligence and good judgment. And even though he described the controversy that was paralyzing the cabinet as "the Eaton malaria," his remark did not blame Margaret for the contagion.

Van Buren's enemies watched sardonically as he took Mrs. Eaton's side, sure that he was promoting himself in order to undercut Calhoun and establish himself as Jackson's political heir. Alone with Margaret, Van Buren saw no need for subtlety and told her that he considered Andrew Jackson the greatest man who had ever lived.

"But," Van Buren added, "don't tell General Jackson what I have said. I would not have him know it for the world."

With gratifying speed, his praise reached the president, who responded in kind: Van Buren was "the most frank man I have ever known," Jackson said warmly. "A *true* man with no guile. It is said that he is a magician—I believe it, but his only wand is common sense, which he uses for the benefit of his country."

To Jackson's dismay, his family became caught up in the feud when the Eatons accompanied the president and his household during a Fourth of July cruise on the steamboat *Potomac.* Emily Donelson, who was pregnant, became faint from the rocking of the boat. Seeing her distress, Margaret Eaton offered her fan and a bottle of cologne to revive her. Emily had been warned against Margaret by the older society women she admired, and she rejected her assistance.

Margaret had already sensed Emily's hostility, which she attributed to jealousy because of Margaret's influence with Jackson. Now she was enraged enough to confront Andrew Donelson, who had not witnessed his wife's behavior. Margaret claimed that his uncle had assured her that if the Donelsons did not behave better toward her, Jackson would send them both back to Tennessee.

The return of Congress meant the launching of Washington's fall social season. Van Buren intended to draw upon his vaunted tact to smooth over a feud that had already blighted the spring and summer. His opening came when Emily commented to him that she had never heard Van Buren say anything at all about Margaret Eaton. From her tone, Van Buren took the remark as a reproach. He was wary because he suspected that the Donelsons resented his own influence with Jackson from their daily horseback riding together.

Emily made no direct reference to the scandal. Instead, she faulted Mrs. Eaton for "possessing a bad temper and a meddlesome disposition." She added that the meddling "had been so much increased by her husband's elevation as to make her society too disagreeable to be endured."

Van Buren found it prudent to acknowledge the truth in Emily's complaints. He reminded her, however, that she was the acting First Lady and should not continue to distress the president by shunning Mrs. Eaton's company. From her silence, Van Buren's reliable instincts warned him that Emily had been offended, and he "asked her permission to drop the subject."

Word of that exchange reached Massachusetts, where the fracas provided John Quincy Adams with momentary relief from the depression that had descended on him since he left Washington. Despite his denials, Adams missed public life. And then in April his son George Washington Adams committed suicide. A heavy drinker and gambler, George had recently added to his offenses by getting a young woman pregnant. Disgraced, he jumped to his death from the side of a steamboat. His father was beset by guilt that he had been too stern with the boy and poured out to his journal his contrition and despair.

With news of the Eaton malaria momentarily distracting him, Adams set down the version he had heard: "Mrs. Donelson said, 'Mr. Van Buren, I have always been taught that honesty is the best policy.' Upon which, he immediately started up, took his hat and departed."

Adams summed up the two factions: "Calhoun heads the moral party, Van Buren that of the frail sisterhood."

At last, President Jackson set the date of November 26, 1829, for his long-delayed cabinet dinner. The setting was the recently redecorated East Room, and every cabinet officer attended. More to the point, so did their wives. Only the Calhouns remained at home in South Carolina.

A resplendent Margaret Eaton arrived with feathers in her hair. When it came time for dinner, Jackson took in the wife of his Treasury secretary, Samuel Ingham. Their tiff forgotten, Van Buren escorted Emily Donelson. But he surveyed the room sadly, sure that Jackson had to notice how hollow his dinner had turned out to be and how early the command appearance was ending.

Van Buren's unease was compounded soon afterward when the time came for him to host his own official dinner. Since he did not want to extend to Mrs. Ingham the precedence due her husband's position, he hit upon the idea of inviting as his guest of honor Thomas Jefferson's surviving daughter, Martha Jefferson Randolph. As the night approached, however, every cabinet officer accepted Van Buren's invitation but made excuses for his wife. Margaret Eaton also sent regrets.

Theodore Frelinghuysen

7 · Theodore Frelinghuysen (1830)

With his social chores accomplished, however limited their success, Jackson turned to writing his first State of the Union report. The Eaton affair had severely drained his energies, and he lamented that the writing was reducing him to a state of "dignified slavery."

The day after Congress reconvened on December 7, 1829, the president delivered a ten-thousand-word statement for a clerk to read. Jackson made a graceful reference to Great Britain—"alike distinguished in peace and war"—before running through a list of nations with pending U.S. disputes to resolve.

The Adams-Clay bargain still rankled, and Jackson called for the president to be chosen entirely by a popular vote. If necessary, a runoff would be held between the two leading candidates. Jackson reneged, however, on a pledge he had made to himself. He did not call for barring cabinet officers or judges as candidates for the presidency. But he repeated his idea of limiting the office to a single term of four or six years.

In his fiscal accounting, Jackson announced that after current receipts and expenditures, the Treasury would have a balance of nearly $4.5 million dollars, despite making a payment of $12.4 million on the national debt and reducing it to $48.5 million. He expected the entire debt to be paid "in a very short time."

Jackson next paid tribute to the concept of states' rights, which served to introduce a statement of his Indian policy: "Professing a desire to civilize and settle them, we have at the same time lost no opportunity to purchase their lands and thrust them farther into the wilderness. By this means they have not only been kept in a wandering state, but been led to look upon us as unjust and indifferent to their fate."

As Jackson continued, his expression of concern took on a harder edge: "Their present condition, contrasted with what they once were, makes a most powerful appeal to our sympathies. Our ancestors found them the uncontrolled possessors of these vast regions. By persuasion and force they have been made to retire from river to river and from mountain to mountain, until some of the tribes have become extinct and others have left but remnants to preserve for a while their once terrible names.

"Surrounded by the whites with their arts of civilization, which by destroying the resources of the savage doom him to weakness and decay, the fate of the Mohegan, the Narragansett, and the Delaware is fast over-taking the Choctaw, the Cherokee, and the Creek. That this fate surely awaits them if they remain within the limits of the States does not admit of a doubt."

Turning to the quarrel between Georgia and her Northern opponents, Jackson noted that Georgia and Alabama enjoyed an equal sovereignty with every other state. Would the people of Maine permit the Penobscot to set up an independent government in their state? Or the people of New York allow survivors of the six Indian nations within her borders to declare their independence? What about the Indians of Ohio? Could they establish a separate republic on each of their reservations?

With that preamble, Jackson stated his implacable position: "I informed the Indians inhabiting parts of Georgia and Alabama that their attempt to establish an independent government would not be countenanced by the Executive of the United States, and advised them to emigrate beyond the Mississippi or submit to the laws of those States."

Jackson immediately pulled back slightly. "The emigration should be voluntary, for it would be as cruel as unjust to compel the aborigines to abandon the graves of their fathers and seek a home in a distant land." But they must understand that, by remaining on lands they had only seen from "the mountain or passed them in the chase," they must submit to their state's laws. They would also receive, however, their state's protection.

Moving on to a reorganization of the armed services, Jackson ended with a muted call for reexamination of the charter of the Bank of the United States, due to expire in 1836. He also voiced support for claims lodged by Commodore Stephen Decatur, his officers, and crew for their role in capturing the frigate *Philadelphia* from Tripoli.

Henry Clay scrutinized Jackson's message for ways to position his National Republican party for the next presidential election. He wrote to Nicholas Biddle, the president of the Bank, to suggest that Jackson's "public disapprobation" would backfire. It had come too early to be effective, Clay assured Biddle, and Jackson's remarks on the tariff would set off a distracting uproar in the Congress.

Meantime, Clay sent suggestions to Charles Hammond, the compliant editor of the *Cincinnati Gazette*, on how to attack Jackson's message. Since Indian Removal offered a promising target, Clay considered invoking religion and claiming that to violate the rights of "those poor children of the woods" would provoke "the maledictions of a more exalted and powerful tribunal." But given his own ambiguous feelings about the Indians, Clay was necessarily vague. He recommended merely that Hammond's newspaper say "something" about Jackson's plan.

Emboldened by President Jackson's speech, Georgia's legislators decided to finish off Cherokee resistance once and for all. They passed the Cherokee Code, which annexed most of Cherokee territory to five neighboring white counties and declared Cherokee law within those areas null and void. The code banned all Cherokee meetings, and any Cherokee who resisted Jackson's removal policy could be arrested and jailed.

The code also forbade Cherokees from testifying against white men or prospecting for gold on the formerly Cherokee territory. All previous contracts between Indians and whites were nullified unless two white men agreed to vouch for their validity.

Massachusetts congressman Edward Everett, a champion of Indian rights, spelled out the consequences of the code for his House colleagues. Everett had been a Unitarian clergyman, and he denounced the legislation in moral terms: White settlers had only to guarantee that no fellow white man was watching and then they could cross the Cherokee line to "burn the dwelling, waste the farm, plunder the property, assault the person, murder the children of the Cherokee . . . and though hundreds be permitted to be looking on, there is not one of them that can be permitted to bear witness against the spoiler."

Everett said that if Jackson's supporters asked what the Cherokee had to fear from Georgia law, Everett said he would answer that "by that law, he is left at the mercy of firebrand and dagger of every unprincipled wretch in the community."

Readers of the *Cherokee Phoenix* knew that Everett's warning had come too late. Long before June 1, 1830, when the code would officially take effect, crimes against the Cherokees had become too flagrant for Washington to ignore. While Jackson was preparing his address to Congress, he had sent his kinsman John Coffee to hear the tribe's side of the controversy. Georgians were outraged that the issue was not already settled in the new president's mind, and the state's current governor, George Gilmer, did his best to discredit the testimony of Major Ridge and the others.

Gilmer claimed that Ridge had induced "some old drunken Indians" to drill holes as false evidence that white Georgians were plundering gold from Cherokee territory. Although Coffee seemed to doubt some of Ridge's information, his confidential report to Secretary Eaton said that he had found no plausible evidence to support the Georgians' claims, either.

And yet, the new evidence of hostility confirmed the administration's feeling that since the conflict could never be resolved, the Indians had to leave. It was the only way to ensure their own safety. The *Phoenix* sought to expose the hypocrisy of Jackson's reasoning: "You are too near to my white children. There will always be difficulties between you and them. Go to the west where I can protect you." That was what the president seemed to be saying. "But, in the name of common sense, we ask, who makes the difficulties?"

For now, Coffee warned the Cherokees not to expect Washington to end the white man's abuses. Coping with them would be up to the chiefs themselves.

Since their pledge of nonviolence had not protected the Cherokees, Coffee's advice led Major Ridge to change the tribe's strategy. On January 4, 1830, Ridge rode out with a posse of about thirty Cherokees to confront a settlement of white squatters at Cedar Creek near the boundary between Georgia and Alabama.

In authorizing the retaliation, John Ross had instructed Ridge's men to show the intruders "all possible leniency and humanity" and forbade the Indians to drink alcohol before or during the raid.

The target was a cluster of houses taken over by eighteen white families when their Cherokee owners had moved west. Major Ridge's posse accused the group of stealing tribal horses and cattle. For the eviction, Ridge put on a horned buffalo headdress, and his men painted themselves for the warpath. They claimed later that they had intended only to intimidate any intruders who might try to fight back.

But the white families did not intend to resist. They obeyed Ridge's order to vacate the houses and then fled as the Cherokees were taking out their furniture and bedding for safekeeping. Once the houses were empty, Ridge's men razed them. They argued that they were committing no crime since the buildings were Cherokee property.

Having imposed their idea of justice, Major Ridge and his men headed home. They left behind four Cherokees who had discovered a keg of whiskey at a house commandeered by a man named Samuel Rowe. When some two dozen armed white men returned the next day, they found three of the four too drunk to fight back. The Indians themselves had tied up one of their group, a Cherokee called Chuwooyee, to subdue him.

The white men seized the others—Daniel Mills, Waggon, and Rattling Gourd—slung them onto horses, and headed for the Carroll County jail. Chuwooyee was still too drunk to stand. But when he tried to refuse to go, he was struck on the back of his head with a rifle butt and loaded onto a horse with the others. During the ride, he kept slipping to the ground until he was discovered to be dying from a fractured skull.

Chuwooyee was left behind to spend a night drenched by a cold sleet; John Ross found his corpse two days later. Mills and Waggon sobered up enough to escape before the posse reached town, but Waggon had been wounded severely in the chest by a butcher knife. Rattling Gourd was held in jail.

The incident came at an opportune time for Governor Gilmer, who sent to Washington a report of white women and infants being driven into a winter storm. Much was made by a Georgian newspaper of Ridge's buffalo headdress. Sarcastically, its editor suggested that a portrait of him "brandishing his tomahawk over suffering females and children" should be added to the gallery of Indian chiefs in Colonel McKenney's office.

Gilmer assured Washington that it had been difficult to restrain his white constituents from "taking ample vengeance" on the Cherokees. Even so, armed white men began riding through Indian territory, making threats and firing rifles.

The explosive aftermath confirmed for John Ross the wisdom in the former policy of restraint. Elias Boudinot wrote in the *Phoenix* that the tribe's enemies had long hoped to provoke just such a desperate act. Now, Cherokees must pledge themselves against further revenge. They had no choice except to trust in the white man's courts.

William Wirt watched with dismay as a showdown loomed between the Georgians and the Cherokees. As attorney general under both Monroe and John Quincy Adams, he had concluded that federal law favored the tribes. But it was becoming clear that the law counted for nothing with the Georgians and for little more with President Jackson or John M. Berrien, the man Jackson had appointed as Wirt's replacement.

Born in Maryland, Wirt had lived for many years in Virginia before his service in Washington. Like Margaret Eaton, he was the child of a tavern owner; in his case, his father had been Swiss, his mother German. When his parents died before he was eight, William had been shunted among guardians until, at fifteen, he could earn his way as a tutor.

Wirt had grown into a husky young man with a quick smile and the blue eyes and fair hair he had inherited. He became a gifted attorney, although hampered initially by a timid courtroom manner. All the same, his skill impressed his neighbors, including both Jefferson and Madison.

In 1803, Wirt, at thirty, had traveled on business to Richmond and was passing the autumn evenings in a tavern room by writing a series of lighthearted essays that provided a pleasant distraction from worrying about his pregnant wife in Norfolk. Wirt framed his genial satire of American life as supposedly written by a British traveler who was observing the customs of the Virginians he encountered.

A magazine published the pieces anonymously. When they were collected into a book, they became a publishing sensation. Wirt wrote to a friend that "very far beyond my expectations, the printer has found it in his interest not only to bind it up in a pamphlet but to issue a second edition." That was only the beginning. *The Letters of the British Spy* would still be in print seven decades later, although looking back on his handiwork, Wirt decided that "the style, though sometimes happy, is sometimes, also, careless and poor."

At first, readers were fooled by the persona Wirt had invented. Some even claimed to have met the Englishman who wrote the volume. But as Wirt's authorship became known—he would not, he said, "deny the brat to be my own"—he acquired a reputation for possessing the very eloquence he had felt eluded him.

Wirt's reputation grew further when he was selected to prosecute Aaron Burr for treason in 1807. Throwing off his shyness, drawing on his gift for vivid imagery, he delivered a summation that became an oratorical model. He did, however, lose the case.

By the time Jefferson and John Adams died on the same day in 1826, Wirt's gifts were sufficiently celebrated that he was chosen to deliver their eulogy before a joint session of Congress. Now, four years later, the Cherokees were convinced that if Wirt could be persuaded to take up their cause in a courtroom, no Georgia lawyer could match him.

Jackson had more urgent political battles to wage before he could turn his full energies to the Indian Removal bill, although one of the debates had become intertwined with the issue. John Calhoun had emerged as the foremost champion of nullification—the doctrine that any state could refuse to recognize a federal law within its own borders. Calhoun's supporters traced the theory to a protest against the Alien and Sedition Acts that were passed during John Adams's presidency. At that time, both Jefferson and Madison had argued for the right of states to reject laws they considered unconstitutional. But they were upholding freedom of the press. In 1830, South Carolina was taking the argument far beyond what either man would have endorsed.

In the Senate, Robert Hayne of South Carolina made a passionate case for nullification if Northerners threatened the institution of slavery. For Hayne, the first step would be for the Southern states to nullify all offending legislation. But if that approach failed, they must then secede from the Union.

In a two-day rebuttal, Daniel Webster had outshone Hayne while voicing sentiments that President Jackson shared. "I go for the Constitution as it is," Webster said, "and for the Union as it is. It is, Sir, the people's Constitution, the people's government, made for the people, made by the people, and answerable to the people."

The president admired Webster's gifts as an orator although he liked Hayne better as a man. Jackson had once expressed himself trenchantly on the issue when he said he would rather "die in the last ditch than see the Union disunited."

A public showdown arose when Jackson's party met on April 13, 1830, for its annual celebration of Jefferson's birthday. Jackson got word that the affair was being advertised as an endorsement of nullification. His own remarks would come near the end of some two dozen toasts.

The president told Van Buren to consult with Lewis Cass and

Andrew Donelson and draft what he should say. When the evening arrived, Van Buren watched a keyed-up Jackson set off for the dinner as though heading into battle.

At the Indian Queen Hotel, Jackson endured the speeches, including Hayne's praise for the way Georgia was dealing with the Cherokees. In conclusion, Hayne toasted "The *Union* of the States, and the *Sovereignty* of the States."

When the president's turn came, many in the crowded hall stood up for a better view, and Van Buren had to climb onto his chair to watch Jackson rise for his rebuttal. The teeth Jackson had lost to age and decay could make him hard to understand in a large hall, but on this night his words rang clearly: "Our Union: It must be preserved."

Jackson had meant to say "our Federal Union." Inadvertently, he had left out the qualification, which made his challenge even more unflinching. Calhoun came afterward, and the president's admirers agreed that his wordier toast paled in comparison.

Jackson's next showdown involved the National Road, a project financed by the federal government that had begun in 1811 in Cumberland, Maryland, and was slowly progressing westward. The next section of the road was scheduled to run from Maysville, Kentucky, to Lexington, and Jackson opposed the extension for at least two reasons: The road would run entirely within the state of Kentucky. Men who favored a strict construction of the Constitution objected to the federal government taking on any project that a state should finance for itself. And since the road would pass through Henry Clay's home state, Jackson suspected a plot to divert money that he intended to use for keeping his promise to pay down the federal debt.

The National Road was popular among westerners, who had not anticipated Jackson's active opposition. After the funding passed both houses of Congress, the president was grateful when Van Buren offered to draft a veto message.

Congressman Richard Johnson, Jackson's longtime comrade-in-arms, came to plead for Maysville Road, but the president challenged him sternly: "Are you willing—are my friends willing—to lay taxes to pay for internal improvements? For be assured I will not borrow a cent except in cases of absolute necessity!"

Johnson was not prepared to back higher taxes. He cried, "No!"

On May 27, 1830, Jackson vetoed the legislation. He had delayed action on Maysville until the Indian Removal bill was safely reported out of committee in Congress because he knew that a veto might have killed his removal legislation.

In another round of cost cutting, Jackson vetoed an additional million dollars in appropriations, although he approved other measures that involved more than one state. In some cases, Jackson simply killed a bill by not signing it before Congress adjourned, making use for the first time of what came to be called the pocket veto.

As Jackson had waited, the Senate Committee on Indian Affairs—guided by men he had chosen personally—reported a removal bill on February 22, 1830. Two days later, a similar bill followed in the House. Their provisions included the president's formula: Territory west of the Mississippi would be allocated and divided into as many districts as the number of tribes required. In exchange, the Indians would cede all land east of the river.

The authors of the House report left no doubt about their thinking. Treaty-making with Indians was only an "empty gesture" aimed at satisfying Indian "vanity." Such agreements were not treaties at all but merely a means to the peaceful ceding of Indian land. The baldness of that language was eliminated as the president's bill moved toward a vote by the full House.

The Indian Removal Act of 1830 would fund negotiations and did not directly authorize seizing Indian land. Opponents, however, saw Jackson's iron hand poised to compel what the Indians would not concede. Presidential allies, like Pennsylvania congressman James Buchanan, claimed that Jackson had never considered the use of force, and Wilson Lumpkin swore that "no man entertains kinder feelings towards Indians than Andrew Jackson."

Those reassurances did not quell the anguished Northern outcry. Leading the resistance was Senator Theodore Frelinghuysen, a former attorney general in New Jersey who had been appointed to the U.S. Senate the previous year by his state's legislature. Frelinghuysen was the great-grandson of a prominent clergyman from the Great Awakening religious movement that had swept over colonial America and deeply influenced many revolutionaries, most notably Samuel Adams. A deeply committed Christian himself, Frelinghuysen had never shied away from unpopular causes. As a young lawyer, he had won dismissal of a murder charge against an indigent Negro accused of killing a white man.

As his law practice grew, Frelinghuysen had become selective about his clients. If he believed that a man was guilty, he said, "I send him to another lawyer." An elector for John Quincy Adams in 1828, he had deplored Jackson's victory.

Political opponents painted Frelinghuysen as an intolerant zealot, a leader not only in the American Board of Commissioners for Foreign Missions but a host of other crusading organizations, including the American Temperance Union. They claimed that he showed more sympathy for Indian tribes than for the white workingman and that he wanted to breach the constitutional wall between church and state.

When Frelinghuysen rose to speak in the Senate on April 6, 1830, he saw a chance to oppose the Jackson administration but, more important, to bear witness to a profoundly moral cause. The hour was late, however, and the forty-three-year-old senator was not feeling well and asked for a delay. Then the next day, his speech was deferred again while the Senate debated the proper rate of pay for U.S. Navy pursers. Disposing of that matter, senators convened as Committee of the Whole and called upon Frelinghuysen, who spoke from 1 p.m. until adjournment two hours later.

After his opening remarks, Frelinghysen cut to the crux of the matter: He regretted that the present chief magistrate "did not pursue the wise and prudent policy of his exalted predecessor, President Washington." Frelinghuysen reminded his colleagues that America's first president had informed the Senate in a special message in 1790 that he intended to protect the Cherokees under the Treaty of Hopewell. That agreement had been signed five years earlier and required that any change of boundaries be negotiated with the tribe.

Instead of that precedent, however, the Jackson administration had "thought proper without the slightest consultation with either House of Congress" to alter the country's obligations and the Indians' rights.

Frelinghuysen reviewed reports from Carroll and Coffee to Secretary Eaton in the War Department with their private recommendation for working with individual chieftains to divide the majority of the Cherokees from their leadership. "I admire the ingenious clothing of a most odious proposal," he said, adding that "a strong hint is suggested to try the effect of terror."

Frelinghuysen noted that the administration was counting on the Senate to reject a Cherokee petition for protection. That negative vote would turn the Cherokees over to the "high-handed, heart-breaking legislation of the States, and drive them to despair."

Tracing the tangled history of the dispute, Frelinghuysen made a sweeping claim on behalf of the Indians: "I insist that, by immemorial possession, as the original tenants of the soil, they hold a title beyond and superior to the British Crown and her colonies, and to all adverse pretensions of our confederation and subsequent Union. God, in his providence, planted those tribes on this Western continent, so far as we know, before Great Britain herself had a political existence."

Arguing that the Indians were entitled to a fair share of what providence had provided, Frelinghuysen spoke of their land: "If I use it for hunting, may another take it because he needs it for agriculture?" But if a growing population did, in fact, require more cultivated farmland, that land had to be obtained under fair contracts and at a fair price.

As his speech entered a second day, then a third, Frelinghuysen paused to apologize for offering tedious details that could "oppress the patience of the Senate." But his main themes had emerged: He objected to a provision in the pending legislation that might threaten prosecution against anyone who urged the Cherokees to stay on their land. He also opposed Indians' being prohibited from testifying in court against white defendants who did not live on Cherokee territory. "For, sir, after the first day of June next, a gang of lawless white men may break into the Cherokee country, plunder their habitations, murder the mother with the children, and all in the sight of the wretched husband and father, and no law of Georgia will reach the atrocity."

Even worse, the pending bill stated that "all laws, ordinance, orders and regulations of any kind whatever, made, passed or enacted by the Cherokee Indians, either in general council, or in any other way whatever, or by any authority whatever, of said tribe, be, and the same are hereby declared to be, null and void and of no effect, as if the same had never existed."

Frelinghuysen reminded colleagues about the partition of Poland by Russia and Prussia between 1772 and 1795, which had eliminated Poland from the map. Now, with the proposed assault on the Cherokees, "history furnishes no example of such high handed usurpation—the dismemberment and partition of Poland was a deed of humane legislation compared with this."

To underscore his resistance, Frelinghuysen offered amendments to Jackson's legislation. All relocation would be truly voluntary. Whether the Cherokees moved or stayed in Georgia, their legal rights would be protected. Finally, if the tribe did move, the Jackson administration must negotiate new treaties to guarantee that the Indians would control their new territory west of the Mississippi.

Frelinghuysen said he was realistic about the vote count against him and expected that his long oration would be "fruitless." But he believed that "defeat in such a cause is far above the triumphs of unrighteous power." He ended by quoting another opponent of removal: "I had rather receive the blessing of one poor Cherokee, as he casts his last look back upon his country, for having, though in vain, attempted to prevent his banishment, than to sleep beneath the marble of all the Caesars."

Frelinghuysen's passion was returned in a furious counterattack by John Forsyth of Georgia. He dwelt on the hypocrisy of Northerners who had been allowed for decades to deal with their own tribes without federal interference.

Forsyth's rebuttal was aimed at reminding senators that the Chickahominys and the Wampanoags of Chief Massasoit were gone, along with many other tribes of the North and Midwest—the Mohawks, Senecas, Pequods, Cheraws, Eries, Hurons—without provoking this sort of national outcry.

When Forsyth had finished, Peleg Sprague of Maine rose to speak in support of Frelinghuysen. At thirty-seven, Sprague had no religious training; he had graduated from Harvard College and studied law in Connecticut. But serving two terms in the House of Representatives had attuned him to congressional oratory, which ran to classical allusions and quotations from Shakespeare. Now Sprague caught out Forsyth for invoking *The Merchant of Venice.*

He reminded his audience that the gentleman from Georgia had capped the claims for his state by exclaiming triumphantly: "I will have my bond; I will have my bond; I will have my pound of flesh."

"A most unfortunate allusion, sir," Sprague said, reminding the Senate that in the current situation, Georgia did not hold the Cherokees' bond. "No, they hold ours, and now they present it to us, and demand payment."

Sprague accused opponents of relying entirely on the right of conquest. Under that theory, he said, "Britain has done no wrong in sweeping India with the hand of rapine, and holding fifty millions of people in thraldom! All the cruelties of the Spaniards in South America; the crimes of Pizarro and Cortez, tracking the fugitive natives in terror and dismay with bloodhounds to the caves of the mountains, and stretching their wretched monarch upon burning coals to extort from him the secret of his treasures, are sanctified in the name of right!"

For good measure, Sprague threw in the examples of the Barbary pirates, Alexander the Great, and Napoleon. "But even this miserable argument of conquest is not applicable to the Cherokees. They were not subjugated. The Southern Indians had sixteen thousand warriors with arms in their hands. They were powerful; their trade was war; they did not solicit peace. We sought for it," and had included in the Treaty of Hopewell the phrase the "United States give peace" to the Indians.

Now the nation that pledged its protection is prepared to send away those native tribes. "And what security do we propose to them? A new guarantee! Who can look an Indian in the face, and say to him, we and our fathers, for more than forty years, have made to you the most solemn promises. We now violate and trample upon them all, but offer you, in their stead, another guarantee!"

Sprague did not invoke the Almighty as Frelinghuysen had done. Instead, he appealed to the senators' innate sense of justice. Let them not sneer at his words as unworthy of a politician. "If, sir, in order to become such, it be necessary to divest the mind of the principles of good faith and moral obligation, and harden the heart against every touch of humanity, I confess that I am not, and, by the blessing of Heaven, will never be—a politician."

Instead he promised that the "still small voice" of conscience "will speak to us—when we meditate alone at eventide—in the silent watches of the night—when we lie down and when we rise up from a solitary pillow—and, in that dread hour, when 'not what we have done for ourselves, but what we have done for others' will be our joy and our strength; when—to have secured, even to the poor and despised Indian a spot of earth upon which to rest his aching head—to have given him but a cup of a cold water, in charity, will be a greater treasure than to have been the conquerors of kingdoms, and lived in luxury upon their spoils."

Robert Adams of Mississippi took John Forsyth's accusations of Northern hypocrisy to a more personal level. In rising, Adams claimed he was embarrassed to be addressing the Senate for the first time, especially since he had not been a member of his legislature at home. But, he said, he was trusting to the "generous indulgence and courtesy for which this body is so distinguished."

With that disarming preamble out of the way, Robert Adams launched into a sarcastic assault on the sincerity of Frelinghuysen and his allies in rollicking language that piled clause upon clause: "If gentlemen are really in earnest in the opinions which they have expressed; if the remonstrants who have loaded your table with their petitions, are really in earnest; if the pamphleteers who have inundated the country with abuse upon the present administration, and pour out phials of their unsparing wrath upon Georgia, are really in earnest, if they really believe that civilized man has lawlessly usurped the territory and dominion of the barbarian, then let them show their sincerity and consistency, by asking for this much injured and almost exterminated race, that ample measure of justice which the magnanimity of their professions purport; let them not only ask, but do justice; call them back from the deep wilderness to which they have been driven; restore to them this fair and happy land, from which they have been cruelly expelled; give them up your fields, houses, cities, temples of justice, and halls of legislation."

Summing up, Adams demanded that the men whose sense of justice was so strong now prove it by surrendering what they controlled directly "and then call upon us to follow an example so worthy." But, he said, he did not expect that to happen. Instead, faced with sacrificing his own possessions, "the pretended philanthropist" would "content himself with permitting things to remain as they are."

Frelinghuysen had been picking up votes from Ohio and Missouri, but Van Buren was holding the New York contingent firm, along with those of New Jersey and Pennsylvania. As a delaying tactic, Frelinghuysen called for putting off the vote until Congress could be assured that the land designated for the removal was sufficient for the Cherokees' needs. His proposal was rejected.

On April 26, 1830, the removal bill came up for final approval. The result was closer than the Jackson camp had anticipated. Twenty-eight senators voted for the removal, only nine more than those who voted against it.

As the debate moved to the House, Henry Clay was not in Washington for the first time in twenty years. At his estate at Ashland, Kentucky, Clay's sympathies lay with the Cherokees, and he saw Jackson's support of the Georgians as no different from the nullification threats coming out of South Carolina. But Clay's eyes were focused on 1832, and he was instructing Charles Hammond how his newspaper could create a groundswell for Clay's next presidential campaign.

With public attention now turned to the House, Frelinghuysen and his allies had reason to be encouraged. Not only had a public outcry arisen against Jackson's policy, but Van Buren acknowledged that his party's discipline in the lower chamber was less reliable than in the Senate. Particularly troublesome were the Quakers and other religious groups who were threatening reprisals against any congressman who voted to uproot the Cherokees.

On Thursday, May 13, 1830, the House debate began with Charles Wickliffe of Kentucky speaking for more than two hours in favor of appropriating the five hundred thousand dollars that Jackson was requesting for removal. Two days later, after a hiatus devoted to trade policy, the issue was taken up again. Speakers covered familiar ground but with a new emphasis on the argument that Jackson was assuming powers entrusted by the Constitution to the Congress. Representative Henry Storrs of New York assured Southern congressmen that Northern protests should not be dismissed as mere factional politics or religious fanaticism.

Storrs claimed that the opposition arose instead from the president's asserting an unprecedented executive power. With that twist, he tried to turn the doctrine of states' rights against its most fervent advocates.

"If the friends of state rights propose to sanction the violation of these Indian treaties," they must be prepared for "the full extent of this thoughtless usurpation. What security exists for the nation's European treaties if the President decided to dissolve them?"

Storrs challenged the apathy of his colleagues: "We are bound to resist these encroachments on the power of Congress at the beginning. This is not a distant alarm—the invader is within this hall—his manifesto is on your table, and at the next step, we, too, shall have surrendered our discretion."

And, Storrs added, do not be misled because this time the president seems to be acting on behalf of a state. "What will be the decision of the Executive in the next case?" He noted that "we have entered into more than two hundred treaties with the Indians"—fifteen of them with the Cherokees alone—and all but one of those since the U.S. Constitution was adopted. Honor demanded that to change policy now required making a clear and persuasive case.

Storrs apologized several times for the length of his remarks before returning a final time to the history of the white man on Indian land:

"We came to these people with peace offerings, and they gave us lands. As we increased in numbers we increased our demands, and began to press upon them. They saw us hemming them in on every side, and furrowing down the graves of their fathers. . . . We were deaf to their reproaches. They implored us to remember their kindness to us, but we turned away from them.

"They resisted at last, and flew to arms. Fierce and bloody wars followed. We felt their power; and if they had been united, or had foreseen what we are now doing, we should not now be in these seats."

Storrs said he did indeed want to negotiate with the Indians again. But if asked when, "I am ready to answer: Never, sir, never, till they are at perfect liberty, and free from all restraint . . . I will not consent to take advantage of men in their situation. I am sick—heart-sick of seeing them at our door as I enter this hall, where they have been standing during the whole of this session, supplicating us to stay our hand."

In a somewhat transparent ploy, Storrs downplayed the stakes, although his opponents knew better: "When it is considered how little, after all these States really have at stake on this question, and how trifling the acquisition of this paltry territory must be, I cannot believe that they will refuse to make some sacrifice or concession of feeling to the reputation of the country."

On Monday, May 17, the House enjoyed a brief respite to take up the question of a duty on salt. Then it was back to the removal debate. Lumpkin of Georgia restated the president's position that the legislation was designed only to help the Cherokees.

"It is a measure of life and death," Lumpkin said. "Pass the bill on your table, and you save them. Reject it, and you leave them to perish. Reject this bill, and you thereby encourage delusory hopes in the Indians, which their professed friends and allies well know will never be realized."

But Lumpkin also wanted to refresh memories of past warfare with the tribes: "The rejection of this bill will encourage and invite the Indians to acts of indiscretion and assumptions which will necessarily bring upon them chastisement and injury, which will be deplored by every friend of virtue and humanity. I therefore call upon you to avoid these evil consequences while you may. Delay is pregnant with great danger to the Indians; what you do, do quickly, before the evil day approaches." For Lumpkin, removal presented no conflict of loyalty. But a Jacksonian like Congressman Joseph Hemphill had to choose between voting with the president or with a sizable number of his constituents in Pennsylvania. He tried to ease his dilemma by sponsoring a substitute bill that would delay the decision for a year to allow for more study. That evasion was attractive enough to split the House, ninety-eight to ninety-eight. The tie-breaking vote fell to Andrew Stevenson, the Virginia congressman who now held Clay's former position as Speaker. A forty-six-year-old graduate of William and Mary College, Stevenson had been in the House for nine years and his second wife was a cousin of Dolley Madison. Jackson knew he could count on his support.

Jackson's allies used the close call to lobby for the removal bill before the final vote. The president had staked the success of his administration upon this measure, they said, and they won over wavering House members from Pennsylvania and Massachusetts who had voted for the Hemphill compromise. With that, opponents recognized that they had lost. The vote for Jackson's removal legislation was 102 to 97. A Senate bill was reconciled with the House version and passed easily. The president signed it on May 28, 1830.

Both sides knew that the debate had not been limited to one tribe of Indians in Georgia. Northerners had avoided talking of abolition, but they spoke repeatedly of "white Georgians" and sometimes of "lawless white Georgians." Wilson Lumpkin acknowledged the South's deepest fears when he protested the influence of religious fanatics. Lumpkin said they were using the Indian question to indict Georgians as "atheists, deists, infidels and sabbath-breakers, laboring under the curse of slavery."

Within the decorous precincts of the U.S. Capitol, salvos had been fired in the nation's first civil war, and the South had won the opening round.

As Henry Storrs had mentioned, Indian leaders had shown up at the Capitol building during the long debate to consult with sympathizers like David Crockett of Tennessee. A veteran of Jackson's militia action against the Creeks, Crockett had drawn on his homespun appeal to win election to the Congress of 1828. There, his unrelenting folksiness charmed some colleagues and grated on others.

For most of his first two terms, Crockett had proved loyal to Jackson until the removal bill. He said he "opposed it from the purest motives in the world" and brushed off colleagues who warned that he was committing political suicide.

Crockett believed "it was a wicked, unjust measure," and he would not be talked out of his opposition. "I would sooner be honestly and politically damned," he announced, "than hypocritically immortalized." At least, his vote would "not make me ashamed in the last day of judgment."

Knowing Crockett's feelings, John Ross unburdened himself to him with the same concern for a final reckoning: "Cupidity and Avarice by sophistry, intrigue and corruption may for a while prevail—but the day of retributive justice must and will come, when integrity and moral worth will predominate and make the shameless monster hide its head."

Ross said the defeat was the more galling because he had known Jackson since his boyhood and had held rank in the Cherokee regiment that fought at Jackson's side against the Creeks. In desperation, he agreed with other chieftains to petition William Wirt to carry their cause to the U.S. Supreme Court.

Before Wirt would agree to take the case, he wanted to appeal to Governor Gilmer, who was a distant relative. Wirt's letter of June 4, 1830, could scarcely have been more conciliatory. He acknowledged that except for the unusual circumstances, his involving himself "might well be deemed officious and intrusive." But if his appeal to the U.S. Supreme Court were conducted "with proper temper, as I trust it will . . . it may prove the means of peace and reconciliation."

Wirt said he regretted differing with Georgia officials but that his opinion in the case was shared "with many of the most distinguished lawyers on our continent. We may be wrong, and as infallibility is not the lot of mortals, those who hold the opposite opinion may possibly be wrong." The high court could settle the issue.

Wirt assured Gilmer that he had instructed the Indians to be peaceable and that he would drop them as clients if the Cherokee Nation approved of violence against white people. That was unlikely since the Indian delegates had assured him that "their people at home have abandoned the habits of savage life."

Two weeks later, Gilmer sent back a snide response couched in the third person: "The Governor of Georgia knows of no reason why he should be notified that professional duty required of you to take fees of all who ask your advice. Georgia claims no jurisdiction over the Lawyers of Maryland."

Wirt had testified to the civilized manners and demeanor of the Cherokee representatives, and Gilmer granted that what Wirt said was "partly true." But he explained why: "They are not Indians, however, but the children of white men, whose corrupt habits or vile passions led them into connection with the Indian tribe."

As for the true Cherokees, they "have lost all that was valuable in their Indian character, have become spiritless, dependent and depraved; as the whites and their children have become wealthy, intelligent and powerful."

Gilmer protested that the suggestion that he join with Wirt before the U.S. Supreme Court, "however courteous the manner, and conciliatory the phraseology cannot but be considered exceedingly disrespectful to the Governor of the State." In fact, Gilmer added, the very idea merely proved how Wirt's faction sought to increase the power of the federal government over the individual states. Gilmer ended with the hope that there need be no further correspondence on the subject.

After a rebuff so uncompromising, Wirt agreed to represent the tribe.

Learning that the Cherokees intended to sue them, the Georgians found a harsh new way to show their scorn for the federal courts. In September 1830, a Georgia judge had found a Cherokee named George Corn Tassel guilty of murdering another Indian in Cherokee territory and sentenced him to be hanged.

Behind the scenes, Wirt was having more success than he had found with Governor Gilmer. On the question of jurisdiction, he sounded out Chief Justice John Marshall through a mutual friend and learned that Marshall sided with the Indians. In fact, Marshall was already on record. In an 1823 case, *Johnson* v. *McIntosh*, he had ruled that Indians' rights were not a question of morality or fairness but firmly based in American law.

Drawing on that reassurance, Wirt filed a writ to ask the U.S. Supreme Court to stop the execution of George Corn Tassel on the ground that the Cherokees, not Georgia, had jurisdiction in his case. On December 12, 1830, Justice Marshall, acting for his Court, signed an order requiring the state of Georgia to appear in Washington to show cause why a writ of error should not be issued that would save Tassel from the gallows.

The Georgia legislature claimed that Marshall's order was "a flagrant violation of her rights" and not only instructed the governor and every other state official to ignore it but told the local country sheriff to expedite Tassel's execution.

On Christmas Day, Tassel was driven to the scaffold sitting on his own coffin. Without a tremor, he spoke calmly to a crowd of spectators, including five hundred Indians. Fearing an outburst from protesters, the state had provided a heavy contingent of guards, but the Indians watched stoically as Tassel was hanged, and then they left quietly.

In Washington, Marshall and his colleagues took note that since Jackson refused to enforce their rulings, they carried no weight. And yet Wirt decided to press on. He advised the Cherokees to seek an injunction that would stop Georgia from enforcing its code of punitive restrictions against them.

While resistance was moving forward in the courts, Jackson had worked personally to speed the process of clearing the Indian land. Four days after he signed the removal law, his office sent word that he and Secretary of War Eaton would be traveling to Tennessee later in the summer and wished to meet with chiefs from the affected territory. The Cherokees were the largest in numbers, but removal also involved remnants of other southeastern tribes.

Chickasaw delegates showed up at Eaton's house in Franklin, Tennessee, on August 11, 1830. Since the Louisiana Purchase twenty-seven years earlier, the United States had signed three treaties with the tribe to acquire tracts of their land in upper Mississippi, Alabama, and southern Tennessee.

Their name had been bestowed by the Choctaw, who called them

Chikkih Asaoh—or "they left as a tribe not a very great while ago." The parting had not been friendly. Because of their belligerence, the Chickasaws had been exiled, which only increased a predilection for warfare. Besides their hostility to the Choctaws, they had become the scourge of the Creeks and Cherokees. French and Spanish colonists found the tribe intractable, but British traders had managed to infiltrate their ranks, court Chickasaw women, and create a mixed race that was loyal to Britain during the American Revolution.

Afterward, Jefferson's administration subdued the survivors with gifts of manufactured goods and—although the president himself disapproved—rum and brandy. By the time of the removal legislation, the Chickasaws had already turned over much of their territory to the federal government and promptly accepted Jackson's terms for a new provisional treaty. The Choctaws had also negotiated a treaty with Thomas McKenney, but its generous terms—including the many millions of dollars for the removal—caused Jackson to recommend that the Senate reject it.

None of the Choctaw chieftains had now made the trip to Franklin. Jackson was infuriated as he rode back to Washington, but John Coffee learned that their absence was not a snub but that a bitter rift in their own ranks had prevented them from naming a delegation.

Eaton and Coffee traveled to Mississippi to confer with Greenwood Leflore, a plantation owner of French and Indian descent, who claimed to have united the Choctaws' dissident factions. Light-skinned, comfortable in dark suits with stiff collars, Leflore had named his estate "Malmaison," in honor of Josephine Bonaparte's villa in the suburbs of Paris.

The western land set aside for the Indians had been marked off for each of the Five Civilized Tribes, the name Washington bestowed on them for accepting white society's customs and practices. Choctaws and Chickasaws were allotted land to the south, Creeks and Seminoles land at the center. Cherokee holdings would end at the western borders of Missouri and Arkansas, plus another seven-million-acre strip of land south of Kansas called the Cherokee Outlet.

Eaton and Coffee arrived at Dancing Rabbit Creek on September 15, to find Leflore and his men on the verge of a battle with Mushulatubbe, a full-blooded Choctaw. Eaton turned for help to George Gaines, a white merchant respected by the tribe for his honesty. Eaton also resorted to the time-honored tactic of bribes. He was proposing a section of land in the new territory of 640 acres for every man and woman with a child. In addition, he offered Leflore, Mushulatubbe, and a third chief, Nitakechi, four choice sections. Fifty other obstinate tribal members would receive two sections each.

Along with that inducement, Leflore was awarded a hundred dollars to send his daughter to the Female Academy in La Grange, Georgia. The Treaty of Dancing Rabbit Creek was duly signed but ratification was delayed until the following February.

Margaret Eaton recalled later in life that she had been visiting her family in Tennessee while her husband and Coffee negotiated the treaty. Normally, Eaton would have been entitled to eight dollars a day in expenses for his part in the talks, but since he was already being paid as secretary of war, Margaret reluctantly granted that he had to turn down the money, along with a tract of the Indians' new land that she estimated was worth ten thousand dollars.

The financial sacrifice did not make her better disposed to the Indians, and she blew up when Eaton instructed her to buy all the lemons for sale in Washington. "Indians are coming to town," Eaton said, "and I want you to entertain them."

Margaret took pride in keeping her house in perfect order and in safeguarding her expensive furniture. She vowed that "no dirty, old, tobacco-smoking Indians are coming into my parlors."

"But, Margaret," Eaton assured her, "this thing won't do you any harm. I have been making a treaty with them, and they are coming to my house, and we must treat our red brethren civilly."

"Oh, plague take your red brethren," Margaret said. "Carry them off somewhere and take care of them yourself."

But Eaton coaxed her—"smoothed my feathers," as Margaret put it—and she bought two of the largest washtubs she could find and made lemonade. "Enough," she thought with satisfaction, "to drown one or two of them."

But she was frowning as she made the preparations, and Eaton remonstrated with her, "Treat them nicely and smoke a peace pipe."

"I would never take one of their nasty pipes in my mouth."

When the guests arrived, Margaret was not reassured. "A hard-looking crowd," she decided, "dressed in the most fantastic style of the forest."

But the Indians had brought an elegant silver set, which they presented to their hostess. "Of course, I was pacified in a minute," she recalled. And they also brought a little Indian child. He was alleged to be related to John Ross and was meant to stay on with them as John H. Eaton Ross.

When the time came for the party to leave, everyone wept, except for the foundling. The child remained cold to Margaret for the three years that he lived with the Eatons until one day he jumped into a river and swam away.

"Let him go," Eaton said. "Let him go."

They never saw him again. But Margaret, always susceptible to masculine good looks, recalled that "he was a beautiful boy."

Since the majority of the Choctaws had not been bribed, they continued to oppose removal, and they elected new leaders to replace Leflore and his allies. What followed came as no surprise to the Cherokees, who had been watching their neighbors capitulate. White settlers immediately flocked to Choctaw territory, causing some Indians to move west independently. George Gaines shut down his business to accompany an exploration by Choctaws and Chickasaws, but Leflore refused to join the expedition. He preferred to stay home and buy up Indian property, which he sold at a profit to the white men streaming into the territory.

Traveling during the icy winter months, Gaines's companions encountered hostile Plains Indians, including Shawnees who had survived the War of 1812, and they endured an outbreak of colic that struck down their horses. But on their return, the Chickasaw explorers pronounced themselves satisfied with land they had seen.

Leflore already had dispatched random groups of Choctaws whose property he had snapped up, but he had no illusions about their fate: "A considerable portion of them are poor, and, leaving with means hardly sufficient to sustain them on their journey, will reach the place of their future residence in a very destitute condition."

The reality was worse than Leflore predicted. For the nearly four thousand Choctaws who began one expedition in October 1831, the ordeal meant slogging for 550 miles through wilderness and swamp. Leflore's nephew accompanied the group, and his studies at a missionary school had produced a more compassionate spirit. "Two hundred and fifty head of horses have died," the young man wrote. "We are compelled to travel slow, as there are so many sick people."

Alexis de Tocqueville, a twenty-five-year-old Frenchman studying America's prisons, saw a party of Choctaws boarding a riverboat for the west. "The whole spectacle had an air of ruin and destruction," he wrote. "It spoke of final farewells and of no turning back."

In Louisiana, a white farmer watched the Choctaws pass by during the worst sleet storm he had ever seen. The march was being made "under the pressure of hunger, by old women and young children, without any covering for their feet, legs or body, except a cotton underdress." One team leader agreed with that bleak report, estimating that three-fourths of the children were naked in temperatures that dropped below zero.

Rough calculations concluded that one of every five Choctaw—perhaps more—died before reaching their new home. Some children had gone as long as six days with nothing at all to eat. Many others died of cholera when floodwater overflowed the banks of the Arkansas River. They had no doctors with them, only the tribe's medicine men.

A reporter from the *Arkansas Gazette* interviewed a Choctaw chief from one of the first wagons to reach Little Rock. Asked about his journey, the chief replied with a phrase that reverberated through the Northern press.

It had been, he said, "a trail of tears and death."

In Washington, it was the financial cost that the Jackson administration found shockingly high. George Gaines and the other civilians were soon fired. In the future, the U.S. Army would be expected to do the job more cheaply.

To save the Cherokees from the Choctaws' fate, Samuel Worcester had been working to convince his fellow missionaries to resist removal. Arguing with the gossipy Reverend Ely, Worcester disputed the Jackson administration's contention that the tribe's reliance on hunting had doomed it to extinction.

"The mass of the Cherokee people," Worcester wrote to Ely, "have built houses and cultivated lands with their own hands. There may be a few families among the mountains who depend mostly on the chase for support, but I know not one of them."

The local missionaries did not want to be seen, however, as the principal cause for the Cherokees' opposing removal. On December 29, 1830, a dozen of them had assembled in New Echota to draft a statement. Like Worcester, the majority were from the American Board in Boston; two others represented the United Brethren Church and one the American Baptists.

Worcester was named secretary since the group wanted their resolutions printed in the *Cherokee Phoenix.* Chairing the session was the Reverend Daniel Sabin Butrick, who opened with a prayer.

At forty-one, Butrick was already distinguished for his piety. After being ordained at the Park Street Church in Boston, he had gone to the Brainerd mission to preach among the Cherokees. Adventurous and physically fit, he had traveled south into Alabama and delighted in exploring the region's caves. He kept meticulous notes about their intimidating sheer surfaces and the tight passages between their rocks.

Butrick was already thirty-eight by the time he married forty-four-year-old Elizabeth Proctor, also from New England, who had come south to convert the Cherokees. In Butrick's journal entries, from the day of their marriage she became "my beloved Elizabeth."

At their meeting, the clergymen insisted that the debate over removal was not merely political or limited to Georgia. Rather, it was a moral question—"inasmuch as it involves the maintenance or violation of the faith of our country—and as demanding, therefore, the most serious consideration of all American citizens, not only as patriots, but as Christians."

Their main concern was to deny that they had used their influence to meddle in Cherokee politics. The resolution concluded that "we therefore solemnly affirm, that in regard to ourselves at least, every such insinuation is entirely unfounded."

Because Andrew Jackson saw himself as a friend of the Indian, he preferred to focus on the benefits for the tribes in removal. After all, he observed, his own parents had crossed an ocean in search of a better life, and he himself had left North Carolina to make his fortune in Tennessee. In his second annual message to Congress, on December 6, 1830, the president pointed out that even now white American children "by the thousands yearly leave the land of their birth to seek new homes in distant regions."

Jackson asked, "Does Humanity weep at these painful separations . . . ? Far from it. It is rather a source of joy that our country accords scope where our young population may range unconstrained in body or in mind."

Jackson announced proudly that, with two major tribes already accepting removal, the benevolent policy of his government was "approaching to a happy conclusion."

To him, Jackson's vision seemed unassailable: "What good man would prefer a country covered with forests and ranged by a few thousand savages to our extensive Republic, studded with cities, towns, and prosperous farms embellished with all the improvements which art can devise or industry execute, occupied by more than 12,000,000 happy people, and filled with all the blessings of liberty, civilization and religion?"

Chief Justice John Marshall

8 · John Marshall (1831–32)

While Jackson had been pressuring the Choctaws and the Chickasaws, Thomas McKenney had concluded that the Indian Board of New York had been a sham and that he had lent his prestige to a group that had no intention of protecting the Indians. In his Washington office, McKenney was approached by John Eaton's brother-in-law, Philip Randolph, who was the acting secretary of war. Randolph informed him that President Jackson wanted McKenney to draft an address to the tribes.

McKenney asked to whom it should be sent and what it should say.

Randolph seemed surprised. "Why, the General said you would know all about it."

McKenney pleaded ignorance and asked for instructions.

"Oh, it is nothing," Randolph replied. "You have the business at your fingers' ends and must know what he means."

McKenney soon returned with a vague policy statement, which Randolph pronounced "the very thing."

But as McKenney was discovering, Randolph was a mere functionary. In Eaton's absence, Attorney General John Berrien was running Indian Affairs. Summoning McKenney, he brandished his draft of the address.

"Colonel," Berrien began, "do you not know that this is not what the President wants?"

McKenney tried to speak up for himself, but Berrien overruled him and handed him a paragraph to add to the document. At a glance,

McKenney saw that it was aimed at breaking up the Cherokee government by isolating its leaders. Under Jackson's new policy, federal money—about twelve hundred dollars—that had been paid into the treasury of the Cherokee Council would go instead to individual Indians.

McKenney took the name of his office off the circular and gave it to an inattentive Randolph to sign as coming only from the War Department.

His subterfuge was aimed at promoting McKenney's long-term goal. For years, he had urged splitting off the Bureau of Indian Affairs from the Department of War, and under John Quincy Adams, he had come close. Secretary of War Barbour, who admired McKenney's dedication, got Adams to agree to a reorganization that would allow the head of Indian Affairs to set Indian policy and hire and fire his employees.

Congress had seemed persuaded. Asked to write out his proposal, McKenney had modestly left blank the line for the new director's salary. James Barbour wrote in three thousand dollars and penciled a notation: "Alter not a word."

But McKenney's enemy, Missouri senator Thomas Hart Benson, blocked the legislation. McKenney was certain that Benton was still doing the bidding of John Jacob Astor's American Fur Company. More fatefully, McKenney had run afoul of the president lately by refusing to approve a bit of graft for Sam Houston, a favorite Jackson protégé.

Houston had applied for a contract to supply rations for those Indians forced to emigrate. Jackson was ready to award it to him even though, by law, the contract had to go to the lowest bidder. McKenney calculated that individual rations would cost $4.4 million, which amounted to less than seven cents a day. By asking eighteen cents, Houston was guaranteeing himself an enormous profit.

Only when Duff Green, the editor, went to the president was Jackson asked directly whether he had considered the political damage to his administration. Checking the price of beef, corn, and other staples in the West, Green said he found that they could be delivered for six cents a day.

Jackson tried to put him on the defensive. "Will *you* take it at *ten*?"

Green said, "No, sir."

"Will *you* take it at twelve cents? If you will, you shall have it at that."

Green explained that he was not bidding on the contract. He understood that immense profits could be made, but he had come only to alert Jackson. He had no wish to speculate.

Green followed up that interview with a letter of protest to Secretary Eaton. Finally convinced, Jackson abandoned the entire plan.

Disappointed and angry, drinking heavily, Houston left Washington boasting that he would rise above this latest humiliation. It was scarcely his worst. In 1829, Houston had married into a prominent Tennessee family, but when Eliza Allen left him after fewer than four months of marriage, the scandal sent Houston on a new bout of drinking that culminated with his resigning the governorship.

Now, in this latest test of wills, McKenney had again preserved his reputation, but at a price.

The Cherokees' reliable champion, Congressman Edward Everett, agreed with McKenney that Jackson's new method of paying the tribes was designed to undercut the authority of the Cherokee Council, and Everett made a stab at forcing the administration to pay the sum in the traditional way.

Despite losing the removal debate the previous May, Everett protested the government's treatment of the Cherokees for two full days early in February 1831. With heavy sarcasm, he suggested creating a huge bonfire of past Indian treaties that had been "annulled and broken."

"Sir," he concluded, "they ought to be destroyed as a warning to the Indians to make no more compacts with us."

John Ridge was in the House gallery with a fellow Cherokee. A New York reporter spotted them and observed that Everett's powerful speech had caused one of the Indians to cover his eyes to hide his tears.

But Everett's eloquence could not move a majority of the House, and his motion failed. John Ross joined with fellow delegates in Washington to declare Sunday, March 6, 1831, a day of fasting and prayer. They met in a room at Brown's Hotel, where they heard a native Oneida preach in English before fasting for the rest of the day. They kept the ceremonies private. They did not want white citizens in the capital to know the depth of their despair.

Along with McKenney's official duties, he had been laboring over a massive history of the North American Indians. Exhausted from the intense political pressures, McKenney took a leave of absence to visit his publisher in Philadelphia and then enjoy a respite in New York City.

On his way home, McKenney stopped at a post office, where he found a letter from Philip Randolph. He was informed that as of October 1, his services would no longer be required. Back in Washington, McKenney confronted Randolph, who acknowledged his expertise but added that "General Jackson has long been satisfied that you are not in harmony with him in his views in regard to the Indians."

Ousted from office, McKenney found himself tarred in partisan newspapers as an embezzler. It took until November 1833 for him to wring exoneration from the government auditor, and it was still later when McKenney read that Judge Berrien of Georgia admitted that he had joined Jackson's cabinet only for the chance to influence Indian policy.

The Northern missionaries based in the South were less easily dismissed than Colonel McKenney had been. The previous December, a band of clergy had met in New Echota to pass resolutions supporting the Cherokees. The group was broadly ecumenical—Baptists, Congregationalists, Presbyterians, Moravians, all following the lead of Methodists who had already drafted a similar statement.

The missionaries were modest about their own role in improving life for the Cherokees, and they praised instead the policies of the administrations preceding Jackson's. They also endorsed the positive effect of marriage between Indians and whites. Sent to Boston, their statement was published in the *Missionary Herald.*

Reaction from the Georgia legislature was prompt and livid. Its members passed a law to ban all whites from living on Indian land unless they were licensed by the governor and swore an oath of obedience to the state of Georgia. Violators could go to prison. As enforcement, the legislators created the Georgia Guard, a military cadre designed to control the Indians and their sympathizers.

Despite the delegates' day of prayer and a sense that they had been humiliated, John Ridge was remaining hopeful. He had supplied his allies in Congress with a five-page memorandum listing the major worries of his people, including Jackson's reluctance to keep predatory whites off tribal land. Ridge took heart from well-wishers like Davy Crockett, and he was especially buoyed by the political prospects of Henry Clay. The former Speaker would surely win the presidential election of 1832 and come to the Cherokees' rescue.

To Elias Boudinot, John Ridge wrote, "From private and public sources, we are induced to believe that Henry Clay is our friend, and will enforce the treaties. Bear up my friends for two years longer, and we are victorious—let the people understand that." And Ridge assured his father that, even within Jackson's party, "there is no question of the Cherokees having a vast majority of the people of the United States in their favor."

Meantime, Ridge was waiting for the U.S. Supreme Court to hear William Wirt argue the Cherokee case. Wirt had already confided to a friend that, with Jackson and the Georgians so determined, he doubted he could prevent removal. Although representing the Cherokees would place him in a delicate situation, he wrote, "I was strongly impressed with the injustice about to be done to these people." He "did not think it right to flinch from any considerations of personal ease and safety."

Before Wirt's scheduled appearance, he circulated the argument he intended to make and received a response from former president James Madison at Montpelier, his Virginia plantation. Madison was sympathetic, although he deplored a tendency by the Cherokees to dismiss the U.S. Constitution—Madison's signal achievement—as irrelevant to their case.

Instead, the former president recommended attacking head-on accusations that the Cherokee were incapable of making full use of the land they were occupying since their accomplishments proved otherwise. But Madison also saw a problem in reconciling their interests with their rights: "It is so evident that they can never be tranquil or happy within the bounds of a State, either in a separate or a subject character, that a removal to another home, if a good one can be found, may well be the wish of their best friends." Madison added that "the removal ought to be made voluntarily" and without begrudging the necessary expenses.

Wirt responded that he agreed entirely and was not acting quixotically. He quoted to Madison his letter to John Ross that he thought "your wisest course" would be to agree to removal. But it was his legal opinion that the Cherokees had the right to remain where they were.

Preparing to hear the case, John Marshall was now a frail seventy-six years old, but he remained a proud son of the American Revolution. At nineteen, he had joined the militia in his native Virginia, fought in several battles, and was wounded at Germantown in 1777. Marshall survived the winter at Valley Forge with George Washington and considered him "the greatest man on earth."

Studying law, Marshall had risen in state politics to become a congressman in the Federalist ranks and John Adams's secretary of state. They were temperamental opposites, a righteous New Englander and a Virginian who enjoyed a drop of rum and sometimes more.

During the interval after Adams lost the presidency in 1800 but before he left office, he appointed Marshall as chief justice of the U.S. Supreme Court. Marshall entered the position determined to resist any attempts by Jefferson, a distant kinsman, to diminish the powers of the Court. Throughout the ensuing years, the two men came to symbolize the struggle between the executive branch and the judicial.

As Wirt and his associates began to plead the Cherokee cause, they felt confident that Marshall personally shared their sentiments. They also knew that his ruling would be based entirely on the Constitution as he interpreted it. In the landmark case of *Marbury* v. *Madison*, Marshall's Court had upheld the proposition that the United States was "a government of laws, and not of men." The chief justice cherished the Constitution as a document "intended to endure for ages to come" and yet as one meant "to be adapted to the various *crises* of human affairs."

On March 12 and March 14, 1831, Wirt repeated many of the strongest points from the congressional debate, reminding the Court that the Cherokees had "fought side by side with our present chief magistrate, and received his personal thanks for their gallantry and bravery."

Wirt and his clients would now have to wait four months for the Court's decision.

While the Court was deliberating, Martin Van Buren was at work demonstrating his loyalty to the president. The *Globe,* a new journal devoted to praising the administration, had predicted that Jackson would disregard his previous statements about serving a single term and run for reelection. Because his decision was tightly held, Washington was alive with rumors, and Van Buren figured in most of them.

John Calhoun had returned to South Carolina to await the next session of Congress. Now, seeing a plot to deny him a future presidency, Calhoun's friends resolved to end the antagonism that Jackson felt toward him.

Their overture came on another day when Van Buren happened to be sitting with the president, but Jackson asked to receive Calhoun's emissary alone. When the president came back to Van Buren, he announced, "The whole affair is settled."

Unnerved by the news, Van Buren was even more taken aback when Calhoun appeared unexpectedly at a formal dinner that Van Buren was giving. Speculation arose that this very public reconciliation with the administration had a price. Calhoun wanted the correspondence destroyed that revealed his criticism of Jackson's actions against the Seminoles in Florida. Or, if the letters were made public, it should be done in a way that did not increase the long-standing distrust between Calhoun and Jackson.

What followed, however, was either a series of misunderstandings or a deliberate deception by John Eaton. Calhoun expected Eaton to get Jackson's approval for the form in which he intended to publish the documents. Instead, Eaton did nothing. He may have been inattentive, or he may have been exacting revenge for the role he thought Calhoun and his wife had played in spreading the Eaton malaria.

In the end, the letters were printed as a fifty-page pamphlet, and they were widely condemned as Calhoun's attack on the popular president. Jackson wrote to a friend that Calhoun had cut his own throat, but the Calhoun faction blamed machinations by Van Buren. A New Hampshire senator called Jackson "an ignorant, weak, superannuated man" and proclaimed that "Van Buren is president *de facto.*"

Van Buren knew better than anyone that the charge was untrue. Even though he had learned how to bring Jackson around to his thinking, Van Buren remained in awe of him. Now he considered that the national uproar over Calhoun's pamphlet gave him the chance to solidify his standing with Jackson by ridding his cabinet of its Calhoun men. He would propose resigning as secretary of state in the interests of harmony and would trust his maneuver to compel the entire cabinet to follow suit—a daring strategy, and one that could easily misfire. For weeks, Van Buren lacked the nerve to set it in motion.

Then one day during their regular ride together, Jackson was nearly thrown from his horse. When Van Buren seized the reins, Jackson responded grandiloquently: "You have possibly saved my life, sir!"

It might have been the right moment to broach his plan, except that Jackson went on to say that he was not sure his life was worth saving—not only was Rachel gone, but the Donelsons had returned to Tennessee rather than receive Margaret Eaton in the White House. For the moment, Van Buren had to settle for offering his commiseration.

But the next time Jackson lamented the loneliness he felt without his family, Van Buren was poised with his solution: The only thing to bring peace to the administration was for him to resign as secretary of state.

Jackson protested with the vehemence Van Buren anticipated. "Never, sir! Even you know little of Andrew Jackson if you suppose him capable of consenting to such a humiliation of his friend by his enemies."

But after Van Buren confided the details of his plan, Jackson was won over and was speculating on the right post for Van Buren once he left Washington. Then, overnight, Jackson's dark suspicions persuaded him that Van Buren was deserting him in much the way his family had done. When Van Buren tendered his resignation, the president received it coldly.

"Mr. Van Buren, I have made it a rule through life never to throw obstacles in the way of any man who, for reasons satisfactory to himself, desires to leave me, and I shall not make your case an exception."

It took Van Buren's emotional plea to persuade the president that he was not defecting for personal reasons—not to avoid calumny from the Calhoun camp, not to look after his New York property in Kinderhook.

After Van Buren had pledged to stay on and see him through his travails, the president, near tears, took his hand and asked Van Buren to forgive him. He had been too hasty, Jackson said.

Because of the discord in his official cabinet, Jackson was consulting regularly with trusted friends—opponents called them his "kitchen cabinet"—including Major William Lewis, once Jackson's quartermaster, and Isaac Hill, one of the rare Jacksonians from New Hampshire. Seeking their advice, Jackson found that all of them endorsed Van Buren's plan with the sole exception of John Eaton. He protested that since Van Buren was the only man fit for his cabinet position, why should he be the one to leave?

Putting the same question directly to Van Buren, Eaton said, "I am the man about whom all the trouble has been made and therefore the one who ought to resign."

Van Buren admitted later that he had been thrilled. Eaton's resignation was—he quoted Shakespeare—"a consummation devoutly to be wished." Now he merely asked what Eaton's wife would say. Eaton assured him that Margaret would not object.

And so it was done. Eaton resigned early in April 1831, Van Buren a few days later. With their letters in hand, Jackson compelled the resignations of Ingham, Berrien, and John Branch, his secretary of the navy. Van Buren influenced Jackson's choice of successors, arguing that his replacement at State be Edward Livingston, who had the virtue of being too old to have presidential ambitions.

John Eaton made one more sacrifice for Margaret. While Van Buren was heading for London to represent the United States in Great Britain, Eaton turned down the governorship of the territory of Michigan because he thought the climate would not be healthy for his wife. Margaret Eaton appreciated his concern, although it did not escape her notice that General Lewis Cass, who was replacing Eaton as secretary of war, had become "immensely rich" as governor of the Michigan territory.

Van Buren's leaving Jackson's cabinet represented no setback for the Cherokees. As a senator during John Quincy Adams's administration, Van Buren knew of the bribery and land speculation that had accompanied dealings with the Indians. He was also keenly aware of the antiremoval sentiment among Northern congregations. But although he had not publicly joined the debate, he was known to support Jackson's policy.

In the past, Van Buren had not only owned a slave in New York, he had also denounced Indians for their "barbaric cruelties." To him, the removal bill was a "most generous" gesture by white Americans.

Henry Clay firmly opposed Georgia's attempt to "usurp powers of legislation over the Cherokee Nation," but he also saw the benefit in taking a stand at odds with the Jackson administration. Clay admitted that he was puzzled by what the Cherokees should do next, although he did "see clearly what they ought not to do." They should not go to war. He looked to the day when the American people would correct the wrongs being done to the tribe. Meantime, the Cherokee nation would become "a civilized, Christian and prosperous community."

At the moment, Clay was far more involved with other issues—preserving tariff protection and renewing the charter of the Bank of the United States. He also urged paying for federal public works—the heart of his American System—with surplus revenues rather than new taxes.

Yet Clay's support in his home state seemed to be slipping. To bolster his candidacy for the presidency in 1832, his allies persuaded Kentucky senator John J. Crittenden to step down, which Crittenden did gladly. Next, the Kentucky legislature elected Clay to the Senate by a margin of nine votes. Even though the job was to be only temporary, Clay was unhappy at the prospect of returning to Washington. He left home "with no anticipation of pleasure."

Once there, Clay began to strengthen a coalition of voting blocs that called themselves Whigs. In opposing Jackson, they claimed to be acting in the spirit of the rebels against George III. His rift with Jackson had made even John Calhoun, for the moment, a Whig.

Daniel Webster was also attracted to the party. The gifted orator, born in New Hampshire, was now approaching fifty. From childhood, his unusually large head topped with coal-black hair had given him the nickname "Little Black Dan."

Webster had swept through Dartmouth College before he was twenty, then read law. Throughout his thirties, he had argued major cases before the U.S. Supreme Court, endearing himself to his alma mater when he fought to ensure Dartmouth's survival during a contract dispute among the college's trustees. Fellow alumni wept at Webster's closing argument: "It is, sir, as I have said, a small college. And yet, there are those of us who love it." When the Supreme Court opened its 1819 term, Marshall and his fellow justices ruled for Dartmouth.

Webster had been first elected to the House of Representatives on the Federalist ticket in 1812 and had opposed the war with Britain. After supporting John Quincy Adams against Jackson, he became a director of the Bank of the United States before going to the U.S. Senate from Massachusetts. Webster's keen determination to preserve the Union against the advocates of states' rights suggested that an alliance between him and Calhoun would be short-lived.

The day of the Supreme Court ruling in the Cherokee case finally arrived. On July 18, 1831, John Ridge was among the crush of spectators to hear John Marshall read his decision from the bench. The chief justice's voice sounded unsteady, but he left no doubt about his personal feelings:

"If courts were permitted to indulge their sympathies, a case better calculated to excite them can scarcely be imagined," Marshall read.

But to claim jurisdiction, Article 3 of the U.S. Constitution required that the Cherokees be considered a "foreign state." Marshall believed that the tribe constituted a "distinct political society" capable of governing itself. That was not enough. The Cherokee territory lay within the boundaries of the United States, and the tribe had acknowledged that it was under federal protection.

To resolve the conundrum, Marshall came up with a new definition: Indian tribes were neither foreign entities nor simply U.S. subjects. They were instead "domestic dependent nations," and their relationship to Washington was that of "a ward to his guardian."

Marshall saw a second reason to rule against the Cherokees. His Court could neither control the Georgia legislature nor restrain its armed forces. All the court could do was await "a proper case with proper parties." Then the justices might decide "the mere question of right."

Marshall showed in another way how dissatisfied he was with his own ruling. He encouraged the publishing of a dissenting opinion, and he allowed the Court reporter to release every argument, including those by Wirt and his cocounsels. Finally, Marshall apologized for not having time to consider all of the lawsuit's ramifications. "As an individual," he added, "I should be very glad to see the whole case."

The Ridge delegation took heart from Marshall's hint that they were in the right and that, in a case less problematical, he was ready to rule in their favor. That expectation made the Cherokees combative enough to request and receive an audience with Jackson himself. A newspaper friendly to the president reported that the Cherokees wanted reassurance from Jackson that he was not angry with them, an accusation that stung John Ridge. He wrote to Boudinot: "Sooner than ask the President *if he was angry with me,* I would cut my tongue out."

Once in Jackson's presence, the Cherokees found him in a mood to reminisce about his friendship with their tribe and to assure them that he desired to do right by them.

"I'm particularly glad to see you at this time," Jackson began. "I knew that your claims before the Supreme Court would not be supported. The court has sustained my views in regard to your nation." Jackson paused for emphasis. "I blame you for suffering your lawyers to fleece you—they want your money, and will make you promises even after this."

His persistent cough forced the president to break off for a moment. When he resumed, his tone was confidential: "I have been a lawyer myself long enough to know how lawyers will talk to obtain their clients' money."

The Cherokees assured him that they considered money spent on protecting their rights as money well spent. The president took a final swipe at greedy lawyers and then announced, "I am a friend of the Cherokees." Given that they had fought at his side to defend the United States, he asked, "How could I be otherwise than their friend?"

But because he *was* their friend, the president urged them to remember the fate of the Catawba tribe.

When Jackson was a young man, he recalled, the Catawbas had been notoriously warlike. "They took some of the Cherokee warriors prisoner, threw them in the fire, and when their intestines were barbecued, ate them. Now," Jackson said, spelling out the moral, "they are poor and miserable and reduced in numbers, and such will be the condition of the Cherokees if they remain surrounded by white people."

Before the Cherokees could protest that they were neither poor nor miserable, a delegation from Georgia was announced. Rather than meet them, the Cherokees rose and prepared to leave. At the door, Jackson shook each hand. When he came to the last man, Richard Taylor, an older, heavyset Cherokee with a persistent air of sadness, the president did not release his hand as he repeated his pledge of friendship. He urged Taylor to tell his people that "you can live on the lands in Georgia if you choose, but I cannot interfere with the laws of that state to protect you."

Ignoring that clear warning, John Ridge and his colleagues returned home convinced that they simply had to wait out Jackson's term until Henry Clay put them again under federal protection. John Marshall reinforced that illusion when he wrote privately to Richard Taylor to express his dismay at the ruling his Court had been forced to make.

Henry Clay was finding his political calculations upended these days by the emerging splinter party called the Anti-Masons. Members held America's first national nominating convention in September 1831 and expected to name Associate Supreme Court Justice John McLean as their candidate. But when McLean abruptly withdrew, William Wirt agreed to run.

His decision astounded Clay, who had considered Wirt a trusted ally. And Wirt himself had once been a Mason. Clay decided that Wirt must have been bought off, influenced by the "magnitude of the fee" he had been offered. But he warned his supporters not to attack Wirt or any other of the Anti-Masons; Clay still hoped to unite them with his Whigs.

The maneuvering of white politicians then got more complicated when Georgia created the sort of legal test case that Marshall had hoped for. In March 1831, twenty-five members of the new Georgia Guard, acting without warrants, arrested three white missionaries and teachers. They first picked up Isaac Proctor from the American Board of Missionaries at the town of Taloney. Proctor was already convinced that missionaries should obey Georgia law on secular matters. He was prepared to take the required oath and then petition the state for permission to remain with his congregation. Despite that position, guards took Proctor into custody and held him overnight at a nearby inn.

The next morning at New Echota, they seized Elias Boudinot's ally Samuel Worcester, and at Hightower, John Ross's friend the Reverend John Thompson. Fife and drum sounded as the men were marched to the civil authorities at Lawrenceville. For the moment, their religious standing guaranteed respectful treatment, and many white Georgians assured them that they disapproved of their arrests.

Only a month earlier, Worcester had become a father for the third time and named his new son Jerusha. But childbirth had left his wife depleted and ailing, and Worcester successfully petitioned a local judge to release him and the other two missionaries on a technicality: He argued that because they were employed as federal postmasters, they were immune from arrest by a state guard.

Worcester returned to his family and from New Echota appealed directly to Governor Gilmer on June 10, 1831. With his wife too ill to be moved, Worcester assumed that writing as one gentleman to another would persuade Gilmer to let him remain in Cherokee territory.

Worcester explained that taking the oath as a citizen of Georgia "would greatly impair, or entirely destroy, my usefulness as a minister of the gospel" among the Cherokees. In that event, it would be better for him to abandon his calling entirely.

To bolster his case for staying on, Worcester sent Gilmer a copy of the Book of Matthew that he had translated into the Cherokee language, along with a hymnal and a tract of other excerpts from the Bible.

"My own view of duty is, that I ought to remain, and quietly pursue my labors for the spiritual welfare of the Cherokee people, until I am forcibly removed." Worcester concluded with a pledge that if he should suffer for preaching the gospel, his conscience and trust in God's judgment would sustain him.

Worcester sent off his appeal and waited for his words to touch Gilmer's heart.

While Worcester was temporarily free, the *Phoenix* published accounts of new outrages by white Georgians. Members of the state guard had gone to jeer at Cherokee Christians being baptized at a river in an area called Tensewaytee. When the ritual was over, three guards saddled up and charged the riverbank, shouting to the congregation to get out of their way or be trampled. As they plunged into the water, they explained that they had been so moved by the Holy Spirit that they wanted their horses to have the same religious experience.

Governor Gilmer wrote to Jackson asking whether the president considered the missionaries to be agents of his government. Acting for Jackson, John Eaton assured Gilmer that the missionaries had no such status, and Postmaster General William Barry dismissed Worcester as postmaster. In late June, Georgia began rounding up the men again. Colonel John W. A. Sanford of Georgia was sent to deliver an ultimatum to Worcester. If he did not swear allegiance to the state, Sanford was there to arrest him.

But when the colonel saw that Ann Worcester and her infant, Jerusha, were both too sick to be moved, he left Worcester at home, and he was not picked up until July 7.

This time, eleven missionaries were charged with dwelling illegally in Cherokee territory. Whatever deference they had been shown in February had vanished. John Ridge described "these unoffending and guileless men" being "ignominiously received like felons—they were chained with horses' trace-chains around their necks and fastened, one to the neck of a horse, the other to the tail of a cart, and thus were dragged with bleeding feet, through the rough and tangled forest."

The men were marched some eighteen miles under the eye of a Georgia Guard sergeant named Brooks, who showered them with profanity. When Dickson McLeod, a feisty missionary who lived over the Georgia state line, rode up to protest the prisoners' treatment, he was first told to "fuck off." But as he was riding away, his horse was seized and Brooks forced him to join the group on foot, prodding him with his bayonet into stagnant pools of water in the road.

As they marched, Sergeant Brooks delighted in turning scripture against his prisoners: "Fear not, little flock," he jeered, "for it is your Father's good pleasure to give you the kingdom."

When Brooks learned that four soldiers had given up their horses and walked for four or five miles so that the more elderly missionaries could ride, he cursed the soldiers and insisted that the captives, including McLeod, who was now limping, continue the march on foot.

Arriving at the jail at Camp Gilmer, Brooks offered a final benediction: "Here is where all the enemies of Georgia have to land—here and in Hell."

On their first Sunday in custody, the prisoners asked permission to hold a service that would be open to any guards who wished to attend. The camp commander, Colonel Charles H. Nelson, rejected their request as impertinent: "If your object is true piety, you can enjoy it where you are; were we hearers, we would not be benefited, devoid as we are of confidence in your honesty."

For the time, the prisoners were receiving long-distance support from the American Board of Missionaries. "William Penn"—Worcester's former teacher, Jeremiah Evarts—encouraged them to hold firm: "If you leave, I fear the Cherokees will make no stand whatsoever" since they could be "easily vexed and frightened."

On July 23, the missionaries appeared before a judge in Lawrenceville and were released until they could be tried by Georgia's supreme court. That prospect sufficiently alarmed nine of the eleven that they ignored Evart's call for courage and accepted the state's terms. Only Worcester and Dr. Elizur Butler refused an offer of clemency.

As the freed missionaries hurried to leave Cherokee territory, Georgia's high court found the two holdouts and their printer guilty of not signing the required oath and sentenced them to four years at hard labor in a penitentiary. Although Worcester was briefly released on a writ of habeas corpus, he did not dare return to his family.

In Tennessee, he learned that his son Jerusha had died but could not get home in time for the funeral service that Elias Boudinot conducted. Then, after two days of mourning, Worcester was arrested again.

With backing from the American Board of Missionaries, Chief John Ross and his Cherokee Council asked William Wirt in Washington to appeal Worcester and Butler's sentence to the U.S. Supreme Court.

Wirt offered to defer his retainer, even to waive it entirely if the tribe could not afford to pay. He also agreed that the Cherokees were being punished by the new method of receiving their annuities. Instead of the money being paid to the council, Wirt explained to a friend that "they are doled out in driblets to the individuals of the nation—as if the design were to disable them from supporting the controversy."

Wirt foresaw the abuse he would be enduring again. He knew several prominent Georgians and considered them to be good men. "But the Indian question is a cord of insanity to many," Wirt concluded. "They are hardly responsible for what they do under the influence of the mania which has seized them."

In his personal life, Wirt suffered a loss that strengthened his bond with Worcester. From Baltimore, he learned that his younger daughter, Agnes, had died unexpectedly at the age of sixteen.

Wirt eased his grief by plunging immediately into another celebrated case—the defense of District Judge James Peck, who had been impeached by the House of Representatives on a political charge. By day, the challenge animated Wirt, but he sobbed throughout the nights and consoled himself that he would be united in heaven with his daughter. He came to detest the inevitable strife in practicing law. "Yet I will do my duty—this is a part of my religion."

By the end of the year, John Marshall had joined the ranks of the bereaved. At seventy-six, Marshall remained mentally vigorous, but the death of Mary, his wife of forty-eight years, had left him shaken.

In court, Wirt observed that, as a widower, Marshall now neglected his grooming. The chief justice arrived one day patchily shaved and "with a quantity of egg on his underlip and chin."

John Quincy Adams had picked up alarming rumors that Marshall might retire. That would allow Jackson to replace him with some "shallow-pated wildcat." Such a man, Adams was sure, would be "fit for nothing but to tear the Union to rags and tatters."

Much to his family's distress, Adams himself was back in Washington. He had yielded to an appeal by friends and run in 1830 for election to the Congress that would convene late in 1831. His wife, Louisa, and son Charles had opposed his return to politics, but running as one of Clay's National Republicans, Adams won his seat with 1,817 votes, against 373 for the Democratic candidate and 279 for a remnant of the Federalist Party. In his journal, Adams wrote that this latest victory gratified him more than being elected president.

Having followed the debate over removal, Adams considered the Cherokee cause doomed. When Edward Everett had taken up the issue earlier in 1831, Adams had written to warn him that Everett could do nothing more than remind Congress of "the perfidy and tyranny of which the Indians are to be made the victims, and leave the punishment of it to Heaven."

As Wirt readied his appeal, Worcester began serving his four years in the state penitentiary. He was informed that whenever he chose to take Georgia's oath of allegiance, he would be released. But he felt that capitulating would betray the Cherokees and remained in prison. Ann Worcester stayed close at hand throughout the first months but then took their two surviving daughters north to stay with her family until the ordeal ended.

John Ross, who had recently survived one assassination attempt by a white Georgian, now was facing division within his own ranks. Since the Georgia legislature had banned meetings of the Cherokee Council, Ross hesitated to endorse a scheduled assembly. Violators could be punished by four years at hard labor, and Elias Boudinot warned him that prominent members of the council would resign rather than meet in New Echota.

Instead, the council met just outside the Georgia state limits in Alabama. Ross attended the session but did not join the delegation of John Ridge, John Martin, and Ross's nephew, William Shorey Coodey, who were authorized to travel to Washington for yet another appeal.

After that mission proved fruitless, John Ridge and Boudinot stayed on to launch a fund-raising tour of Northern cities. They intended to publicize the case of *Worcester* v. *Georgia* as it wound its way through the Court, and by now, Boudinot could speak from experience about persecution. He had been rousted twice by the Georgia Guard and harassed for printing "abusive and libelous" articles in the *Phoenix.*

In Philadelphia, Boudinot had collected small sums for his newspaper when he and his cousin crossed paths with Colonel McKenney, who had become an outspoken opponent of Jackson's Indian policy. McKenney asked the two men to sound out John Ross about writing a biographical sketch of Sequoyah for a collection of his lithographs of Indian chiefs.

The Northern press was warmly praising John Ridge's speeches. One reporter noted approvingly that "his metaphors were rarely drawn from the forest" and that he did not employ the bombast "that characterizes the oratory of uncivilized tribes." After appearing at the Old South Church in Boston, Ridge and Boudinot went to relax at the offices of the American Board of Missionaries.

For days, they had been awaiting the Marshall Court's decision. Boudinot described their state of mind to his brother, Stand Watie, who was editing the *Phoenix* while Boudinot was in the North: "Expectation has for the last few days been upon tip-toe—fears and hopes alternately took possession of our minds."

At that point, a friend named John Tappan sought them out at the offices in Pemberton Square. Fresh from Washington, he asked teasingly whether Boudinot and Ridge were prepared to hear bad news.

No, Ridge said wearily, they were not.

Tappan relented and told them that he had been joking. The truth was that the U.S. Supreme Court had struck down as unconstitutional the Georgia law imprisoning Worcester and Butler and demanded that they be set free at once. Even better, the Court had ruled against Georgia's entire Indian Code.

Ridge was pronouncing the decision "glorious" when Dr. Lyman Beecher entered the office. Beecher had been a strong ally from the days Ridge courted Sarah Northrup at the Cornwall School, and the local newspaper had reviled him then as one of the clergymen who abetted their marriage. Boudinot asked Beecher whether he had heard the news.

"No," Beecher said suspiciously. "What is it?" The downward curve to Beecher's mouth spoke of a man who had spent his life fighting frivolity, a crusade so unrelenting that he forbade his family to celebrate Christmas. And yet when he heard the Court's ruling, Beecher jumped to his feet, clapped his hands, and cried, "God be praised!"

He hurried away to tell his large family, which included his twenty-one-year-old daughter, Harriet, an aspiring writer.

John Ridge was convinced that the Marshall Court had "forever settled as to who is right and who is wrong." He added, "It is not now between the great state of Georgia and the poor Cherokees, but between the United States and the state of Georgia, or between the friends of the judiciary and the enemies of the judiciary."

But at the White House, Jackson refused to pick up the gauntlet. The president's displeasure with the ruling became widely known, and in New York the editor Horace Greeley compressed the president's reaction into two sentences. Jackson may not have put it so tersely, but Greeley's version reflected his sentiments: "John Marshall has made his decision. Let him enforce it now if he can."

That defiance provoked a bitter response from Junaluska, a Cherokee chieftain who had fought with Jackson against the Creeks and now lived across the state line in North Carolina: "If I had known that Jackson would drive us from our homes, I would have killed him that day at the Horseshoe."

Legal opinion was divided, in fact, over the extent of the president's power to intervene. Some lawyers held that Jackson could act only after the Supreme Court issued a writ of habeas corpus or cited Georgia's officials for contempt. Since the Georgians refused to acknowledge the Court's ruling, their contempt might be flagrant but still not move the Marshall Court to action.

Ridge and Boudinot were making their final public appearances in Salem and Newburyport when they read in a Washington newspaper that Jackson was refusing to act. Ridge's euphoria evaporated. He returned to Washington and sought a meeting with the president. Jackson agreed to meet but only to dash his last hopes. Declaring flatly that he would not intervene, Jackson pressed Ridge to go home and convince his people that their only future lay in abandoning their nation.

Ridge was shaken to find the president so unyielding, and Jackson was heartened by his evident despair. He wrote to Coffee that he thought Ridge was coming to accept the inevitable.

The president's intuition was correct. Speaking in confidence to his cousin, Ridge learned that Boudinot had also become convinced that their cause was lost. They must now strike the best possible terms with the federal government. But if they made that opinion known, they would risk banishment, or worse. For the moment, they could only work privately with trusted friends and chip away at their tribe's adamant resistance.

The Cherokees had first looked to Congress and been disappointed. Now a victory in the nation's highest court seemed to count for nothing. With Worcester and Butler held in prison, evidence was mounting that even those who sympathized with the tribe had wearied of the debate and that the combative spirit was draining from their most vocal allies.

From Boston, David Greene, secretary of the American Board, objected to the militancy he detected in the *Phoenix*. He found Boudinot's blunt news reports on white Georgians detrimental to the Cherokee cause and urged that they be less "irritating."

In Washington, Justice Story was clearly relieved when he wrote to his wife that "the Court can wash their hands clean of the iniquity of oppressing the Indians and disregarding their rights."

Justice John McLean, Story's colleague who had declined to run for president, agreed but also offered Ridge and Boudinot a crushing analysis of their situation. The Cherokees had long considered McLean a friend, and they listened stolidly as he assured them that his Court was powerless in the face of Jackson's obstinacy.

McLean's advice was to get the best possible terms now because there would never be a better chance. He offered his own services in future treaty negotiations and agreed to Ridge's request that he put his recommendation in a letter to John Ross. McLean left for his home in Cincinnati convinced that he could bargain successfully on the tribe's behalf.

Rather than being persuaded, however, Ross denounced McLean's suggestion as "one of the most consummate acts of treachery" in Cherokee history.

On their side, the Georgians had resurrected their investigation into Ross's ancestry and were charging that he and other mixed-blood chiefs "had but slender claims to be classed" as Cherokees. Samuel Worcester disagreed. He had always held that the tribe's loyalty to its chiefs was based on their policies, not their bloodlines. If John Ross were to advocate removal, Worcester was convinced that he would soon be deposed by the rank-and-file Cherokees.

Worcester's judgment contradicted the view that Andrew Jackson found most comforting. The president had persuaded himself that John Ross and his allies represented the sort of arrogant aristocracy he had fought in his 1828 campaign against John Quincy Adams. Jackson could frame his removal crusade as one more populist issue, like his attacks on the Bank of the United States.

By insisting on removal, Jackson could see himself as taking the side of the beleaguered masses against their wealthy oppressors. Privileged Cherokees might paint him as an enemy of their people, but Jackson knew that he had always championed the ordinary man, whether a white farmer in Georgia or an Indian prevented from moving west by a grasping tribal elite.

Jackson could be unbending on removal because he knew he was not the enemy of the Indian that he was being painted as. He was simply following what he termed "the dictates of humanity." His conscience was clear.

Convinced that the Cherokees were now discouraged enough to leave Georgia, Jackson appointed Benjamin Currey of Tennessee to oversee their exodus. He provided funds for hiring assistants, and Currey hired men recommended by Georgia's governor. Filing a hopeful report, Currey said that, yes, some Cherokees wanted to end the tensions of their daily life and move west. But he confirmed Worcester's point that they were being prevented by pressure from the majority of their tribe, not from a few chieftains.

To persuade diehards in the Ross camp, Currey paid several willing Cherokees a sizable fee to mingle with the tribe and promote the advantages of going west. The effort was undercut, however, by those Cherokees who had already made the trip. They were returning to Georgia disillusioned by the land designated for them across the Mississippi. "Extensive prairie badly watered," they reported to Ross, which yielded only "corpses of wood."

White predators, however, were making a more persuasive case than Currey's. Emboldened by Georgia's law that banned Indians from testifying in state courts, they had increased their raids on Cherokee property. Even so, the antiremoval chieftains continued to promise, at least publicly, that help would be forthcoming from the next Congress.

After a summer of threats and bribes, Currey had managed to enroll only seventy-one families. He hoped to have a thousand more emigrants ready to leave by April 1832, but he complained to Washington that his Cherokee opponents had stepped up their efforts to thwart him. He claimed that they were getting tribal members drunk so they would be encumbered with debts and that decades-old warrants were being resurrected to prevent them from leaving. As he waited for volunteers, Currey received sixteen U.S. flatboats for the migration by river that he expected.

9 · Elias Boudinot (1832–34)

THROUGHOUT THE SPRING, Benjamin Currey oversaw the repair of his flatboats, or arks, and by April 16, 1832, he was ready to sail west, even though the number of emigrants had fallen far short of his estimate. And he had found that even those Cherokees resigned to making the trip were dreading the long voyage; disease was their major worry.

When Currey cast off from Calhoun, Tennessee, he had fewer than half of the passengers he anticipated, and many of those were not Cherokees. His final total was 380—40 whites, 108 blacks, a few full-blooded Indians, and the rest of mixed races. Moving them required only nine of the sixteen vessels Currey had requisitioned.

After a week of sailing the Tennessee River and weathering the rapids at Muscle Shoals, the passengers transferred to a steamboat called the *Thomas Yeatman*. Two more weeks of traveling took them to Little Rock, Arkansas. Some passengers left for an established Cherokee settlement on the left bank of the Arkansas River, above Fort Smith. The rest sailed to the mouth of the Illinois River.

But by the time they landed, they had neither provisions nor the money to buy them. Currey could rustle up rations only for the Indians, not their slaves. He also turned away whites who had married Indians. Leaving them to scavenge for food as best they could, Currey returned to Georgia to recruit more Cherokees for another trip in the fall.

As he edited the *Phoenix,* Boudinot found the letdown after his euphoria from the Marshall decision particularly severe. Since he was coming to question the wisdom of fighting removal, he wanted to make his newspaper a forum for reasoned discussions.

John Ross vehemently disagreed, afraid of a weakening spirit he already sensed around him. One example was John Walker, Jr., Ross's longtime foe, who had led a renegade delegation to Washington to pursue negotiations. Walker enjoyed little prestige, but for Ross his trip was one more proof that the times were far too dangerous to be conducting policy debates in the pages of the *Phoenix.*

Even though Boudinot, the Ridges, and their friends were now being termed "the Ridge faction," John Ridge still wanted to consider Ross an ally in their common struggle. He wrote to remind Ross of the way white Georgians were robbing and whipping the Cherokees.

In his letter, Ridge acknowledged Ross's position as "chief of the whole Cherokee Nation, upon whom rests under Heaven, the highest responsibility and well being of the whole people." And he remained convinced that Ross was capable of acting as a statesman. But if the Cherokees could not maintain their nation on its ancient land, they must try to establish it someplace else. Ridge added, "*Where,* the wisdom of the nation must try to find."

For Ross, the letter was one more sign that the Ridge faction was yielding to the unthinkable.

When Ross returned from Washington, he convened a special session of the Cherokee Council to tell them of Jackson's final offer. The president would agree to a treaty with an allowance of $2.5 million for removal. He would add another half-million dollars if the Cherokees managed the migration on their own, without federal assistance. Ross indicated that his delegates had also been offered a bribe of eighty thousand dollars to sign the new agreement.

Ross said he had made a nervy counteroffer: Let the federal authorities buy out the white men who were usurping Cherokee property instead and pressure *them* to move west.

To Boudinot, Ross was looking less like a tribal chief these days and more like a dictator. Despite Jackson's efforts, Ross still controlled the greater share of the tribal annuities that the U.S. government paid for land ceded under past treaties. And for Boudinot, the stern warning the Cherokees had issued when their constitution was drafted now was taking on a sinister aspect: "Resolved by the National Committee and Council, that any person or persons, whatever, who shall be found guilty of forming unlawful meetings or encourage rebellion against the laws and government of the Cherokee Nation, shall receive one hundred stripes on the bare back."

The threat had been intensified three years ago by putting in writing the death penalty for violating the blood law, a warning that no longer seemed aimed only at outright traitors like William McIntosh.

By September, John Ross was feeling beleaguered. As the leading Cherokee voice against removal, he denounced Boudinot's "toleration of diversified views" in the *Phoenix* as fomenting confusion. Ross called instead for a "unity of sentiment and action for the good of all." Working through the Cherokee Council, he forced out Boudinot as editor of the newspaper he had founded and installed in his place Ross's brother-in-law, Elijah Hicks.

Boudinot framed his ouster as a matter of principle. He believed in the free expression of ideas, he wrote, but his "usefulness would be paralyzed by being considered, as I already have been, an enemy to the interests of my country and my people."

For Major Ridge, the division within the tribe reflected an upheaval in his personal life. For years, he had stood aloof from the religious conversions inspired by the presence of John and Anna Gambold and their Moravian Church. John Ridge and Elias Boudinot had both joined the congregation, and more than a decade earlier, Major Ridge had been proud when his wife also accepted the faith. Ridge said then that although he was not ready to become a Christian, he was glad that "Susanna has chosen the *good* part."

The Gambolds were both gone. When Anna died from a heart attack, John Gambold's church had decreed that he required a wife for his missionary work. At that time, Ridge had welcomed the newlyweds to a new mission in Oothcalooga, where the elderly clergyman converted both Stand Watie and his mother, Ridge's sister.

But Father Gambold had also died, replaced by a Brother Clauder. With his political certainties failing him, Major Ridge sought out the Moravian Church for a form of confession.

He reminded Clauder that while his friends and relatives had joined the white man's church, he had not. "I am still a bad man," Ridge said. But he started showing up more often at church services. He explained that he had been a young man when the missionaries first arrived, but they were dead and he knew that he himself would not live much longer.

"Many of my countrymen are now Christians," Ridge said. "They no longer drink and are better men than they were before. I too want to seek the good now."

Clauder accepted Ridge for religious instruction. After two years, Ridge chose the Presbyterians over the Moravians, and in 1832, he was baptized.

Major Ridge's conversion did not deflect attacks from John Ross, although Ross did not need to name him directly. The tribe understood his target when Ross charged that "a man who will forsake his country" was "no more than a traitor."

Boudinot also found himself denounced by Elijah Hicks in the columns of his former newspaper for a lack of patriotism. Boudinot struck back with his own definition of the word. "Patriotism" was not only love of country, he said, but love for its people. "Now, as a friend of my people, I cannot say *peace*, *peace*, when there is no peace. I cannot ease their minds with any expectation of a calm, when the vessel is already tossed to and fro, and threatened to be shattered to pieces by an approaching tempest."

To serve the Cherokee people best, Boudinot concluded, was "to weigh the matter rightly, act wisely, not rashly, and choose a course that will come nearest benefiting the Nation."

As part of his lead-up to the coming presidential campaign, Henry Clay decided to oppose Van Buren's appointment as minister to Great Britain. Clay may not have returned to Congress gladly, but he was greeted in the Senate as a formidable force. Colleagues found him looking somewhat older since they last saw him but still possessing undeniable charm and a melodious voice.

Privately, Clay granted that his motive in going after Van Buren was entirely political. If his appointment was rejected, the result "would cripple him and weaken the Administration."

Van Buren had sailed off to his English mission in August 1831, relieved to be trading the turmoil in Washington for the tranquility of an ocean voyage. He used the long, empty days to review his behavior in the political maelstrom and concluded that he had been blameless. Van Buren was sure, though, that his voluntary exile was ending whatever chance he might have had for the presidency, and he had said as much to Jackson.

Van Buren knew he was called "the magician" and thought to be never happier than when "concocting and advancing political intrigues." He felt he knew himself better than that. He was convinced that he had never sought power for its own sake.

By the time his packet ship—coincidentally called the *President*—docked in England, Van Buren had resolved to serve out his time in London and return to private life. Meantime, he considered his most important priority the retaining of "pacific and cordial relations" with Britain.

As his first point of attack, Henry Clay castigated Van Buren for undermining the successful trade and foreign policies of the Adams years and linked him to the "detestable" spoils system. As the political charges grew more heated, Margaret Eaton's reputation once again became fair game, and the choicest innuendoes were repeated on the Senate floor. On the day the confirmation vote arrived, Clay choreographed a tie so that John Calhoun would cast the deciding ballot against Van Buren.

When Calhoun broke the deadlock and defeated the nomination, he was said to have exulted to Senator Benton, "It will kill him, sir, kill him dead."

To which Benton, who understood Jackson's towering sense of loyalty, was said to reply, "You have broken a minister, and elected a vice president."

On the evening before the queen's first Drawing Room of the season, news reached London that the U.S. Senate had refused to confirm Van Buren's appointment. He had been spending the day in bed, recovering from a passing indisposition, when his servant brought him a packet of urgent letters.

His friends' accounts from Washington suggested that the rejection had been bungled in a way that could confound his enemies. One predicted, "You will be V.P. in spite of yourself."

Instantly feeling better, Van Buren dressed and went to breakfast with the writer Washington Irving, who was staying with him. With Irving's encouragement, he headed for Buckingham Palace, where Lord Palmerston, the foreign secretary, took him aside to commiserate. The king wanted Van Buren to know, Palmerston said, that he never meddled in the affairs of other governments but that nothing had changed the respect his majesty had for him. The king underscored his words by inviting Van Buren for a two-day visit with the royal family at Windsor Castle. Van Buren, from Kinderhook, New York, was overwhelmed.

For tactical reasons, Van Buren wanted to delay his return to the United States until after the Democrats had held their nominating caucus in Baltimore. He gave Jackson a list of housekeeping trivia that would keep him a little longer in London—settling the lease on his quarters in Stratford Place, selling his horses and carriage, arranging suitable positions for his servants. Jackson agreed and turned over the choice of his vice president to his kitchen cabinet and to Van Buren's allies in New York.

Van Buren packed for home, taking away a lifelong regard for the simplicity with which the English nobility carried their honors. "No one can doubt," wrote the champion of the people's party, "that the form of government recognized by the English Constitution is as much the choice of her people as that under which we have the happiness to live is the choice of ours."

Just before Van Buren boarded the packet *New York* to spend more than a month at sea, he was notified that his party's convention had nominated him for vice president by a vote of 208 to 75.

The presidential campaign of 1832 started as explosively as the race four years earlier. A harbinger came when a cholera epidemic struck Canada before sweeping down to New York City and threatening to move south. Seeing an opportunity to court religious voters, Clay proposed a day of fasting and prayer that God might protect the nation.

Since his personal behavior was too flagrant for him to pretend to a new piety, Clay did the next best thing: "I am a member of no religious sect," he told his Senate colleagues unnecessarily. "I regret that I am not. I wish I was, and I trust that I shall be."

But he assured them of his profound respect for Christianity and, by a vote of thirty to thirteen, the Senate ignored any hypocrisy and approved his resolution.

Jackson agreed with Clay's enemies that his measure had been a political stunt. One critic claimed that if Clay could gain votes from it, "he would kiss the toe of the Pope and prostrate himself before the grand lama."

Jackson also regarded Clay's proposal as a violation of the Constitution, but John Quincy Adams resolved the issue by successfully tabling the House version.

On the economic front, Clay was determined to block Jackson's secretary of the Treasury from paying off the national debt by selling public land and unloading the government's share in the Bank of the United States. The Bank debate dated to a 1791 initiative by Alexander Hamilton when Jefferson and his faction had fought the Bank as the tool of the country's moneyed interests.

Twenty years after its creation, the Bank had not been rechartered immediately. After the War of 1812, however, a Second Bank of the United States was established with an expanded capital of $35 million. When a financial panic struck in 1819, the Bank had been blamed for an increase in easy credit. Only the installation of Nicholas Biddle as its head four years later restored the Bank's reputation in the nation's financial circles.

Jackson was among the westerners who believed with Jefferson that the Bank of the United States was a mechanism for defrauding average Americans. His distrust of all banks went back to his youth, when Jackson had learned to put his trust in the coins of hard money rather than in paper.

As Biddle's friend, Clay hoped to embarrass Jackson's reelection effort with some sly legislative maneuvering. His chance came when Jackson's supporters became alarmed by a report that his administration was ready to modify the Bank's charter and then extend it. Clay decided that the rumor was a feint, that Jackson was "playing a deep game" to avoid deciding an explosive issue before the election.

To foil that strategy, Clay led a move for an immediate rechartering. That challenge caused Jackson to reverse himself and promise to veto any bill that kept the national bank alive.

Daniel Webster had been spearheading the Senate campaign to recharter the Bank, and his effective arguments led to a 28-to-20 favorable vote in the Senate and 107 to 85 in the House.

Van Buren had arrived in Washington in time to review the veto

Daniel Webster

message Jackson was preparing to send. He understood the banking system better than many of Jackson's advisers and had first recommended delaying the issue. But he had become persuaded that a veto would be good politics.

Even though the Marshall Court had ruled in *McCulloch* v. *Maryland* that the Bank was constitutional, Jackson was no more willing to bow to that decision than he had been in the Cherokee case. With the help of Van Buren and his kitchen cabinet, the president drafted a veto message to remind the country that he was the protector of the average citizen.

"It is to be regretted," Jackson wrote, "that the rich and powerful too often bend the acts of government to their selfish purposes." When that happened, farmers, mechanics, and laborers had the right to appeal to their government for justice.

At the president's request, Van Buren showed up in the Capitol for the reading of the veto message. Clay greeted him cordially, and Van Buren, who had always liked Clay personally, returned the geniality. Van Buren's presence on a visitors' sofa indicated unmistakably that Jackson was determined to end the Bank.

Webster opened the argument for overriding Jackson's veto. But it was Clay, although seeming rather indifferent during the earlier debate, who unleashed his most emotional oratory. He agreed with the judgment of Nicholas Biddle that the veto message was "a manifesto of anarchy."

Clay claimed that the framers of the Constitution had intended the veto to be used sparingly, and yet Jackson had already vetoed four bills in three years.

Defending the veto, Thomas Hart Benton chastised Clay for his "disrespectful" language about Jackson. At that, Clay reminded the Senate of a scuffle from 1813, when Jackson had tangled with Benton's brother, Jesse.

Purporting to quote Senator Benton from twenty years ago, Clay said that at least he himself had never called Jackson a murderer and a coward nor predicted that if Jackson were ever elected president, congressmen would be forced to carry guns and knives to protect themselves.

Benton jumped up and shouted, "That's an atrocious calumny!"

Clay challenged him to deny making those charges. When Benton did, Clay said, "Then I declare before the Senate that you said to me those very words."

"False! False! False!" Benton cried.

It took repeated gaveling by the chair to end the hooting from the galleries and restore order on the floor.

Each man then told the Senate that he regretted his outburst but added contemptuously that he was not apologizing to the other. Half an hour later, however, the men obeyed the code of the West and shook hands.

In its anticlimactic vote of twenty-two to nineteen, the Senate failed to muster the two-thirds vote to override Jackson's veto.

Sam Houston had also contributed to the incendiary atmosphere when he came back to Washington earlier in the year. After the scandal with his first wife, he had sought comfort among the western Cherokees and opened a trading post at Fort Gibson in a section of the Arkansas Territory. Risking a second marriage, he had taken as his bride a part-Cherokee woman named Tiana Rogers.

When the tribe asked him to promote its fortunes by drawing on his friendship with Andrew Jackson, Houston readily agreed. But once in the capital, he read an account in the *National Intelligencer* that Ohio congressman William Stanbery had described as fraudulent the bid Houston had made for the removal contract.

Houston wrote to Stanbery for clarification and got instead a dismissive response. At that, Houston began making threats so dire that Stanbery took to walking to the Capitol with two pistols and a dirk.

Then one day, Houston caught him unawares on the street. The congressman did not recognize him, since his hostile remarks had not been personal, only one more salvo against the president. In recent years, Stanbery had gone from being a Jackson Democrat to being a National Republican, largely because of the Cherokee question.

Approaching him mildly, Houston asked, "Are you Mr. Stanbery?"

Stanbery bowed courteously. "Yes, sir."

"Then," Houston shouted, "*you* are the damned rascal!"

At thirty-nine, Houston was five years the younger man. He struck Stanbery repeatedly with a hickory stick that Jackson had once given him. Stanbery staggered back and pleaded, "Oh, don't!"

The two men tussled and fell to the ground. Stanbery drew a pistol and pulled the trigger. It misfired. Houston wrested it away and kept striking Stanbery until he lay motionless. An onlooker moved belatedly to stop the assault, but Houston had already begun to wander off.

The next day, Stanbery wrote to Speaker Andrew Stevenson, no political ally, to demand that Houston be tried by the House of Representatives. Claiming self-defense, Houston engaged Francis Scott Key as his attorney, with assistance from James K. Polk of Tennessee. After a month's trial, Houston was reprimanded, but no one could doubt that Speaker Stevenson's sympathies lay with the assailant.

Sam Houston

Stanbery next took his grievance to civil court, where Houston was fined five hundred dollars, which he refused to pay. Nor did Stanbery's beating move Andrew Jackson. The president told a friend that after a few more examples like that one, members of Congress would learn to keep a civil tongue in their heads. He remitted Houston's fine and gave him a small contribution of his own for Houston's proposed plan "to cast my bread upon the waters" in Texas.

In the end, William Stanbery was also publicly rebuked, in his case for criticizing Stevenson because he "frequently turned from the chair you occupy to the White House." For that suggestion that the Speaker was too deferential to Jackson, Stanbery became one of its first members to be censured by the full House.

Jackson increasingly saw the coming presidential vote as a national referendum on the Bank and felt secure that the voters would validate his judgment. He retired to the Hermitage for the summer, relieved to be out of Washington, especially given the cholera epidemic, and leaving his lieutenants to carry out campaign strategy. Newspaper editors committed to Jackson's Democrats began to accuse the Bank of bribery and other corruption.

The National Republicans fired back with a pamphlet, *A Retrospect of Andrew Jackson's Administration,* that denounced its offenses—the spoils system; Jackson's opposition to federal works that would benefit the country; even the eighteen thousand dollars the president had wasted by sending Van Buren to London without waiting for Senate confirmation.

As for the Cherokee removal, the pamphlet briefly mentioned "the wretched half-starved Indians" but only as part of a more sweeping accusation about Jackson's tyranny, which had "gone very far to discredit the whole system of popular government."

Mild weather in Tennessee rejuvenated Jackson, who reported walking one day for four miles without stopping. Contributing to his sense of well-being, his daughter-in-law, Sarah, gave birth to a girl that autumn, and Jackson let the new parents understand that he expected the baby to be named Rachel.

The president's one policy concern was the Tariff of 1832, passed in the final moments of the Congress. How would it play with John Calhoun and his supporters in South Carolina, who seemed ready to nullify the Constitution over their grievances? How much was Jackson exaggerating when he threatened to march ten thousand volunteers into South Carolina to "crush and hang" the nullifiers? Concerned that the rebels might seize the state's forts, Jackson authorized General Winfield Scott to take all necessary precautions.

By now, Jackson's Cherokee policy made it unlikely that Georgia would join South Carolina in any revolt. The governor had, in fact, pledged his opposition to nullification.

For the coming election, the Democrats were organizing as never before and funding a host of Hickory Clubs in honor of Jackson's nickname, "Old Hickory." Another successful tactic was their political parade—a good-natured march of a mile or so with torches and banners. The parade would stop at the doors of Jackson supporters and give a cheer, then move on to the houses of opposition leaders for a round of disapproving groans.

From before Independence, food and drink had been a staple of elections, and now the Democrats laid out barbecues of turkey and pork for the president's supporters. When Jackson occasionally showed up at those events, opposition newspapers chided him for breaking with the tradition that kept candidates—particularly for the presidency—from descending into the political arena.

Yet as Jackson passed through Kentucky on his return to Washington in mid-September, he found five thousand frenzied admirers gathered in Lexington. Since they were residents of Henry Clay's home state, Jackson could write to Andrew Donelson that "the political horizon is bright as far as we have seen and heard."

Clay's National Republicans struck back with derogatory cartoons. The most celebrated showed "King Andrew the First" dressed in regal robes and carrying a battered copy of the Constitution and a document labeled "Veto."

Traveling home from Washington, Clay had been encouraged by the crowds of friendly voters, an outpouring that led him to speculate that Jackson would get fewer than a hundred electoral votes. Soon afterward, however, Clay's candidate for governor of Kentucky was defeated by a Jacksonian. Clay termed the loss a "public mortification" but persuaded himself that it was not a harbinger of the presidential election to come.

Like the Democrats, Clay appreciated strong party organization. He backed Nicholas Biddle's plan to reproduce thirty thousand copies of the Jackson message vetoing the Bank of the United States. Clay had warned that voters should be treated "as if they know nothing" and must be informed in "plain, intelligible and forceful language." Biddle was sure that Jackson's argument was so flimsy it would be taken as proof of his incompetence, and Clay agreed that the Bank was a winning issue for their party.

Since the Bank was based in Philadelphia, Clay expected to carry Pennsylvania, and he had hopes for Ohio or New York, despite Van Buren's place on Jackson's ticket. If he lost both Pennsylvania and Ohio, however, "we must be defeated."

To the end, Clay expressed confidence that Jackson would lose and that ousting him from the White House would "heal the wounds of our bleeding Country, inflicted by the folly & madness of a lawless Military Chieftain!"

But as the election approached, portents of a Jackson sweep became too strong to ignore. Even if that happened, Clay wrote to an ally, the National Republicans would bring to Congress "a fresh infusion of vigor and power" that would "check the mad career of the tyrant."

When the returns were counted, Andrew Jackson had received more than 700,000 popular votes, besting Clay by 54 percent to 37 percent. William Wirt surprised both camps by drawing 101,051. In the Electoral College, Clay won only Massachusetts, Connecticut, Delaware, Rhode Island, and a majority of Maryland's electors. He did, however, carry Kentucky.

Jackson took everything else except for Vermont, which he lost to Wirt, and South Carolina, which gave John Flood of Virginia its eleven protest votes. The breakdown of the 286 electoral votes was Jackson, 219; Clay, 49; Flood, 11; Wirt, 7. As the vice presidential candidate, Van Buren could not match Jackson's total, but his 189 electoral votes established his clear win over five other candidates.

Clay's usual ebullience finally gave way to reality. He wrote to a friend, "Whether we shall ever see light and law and liberty again, is very questionable." He lamented, "We had suffered a perfect Waterloo defeat" and for a moment considered resigning from the Senate. But within days, Clay was writing, "We must bear it with what philosophy we can."

During the campaign, John Ross thought he had figured out the white man's tactics. David Greene informed him from Boston early in 1833 that, after sixteen months in prison, Worcester and Butler had accepted a pardon from Georgia's current governor, Wilson Lumpkin, and that Worcester intended to leave New Echota for Arkansas.

With the defendants now free, the American Board did not intend to pursue their case in court. Indeed, Greene announced that there would be no further political support for the Cherokees. "It makes me weep to think of it," Greene added. But since their friends in Congress think further effort would be useless, "you must make the best terms you can & go."

Ross planned to explain to the Cherokee General Council that Jackson had faced a hard choice from the time that Cherokee tribal rights became caught up in the Southern clamor over states' rights. Ross saw both South Carolina and Georgia as posing a threat to the president's principles by claiming the right of a state to defy the federal government. The difference was that so far South Carolina had asserted nullification merely as a theory, Ross said, while Georgia "has reduced it to practice."

He was convinced that the early release of Worcester and Butler had been arranged to prevent Georgia's defiance from encouraging Calhoun and his nullifiers to carry out their threat.

In Congress, events were moving so quickly that Henry Clay could not take the time to indulge his disappointment. South Carolina had passed an ordinance nullifying the tariff acts of 1828 and 1832 but had put off enforcement until February 1, 1833. Jackson's annual message to Congress included a conciliatory retreat from the protectionist aspects of the latest tariff. That bow to the nullifiers alarmed John Quincy Adams, who called it a complete surrender to South Carolina.

Then six days later, Jackson issued a proclamation that reversed his earlier approach and warned that "disunion by armed force is treason."

To resolve the mounting danger, Congress turned to Clay for another compromise. The erratic John Randolph announced, "There is one man, and one man only, who can save the Union—that man is Henry Clay."

Clay answered the call. He proposed extending the 1832 tariff seven years. But after March 1840, taxes would be levied only to finance the government with no regard for protecting any industry. When Daniel Webster and other Whigs denounced the compromise as a retreat from party principles, Clay threatened to walk away and let the two camps "fight it out."

Meantime, John Calhoun had been working himself and his supporters into a frenzy. And Jackson was asking for new powers—the Force Bill, it was called—to put down a possible insurrection.

To oppose the president, Calhoun, now fifty, gave his first major address in sixteen years. Clay—his ally in 1812, his opponent thereafter—described him as haggard and careworn, wracked by the abstractions "which sprang from his metaphysician's brain, and muttering to himself, 'This is indeed a real crisis!'"

For all his nervous pacing, Calhoun bested the passionate Webster in the legalistic aspects of their debate. Yet Clay, the cardsharp, had always argued that the nullifiers were bluffing. Now he put forth an amended version of his tariff compromise and lobbied effectively for its passage. He also sent an ally to remind Calhoun that Jackson was talking of hanging him for treason.

On March 2, 1833, in the waning hours of the Twenty-seventh Congress, Andrew Jackson signed into law Clay's tariff compromise. Two days later, he was sworn in for his second term as president. A week after that, the South Carolina legislature rescinded its nullification ordinance. The Force Bill, which had passed in the Congress, was no longer necessary.

But in Georgia, defiance was going unchecked. During the tariff debate, a score of white Georgians invaded Cherokee territory at a former missionary community called Spring Place and seized the buildings. They claimed to have won the property in a new Georgia lottery that state officials were running even before title to the disputed land had been cleared.

One Northern missionary remembered Spring Place as the site of the baptism of the first Cherokee who had converted to Christianity. Giving up that center of joy and prayers, he wrote bitterly, was "far more painful than any amount of unrighteousness inflicted upon us by the miserable wretches around us."

A British traveler, paddling through the territory by canoe, shared that low opinion of the Georgian squatters: "Tall, thin, cadaverous-looking animals," he wrote. They were melancholy and lazy and "formed a striking contrast to some of the swarthy, athletic-looking Cherokees."

In Milledgeville, Shadrach Bogan, a white commissioner, was discovered to have substituted his own handwritten lottery tickets for the official entries, and Georgia's lottery was suspended while charges of fraud were investigated. Among the prizes Bogan had awarded to a crony were John Ridge's house and 160 acres of his plantation.

Bogan was tried and convicted, fired from his appointment, and deprived of his civil rights for twenty years. But the *New York Spectator* advised Georgians not to congratulate themselves on seeing justice done. Bogan's offense was minor, the newspaper observed, "compared with the *fraud* in which the Government of Ga. engaged against the Cherokee community."

Nor did Bogan's conviction spare the Ridges their loss. John Ridge's property was entered into a new lottery and won by a Georgian named Griffin Mathis. Major Ridge's estate was won by Rachel Fergason, a widow whose husband had been a Revolutionary War veteran.

By now, however, the sentiments of the Ridge faction were well enough known to white officials that not only were they permitted to remain temporarily in their houses, but Governor Lumpkin asked U.S. agents to see that they were undisturbed. And the Georgia legislature specifically exempted Major Ridge's lucrative ferry business from a white takeover.

Lumpkin's favors cut two ways. John Ross was fostering resentment against this special treatment being given to men he called traitors for selling out their tribe.

With the arrival of spring, Cherokees found Benjamin Currey playing an expanded role in their affairs. The Georgians were pressing Jackson not to wait longer for voluntary migration but to act now to force the Cherokees from their land. Despite his biases, Currey's reports to Washington as a federal agent gave a realistic view of what had been happening in Georgia since the state law forbade Indians to challenge white men in court.

Currey observed that, before the law, the few white men in Cherokee territory were usually thieves or fugitives. Now there were at least five hundred families, who were honest enough in their dealings with fellow whites but not with the Indians. Under the new legislation, Cherokees could no longer sell their livestock for cash but could sell only on credit, which was "equal to giving it away."

Currey had thoroughly embraced the Ridge-Boudinot faction, and when he showed up uninvited at Cherokee meetings, his reports afterward were invariably critical of John Ross. Reading those reports in Washington, Secretary of War Cass intercepted Ross's latest bargaining proposal, even through the Cherokees had addressed it personally to the president. Cass rejected new terms under which the tribe would give up a portion of its land to Georgia if, in return, the United States would guarantee the Indians their rights on the territory they retained.

Ross tried again. Could the Cherokees stay if they submitted to the jurisdiction of states such as Georgia and eventually merged with them? When the administration turned down that offer as well, Samuel Worcester explained to his missionary board in Boston why he also opposed it: The Indians would "be perpetually made drunk by the whites, cheated, oppressed, reduced to beggary, become miserable outcasts, and as a body dwindle to nothing."

To Andrew Jackson, that wretched condition had already come to pass. By his fifth annual message to Congress on December 3, 1833, Jackson's tone had changed drastically from his earlier messages. From 1829, his assurances of goodwill toward the tribes had always figured in his brief mentions of the Indian question. In his second address,

Jackson had even echoed Wilson Lumpkin: "Toward the aborigines of the country no one can indulge in a more friendly feeling than myself."

But after the Supreme Court challenges, the acrimonious arguments in the Congress, and the determined refusal of the Cherokees to bend to his will, Jackson dropped any show of respect for his adversaries.

Georgia's Cherokees, Jackson wrote, "have neither the intelligence, the industry, the moral habits, nor the desire of improvement which are essential to any favorable change in their condition. Established in the midst of another and a superior race, and without appreciating the causes of their inferiority or seeking to control them, they must necessarily yield to the force of circumstances and ere long disappear."

With the president rallying sentiment against him, Chief Ross's position was further undercut early in 1834, when the Ridge faction openly defied his leadership and elected William Hicks as a rival chief. In past years, Ross had served as Hick's deputy before the schism, but now Hicks joined with John Ross's brother, Andrew, in a delegation that was publicly committed to removal. As a result, the Ridges and Boudinot became even more isolated. If they found John Ross inflexible, they considered Andrew Ross too weak and compliant.

On June 19, 1834, Andrew Ross, claiming to speak for eighteen hundred Cherokees, agreed to turn over all Cherokee land east of the Mississippi in exchange for a twenty-four-year annuity of twenty-five thousand dollars. That sum included allotments for school, plows, and other farm implements, as well as for rifles, blankets, and brass kettles. Liquor would be allowed to enter the Cherokee Nation, provided it was brought in by the Cherokees themselves. In addition, Andrew Ross would receive a thousand dollars toward construction of a turnpike road.

Even Andrew Ross's allies agreed with the Ridges that he had given away too much. They refused to put their names on his draft, and in the end only three other Cherokees would sign the treaty. John Ross lobbied strenuously against his brother's proposal in Congress, pointing out to senators that the signers "have no authority whatever from the nation to do what they have done."

For once, Ross's protest was effective. The Senate rejected the treaty, and Andrew Ross returned home in August to confront threats against his life. Yet the greatest resentment was still directed against the Ridge faction for making the first contacts with the administration.

At a Cherokee Council meeting in August at Red Clay, Tennessee, John Ridge listened bitterly to his faction being described as the villains of recent events. Tom Foreman, the territory's emotional sheriff, was especially venomous. He reminded council members that Major Ridge had once traveled far and wide urging Cherokees to love their land, and he mocked the way Ridge had emphasized his point by stamping on the earth. But now Ridge was talking for removal.

"These men have good clothes on," Foreman said of the Ridge faction. "Why could they not be satisfied with their property and not try to suck for more in the veins of their country?"

Another treaty proponent, John Walker, Jr., watched the mood become menacing as one man in the audience was heard to whisper "Let's kill them!" With the speeches dragging on, Walker left with a friend to ride home to Cleveland, Tennessee.

By leaving, they missed John Ridge's impassioned praise for his father's "distinguished zeal and ability" in serving his country. "But was a man to be denounced for his opinions?" If he saw a storm cloud threatening overhead, was he to be hated—or respected—for warning his countrymen to take cover?

John Ridge asked what if everyone behaved like Tom Foreman? "We should fall together and twist each others noses. Our eyes would not remain in their sockets"—they would be gouged out.

When Major Ridge spoke on his own behalf, he remained dignified as he railed like a prophet against the council: "We have no government," Ridge said. "It is entirely suppressed. Where are your laws? The seats of your judges are overturned. When I look upon you all, you laugh at me."

Major Ridge added that for his part, he felt only "oppressed with sorrow." He was not angry at the people, but he scorned those council members who knew better than their arguments suggested.

The Ridges were not easing the tension, and threats against them began to be spoken aloud: "If some men did not take care they would drop from their ponies."

At the height of the agitation, Elijah Hicks offered a petition signed by twelve dozen Indians from six districts, demanding that the Ridges and David Vann be impeached for their opinions and policies that would end Cherokee life on the land of their fathers.

The council voted that the three were indeed guilty and should be removed, and the clerk notified them to return in October to answer the charges. Before the council adjourned, however, members got startling news that upended their October agenda.

President Jackson was home at the Hermitage when he was told that John Walker, Jr., had been assassinated. What he knew about Walker was that he had married a niece of the late government agent Return Jonathan Meigs, and was using his standing among the Cherokees to promote removal. Jackson had once paid his way to Washington as part of an unauthorized delegation.

At that time, Walker had been promised protection by Jackson's government. Yet it now appeared that his Cherokee rivals had succeeded in murdering him.

After leaving the council meeting, Walker and his companion had been riding home when a bullet struck him from behind and dropped him from his horse. He was able to take up his rifle and fire back, but when he reached his wife's house, he collapsed and died.

Besides Emily Meigs, Walker had married another woman and had fathered children with her. His marriages required that he be buried with two rituals—one Cherokee, one Masonic. Maddened with grief at the loss of his son, Chief Walker blamed John Ross and threatened to kill him.

Questions would arise later about whether the motive for slaying

Walker had been personal, not political. But Jackson agreed with his father that Ross had been responsible. Expressing his own fury, the president wrote to Benjamin Currey: "The Government of the U.S. has promised them protection. *It will perform its obligations* to a tittle." Jackson told Currey to investigate the circumstances of Walker's murder and warn Ross and his council that they would be held responsible for any further harm to those leaders willing to migrate.

After Currey established which two men had staged the ambush, they were arrested and brought for indictment to the criminal court in Athens, Tennessee. That court ruled it had no jurisdiction since the murder had been committed by Cherokees on Cherokee territory. But when Georgia's supreme court agreed to hear the case, John Ross raised money for the defense. Before a trial could begin, however, the defendants were mysteriously released from prison. One of them, James Foreman, admitted that bribery had freed him: "By God, sir, I was let out with a silver key."

The events in Athens had exposed the limits of Jackson's ability to protect his Cherokee allies, but it also strengthened his conviction that he was the Indians' friend. At one point, he unburdened himself to Henry R. Schoolcraft, a noted explorer and naturalist. As Indian agent to the Upper Lakes Tribes, Schoolcraft had negotiated treaties that secured extensive holdings in what became Michigan. His wife was part Ojibwa but educated in Europe, and Schoolcraft was convinced that the president's policy was a benign one.

After his meeting with Jackson, he recorded the president's instructions for dealing with white men who came to Washington with claims against the Indians.

"Don't pay them one dollar," Jackson said. "Pay the Indians honorably for their lands, their full value, in silver—not blankets, not rifles, not powder, but hard cash. And let their creditors collect their own debts. Don't you pay one of them, neither now nor at any future time.

"When white men deal with Indians, the Indians are sure to get into debt to the white man; at least, the white men are sure to say so. I won't hear of paying any of their 'claims.'"

John Howard Payne

10 · John Howard Payne (1835)

Disappointment and humiliation had dogged John Ross from the beginning of 1835. Returning to Secretary Cass's office, Ross was driven to make a desperate offer: The Cherokees still sought federal protection to stay on their land, he said. But if that was impossible, the tribe would accept $20 million, plus reimbursement for losses from earlier treaties and a guarantee that federal troops would safeguard them during the five years it would take to organize their trek west.

Ross reminded Cass that Jackson had promised to pay the Cherokees as liberally as the U.S. Senate would allow. At that point—depending on whose later version one believed—Ross either pledged to accept whatever figure the Senate set, or, given his devotion to the Cherokee constitution, Ross explained that he was not authorized to make such a promise.

Lobbying began in earnest, with friends of the Cherokees pressing well-disposed senators to accept Ross's figure. But members found it simply too expensive. They would go no higher than $5 million. And Cass refused to make good on his earlier assurance that Ross could see a full transcript of the Senate deliberations.

Ross was shaken enough by the latest setback that he wrote to Mexico's chargé d'affaires in Philadelphia to explore whether establishing a Cherokee colony south of the border might be more desirable than moving across the Mississippi in the United States.

Meantime, John Ridge was preparing another delegation of his own. At the last Cherokee Council, members had declined to proceed further with impeachment against the Ridges and David Vann, but they also declined to withdraw the charges, leaving the Ridges suspended in a compromised state. Ridge drafted a resolution open to the possibility of a move west, and after fifty-seven Cherokees had signed it, Ridge handed the document in person to Edward Everett, the tribe's most loyal voice in Congress.

On February 4, 1835, Henry Clay was in the awkward position of bringing John Ridge's resolution to the Senate floor. Clay had opposed Jackson's removal policy. Now he would seem to be endorsing it, but not without a mournful preamble: "It is impossible to conceive of a community more miserable, more wretched. Even the lot of the African slave is preferable to the condition of this unhappy Nation. The interest of the master prompts him to protect the slave. But what mortal will care for, protect the suffering Indian, shut out from the family of man?"

Ridge's pliancy earned him a warm reception in Washington. Since Jackson was still said to be unbending, Ridge recommended a preliminary treaty that his delegation could sign and take afterward to the Cherokee Nation to be ratified.

To work out the details, Lewis Cass appointed a New York clergyman named John F. Schermerhorn.

The Reverend Schermerhorn had come to Georgia to break John Ross's hold over the Cherokees. Born in Schenectady, New York, Schermerhorn had graduated from Union College before being sent out as a missionary, first for the Congregationalists, then for the Dutch Reform Church. As a preacher, he had traveled as far south as New Orleans and later met and impressed Jackson at the Hermitage. In 1832, when Schermerhorn was forty-six, the president had appointed him as an Indian commissioner.

Schermerhorn made good use of that position. He bought up four hundred thousand acres of land in four Virginia counties, although the deeds were murky enough to send them to court. Three years later, those negotiations remained at an impasse when the Jackson administration dispatched Schermerhorn to Georgia. There his ecclesiastical air at first reassured those Cherokee men who considered Northern clergymen their staunch protectors.

Women of the tribe quickly formed a different impression. Schermerhorn plunged among them with such randy vigor that although his advances were rejected, Cherokee women giggled at the mention of his name.

Seeking out the Ridge faction, Schermerhorn proposed terms that would exchange the Cherokee Nation for $4.5 million and 13 million acres in the west. To bring those figures closer to what the Senate had authorized, the treaty would throw in another eight hundred thousand western acres, estimated to be worth half a million dollars. Given their reverence for education, John Ridge and Boudinot were able to include a perpetual annuity for Cherokee schools.

On March 14, 1835, the Ridge faction signed a tentative agreement, with the understanding that the full Cherokee Council would ratify the terms before the treaty could take effect.

John Ridge wrote to assure his father that the terms were "very liberal," that "the poor Indian enjoyed the same rights as the rich—there is no distinction."

During this latest round of talks, John Ridge had become persuaded that Jackson was, after all, a friend of his tribe. He paid the president the ultimate compliment by naming his new son Andrew Jackson Ridge.

White families moving onto Cherokee property were sometimes surprised and annoyed to find that their new Indian neighbors resented them. Zillah Haynie Brandon had arrived in Cass County on the Etowah River only because her husband had failed as a merchant. Next he had bought thirteen chances in the Georgia lottery and come up empty every time. Finally, in 1835, he scraped up enough money to buy a small property and move his family.

Zillah Brandon considered the winter weather disagreeably cold, but worse, as she noted in a memoir, was finding "a family of *Indians occupying our house*, which, by the way, was a very poor one without floor or loft.

"The Indians set about moving out, tho, with looks as magisterial as if they had been kings seated upon thrones in royal robes with a retinue about them, leaning upon the sceptres. They would not deign to look at us, much less speak to us."

As she went about spreading her family's carpets over the dirt floors, Mrs. Brandon remained disconcerted by the three families of Indians living sixty yards away and looking "as if the very shafts of desolation was hanging around them."

Mrs. Brandon knew that the Indians were to blame for their fate since the tribe had murdered "one of their noblest chiefs, McIntosh." In time, she decided that the women "were chaste and very civil, but their husbands would drink to the point of drunkenness and were very cruel when under the influence of the fire water."

She concluded that "when they were sober, we were not afraid of them," but a whiskey shop owned by a white man was only a quarter of a mile away. Drunk, "the men would look like the cord of their souls was torn asunder." They would stand around outside, weeping and looking so doleful that even Mrs. Brandon was moved to pity.

A devout Christian, she became sufficiently accepted in the community to attend the dying moments of an old Cherokee neighbor, who railed against McIntosh and Major Ridge as traitors who had plunged the tribe into its current wretchedness. "He said he 'had lived a long time, had done much but had never done much harm.' He said he 'had sometimes drank too much but he had not been bad while drinking.'"

Mrs. Brandon set down his thoughts to show that God's spirit "had been doing its work even in the heart of the heathen."

All the same, she continued to fear for her life whenever an Indian, maddened by drink, seemed determined to kill the white people around him. That anxiety went on until "to our great comfort the liquor shop was demolished, and from that time, we had less to fear."

Not all white settlers moved into homes as primitive as Mrs. Brandon's. When John Ross's last overture came to nothing, he had returned home, where he found that his elegant house had been handed over to another Georgian. Since Wilson Lumpkin would not extend to Ross the temporary relief he had granted the Ridges, Ross gathered up his family and moved to a two-room log house across the Tennessee border.

In mid-May 1835, nearly a thousand Cherokees gathered to hear Ross's latest report. He put the best possible interpretation on his negotiations, and the Ridge faction believed that Ross was duping the council by not divulging the better terms they had already reached.

When the moment seemed promising, John Schermerhorn was planning to reveal his understanding with the Ridges. His best opportunity seemed to come during a speech in July before more than twenty-five hundred Cherokees, who had gathered to debate once again how annuities should be paid. Schermerhorn ordered a speaker's platform built to resemble a pulpit, and for three and a half hours he extolled President Jackson's policies. But the vote rejecting individual annuity payments went against him by a lopsided margin of 2,225 to 114, and Schermerhorn did not disclose the Ridge treaty.

He asked for permission from Washington to offer bribes to chiefs who were holding out. But the administration was convinced sentiment was moving toward Jackson's position, and Cass refused his request. Schermerhorn resolved to exercise patience until the next council meeting in October.

That session promised to be harmonious for the first time in recent years. John Ross had written in a brotherly spirit to Major Ridge, urging that they present a united front against Schermerhorn and Benjamin Currey. With their own treaty proposal in limbo, the Ridge faction agreed, and a twenty-member committee was formed to fend off the agents from Washington.

From the sidelines, Currey was not impressed by rumors of a reconciliation. "Ross holds out the olive branch of peace to Ridge," he informed Washington, "while his confidential friends speak of slaying Ridge because they say he has forfeited his life by the laws of the nation."

Currey could point to the murder of a man named Crow from the Ridge faction who had been stabbed repeatedly when he argued for removal. At a party, two other Ridge adherents were also fatally stabbed and another beaten to death.

John Ridge wrote despairingly that "it is dreadful to reflect on the amount of blood which has been shed by the savages on those who have only exercised the right of opinion."

Ridge's right to publish his opinions had been at the heart of the debate over the *Cherokee Phoenix,* and in August 1835, the newspaper provoked a rupture that threatened the new unity. A few hours before John Ross's men arrived to move the paper to Tennessee, the Georgia Guard descended on Elijah Hicks's house and carted away the printing press, along with its type and newsprint. To keep the press out of Ross's hands, Elias Boudinot's brother, Stand Watie, had joined forces with the Guard to seize the paper's property.

Ross appealed to Currey, who sided with Watie. After all, Currey said, the paper really belonged to Boudinot, and it could now be impartial again on the subject of removal. But since Currey did not release the press, the *Phoenix* did not rise again.

When the Cherokee Council met at Red Clay in October, members were visited by a Northerner who enjoyed a remote but very real fame. John Howard Payne, a forty-three-year-old itinerant actor and playwright, was back in America after two decades in Europe.

In his youth, Payne had briefly attended Union College in Schenectady, where he crossed the path of John Schermerhorn, who was five years older. Dropping out of college for a career on the stage, Payne embarked on what would prove to be a tumultuous life. Traveling to Baltimore during the War of 1812, he was on hand when a mob of James Madison's supporters attacked the offices of an antiwar newspaper published by Payne's friend Alexander Hanson. Payne offered to help Hanson rebuild, but the embittered editor advised him to head for Europe and a climate more receptive to the arts.

Arriving in England, Payne was detained for two weeks in wartime Liverpool as an American. He already had developed a knack for adapting to his circumstances and pronounced his confinement entirely comfortable.

Armed with letters of introduction, Payne soon made his British stage debut at the age of twenty-one. In time, he could boast of being the first American to play Hamlet in England. During his travels, he met Lord Byron and roomed briefly with Washington Irving. He admired Junius Brutus Booth as the Iago to Edmund Kean's Othello and predicted for Booth "a large place in the future history of the English stage." But a few years later, Booth deserted his wife and son to run off to America and begin a new family that included a son he named John Wilkes.

In Paris, Payne was befriended by the French tragedian Talma and began to write and adapt plays of his own. By the time Payne was twenty-seven, Kean was starring in his amalgam of seven history plays, *Brutus: or The Fall of Tarquin.*

But Payne was a notoriously bad manager of money. He leased the Sadler's Wells Theater for a season, lost seven thousand pounds, and ended up in a British debtors' prison. He was released only after his fortunes were restored by his translation of a French play, *Therese, the Orphan of Geneva.*

John Howard Payne secured his lasting reputation, however, as he whiled away one drab October afternoon by writing a song for a new contemporary play, *Clari, the Maid of 1822 Milan.* Since the death of his mother when he was sixteen, Payne had suffered from bouts of depression. Now he tried to capture the haunting nostalgia that could overcome him:

'Mid pleasures and palaces though we may roam,
Be it ever so humble, there's no place like home!

His verse went on to celebrate "the love of a mother, surpassing all other" and the memories of a thatched cottage dearer than any splendid halls. Set to a melody from a Sicilian vesper, the song became popular overnight—a hundred thousand copies of the sheet music sold within a year. But Payne's luck ran true to form. Although he was able to live luxuriously in Paris, his name did not appear on his song's title page, and he did not share in the publisher's windfall.

In the summer of 1832, Payne sailed back to New York, where friends welcomed him with a gala benefit at the Park Theater. The house sold out at a steep five dollars for a box, one dollar for the gallery. The evening's fare began with Payne's *Brutus,* followed by a singing of "Home Sweet Home," and then Charles Kemble and his daughter Fanny recited selections from *The Taming of the Shrew.* Closing the bill was Payne's comedy *Charles II.* The benefit raised seven thousand dollars.

During the next two years, Payne foundered. He launched a literary journal but attracted few subscribers. He wrote a *Life of Our Savior* only to find the market preempted by a clergyman with a similar book. He did better with a Southern tour, where a production of his plays in New Orleans brought in another three thousand dollars.

Heading back to New York, Payne resolved to publish a journal dedicated to the wonders of America and the ideals of its people. As research, he planned to visit every state in the Union and had already traveled through seven of them when he stopped over in Georgia.

Payne had been abroad during the congressional debate over the Cherokees. Now he listened with growing excitement to their story and resolved to incorporate their history in his new project. To his sister, Payne sent back one of his long and evocative letters describing a

Creek corn dance. He had heard about the murder of William McIntosh eleven years earlier and found its echoes in the pageant when young Indian men brandished corn stalks as guns. A naked chief, swinging a stalk painted red like a bloody saber, was mowed down by the others.

"He was," Payne wrote, "the chief who made an objectionable treaty, and whose house was burned."

Payne confessed to his sister that he had brought gifts of beads and tobacco but had been too bashful to offer them. Instead, he asked a chief to pass out the presents on his behalf and was pleased when the man returned to say, "The chiefs are mighty glad, and count it from you very great friendship."

Reluctantly, Payne rode on to his next destination, reflecting "that this ceremony, so precious to them, was now probably performing in the land of their forefathers for the last, last time."

In that sympathetic spirit, Payne arrived at John Ross's modest cabin, where Ross was known to possess manuscripts on Cherokee traditions that Payne hoped to examine. At their meeting, Payne found Ross shorter, milder, and more unassuming than he had expected. Ross received him cordially, apologizing that he could offer only the hospitality of a log cabin. But he invited Payne to stay with him while he made copies of old documents and to attend the October General Council session.

Touched by the way Ross's fortunes had been reduced, Payne saw his story as a metaphor for the suffering of an entire people. And when Payne met Daniel Butrick, the missionary interested him in the theory that the Cherokees had descended from one of the Ten Lost Tribes of Israel. They agreed to work together to confirm the Cherokees' Hebrew ancestry.

As the council date approached, Payne also became acquainted with the Ridge faction, including Elias Boudinot. He noted that Boudinot had "married a Gold" and judged them "a very intelligent and amiable couple."

On the day before the meeting, Payne watched hundreds of Cherokees pass Ross's gate on their way to the nearby Red Clay council ground. What impressed him most was their silence as they lined up with their tin drinking cups attached to blankets flung loosely over their shoulders. Long lines formed to take Ross's hand in a gesture of fealty.

In his notes, Payne was already likening the Cherokees to a lost tribe of Israel: "Their dress was neat and picturesque; all wore turbans, except four of five with hats; many of them, tunics with sashes, many long robes, and nearly all some drapery so that they had the oriental air of the old scripture pictures of patriarchal processions."

Payne admitted that the prevailing feeling of anticipation had touched him as well. Perhaps because John Schermerhorn was a clergyman, both sides were casting the showdown in theological terms. Schermerhorn considered John Ross the "Devil in Hell." The Cherokees played off Schermerhorn's name to coin a version that particularly amused the women of the tribe. They called him *Skaynooyaunah,* "Devil's horn."

When the council convened, Schermerhorn waited in the wings to make his new appeal, but the meeting dragged on through a litany of complaints from individual Cherokees about their latest abuse at the hands of Georgian whites.

Payne had introduced himself to Schermerhorn and reminded him of their days at Union College. But they were now on opposing sides. When Payne said he doubted that the council would approve the Ridge treaty, Schermerhorn cut him off: "I'll have a treaty within a week."

But he resented Payne's presence and wrote angrily to the Office of Indian Affairs afterward that Payne "has been very busy meddling with Cherokee affairs, and did what he could to prevent an arrangement with the Government."

When John Ross could stall no longer, he asked Schermerhorn—very politely—for proof that he had been authorized to broker a treaty. The best Schermerhorn could produce was a casual letter from Secretary Cass. Ross looked it over, thanked him, and said that now he would like to see his formal commission.

Schermerhorn admitted that he had no such document. Ross ruled that since no commissioners were present, his Committee of Twenty would have to return to Washington.

Just before the council meeting broke up, Ross asked the assembled Cherokees whether they were willing to sell their land for $5 million.

"No!" they shouted.

Looking on, John Ridge reflected bitterly that the men yelling loudest did not know the difference between five thousand dollars and five million. He concluded that their opposition was the inevitable result of "double dealing with an ignorant people." But the crowd's anger was unmistakable, and neither he nor Boudinot challenged John Ross publicly.

Next, Ross asked whether they agreed that the Committee of Twenty could negotiate for them with the United States.

The answer, equally spirited: "Yes!"

For the moment, John Ridge and Boudinot felt they had no choice but to stay on as members of the committee and hope that, away from the high emotion, a treaty could still emerge.

Schermerhorn was stunned by his rout. Reporting to Cass, however, he expressed his confidence in a favorable outcome: "The Lord is able to overrule all things for good." He intended, however, to help Providence along. Even though Ridge and Boudinot advised him against it, Schermerhorn called a meeting for December 21 at New Echota. He distributed notices that anyone who failed to attend would be bound by whatever was decided there.

Schermerhorn faced one complication. John Ross's delegation had been authorized to travel to Washington. Unless he could be prevented, Ross might yet overturn Schermerhorn's plans.

As midnight approached on Saturday, November 7, 1835, Ross was chatting with John Howard Payne while Payne copied minutes of a 1794 meeting between the Cherokees and George Washington. Suddenly, they heard barking dogs, galloping horses, and a voice shouting, "Ross! Ross!" Twenty-five troopers from the Georgia Guard had crossed the Tennessee state line to seize Ross.

He received them calmly. "Well, gentlemen, I shall not resist. But what have I done?"

"You'll know that soon enough," the Guard's leader answered. "Give up your papers and prepare to go with us."

At that, Payne, with a pistol poking at his chest, protested when the Guards began sorting through his belongings. "Hold your damn tongue," the leader said. "You are here, up to no good."

The Guards saddled up to take their prisoners the twenty-four miles to the Georgia state line. The night had been bright and clear until a wild storm arose. As their horses rode through the downpour, Payne heard one guard humming the tune to "Home Sweet Home."

When he came alongside, Payne asked, "What song was that I heard you humming?"

"That? 'Sweet Home' they call it, I believe. Why do you ask?"

"Merely because it is a song of my own writing, and the circumstances under which I now hear it struck me as rather singular."

The Guardsman would not be fooled. He had learned the melody from a well-known anthology. He said crushingly, "It's in *The Western Songster*."

The group stopped for a meal at an inn owned by one of the Guard, who relaxed enough in front of his own hearth to ask Payne, "Was Tom Paine any kin of yourn?" and seemed disappointed by the answer.

Once at the prison, the two men were not charged. From what could be determined, Ross was being accused—apparently by Benjamin Currey—of hindering a census of the Cherokees. Payne was pegged as a Northern abolitionist or possibly a French spy.

When Payne recited his rights under the Constitution to the Georgia Guard captain, the man said, "That might have done very well once. But, Lord! Don't you know that's all over now?"

Hearing of the arrests a few days later, John Ridge hurried to the prison and was dismayed to learn that the charges were serious. After eight days, Ross secured his own release by pointing out that no legitimate treaty could be negotiated until he reached Washington. Ross left confinement with neither an explanation nor an apology. With him gone, Payne paced his cell for another four days until he was led before the ranking Guard officer.

"The minute you hear the tap of the drum," the captain said sternly, "I tell you to cut out of here, and I order you never, while you exist, to be seen in this State of ours any more. For if you are, I'll make you rue it.

"Let this be a lesson to you—and thank my sympathy for a stranger that you have been treated with such extraordinary kindness. And now, sir, clear out of this State forever and go to John Ross, God damn you!"

The harmony Ross had hoped to foster in Washington quickly vanished. First, Boudinot resigned from the commission even before they left, followed by John Ridge's threat to follow him. Ridge was angered by Payne's articles in a Knoxville newspaper that asked the people of the United States, in the name of the Cherokee Nation, to support Ross's position, which Ridge called "diametrically opposite" to his own. Only after Ross assured him that Payne had spoken solely for himself did Ridge agree to remain a commission member.

As Ross's delegation prepared to leave for Washington on December 2, 1835, he received a harsh letter from Secretary Cass insisting that he give up any hope for new negotiations and advising him that it would be "utterly useless" to make the trip.

Ross found himself in a position somewhat like that of George Washington nearly sixty years earlier when Washington had to weigh whether to go to Philadelphia for the Constitutional Convention. In both instances, a nation was falling apart on all sides, leaving its people open to predators with no respect for its sovereignty. For each man, the risk in attending was substantial and yet each felt that only he could provide an essential rallying point. Ross decided, as had Washington, that duty demanded he act. He disregarded Cass's warning and headed for the capital.

Meanwhile, John Schermerhorn was going forward with his unauthorized meeting in New Echota on December 21.

Schermerhorn had worked during the past two months to guarantee a crowd at his renegade conference, offering as inducement free blankets and food. Even so, only a small number of Cherokees were on hand—Schermerhorn's own estimate was three to five hundred, while the latest Cherokee census had recorded a population of seventeen thousand. And Schermerhorn's figure included women and children.

In the audience was Elias Boudinot, who had lost all hope that by adopting the white man's culture the Cherokees could survive in Georgia. He had seen too many unscrupulous white men abuse his people. But he also understood the appeal in John Ross's adamant rejection of removal, and he knew how remote the lands west of the Mississippi seemed to families that had never left the Blue Ridge Mountains. Although he had converted to Christianity, Boudinot could appreciate the reverence of the mountain Indians for their ancient gods—the Immortals—and their faith that the Immortals would descend upon Georgia to save them.

Major Ridge was also at New Echota to hear Schermerhorn treating the audience to hours of fire and brimstone. One of Ross's men, present to monitor the event, described the clergyman's speech as "his usual style, only a little more so."

More drama underlined the occasion when the roof of the gathering place caught fire while Benjamin Currey was reading the government's terms. As his listeners bolted to safety, Ross's men took it as heaven's judgment on the proceedings.

From its opening phrase, the Schermerhorn treaty was worded to imply that it had been drafted at the request of the entire tribe:

"Whereas the Cherokees are anxious to make some arrangements with the Government of the United States . . ." The provisions that followed were little different from those the Cherokees had rejected twice that year.

The tribe would get its $5 million and the land west of the Mississippi that had already been guaranteed in 1828 and 1833. Five hundred thousand dollars would be deducted, however, for another eight hundred thousand acres designated as Neutral Lands. The United States would either move the Cherokees to their new homes or contribute twenty dollars for each member of any family that chose to make the move on its own.

Washington would also pay for a year's subsistence in the new lands. And the federal government would put $150,000 into an account for Cherokee schools. Andrew Jackson had demanded the striking out of an earlier provision that would have given John Ross the authority to approve individual payments for claims under past treaties. Instead, a flat $600,000 was set aside for those claims.

The treaty held out one intriguing possibility. The Cherokees might be entitled to a delegate in the U.S. House of Representatives. But only if Congress approved the idea.

As the terms were read out, the Cherokees puffed on their pipes and said nothing except for an occasional grunt. When the time came for a response, Major Ridge led the discussion, with Boudinot interpreting for the government officials.

"I have hunted the deer and turkey here more than fifty years," Ridge reminded them. "I have always been the friend of the honest white man. But the Georgians have shown a grasping spirit lately. They have extended their laws to which we are unaccustomed, which harass our braves and make the children suffer and cry."

The Georgians expected their president in Washington City to secure our land for them, Ridge continued, even though "we obtained the land from the living God above. Yet they are strong and we are weak. We are few, they are many."

The Cherokees will never forget their homes, Major Ridge concluded. "But an unbending, an iron necessity, tells us we must leave them. I would willingly die to preserve them, but any forcible effort to keep them will lose us our lands, our lives, and the lives of our children.

"There is one path of safety, one road to a future existence as a nation. That path is open before you."

Old chiefs were weeping as Ridge finished. They surrounded him and pledged to follow him even if it meant leaving the graves of their dead.

When Boudinot spoke next, he struck a different note. He acknowledged the fierce and bitter feelings of John Ross and his allies and knew that he was taking his life in his hands. Boudinot offered a Christian consolation that many in his audience could not share: "We can die, but the great Cherokee nation will be saved." If they paid with their lives in this heroic struggle, "the captain of our salvation will command us, and we will sing His praises forever and evermore."

With emotions running high, Schermerhorn recommended naming a committee of twenty-one members to weigh the treaty's terms.

On December 28, 1835, that committee announced its unanimous approval. Late the following night, delegates met in Boudinot's parlor to sign the last of the many treaties between the United States and the Cherokee Nation.

Every man in the room knew the potential consequences of his action, and members hung back, reluctant to be the first to sign the document. Then John Gunter from Gunter's Landing on the Tennessee River marched to the table with the treaty, took up a pen, and signed. The others followed suit, a defiant group of leaders including John Ross's estranged brother, Andrew, but also other men of mixed blood and a few white men who had married Cherokee women.

A thirty-year-old Methodist circuit rider, Robert R. Rogers, added his name to the document. Rogers considered himself a full "native Indian" and deplored the "merciless breed of locusts"—the white Georgians—swarming over Indian territory. He knew, however, that others would see him as "the Benedict Arnold of the Cherokee race."

John Ridge shared with Schermerhorn his feeling that he might "someday die by the hand of some poor infatuated Indian, deluded by the counsel of Ross and his minions."

His father put it more simply. He not only understood the penalty for his action, he had once enforced it.

Major Ridge said, "I have signed my death warrant."

Chief John Ross

11 · John Ross (1836)

While the treaty faction was signing with the Reverend Schermerhorn, John Ross was making a desperate trip to Washington. Stopping over briefly in Salem, North Carolina, to visit his daughter, Jane, a student at the Moravian Female Academy, he reached Washington on January 2, 1836.

After presenting his credentials at the Bureau of Indian Affairs, Ross asked to speak with President Jackson and Secretary Cass. Four days later, Cass met with Ross and his delegation to pass along what his letter had already made clear: The president would not be moved. His offer remained the $5 million that Congress had approved. Jackson would not permit individual gifts of land in the new territory, but he remained adamant that federal money be paid to individual Cherokees, not to the tribal council.

Delivering that news, Cass bemoaned the fact that the government had now incurred the expense of Ross's futile trip. He said that Schermerhorn had suggested sending his partisans to Washington, too, but Cass had forbidden him to pay for a single person.

At 11 a.m. the next day, Ross and his allies were granted a final audience with Jackson, who yet again recited his friendly motives for insisting on removal but assured Ross that he was limited in the amount his government could pay.

While he was staying in Washington, Ross heard of the Treaty of New Echota and summed up its signers as "men of no influence and of infamous moral characters." By early February, messengers were bringing Ross protests signed by 3,250 Cherokees opposed to the Schermerhorn treaty. All the same, Cass's commissioner of Indian

Affairs, Elbert Herring, sent a note cutting off further communication with Ross and his delegates.

In Georgia, federal advisers to the Ridge faction were urging strongly that they reconcile Ross to their treaty, and Boudinot and Major Ridge agreed to send him a placating letter. Ross ignored it. He considered that any response would legitimize what had been done at New Echota.

Cherokee protests kept arriving until Ross had received almost sixteen thousand signatures endorsing a statement written by John Howard Payne. Even though many of the signatures were dubious—including Xs for infants—the outpouring was impressive. Ross calculated that ninety-nine out of every hundred Cherokees opposed the treaty.

Hearing that Schermerhorn had tried to convene a meeting of the North Carolina Cherokees, Ross jeered when, despite the lure of a free barbecue, only two men showed up. Even those two, according to Ross, had come "from curiosity or accident." But he predicted that Schermerhorn would misrepresent his gathering as a success.

As soon as they received news of the New Echota treaty, John Ridge and Stand Watie had moved out of the boarding house where the rest of Ross's delegation was staying. Ross ridiculed Ridge's willingness to sign the treaty as representing his fourth change of heart in as many months. Ridge was "varying as often as the moon," Ross said, "without the excuse of lunacy for his changes."

Compiling a chronology of recent events for the U.S. Senate, Ross said he was not doing it "to arouse at this late day a useless sympathy, but only as a matter of history." He had decided that, rather than have the Cherokees accept the New Echota treaty, they should let themselves be "expelled and removed by an act of Congress." That way, "they or their posterity, in after times, may have some claim on the magnanimity of the American people."

Henry Clay remained steadfast in attacking Jackson's removal policy and was writing sympathetically to John Howard Payne. On the Senate floor, Clay had once lamented, "Alas! Poor Indians, what rights can they assert against the state of Georgia, backed by the tremendous power of General Jackson?" The speech had been among Clay's most moving, and an English visitor reported that tears fell among his fellow congressmen. Presiding over the Senate, however, Vice President Van Buren was seen to yawn.

When the New Echota treaty came before the Senate in May, Clay repaid the Cherokees' confidence in him by trying to amend the treaty in ways that would scuttle it. Once more John Quincy Adams sided with his former secretary of state, calling the treaty an "eternal disgrace upon the country." But neither man was president, merely another congressman, and Clay's amendment was defeated.

The final vote came on May 18, with thirty-one in favor of the treaty and fifteen opposed. Because two senators were not present, the treaty passed by a single vote more than the required two-thirds majority.

Jackson signed the treaty on May 23, 1836. Its terms gave the Cherokees two years to make their move across the Mississippi.

Harriet Boudinot had always been able to reassure her family in the North that she was happy in New Echota with her "kind and affectionate devoted husband." These days, however, Harriet was being ostracized by those Cherokees who saw Boudinot as a traitor.

After bearing three sons and three daughters, she was pregnant again. When that child, a son, was born dead, she never recovered her strength. On the day Ann Worcester left New Echota with her missionary husband, Harriet had assured her that they would soon meet again in the new Cherokee territory. By August, however, Boudinot knew that his wife would not be making the trip.

Suffering from pain that clouded her mind, Harriet complained of a darkness that was causing her to question her faith. Then one day she awoke to say that the obstruction had lifted and once again she could see clear sky between her and her Redeemer. But her physical pain did not let up. After a distressing night, she called her family to her bedside.

She told Boudinot, "I hope this is the last night I shall spend in this world. Then how sweet will be the Conqueror's song."

Boudinot asked, "Are your doubts removed?"

Harriet answered, "Yes."

Her husband was a convert to the faith that she had been born into. He persisted, "Are you happy, notwithstanding all your bodily pain and affliction?"

"I am happy," she assured him.

Boudinot chose a hillside near their home and buried his wife beneath a headstone that read, "We seek a rest beyond the skies."

As with Rachel Jackson's death, the loss of Harriet seemed to release in her husband new depths of bitterness. Boudinot's response to critics usually had been restrained, but after August 1836, he struck back more fiercely. His belligerence was evident in a pamphlet he distributed among those Cherokees and white Americans who remained persuaded by John Ross's arguments.

Addressing his adversary directly, Boudinot wrote that he was aware of his disadvantage as a humble individual challenging the "Principal Chief." But he resented accusations that he was benefiting from the treaty he had signed. He detested the widespread buying up of Cherokee possessions for a pittance, Boudinot wrote. It was "vile speculation."

Boudinot threw the charge of greed back at Ross: "You seem to be absorbed altogether in the pecuniary aspect of this nation's affairs—hence your extravagant demands for the lands we are compelled to relinquish—your ideas of the value of the gold mines (which, if they had been peaceably possessed by the Cherokees, would have ruined them as soon as the operation of the State laws have done), of the value of our marble quarries, our mountains and forests."

He accused Ross of ignoring the "depression of the mind, and the degradation and pollution of the spirit" that the Cherokees had suffered in recent years. Instead, Ross had opposed all treaties, and now he opposed this treaty solely because it was not as lucrative as his unrealistic hopes.

Boudinot, in his wrath, was sounding like Andrew Jackson.

Yes, he granted, the descendants of whites who had intermarried with Cherokees might lose under the treaty. But what about the others? By now, Boudinot said, he did not care whether he was considered a slanderer of his country's reputation. He must speak out about the condition of the average Cherokee, which was wretched. "We are making a rapid tendency to a general immorality and debasement."

Boudinot summed up his solution: "My language has been, 'Fly for your lives'—it is now the same. I would say to my countrymen, you among the rest, fly from the moral pestilence that will finally destroy our nation."

Ross was not listening. Although the two years were slipping away, he could not believe that the government of the United States would forcibly dispossess fifteen thousand of the continent's original owners.

As the months passed, and the treaty faction prepared for the move, the Jackson administration sent U.S. troops to the Cherokee Nation to disarm the Indians. Their commander, General John Ellis Wool, was a fifty-two-year-old New Yorker who had won praise for his heroism in the War of 1812. When the British had stymied the Americans at Queenston Heights, Wool had led his unit up an overgrown fisherman's path and seized control of their position. Two years later, for holding firm in the face of a British assault at Plattsburgh, New York, Wool was promoted to major of the Sixth United States Infantry.

Orphaned early and sketchily educated, Wool had chosen to stay in the army, where his intelligence and ability had been recognized. The struggle under way at his new command would challenge those qualities, along with Wool's sense of fair play.

John H. Garrett, a white man who had claimed John Ridge's holdings in Alabama, had driven out Ridge's tenant and taken over both the Ridge farm and its ferry. Sarah Ridge had appealed for help to Benjamin Currey, but he proved ineffectual. When Wool arrived, he sent his troops to remove Garrett and restore the property to Ridge's tenant.

Garrett then obtained a writ of possession from an Alabama court and returned with a larger force of men. At that show of defiance, Wool urged John Ridge to avoid bloodshed. Better that Ridge accept the situation and apply for government reparations under the new treaty.

Wool was equally cautious during his meetings with John Ross in mid-August 1836. When Ross said he intended to call a new meeting of the Cherokee General Council, Wool knew what response President Jackson expected from him. He had already been rebuked the previous December for forwarding a Cherokee Council resolution declaring the Treaty of New Echota to be void. At the time, Jackson ordered that "no council should be permitted to assemble to discuss the treaty."

As Wool was faced with Ross's disobedience, his letter to Washington acknowledged that "no good will result from it and much evil may be anticipated." But he also warned that Ross could unite a large majority of the Cherokees in an all-out war against Wool's outnumbered men. He granted that the prospect was unlikely, but he used the threat as his excuse for giving permission for the September 5 meeting. When three thousand Cherokees descended upon Red Clay, Wool kept his soldiers a quarter of a mile away.

Benjamin Currey, who did not attend the meeting, disapproved of Wool's actions. He wrote to the Office of Indian Affairs that if he had been in charge, "Mr. Ross and his pretended authorities" would now be in jail.

To Currey, it could seem that Wool had become personally beguiled by Ross, even though the general remained committed to the treaty. Wool believed that the tribe should move far from the white men, "who, like vultures are watching," ready to strip the Indians "of everything they have or expect to have from the Government of the United States."

Already, pickings had become scant. To oversee the treaty for his administration, Jackson had commissioned Tennessee governor William Carroll and Wilson Lumpkin, who had ended his term as governor of Georgia anticipating a quiet retirement on his plantation in Athens, Georgia.

When Lumpkin arrived in New Echota, he found the buildings so dilapidated that he ordered the Cherokee to build two new cabins, one for him and Carroll to live in, the second for transacting business. Carroll, however, had been stricken with rheumatism and did not appear. Lumpkin passed the days sorting through claims filed under the treaty, but acting alone he could not process the masses of paper from Cherokees who had already sold their belongings and bought wagons for the trip west.

Because some Indians were too poor to afford food, Wool had been feeding them, without authorization, from his troops' rations. Lumpkin agreed to take on that responsibility in order to ward off starvation, but the delay continued to drag on until Jackson finally named Carroll's replacement, Colonel John Kennedy, also from Tennessee.

John Ridge had been appointed chairman of a committee to act on behalf of those Cherokees willing to move. He negotiated a salary of six dollars a day for himself and four dollars for the other committee members. Lumpkin wrote to Washington that he "shall never cease to bear witness to the honor and fidelity of Ridge and his party," but also that he felt he had to guard against their "gross improprieties and extravagances."

In Lumpkin's view, the Indians' trips to Washington at government expense had cultivated a taste for high living. He accused members of Ridge's committee of wanting to keep getting their four dollars a day by making their meetings "interminable." In fact, Lumpkin complained, they had begun to assume the airs of gentlemen. "It became necessary to correct their high notions and set them straight."

These days, protests against the treaty were no longer coming only from the Cherokees. In recent years, an army major named William M. Davis had been put in charge of enrolling Cherokees to emigrate. But after watching Schermerhorn's tactics, Major Davis was moved to protest to the secretary of war. Schermerhorn had been "a most unfortunate selection," Davis wrote; the clergyman's policy had been "a series of blunders from first to last." Davis was especially critical of the fact that, rather than promoting harmony between Ross and the Ridge faction, Schermerhorn and Currey had actively sought to inflame their disagreements.

Davis explained that he felt it was his duty to the president, to Secretary Cass, and to his country to state the facts as he saw them. Schermerhorn had vastly exaggerated the number of Cherokees present at New Echota, and the delegation he had recognized had no more authority than any other dozen Indians picked at random.

At about that time, another commander, General R. G. Dunlap, commanding the Tennessee troops on alert against any Cherokee uprising, learned of the treaty's history and announced that he would never dishonor his state by executing its terms at bayonet point.

And General Wool had begun to echo those opinions. He said it was futile to talk with the overwhelming number of Cherokees who were "almost universally opposed to the treaty and who maintain they never made such a treaty." Many Cherokees were poor, even destitute, Wool continued, but they refused his offer of food and clothing because to accept them could be seen as endorsing the treaty.

During the past summer, Wool had encountered a similar sentiment among the Cherokees of North Carolina. They "preferred living upon roots and sap of trees, rather than receive provisions from the United States," Wool wrote. "They will die before they will leave the country."

For Wool, his duties were heartrending. With the white man ready to pounce, "nineteen-twentieths, if not ninety-nine out of every hundred, will go penniless to the West."

Even so, Wool's troops at New Echota were encountering few disciplinary problems with the Cherokees unless they got hold of whiskey and became belligerent. Currey took heart from the peaceful scene and once again inflated the number of prospective emigrants. "About fifteen hundred or two thousand Indians would leave this fall," he reported to the army's commissary general. He promised that Major Ridge would be in that number.

All but ignored during recent months in the Cherokee Nation were the elections taking place elsewhere throughout the United States. Whatever the result, Andrew Jackson, scourge or savior, would be leaving the presidency.

Martin Van Buren

12 · Martin Van Buren (1836–37)

Martin Van Buren had been positioning himself for the 1836 presidential election for the past two years. He had seen Andrew Jackson through to success in the debate over the Bank of the United States and the brief economic panic that followed its shutting down. On tariffs and other issues, Van Buren had steered his own course between Jacksonian ideology and the growing clamor from South Carolina for states' rights. He could never match Jackson's stature, but his moderation on explosive issues seemed to suit the country's mood.

With America rapidly expanding, Van Buren's policies reflected the westward tilt. The populations of Michigan and Ohio had soared, and the first railroad had opened in 1827. Federal land sales rose in the West during Jackson's administration from about two million acres to twelve and a half million. After the dismembering of the Bank of the United States, Washington had turned over money-lending to state banks—derided by the Whigs as "pet banks"—and in Mississippi, capital funds in banks favored by Jackson had jumped from $3 million to more than $50 million as he prepared to leave office.

If the nation's look had changed, so had Van Buren's. He was dressing less colorfully and, with his scant white hair and expanding waistline, looked the solid statesman. His makeover did not protect him, however, from gibes about his former preening. An 1835 biography attributed to David Crockett described Van Buren as he presided over the Senate—"laced up in corsets, such as women in a town wear, and, if possible, tighter than the best of them." The book added that whether Van Buren was a man or a woman would be hard to tell except "for his large *red* and *grey* whiskers."

Crockett's break with Jackson over the Cherokee Removal had been a factor in his defeat for reelection to Congress, and his bitterness extended to Van Buren. But the vice president did not need to fear further mockery from him. Running again for Congress, Crockett had issued a defiant message to his constituents. If they did not vote for him this time, he said, "You may all go to hell, and I will go to Texas."

Crockett lost the election and made good on his threat. He rode off to join a band of settlers and soldiers of fortune that succeeded in driving Mexican troops from an area called Mexican Texas. When Mexico's president Antonio López de Santa Anna brought soldiers to regain control, Crockett holed up with some 250 Texans inside the Alamo, a former mission converted to a fort.

General Santa Anna's men scaled the Alamo's walls on March 6, 1836. Crockett was among those killed, five months short of his fiftieth birthday.

The fate of those Texans generated a cry for revenge from a contingent of soldiers led by Sam Houston. In the years since his censure by the House of Representatives, Houston had found his destiny in Texas. The Stanbery scandal had given a boost to his national reputation, and Houston acknowledged that if the House had simply fined him ten dollars, "It would have killed me." Instead, Jackson's enemies "gave me a national tribunal for a theater, and that set me up again."

Leaving his Cherokee wife behind, Houston had settled in a Mexican province of Texas and opened a law office in Nacogdoches. After Mexico achieved its independence from Spain in 1821, its government had lured settlers to its barren northern wastes by promising land to anyone who would work it. By 1830, the offer had attracted so many Americans that they outnumbered the Mexican population, and measures to reduce that imbalance set off furious protests. Houston joined a movement calling for Texas statehood. After a rocky start in managing the headstrong volunteers, he became commander in chief of the American forces.

On April 21, 1836, Houston's troops—fewer than eight hundred men—attacked during a Mexican siesta and caught twice that many of Santa Anna's men by surprise. Rushing into battle, Houston's men shouted, "Remember the Alamo!"

Only six weeks had passed since Crockett and his comrades had been annihilated in the small fort. Now Houston's eighteen-minute victory at San Jacinto made him a military hero all over again.

He took Santa Anna prisoner and forced him to sign the Treaty of Velasco, which spared his life in exchange for Texas independence. That was how it happened that Sam Houston, knockabout and failed governor of Tennessee, became president of the Republic of Texas.

Van Buren's political nemesis remained Henry Clay, but in presiding over the Senate, Van Buren had found an effective way to deal with him. In the wake of the furor over the Bank of the United States, Clay had persuaded the Congress to censure President Jackson for his actions. During his powerful harangue, he had also heaped ridicule on Van Buren.

After Clay finished, Van Buren put aside a book he had been pretending to read and stepped down to the floor. From the gallery, spectators watched in suspense as he strode up to Clay, who towered over him.

Speaking courteously but with an undertone of mockery, Van Buren said, "Mr. Senator, allow me to be indebted to you for another pinch of your aromatic Maccoboy."

At a loss, Clay gestured to the gold box on his desk. Van Buren took a bit of the high-quality snuff between his thumb and forefinger and sauntered back to his seat.

Another of Van Buren's fellow Democrats was less adroit. Clay did not hide his contempt for the slow and lumbering James Buchanan of Pennsylvania, who was afflicted with deficient humor and an eye that could look crossed.

During a debate, Clay complained that the Jacksonians had not stated their positions on important issues. "Let us hear from you," Clay baited them. "I call for the leaders of the party."

When Buchanan rose to protest that he had indeed given his position, Clay claimed silkily that he had not been addressing Buchanan. "Far from it," Clay said. "I called for the *leaders* of the party."

As Buchanan fumbled for a response, Clay could not resist a final jab. He sympathized with Buchanan's erroneous thinking that he had been Clay's target, he said, because "I often suppose that the gentleman is looking at me when in fact he looks quite the other way."

A colleague murmured to Clay that while his first sally had been cruel but magnificent, the second was "savage warfare—tomahawking."

"Ah, damn him," Clay replied. For twelve years, he had never forgiven Buchanan for repeating the accusations of Clay's bargain with John Quincy Adams.

But playing to the Senate gallery these days offered Clay little satisfaction. He still craved the presidency. And yet sounding out state representatives had convinced him that getting the Whig nomination would require more effort than he was prepared to make.

And Clay's family life was painful. His wife, Lucretia, had barely survived a wasting disease when his favorite daughter, Anne, died in delivering a son. That news came to Clay by letter from Lexington. He read it and fell to the floor as though he had been shot. For days, he could not stop weeping and often felt that he could not breathe.

To his wife, Clay wrote that his heart would never mend. "Never, never can its wounds be healed."

With Clay retiring from active leadership, the Whigs' volatile alliance seemed more united by hostility to Jackson than by any common goal. National Republicans like John Quincy Adams and Daniel Webster shared little beyond their party label with the anti-Masons or with states' rights Democrats like Calhoun.

But within his Democratic Party, Van Buren also faced divisions so severe that Millard Fillmore, a rising young Whig in Buffalo, could hope that Van Buren's New York base had eroded. Van Buren himself saw Virginia as another trouble spot, which galled him, given his past backing of its state leaders.

"God knows I have suffered enough for my Southern partialities," Van Buren complained to the wife of his longtime Virginia friend, William Rives. "Since I was a boy I have been stigmatized as the apologist of Southern institutions. Now forsooth you good people" were suggesting that he was an abolitionist.

Any defections plagued a man as ambitious as Van Buren, although he was also drawing new followers from the West, including Stephen A. Douglas, only in his early twenties but already on his way to a political career in Illinois. In the end, Van Buren had Jackson's support and that was enough. By the time the Democrats held their convention in Baltimore, he was unopposed for the nomination.

Van Buren immediately demonstrated again the extreme flexibility that could disturb even his friends. William Rives and his allies in the slave states believed they had his firm commitment to offer Rives the vice presidential nomination. But Jackson and other western leaders had decided that the ticket needed to balance Van Buren's urban appeal with a voice from the frontier. Van Buren might have stood by Rives except that Hugh Lawson White, a Tennessee senator and former Jackson intimate, had fallen out with the administration and become a formidable candidate for the Whigs.

Van Buren left it to his campaign manager, Silas Wright, to break the news to Rives that he was being replaced. At their meeting, Wright had to retract his own promise that the New York delegation would back him. He assured Rives that the delegates still preferred him personally. But "if compelled to vote, they must take a man who would bring the greatest strength to the party."

When the new choice was revealed, Cherokees in Georgia understood that Van Buren would be no more sympathetic to their cause than Jackson had been. He had been persuaded to name Richard Mentor Johnson, the Kentucky senator who had built his political career on the claim that he had killed Tecumseh.

Johnson's nomination aroused opposition from slave owners since he had made no secret of his mulatto mistress or their two daughters. Tennessee's chief justice derided the woman for claiming equality with whites and accused Johnson of trying to "force his daughters into society." Like Clay scoffing at Jackson's military exploits, the judge observed that even if Johnson had killed Tecumseh, one random shot did not qualify a man for the vice presidency.

At their convention, Van Buren had to draw on his political legerdemain to nominate Johnson over the adamant Virginians holding out for Rives. Van Buren's allies expected Tennessee's votes to go to Johnson, but the state had refused to send delegates. To cool tempers, Van Buren rode to Tennessee and worked his magic.

As Van Buren anticipated, the campaign against him focused on his reputation as a sly self-promoter. When Calhoun described Andrew Jackson in the Senate as a lion or a tiger it was only to contrast him with Van Buren as a fox and a weasel.

The Democrats responded with a twenty-page party manifesto that dealt in generalities and avoided controversy. It mentioned Jackson fifteen times, Van Buren once. Nowhere did it mention Indian Removal.

All the same, Van Buren's campaign got a boost from the continuing dissension among the Whigs, who proved too divided to hold a national convention. Instead, the states held separate nominating conclaves and came up with Hugh White in Tennessee and Daniel Webster in Massachusetts. At a state session in Pennsylvania, delegates selected William Henry Harrison of Ohio. Clay felt it was important for the Whigs to have one candidate who could appeal to both the North and West while Hugh White was drawing voters in the South.

Clay held no high opinion of Harrison, even though he had been promoting the general's career since Harrison had won his highly publicized victory over Tecumseh's Shawnees at Tippecanoe in 1811. Clay agreed with John Quincy Adams that Harrison, who had a large family to support, showed an unbecoming lust for well-paying jobs and did not seem to care which party could provide them.

During the Adams administration, Clay had urged the president to appoint Harrison as the U.S. minister to Colombia. At the time, skeptics suggested that Clay merely wanted to sidetrack a popular figure and prevent his running as Adams's vice president in 1828. In Colombia, Harrison had created a stir by reproaching Simón Bolívar for antidemocratic policies. Bolívar's rebuttal had echoed through the hemisphere: "The United States," Bolívar wrote, "seems determined by Providence to plague America with torment in the name of freedom."

Upon Jackson's election, Harrison had confirmed Adams's opinion by trying to ingratiate himself with the new administration. Rebuffed, Harrison retreated to his farm in North Bend, Ohio, growing corn and distilling whiskey. Sinking further into debt, he accepted a low-level post in the Cincinnati court system.

As Clay surveyed the field, he decided that Harrison might be "weak, vain, far inferior to Webster," but at least he seemed to be honest and well-intentioned. It did trouble Clay that Harrison, like Jackson, based his claim to the presidency on his battlefield renown.

As for himself, Clay fended off inquires about a possible candidacy: "The only condition upon which it would have been acceptable to me, that of my being desired by a majority, did not I thought exist; and I felt no inclination to engage in a scramble for it."

During the campaign, Van Buren found himself navigating his own treacherous shoals. As secretary of state, he had defended the right of

Catholics to worship as they pleased. But Protestants in Philadelphia were alarmed by an influx of workers from Ireland and accused him of being part of a "popish plot." Van Buren had to reassure voters that he was not a Roman Catholic.

Nor was he an abolitionist, even though his home state of New York had more than two hundred societies dedicated to ending slavery. Van Buren defused the issue by pointing out that the federal government had no power to abolish slavery almost anywhere in the United States. The exception was within the District of Columbia, which was federally governed, and Van Buren said that he opposed action even there.

To maintain Southern support, Van Buren went further. He called slave owners "sincere friends to the happiness of mankind" and denounced abolitionists as no more than onetime Federalists trying to sow dissension.

Van Buren's strategy worked, if not brilliantly. He took 50.9 percent of the popular vote, with the splintered Whigs claiming the other 49.1 percent. Although it had been a quarter-century since Tippecanoe, William Henry Harrison's war record helped him to carry six states—not only Ohio, Kentucky, and Indiana, but also New Jersey, Vermont, and Maryland.

Hugh White won Tennessee and Georgia. He also took South Carolina, but when the legislature appointed its electors, they gave their eleven votes to an anti-Jackson senator from North Carolina. Daniel Webster received only the fourteen electoral votes of his own Massachusetts.

One of Van Buren's New York enemies saw ominous portents in the results. "I have no confidence in a People who can elect Van Buren President," he wrote. "Depend on it, his election is to be the 'beginning of the end.'"

In recent months, the federal government had replaced its representatives to the Cherokee Nation. Benjamin Currey had died, succeeded by

Brigadier General Nathaniel Smith. And General Wool had become increasingly frustrated as he defended the Cherokees against rapacious white settlers from Alabama. Wool drove them from tribal property and returned it to its Indian owners, but he concluded at last that his duties were violating his sense of honor.

Just as Wool was requesting a transfer, local white officials demanded that he be reprimanded for favoring the Cherokees. By the time a military tribunal cleared Wool of that charge, a Colonel William Lindsay had taken his place.

In Washington, the president-elect felt he needed a secretary of state from the South and retained in the job John Forsyth, Georgia's former governor. To Van Buren's dismay, William Rives declined the consolation of secretary of war and kept angling instead for the State Department. Van Buren held firm for Forsyth, and the War Department went to Joel Poinsett of South Carolina. Poinsett was the ally John Calhoun had unsuccessfully pressured John Quincy Adams to appoint secretary of state in 1825. More recently, Poinsett had resisted the nullification movement in his state and had gone to Mexico as America's first ambassador. Now Poinsett inherited the distinction once bestowed on Van Buren—he was considered the most able appointment in the new cabinet.

Poinsett had also won a reputation as an amateur botanist by bringing home from Mexico a gaudy red plant, the *Euphorbia pulcherrima.* It was named "poinsettia" for him. But as an honor, it could not match the naming of the ancient trees of California as *sequoia gigantea* for the man who had given the Cherokees their written language.

The night before Van Buren's inauguration, he went to spend the night at the White House as Jackson's guest, along with Roger Brooke Taney, the nation's chief justice. When John Marshall died in July 1835, just short of his eightieth birthday, Jackson became the first president to name a chief justice since John Adams had picked Marshall in 1801.

Dour, addicted to cigars, Taney had served Jackson as attorney general and then as a recess appointee in the Treasury during the Bank Wars, where he oversaw the transfer of government deposits to the pet banks. By the time Jackson nominated him formally as Treasury secretary, the Senate had censured his practices, and Taney became the first cabinet nominee to be rejected by the Senate.

After that rebuff, Taney returned to Baltimore to practice law. Years before, he had married Francis Scott Key's sister and shared a legal office with Key. Then, eighteen months after the Senate rejection, Jackson nominated him as chief justice. Despite vociferous opposition, Taney was confirmed early in March 1836.

Jackson's last night in the White House was spent receiving gifts from a grateful nation. A Jacksonian from New York brought a wheel of cheese four feet in diameter and two feet thick that weighed fourteen hundred pounds. Jackson wanted to believe that his eight years as president had broken the stranglehold of the moneyed elite on the United States. But the memory of Thomas Jefferson's disdain for him still rankled. He was assured that this gift was twice the size of the cheese presented to Jefferson when he retired to Monticello.

Jackson's farewell address summarized his eight years in office without mentioning the Cherokees. Invoking Washington's famous remarks, Jackson concluded, "And filled with gratitude for your constant and unwavering kindness, I bid you a last and affectionate farewell."

His presumption in quoting America's first president gave Jackson's enemies a final chance to strike. The *New York American* was unforgiving: "Happily it is the last humbug which the mischievous popularity of this illiterate, violent, vain, and iron-willed soldier can impose upon a confiding and credulous people."

On the morning of March 4, 1837, Martin Van Buren was sworn in under a sunny sky. The public mood reflected the changes in the United States during Jackson's eight years. With his Democrats now in charge of the legislature, the desperate fervor that had marked Jackson's first inaugural had subsided. This time, the crowd was silently respectful as Jackson emerged from his phaeton—another gift, built with timbers from the USS *Constitution.* Jackson's bearing was still erect, his white hair visible to onlookers who could not see Van Buren's balding head as he followed along to the Senate chamber.

After Richard Johnson was sworn in as vice president, Taney accompanied the retiring president and his successor to a platform on the Capitol's east portico. Because of the hush, many in the audience of twenty thousand could hear Van Buren pledge that he was "the inflexible and uncompromising opponent of every attempt on the part of the Congress to abolish slavery in the District of Columbia." More sweeping was his promise "to resist the slightest interference with it in the states where it exists."

Agitation over the issue threatened the destruction of the government, Van Buren continued, "but neither masses of the people nor sections of the country have been swerved from their devotion to the bond of union and the principles it has made sacred."

Taney administered the oath, Van Buren kissed his family Bible, and his four sons drew closer amid cheers from well-wishers. The reception that followed at the White House was crowded but restrained, although an odor of cheese permeated the hallways.

On the day before Van Buren took office, Major Ridge left New Echota for the last time. It was fourteen months before the treaty deadline, but life at home had become intolerable. Fellow tribesmen refused to speak to him and often spat as he walked by. With his health declining, Ridge compounded his sins in the eyes of Ross's faction by accepting transportation from the government rather than making the trek west on his own. Going with him would be his wife; Clarinda, a slow-witted granddaughter; one of Boudinot's children; and eighteen slaves. They were being joined by nearly five hundred Cherokees who were also yielding to the treaty.

Taken to fifteen open flatboats, the group sailed away with their eyes still fixed on the land they were leaving. After six days raw with wind, the boats put in at a landing and transferred their passengers to a steamer, the *Knoxville,* that was scheduled to take them to Arkansas.

The trip had so weakened Major Ridge that many in his party worried that he would not live to see his new land. The army general in charge of the passage had been allotted twenty dollars for each Cherokee, and he had put aside three hundred dollars to allow Ridge and his family to travel in the comfort of a cabin.

At Decatur, Alabama, the Tennessee River was running too low for the steamer to navigate Muscle Shoals. The Indians were moved onto the open cars of a private rail line run by the Tuscumbia, Courtland, and Decatur Railroad. At Tuscumbia, they waited with their supplies of cornmeal and bacon for another steamer, the *Newark*, to take them to Paducah, Kentucky. After more windy, wet days and another transfer to riverboats, the passengers reached Fort Smith, Arkansas. A doctor traveling with them had treated both Major Ridge and his wife for worrisome coughs. But not only had they recovered, no other passenger had died during the twenty-four days.

Major Ridge had chosen land about two miles north of Fort Smith, near the border of Arkansas and Missouri. The mouth of Honey Creek lay within the Ridge property, and Washington Irving, scouting out the landscape, had written rapturously about the swarms of wild honeybees: "It seems to me as if these beautiful regions answer literally to the description of the land of promise, 'a land flowing with milk and honey.'"

Ridge purchased the richly productive land with its rolling prairies and groves of cedar, oak, pine, and wild grape. He bought imported livestock and equipment and set his slaves to work on what promised to be an estate to rival the one he had left behind.

It had taken Elias Boudinot months to recover from the loss of his wife. In a letter to her brother, he described his "deeply wounded heart" and his worry over coping with their six children. Boudinot said his consolation was the sterling memory Harriet had left behind, even among the whites of Georgia who had come to know her, people "not infrequently carried way with overwrought passions and prejudices against our race."

By early 1837, Boudinot still grieved, but he was satisfied with the arrangements he had made for the children. Cornelius, who was lame, had become the pet of a family that sent the boy to a respected doctor in Huntsville, Alabama. But it looked as though he would be crippled for life. One child had gone with Major Ridge, the others were flourishing at school in Brainerd, Tennessee, where Boudinot could leave them if he traveled from Cherokee territory. He was planning a trip north with his sister and his daughter, Eleanor, before the Treaty of New Echota became law. To Harriet's parents, Boudinot mentioned casually that he would be joined by the daughter of a New England doctor, a "Miss Sargent, formerly a teacher here," who was "returning to see her friends in Vermont."

When Boudinot wrote again to the Golds two month later, he announced that he had decided "to change my situation." He was sure his former in-laws would approve of his remarriage since his bride, thirty-seven-year-old Delight Sargent, "is about my age, of small person, excellent acquirements and most lovely disposition." And "the children are delighted with her and feel they have a home once more."

By September, John Ridge was preparing to join his parents and would be traveling west with the Boudinots. Ridge had received $19,741.67 for the improvements to his property and another $1,745 from the farmer who bought his crops. He thanked Wilson Lumpkin and other committee members for their kindnesses to the Cherokees but granted that his family's reputation might have been permanently sullied by those Cherokees too short-sighted to see the wisdom in their actions. Committee members, in turn, praised Ridge's efforts to "save your people from certain impending ruin and destruction" and wished him a long life of service to the Cherokees.

Ridge sent ahead most of his slaves and horses and traveled to Arkansas with only his own family, the Boudinots, a few other friends, and three slaves to cook and drive their carriage. On the route, their party stopped at the Hermitage to call on Andrew Jackson, nearly deaf now and all but blind in his right eye. But he was unfailingly gracious to these Cherokees who had bowed to his will.

After seven weeks of travel through hills and marshland, Ridge and his contingent reached his parents and predicted that in a few years the new Cherokee Nation centered on Honey Creek would be "the garden spot of the United States." As for now, "perfect friendship and contentedness prevail over this land."

In Washington, Van Buren's first days in office did not offer the same sort of respite. The new president first had to put his personal house in order. Two of his sons were returning to Albany: John—clever and equally energetic in pursuing a prosperous legal career and New York's society women—and Smith, shy and charming but unambitious and perhaps best suited to marrying an heiress.

Abraham, the eldest son, had resigned his U.S. Army commission the day before the inauguration to take a post in the Treasury Department that would let him serve as his father's secretary. The president would pay his namesake, Martin, Jr., out of his personal account to copy official correspondence until Van Buren could find a spot for him on the government payroll.

Then, less than two weeks after Van Buren took office, the nation's economy collapsed. The failure of the New Orleans cotton market led to the default of a large New York City exchange. The threat of bankruptcy soon had bankers urging Van Buren to rescind a Jackson order called the Specie Circular, which required the use of only hard money in buying western land. Since many of the pet banks did not have enough gold or silver coins to exchange for their notes, they quickly failed.

Senators joined in urging a change of direction, but Jackson warned from his plantation that abandoning his Specie Circular would set off land speculation and add to the collapse.

Initially, Van Buren thought he might have to challenge his powerful patron. He wrote to Jackson that he was getting "bundles of letters" from their political friends, all men well disposed to Jackson, who argued that his circular must be revoked.

Van Buren knew his cabinet was divided. Rather than provoke a face-to-face showdown, he solicited their judgment in writing. Most, including his Treasury secretary, Levi Woodbury, urged changes or outright repeal of Jackson's policies. Other advisers told Van Buren that the problems had arisen from the greed of speculators, who should be allowed to fail.

At last, Van Buren decided he must take responsibility. He upheld Jackson's circular. Aghast, New York bankers and merchants called for a special session of Congress to implement emergency measures. Van Buren denied that the crisis required such drastic action.

Within weeks, there was a run on New York City banks. In one day, depositors withdrew more than $2 million in hard currency. Soldiers patrolled New York streets as all but three banks suspended specie payments. Those suspensions then spread throughout the nation.

By May 1, the economic upheaval had become the Panic of 1837. Prices and profits plunged. A New York City lot at Broadway and 100th Street that had brought $480 eight months earlier now went for $50.

Unemployment rose to one-third—in some areas one-half—of the nation's workers, but the suffering was not uniformly shared. Tax assessments showed that in Boston, for example, the city's wealthiest speculators were getting still richer from the financial upheaval.

On May 15, 1837, Van Buren yielded to pressure and called a special session of Congress for September to deal with the excesses of the Jackson years.

While Washington was convulsed by the economic panic, time was running down to May 22, 1838, when the Treaty of New Echota would become law. Although facing that deadline, John Ross was distracted by an unexpected deal put forward by Joel Poinsett.

Ross had brought his delegates to Washington again early in October 1837. They were granted an audience with Van Buren, but their exchange was stilted and led nowhere. Soon afterward, Poinsett offered his attractive proposition. He said that official Washington appreciated the way Chief Ross had kept his people from exploding in violence. Now Poinsett was sure that Ross could demonstrate the futility of rebellion to a Seminole named Osceola and his band of renegades in Florida. If Ross were able to persuade Osceola to give up his war against the United States, the Cherokees could expect handsome rewards.

The same suggestion had already been broached to Ross three months earlier by Poinsett's aide, Colonel John H. Sherburne, who promised that money would be no object in underwriting a peacemaking mission. By then, Ross had become canny enough not to agree until he received Poinsett's personal assurance: "Are you authorized by the President of the United States to guarantee safety and protection to the lives of Osceola and others of the Chiefs as may compose the Seminole delegation?"

Ross knew Osceola by reputation. His mother was part Muskogee Indian, and he had been raised by William Powell, an English trader who was either his father or his stepfather. White settlers around his village of Tallassee, Alabama, had called the boy Billy Powell. After renegade Creeks fled to Florida during the War of 1812, Powell's mother took her ten-year-old son to join them. There he received his Indian name of Osceola—a combination of the Creek words for "shouter" and for a ceremonial drink made from holly.

When hostilities flared again between the Seminoles and Washington, Osceola threw his lot in with the Indians, objecting to a proposed treaty that he claimed would reduce the Seminoles to slaves. Osceola had married a black woman, and the issue had become urgent to him.

Given the simmering unrest among the Seminoles, the government's agent, Wiley Thompson, had forbidden the sale of guns and ammunition to them. But Thompson considered Osceola a friend and made an exception for him.

In December 1835, Osceola and a cadre of Seminoles staged an ambush that killed seven white men. Wiley Thompson was among them.

For the next twenty-two months, the assailants eluded capture. When other Seminole leaders signed a "Capitulation" and agreed to leave Florida in exchange for land in the West, Osceola not only refused to sign but staged a raid against a badly guarded camp and led away seven hundred Seminoles who had surrendered.

Enraged, Major General Thomas Jesup used the escape to justify his own breach of trust. The U.S. government announced peace negotiations, but when Osceola and others approached under a white flag, Jesup had them arrested. It was that tangle of bloodshed and bad faith that Poinsett wanted Ross to resolve.

Ross went with a Cherokee delegation to St. Augustine, Florida, in mid-November 1837 and offered Jesup's prisoners the same realistic advice that Ross had found hard to accept for himself: "I know that a brave people when driven to a state of desperation would sooner die under the strong arm of power than to shrink and die the death of a coward. But I will speak to you as a friend, and with the voice of reason advise you, as a small but brave people, to act the part of a noble race, and at once throw yourselves upon the magnanimity and justice of the American people."

Taking his message to rebel Seminole enclaves, Ross was more convincing with them than with General Jesup. When the Indians showed up at Jesup's camp carrying aloft a white scarf of peace, the general again violated the truce and shipped them to join Osceola in custody. Ross followed after them, desperate to convince the Seminoles that he had had no part in their betrayal.

Ross's discussions with local white soldiers and civilians had persuaded him that they were "heartily sick of the war." If allowed a free hand, Ross promised to end the strife within two weeks. But the arrests had made Jesup's objective clear. He was not seeking peace but expulsion of the Seminoles from Florida.

In the white community, Osceola was generating sympathy, and Jesup's deceit was widely denounced. When Osceola was moved to Fort Moultrie in South Carolina, he was visited by artists who painted him in oils, engraved his portrait, and fashioned a cigar-store Indian in his likeness.

Ross went back to Washington to complain angrily to Poinsett about Jesup. Poinsett explained that, given his distance from Washington, Jesup had been given broad discretionary powers. Not only would Poinsett not support Ross in any further negotiations, he authorized his government to pay less than one-tenth of the expenses that Ross's party had incurred.

Ross's negotiations on behalf of his own tribe were not going any better. In Washington, he found himself competing for attention with Samuel Morse, whose new telegraph had captivated legislators. By now Ross was prepared to make further concessions. He pointed out that the U.S. Senate could be more generous and still save a great deal of the money that would be required to evict the tribe by force. But he learned that the Van Buren administration was firmly committed to the Treaty of New Echota.

To Ross, it was proof that newly installed officials of the Democratic Party were "doubtless afraid from the Old Hickory stubble." Yet, against all evidence, Ross went on believing that the Senate would somehow rescue his people.

That misplaced optimism infected even those Cherokees who were resigned to the move. One group had traveled thirty miles along the route to their new land when they got word that Ross had negotiated new and better terms. They turned around and went home.

To assist him in the propaganda wars, Ross paid the expenses of John Howard Payne to bring his literary talents to Washington. It was to no avail. Two days after Christmas, Poinsett wrote to chastise Ross for holding out false hope. As a result, Poinsett said, the Cherokees had refused to emigrate during "the season of the year best suited for their comfortable removal."

When Samuel and Ann Worcester packed up after his release from prison, they first lived in Tennessee, where they became resigned to removal. In 1836, they began to travel west to their new home. But swamps created by spring rains blocked their two-seat wagon. Ann Worcester contracted a fever, and a steamboat sank, destroying the household goods they had sent by river. After seven weeks riding through Kentucky, Illinois, and Missouri, the Worcesters arrived at the Dwight Mission in the Oklahoma Territory.

The American Board of Foreign Missionaries sent a printing press from Boston to replace the one confiscated from the *Cherokee Phoenix* and also furnished a printer and his apprentice. The Worcesters opened a church and school, and Worcester began to publish quotations from the Bible and copies of Sequoyah's alphabet.

Applying for permission to establish himself in the new Cherokee territory, Worcester had to live down suspicions from his previous contact with the Ridge party. The tribal council gave permission for his house and school but struck down Worcester's initial request for fifteen acres of land and allotted him five acres instead, along with the right to raise twenty-five head of cattle, not the fifty he had requested.

More significantly, Worcester was instructed that he "must stand aloof from all political affairs of the Nation."

As he took up his work again on the Cherokee dictionary, Worcester regretted the absence of his partner. Try as he might, he could not understand why Boudinot had signed the Treaty of New Echota. In mid-December 1836, he wrote a plaintive letter to assure Boudinott—Worcester spelled it with two final t's—that he was convinced of his friend's sincerity and upright character and yet was not satisfied that he had acted lawfully.

Despite those misgivings, Worcester defended Boudinot to the American Board. He was certain that the tribe's resentment would ease once "they find themselves undeceived as to what Mr. Ross can do for them, and as to the character of the country to which they are sent."

Worcester had not expected to find the rolling hills and lush foliage that surrounded his new home, and he reported that other recent emigrants also "expressed great surprise on their arrival, or soon after, at the goodness of the country." He quoted one as saying, "This is a very different country from what our leading men have told us." As that feeling spread, the Cherokees would change their attitude toward Boudinot and consider themselves "grossly deceived by Mr. Ross."

All the same, Worcester felt compelled to add that the New Echota treaty had been a "fraudulent and wicked transaction."

When Boudinot arrived with his new wife, Worcester persuaded the American Board to approve five hundred dollars for him to build a house. Boudinot chose a lot a quarter of a mile from the Worcesters and began construction.

That proximity complicated the missionary's position. Some Cherokees had already identified Worcester with the hated treaty because of their friendship, and Boudinot was now justifying himself aggressively in a pamphlet that was widely reprinted.

Boudinot conceded that the Ridge faction might have been small, but sometimes a minority must act as the majority "*would* do if they understood their condition, to save a *nation* from political thralldom and degradation."

That sort of self-serving argument only aroused more anger from the Cherokee Council, which warned Worcester that Boudinot was so despised he should not be identified on any publication as Worcester's translator. The council "respectfully requests you not use his services or his name in your printings, in order that nothing unpleasant may occur."

Although he was concerned about being banished, Worcester went on maneuvering on Boudinot's behalf. Yet he asked himself whether his years among the Cherokees had led them any closer to Christianity.

At the least, Worcester could wage a continuing battle against liquor. He organized the "Cherokee Cold Water Army" and composed a song for Christian converts and their children to sing as they marched through town carrying temperance banners. It was to be sung to the tune of "Yankee Doodle."

We will not fight with guns or swords,
Nor kill one son or daughter;
Our weapon shall be pleasant words
And cool, refreshing water.

Then, with King Alcohol on the run, Worcester's marchers sang out their final triumphant verse:

Sweet cold water now we sing!
Water is the dandy!
Give me water from a spring,
And fling away the brandy.

In Washington, George Gilmer, elected Georgia's governor once again, denounced Chief Ross for remaining in the capital during the past several months even though he had no hope of success. Rather, Gilmer said, Ross should return home to prepare his tribe for the inevitable. Ross replied that he was where the Cherokees wanted him to be, but he also reassured Gilmer that there was no possibility that his people would resort to violence.

In fact, it was Gilmer who was advocating force. He implored Poinsett to send to Cherokee country "in as short a time as possible, the whole of the United States army."

On April 9, 1838, Ross's last appeal to Congress was stamped "Laid on Table," which meant that no action would be taken. Yet Ross stayed on in Washington. Writing from the Cherokee Nation, Lewis Ross chided his brother for not sending home more information. "There is a great many of our people here every mail day and where there is no letter the disappointment is visible in every countenance."

But Ross retained faith in his economic argument. Although the Senate had rejected his estimate that removal and compensation would require $13 million, Poinsett had agreed to additional appropriations that approached $1.2 million, bringing the total to $6,647,067. The Senate approved that new figure but rejected Ross's appeal that the treaty deadline be extended.

As the May date approached, however, Van Buren saw merit in Ross's request. Unlike Jackson, he did not feel personally committed to removal. It was simply a chore he had inherited. Given the devastating financial crisis, the opportunity to paper over a dispute suited Van Buren's temperament, and he gave the Cherokees two more years in Georgia. But come May 1840, they must definitely move west.

The president's concession infuriated Gilmer. He said that hearing the news had led to only the second time in his life that he had lost his temper. The governor announced that the patience of the Georgians had been exhausted, and they were determined to claim the land that was due them. If Van Buren did not reverse his extension, Gilmer would call out his state militia of two thousand men. Let the president delay and "the consequences must be upon his head."

Like John Quincy Adams before him, Van Buren would not risk going to war against the state of Georgia. He ordered the original treaty terms enforced, starting on May 23, 1838.

During the past decade, the white population of the South had increased by 2.5 million. To assist in providing for them, Van Buren called on General Winfield Scott to evacuate the Cherokee Nation.

General Winfield Scott

13 · Winfield Scott (1838)

Before Winfield Scott could begin to carry out his assignment, a young philosopher in Concord, Massachusetts, challenged the general's sword with his own brash pen. In recent years, Ralph Waldo Emerson had become celebrated for developing a quintessentially American creed called Transcendentalism. Emerson, about to turn thirty-four, was drawing crowds to his lectures with his resonant baritone and unquenchable enthusiasm.

Since high spirits did not come naturally to Emerson, they testified to the willpower that his speeches were extolling. In 1831, when his first wife, Ellen Tucker, died of tuberculosis at the age of twenty, he had been inconsolable. Unwilling to accept that she was gone, he first insisted on reopening her coffin, then mourned at her grave every day for months.

Emerson had expected to be a preacher like his father, but religion offered no comfort in his loss, and he resigned his ministry. He found that he could accept Jesus as a great man but not as the son of God.

With the soothing passage of time, Emerson took a second wife in 1835. A practical, somewhat formal woman named Lydia Jackson, she addressed her husband as "Mister Emerson." He called her "Lidian." When they had a daughter, the new mother suggested that they honor Emerson's first wife by christening the infant Ellen.

From his late teens at Harvard College, Emerson had been keeping a journal of his reading and his random thoughts, and when he returned to lecture before Harvard's Phi Beta Kappa Society, Emerson recalled his bookish habits. "Meek young men grow up in libraries," he told his audience. He urged them to break free and follow their intuition.

The aphorisms in an Emerson lecture were challenging: "Make the most of yourself, for that is all there is of you" and "Nothing is at last sacred but the integrity of your own mind." Other times he could be lighthearted. Skewering a hypocrite, he wrote, "The louder he talked of his honor, the faster we counted our spoons."

But when he set out to shame the president of the United States, Emerson was entirely serious.

Six years earlier, he had become acquainted with the plight of the Cherokees from hearing Major Ridge speak at Boston's Federal Street Church. Writing to his younger brother, Charles, Emerson praised Ridge's powerful oratory, and Charles suggested that they take up Ridge's cause as their own.

In 1836, the scourge of tuberculosis claimed Charles, but his memory remained vivid as his brother wrestled with the Indian question. In a lecture the following year titled "Manners," Emerson described the rustic Indian in terms that he considered complimentary, including their "infantile simplicity."

But friends and family were pressing Emerson to do more. At first, he was resentful. "I can do nothing. Why shriek? Why strike ineffectual blows?" He wondered to himself whether the Cherokees' "eternal inferiority" made it impossible for them ever to adapt to white America's culture. But at last he concluded that he must take up his late brother's challenge and speak out.

Emerson's earlier misgivings were not apparent from the tone of his letter to the president, which began with a ringing challenge to Van Buren about the obligations of his office: "By right and natural position, every citizen is your friend," Emerson wrote, which meant that each American could expect to trust in his government. He granted that his name would "be utterly unknown to you" but hoped that his lack of renown would guarantee that his letter could be judged solely on its merits.

Speaking of the Cherokees, Emerson wrote that even in distant Massachusetts "some good rumor of their worth and civility has arrived." He traced the recent history of what he called the sham treaty of 1835 and deplored the willingness of the president and his government "to put this active nation into carts and boats, and to drag them over mountains and rivers to a wilderness at a vast distance beyond the Mississippi.

"In the name of God, sir, we ask you if this be so. Do the newspapers rightly inform us?

"Sir, does this government think that the people of the United States are become savages and mad?"

Was his heated language overstepping the bounds of decorum? Emerson supplied his own answer. It would be a "higher indecorum coldly to argue a matter like this.

"You, sir, will bring down that renowned chair in which you sit into infamy if your seal is set to this instrument of perfidy; and the name of this nation, hitherto the sweet omen of religion and liberty, will stink to the world."

Emerson acknowledged that the nation had been beset during the past year by economic questions of hard currency and trade. But those debates were "the chirping of grasshoppers beside the immortal question whether justice shall be done by the race of the civilized to the race of savage man."

He cited the opinion of statesmen—by which Emerson meant his friends among New England's prominent families. He said that they believed that ten years ago—before Andrew Jackson—Indian Removal would never have been proposed. Did not Van Buren, as a New Yorker, understand the power of high principle? "A man with your experience in office must have seen cause to appreciate the futility of opposition to the moral sentiment."

Emerson offered a prayer that his single voice might move the president, "whose hands are strong with the delegated power of fifteen millions of men," and that Van Buren would use that power to stave off "the terrific injury that threatens the Cherokee tribe."

Emerson concluded, "With great respect, sir, I am your fellow citizen,

"Ralph Waldo Emerson."

Unlike the message that Worcester sent to the governor of Georgia, Emerson's open letter was meant to be published, and it appeared on May 19, 1838, in *The Yeoman's Gazette,* his local Concord newspaper. Emerson expected no reply from the White House and got none.

When Winfield Scott met John Ross in Washington before Scott left for Georgia, he made an emotional pledge: His greatest objective was to oversee the removal without bloodshed. In fact, as Ross recounted the conversation to his brother, Lewis, the general claimed that "should it happen that one drop of Cherokee blood be spilt *he* will *weep*!"

Ross assured him that Scott had no more need to send a large militia force into Cherokee territory on the pretext of protecting white Georgians than President Van Buren needed a guard to protect him from his own children.

Scott persisted: What of reports that the Cherokees were planting corn on their property? That would suggest they had no intention of leaving. Ross responded with his latest terms. Secretary Poinsett must notify General Scott to put the Cherokees in charge of their own emigration. And if President Van Buren wanted removal to proceed, he must resolve the outstanding matters of restitution.

As wrangling continued, an ally in Philadelphia warned Ross that the Indian question was being linked to an increasingly violent debate over slavery. Even in the North, memories persisted of the slave revolt in Virginia led by Nat Turner in August 1831, when his followers slaughtered fifty-seven men, women, and children before Turner was captured and executed. After that, a Boston mob opposed to abolition had broken up a meeting of the Anti-Slavery Society and chased William Lloyd Garrison through the streets, determined to lynch him. Although Garrison preached opposing slavery nonviolently, he had to take refuge overnight in the Leverett Street Jail and then disappear from the city.

Now a minister scheduled to speak in Pennsylvania Hall on May 17, 1838, had announced that he would prove that slavery was always a sin. Again a mob descended, demolished the hall, and set it on fire. Ross's correspondent concluded that "this mixing of white and black is no-go in Philadelphia," and since Wilson Lumpkin "is a cold-blooded hypocrite" who would resort to any untruth to hurt the Cherokees, it was best that Indians remain silent on the race issue.

Winfield Scott had grown up the delight of his widowed mother. The result was his high opinion of himself and his conviction that he could talk his way out of any corner. Scott emerged from an indifferent education in Virginia schools with an ability to read French and a glancing familiarity with Greek and Latin. Dropping out of the College of William and Mary, Scott studied with a local lawyer and passed the Virginia bar at age twenty. Two years later, in 1808, he was commissioned as a captain in the U.S. Army.

Handsome, dark-haired, standing six-foot-five, Scott had struck Aaron Burr during his trial for treason in Richmond as "the most magnificent youth in Virginia." But Scott's gifts seemed compromised by an instinct for controversy. Serving under corrupt Major General James Wilkinson in New Orleans, Scott had been loud in his denunciations. A tale-bearer repeated to Wilkinson that Scott had told a crowd of fellow officers that "he never saw but two traitors—General Wilkinson and Burr" and had added that Wilkinson was a liar and a scoundrel.

Scott's charges may have been true, but Wilkinson was his commander. After less than two years in the army, Scott was court-martialed. He acted for his own defense, was convicted of charges that included disrespectful language, and was suspended for twelve months. When Scott tried to avenge himself on the man who informed against him, he came out of their duel with a painful head wound.

As a result, Scott soured on the army and the "coarse and ignorant men" it attracted. But he remained fascinated by the study of war itself. To him, the War of 1812 underscored the need for the professionalism that he had been advocating.

He was captured in a battle at Queenston Heights and released in a prisoner exchange, and later he fought along the Niagara River at Chippawa. In both engagements, Scott distinguished himself for his rash bravery.

Then came the Battle of Lundy's Lane, which made his reputation. With a stubborn resolve, Scott rallied his outnumbered men and broke the British line before a rain of bullets left him unconscious and badly shot up. He awoke to find his countrymen comparing his exploit to the Revolution's great moment at Bunker Hill.

The nation lavished on him a gold medal, together with commemorative swords from New York and Virginia and an order promoting him to major general. Scott's new prominence also resulted in an 1817 society marriage to Maria De Mayo, a protégée of Dolley Madison. Maria Scott added regularly to their family, Scott to an expanding waistline.

General Scott's temperament was not suited to peacetime, and his steady rise in the army was stalled after a clash with an even greater military hero. The cause was minor; the repercussions were not. An engineer had been transferred out of Andrew Jackson's military command without notifying Jackson. Outraged by the perceived slight, Jackson ordered his officers to disregard any further orders they received from Washington.

That insubordination gave Jackson's rivals their opening, and they called for his court-martial. When Scott was asked his opinion, he said that Jackson should be admonished but not put on trial. Hearing a garbled version of that qualified defense, Jackson wrote to Scott to demand clarification.

By now, Scott's men were calling him "Old Fuss and Feathers," mocking both his insistence on discipline and his delight in showy uniforms. What Jackson got back was a patronizing letter, which Scott ended with typical self-congratulation. He had expected Jackson's praise for his judgment, he wrote, because "in my humble opinion, refutation is impossible."

Jackson proved him wrong. He challenged Scott to a duel, but his wording was oblique enough that Scott could ignore it. From the sidelines, John Quincy Adams worried about Scott, a man he admired. He wrote in his journal that "Scott's vanity" was "leading him to ruin."

Jackson's hostility temporarily blocked Scott's career, but his abilities continued to propel him forward. Although a campaign against the Seminoles in Florida ended badly, Scott went next to the northern border, where Canadian rebels were using upstate New York and Vermont as havens for raids against the British command. To recruit Americans to their cause, the rebels were promising each volunteer three hundred acres of land around Ontario. Among those heeding the call was Rensselaer Van Rensselaer, whose father, Solomon, had been wounded in Canada during the War of 1812.

Late in December 1837, British soldiers struck back by boarding an insurgent ship, the *Caroline,* even though it was docked on the U.S. side of the Niagara River. One American was killed in the assault. Van Buren had given Scott carte blanche to avoid yet another war with Great Britain, and now he was expected to enforce border neutrality.

Stumping along the disputed frontier, Scott persuaded upstate New Yorkers to end their support for the Canadian battle for independence. When he got reports that another raid might be in the offing, Scott led a U.S. Army detachment along the Michigan-Ohio frontier to discourage local enthusiasm for the rebels.

In Washington, Congress was being diverted from its northern problems by John Calhoun's series of resolutions defending slavery. It fell to Van Buren to dun Great Britain for reparations in the *Caroline* affair and to offer assurances that the United States would remain neutral in the clash between Canadians.

American governors along the border praised Scott for negotiating the edgy commitment to peace. That Van Buren sent him next to oversee the Cherokee Removal reflected the president's confidence in Scott's adroit diplomacy.

For his part, Scott embraced the assignment. "I like difficulties!" he said.

On May 10, 1838, Scott assembled Cherokee elders for an address at his new headquarters on the Hiwasse River near Athens, Tennessee. He had written out his remarks, which he read to the sixty chiefs. Despite the reassurance from John Ross, Scott was nervous about armed resistance and determined to discourage it.

"Cherokees!" Scott began. "The president of the United States has sent me, with a powerful army, to cause you, in obedience with the Treaty of 1835, to join that part of your people who are already established in prosperity on the other side of the Mississippi."

Scott announced that "the emigration must be commenced in haste, but, I hope, without disorder." Every Cherokee man, woman, and child must be on their way west before the next full moon passed.

Next came a show of his determination: "My troops already occupy many positions in the country that you are to abandon; thousands and thousands are approaching from every quarter to render resistance and escape alike hopeless." But Scott wanted to intimidate the Cherokees without panicking them. "Solders are kind hearted as they are brave, and the desire of every one of us is to execute our painful duty in mercy."

He put the choice to them. "Will you then, by resistance, compel us to resort to arms? God forbid! Or will you, by flight, seek to hide yourself in mountains and forests, and thus oblige us to hunt you down?"

Scott called on the Cherokees not to offend his sensibilities. "I am an old warrior," he said, "and have been present at many a scene of slaughter. But spare me, I beseech you, the horror of witnessing the destruction of the Cherokees."

Scott ended with an appeal to God that the Americans and Cherokees might both prosper "and preserve them long in peace and friendship with each other."

Scott's remark about his kindhearted soldiers was wishful thinking, spoken before he learned of the differences among the white settlements that surrounded the Cherokees. The people of North Carolina and Tennessee were pleased by the prospect of removal but not so hostile to the Indians as the people of Alabama. And it was the Georgians who seemed angry, even murderous. Mobilizing at New Echota, members of the Georgia militia were vowing to kill at least one Cherokee each before they returned home.

Scott's command also included the First and Second regiments of the artillery and the regular army's Fourth Infantry, together with six companies of dragoons. He addressed his order to them as well as to the Georgia militia.

Unaware of the Georgians' long-standing hostility to Northern missionaries, Scott appealed to the religious upbringing of the militia, who were largely Methodists and Baptists. "Every possible kindness," Scott decreed, "must be shown by the troops." He went further: "And if, in the ranks, a despicable individual should be found capable of inflicting a wanton injury or insult on any Cherokee man, woman or child, it is hereby made the special duty of the nearest good officer or man" to seize "the guilty wretch" and subject him "to the severest penalty of the laws."

The general's pledge did not reassure Daniel Butrick, who had remained behind even after the American Board of Foreign Missions wrote off the Cherokee cause. Outraged by the Treaty of New Echota, Butrick urged his congregation to vow never to worship again with the Ridges, Boudinot, and their allies until they confessed freely to the wrong they had committed. Since he was resolved to share the fate of his Cherokee parishioners, Butrick was on hand to witness the rounding up of the tribe. He paused as he recorded events of the day to make anguished appeals to his Redeemer for strength to face the ordeal ahead.

On one Sunday in May 1838, Butrick reported that a gang of Georgians had herded sixteen Cherokees into General Scott's fort and requested Scott's permission to whip them. Although Scott refused, Butrick knew that the drama had been staged to demonstrate the Georgians' anger over Scott's slow progress in rounding up the

Cherokees. They were warning him that they would not tolerate further delays.

Their tactic worked. On May 26, 1838, three days after the treaty deadline, Scott's troops began coercing the Cherokees into centers for evacuation. Or, as Pastor Butrick put it, the soldiers "now commenced that work which will doubtless long eclipse the glory of the United States."

General Scott had drawn up a logistical plan for collecting the Cherokees. In the eastern district, troops would seek out Indians from North Carolina and east Tennessee; in the central district, from most of Georgia; and in the western district, from Cherokee property in Alabama, Georgia's Dade County, and the remainder of Tennessee. Before his arrival, the federal government had built twenty-three military stockades throughout the Cherokee Nation. Scott intended for the militia to go out each day to capture all resisting Indians, hold them in the temporary stockades, and then deliver them to detention camps in Alabama and Tennessee.

The general's orders were devised for efficiency. He told his men to seize Cherokee women and children first since they would serve as hostages for bringing in their men to the stockades. Scott explained that his method would also have the laudable result of keeping families together.

Scott recognized, though, that some members of the tribe might present unique problems. "Infants, superannuated persons, lunatics and women in a helpless condition," he wrote, "will all, in the removal, require particular attention, which the brave and humane will seek to adapt to the necessities of the several cases."

Scott suggested that the Georgians should be praised "for their humanity and their tenderness." When the first captives arrived at his base, however, he found that one of his significant orders had been disobeyed. Scott had directed that any Indian judged by an army surgeon to be too sick to be moved should be allowed to remain at home with at least one family member and ample food and medicine.

And yet, on that first night, Scott was finding sick Cherokees mingling with their healthy fellow captives. Worse, the condition of even the healthy prisoners was distressing.

"Poor creatures!" Scott wrote later. "They had obstinately refused to prepare for the removal. Many arrived half-starved, but refused the food that was pressed upon them. At length, the children, with less pride, gave way, and next their parents."

Scott said he had never witnessed a scene of a deeper pathos. But his spirits were soon revived by the way his militia responded: "Some cheerfulness, after awhile, began to show itself, when, counting noses, one family found that a child, another an aged aunt, etc. had been left behind. Instantly dozens of the volunteers asked for wagons, or saddle horses, with guides, to bring in the missing."

Returning from Washington, John Ross confronted an inescapable decision. He heard painful stories about the sweep by Scott's soldiers across his territory and about the way Georgians were following the troops as they rounded up the Cherokees and confiscating their possessions and livestock.

Before the Cherokees could be led away, they saw their houses stripped bare and set on fire. Marauders were digging up graves to make off with any silver jewelry that might have been buried with a Cherokee corpse.

Those same accounts were appearing regularly in *Niles' Weekly Register,* founded by a Baltimore Quaker. Eyewitnesses told the paper that when the Cherokees were arrested, many of them were not allowed to gather up their clothes before they were herded away like cattle. As they went, Scott's soldiers were whooping and bellowing at their side.

At Ross's Landing, some Cherokees had refused to board for the river crossing. "The soldiers rushed in," according to one letter to the newspaper, "and drove the devoted victims into the boats regardless of the cries and agonies of the poor helpless sufferers. In this cruel work the most painful separations of families occurred. Children were sent off and parents left."

Scott's men were depending on shock and surprise to hold down any possible resistance, but they found the Cherokees as docile as John Ridge and David Vann had promised years earlier.

One old man, about to be marched off, asked for a moment with his children and grandchildren so they could kneel together and pray. Troops surrounding another house found that a woman had gathered up her infant and two children, pausing only to feed her flock of chickens before they fell into the hands of strangers.

Still other Cherokees, however, went on tilling their fields and playing the ball games, even as they knew that soldiers would be coming for them. A white farmer explained their mood: "They say they prefer death to Arkansas."

During the roundup, a young lieutenant called upon the Reverend Butrick and asked permission for two hundred Cherokees to stay on his land overnight before they pressed on to a camp two and a half miles away. Butrick welcomed them, and the exiles were prodded up the lane to his home shortly before sunset. It had been a rainy day, and the Cherokees were soaked but with no change of clothes.

Butrick felt he must get approval even to invite inside those mothers with children. When the lieutenant agreed, Butrick and his wife guided the women to their fire to warm infants whose lips were blue with cold. The clergyman had no doubt the children would soon die. He wept when they smiled and thanked him for his kindness.

As night fell, the guard captain addressed the Cherokees who had been allowed into Butrick's meeting house. He warned them that if they tried to escape, they would be shot. His interpreter explained that many Cherokees had dysentery and would have to go outside during the night.

The captain relented. All right, but they must call to his men and ask permission or they would be killed.

The next morning, the Cherokees were moved to a camp. As more Indians arrived at the Butrick mission, another young officer tried to ease their discomfort. He advised them not to wait there to be herded to the camps. If they went directly to General Scott's headquarters in New Echota, they would fare much better.

Butrick watched them set off, and he watched again two days later as they straggled back, wet and exhausted. The officer's commander had overruled him and insisted that the Indians return and follow the official procedure for marching to camp. This time it was not the infants who touched Butrick most deeply; it was a Cherokee woman who looked a hundred years old and who had been walking for two days and all night.

Protests were reaching a pitch that General Scott could no longer ignore, although he continued to absolve his troops. He claimed that the Indians themselves were to blame for their plight since, instead of obeying his orders, they were clinging to the false hopes spread by John Ross. In early June 1838, Scott wrote to General Nathaniel Smith, the Indian agent: "The distress caused the emigrants by their want of bedding, cooking utensils, clothes and ponies, I much regret, as also the loss of their property consequent upon the hurry of capture." But, Scott continued, "All this I am sorry for, and much of it, I am persuaded, was unavoidable, as far as the troops were concerned."

On June 16, a Baptist preacher named Evan Jones sent a different report from Tennessee to his church magazine. "The Cherokees are nearly all prisoners," Jones began. "The poor captive, in a state of distressing agitation, his weeping wife almost frantic with terror, surrounded by a group of crying, terrified children, without a friend to speak a consoling word, is in a poor condition to make a good disposition of his property, and in most cases is stripped of the whole, at one blow."

Cherokees with a comfortable living only a few days before had been reduced to abject poverty. Jones assured readers that "this is not a description of extreme cases. . . . It is the work of war in time of peace."

At one stockade, John Ross's ailing wife, Quatie, tried to comfort the frightened children. William Shorey Coodey, a Cherokee who had become friendly with John Howard Payne, described for Payne the scene around him as the first detachments moved west. "The teams were stretched out in a line along a road through a heavy forest, groups of persons formed about each wagon, others shaking the hand of some sick friend or relative who would be left behind . . . the day was bright and beautiful, but a gloomy thoughtfulness was depicted in the lineaments of every face."

John Ross responded to the misery on every side by assuming full responsibility for his people. On July 27, 1838, he informed Scott that his council had passed a resolution putting Chief Ross and his Washington delegation in charge of "the entire removal & subsistence of the Cherokees."

Scott readily agreed to Ross's request that he be given the months of September and October to get ready. An extended summer drought had already made further migration impossible until after October's annual rains. But in negotiating with the Cherokee Council over the necessary funds, Scott ran into angry protests from white shipowners and other merchants who saw their lucrative contracts disappearing. Although they vilified Scott, he held to his commitment to the Cherokees.

On his side, Ross supplied a detailed breakdown of the expenses he anticipated for transporting at least fifteen thousand Cherokees. His goal, he said, was "the comfortable removal of our people." Ross calculated that it would require one wagon for the possessions of four or five families, perhaps twenty persons. That would involve "bedding, cooking utensils and other indispensable articles." To the list of rations that Washington had drawn up, his tribal council added sugar and coffee. Then they realized that earlier estimates had neglected soap and added three pounds for every one hundred rations, at fifteen cents a pound.

Ross drafted a contract that called for his brother Lewis to supply those rations at a rate two cents a day less per person than the eighteen cents Sam Houston had requested from Andrew Jackson. Lewis Ross was expected to deliver at various points along the removal route "one pound of Fresh Beef or Pork, or three quarters of a pound of Salt Pork or Bacon, three half pints of corn meal, or one pound of wheat Flour (and if any point on the route it should be impracticable to procure either Flour or Meal, the said Lewis Ross is permitted to furnish in lieu of the Ration of Flour or Meal Three half pints of Corn) also four pounds of Coffee, eight pounds of brown sugar and four quarts of Salt to every hundred Rations."

Animals making the journey had their own fee schedule. Each horse, ox, or mule was allotted forty cents per day for corn, oats, and hay.

Possibly because his brother would be the supplier, Ross concluded that it was "our anxious wish in the management of this business to be free at all time from the imputation of extravagance."

Even so, Washington's commissioners in New Echota protested that there had been no publicity and no competitive bidding. They cited a complaint from dissident Cherokees that Lewis Ross's contract could "make the enormous profit of $180,000."

Agreeing with the criticism, Scott wrote that he had contacted "a company of highly respectable citizens"—white suppliers—who offered terms that would shave a hundred thousand dollars from Ross's estimate. Scott complained that he had authorized only *reasonable* expenses and was disappointed that Ross's council had "thrown away $180,000" of the Cherokee Nation's money.

After three days of brooding, John Ross responded on August 25, 1838, that Scott's letter "has produced in our minds the most painful feelings" and hardly reflected "the repeated instances of magnanimity and humanity which has characterized your intercourse with our people." Ross agreed that competition for the contract would have attracted white bidders but to be removed by them "was utterly abhorrent" to the tribe's feelings.

He rejected Scott's claim of a $180,000 profit. "It seems strange that these economical projectors should have maintained a dead silence about these great savings until the business of emigration was turned over to the Cherokees."

Buttressing Ross's argument was the offer white speculators had made to his brother. They would pay Lewis Ross forty-five thousand dollars immediately if he would turn over to them his contract for supplies.

When Ross and his committee recalculated costs, they found that their original estimates had been not too high but too low, and they brought Scott around to their figures. Before Ross took charge, the federal government had already run through the six hundred thousand dollars specifically set aside for removal. During the past June, however, Congress had allocated another $1,047,067 to pay the balance of the costs.

On August 31, Scott forwarded to Ross an order from Secretary Poinsett that "the whole cost of removal"—amounting to about sixty-six dollars for each Cherokee to be deported—should be paid to Chief Ross and his council.

14 · Daniel and Elizabeth Butrick (1838–39)

While Scott and Ross were haggling over costs, Daniel and Elizabeth Butrick visited Cherokee prisoners in their stockades and deplored what they found there. When they came upon the very old and infirm, the Butricks asked permission to bring them to their own house for warmth and nourishment.

Cherokees kept trying to escape in groups of ten and twenty but quickly became famished from the lack of food. The Butricks were told about fugitives who attempted to cross the river not far from the government boat they were trying to evade. When a soldier approached, they fled, leaving behind a woman who "was very sick, unable to sit up." The soldier discovered her "and kicked her in the side and drove her into the boat," but she soon disappeared and was presumed dead.

"It is said," Butrick wrote in his journal, "that many old women, driven in this company, cried like children when they started, saying they never could live to walk that journey in this hot season. But their cries could not be heard. They were driven on."

At the camps, Butrick encountered a hostility he had not expected. Some Cherokees refused to shake his hand, and he learned that they had been convinced that Samuel Worcester and Elizur Butler, while in prison, had drafted the New Echota treaty that John Schermerhorn then circulated. Butrick protested the canard and assured everyone that Butler had papers that would exonerate him.

"The Trail of Tears"

Other troubling events at the camps were due to Cherokee habits that Butrick had been fighting for years. He believed that preventing Cherokee leaders from enforcing their own laws had resulted in card playing and heavy drinking. He had watched white gamblers "strolling through the country, seeking whom they could destroy." As a result, "gambling spread like wild fire throughout the country," and it was white men who were pushing the sale of liquor.

Widespread drunkenness on Saturday nights led every week to murders. Dispassionately, Butrick recorded the fate of a young Cherokee—"engaged in a drinking frolick"—who went to ask his sister for money. When she refused, he stabbed her to death. "He was seized and bound, but two of his brothers, being enraged at the death of the sister, sprang upon him with clubs, and beat him to death."

Butrick was describing the conditions that had persuaded Boudinot that if the Cherokee did not move west, they would be destroyed by the rot in their own community. The missionary saw young people in the tribes treating the Bible, the Sabbath, and the clergy with contempt. He grieved that they had become "the Voltaires of the present age."

For Butrick, however, the worst offenders were the soldiers. He filled his journal with sexual assaults, past and present, against Cherokee women—a young married woman had been raped by Scott's soldiers and was now an outcast to her family. Another woman, traveling with her grandmother and younger brother, was kidnapped by two soldiers and raped by one of them while his companion fought off her frantic relatives. "After abusing her in this manner as long as they wished," Butrick wrote, "they took her to a vacant house near by and frightened her friends away, and it was not, I believe, till the next day that she was permitted to wander, in shame, to her house."

And always the deaths. Butrick counted them up by the twos and threes he witnessed and added reports of others that he had received from the stockades and from earlier migrations. "We understand that a letter has been received from a physician in Waterloo saying that one thousand of those who were sent in the fore part of the summer to the West, are dead.

"The question occurs whether these thousand deaths may not be viewed in the light of deliberate murder?"

The suffering around him unleashed in Butrick a biting sarcasm. He likened the white agents who had skimmed off money from the congressional allocation to hunters who chased "a little trembling hare in the wilderness, merely to take its skin, and send it off to broil in the scorching deserts of the West."

He concluded, "O how Noble! How magnanimous! How warlike the achievement! O what a conquest! What booty! How becoming the glory and grandeur of the United States!"

On another day, the sight of two Cherokee children being buried aroused in Butrick a fierce vision: "Suppose the President of the United States had ordered his most mighty officers to go to every house and measure every infant under four years of age, and every old person over sixty, in order to make the resident willing to forsake the inheritance of their fathers, and leave it a booty to robbers, how glorious would he appear!"

Butrick knew who deserved the blame: "The plan for getting the Cherokees away, if I mistake not, originated in the mind of General

Jackson as early as A.D. 1818," and it was adopted when Jackson became president "with none to put it down."

Butrick also condemned Jackson for tolerating slavery. His missionary service in Georgia had confirmed Butrick's view that "there is no mercy in slavery. The kind master is a tyrant and a usurper." Every day the scene around him furnished new evidence. Butrick wrote of a slave named Nanny, who belonged to a white man he knew. Since Nanny's ninety-year-old mother could no longer work, she wanted to take the old woman to live with her and her brother, Peter.

But useless as the woman was to him, her owner demanded thirty dollars to release her. The brother and sister, slaves themselves, worked at extra jobs to scrape together the price and "had the pleasure of saving their dear mother from the shackles of slavery before she died." But Peter could not take satisfaction for long. Butrick learned that he and his wife were then "sold to Negro speculators."

On August 27, 1838, Butrick got word that Chief Ross had given permission for him and his wife to go west with any detachment they chose and draw their rations along the way as though they were a Cherokee family. That show of acceptance elated Butrick: "This is all we could desire."

The problem, however, continued to be the lack of rain. "The Chickamauga creek is probably lower than it has ever been known to be by the oldest person living."

Butrick and his wife had chosen to travel with the party led by Richard Taylor, the man who had interceded for them with Ross. Their northern route would begin at the Brainerd mission west of Calhoun, Tennessee, and head up through Kentucky, southern Illinois, Springfield, Missouri, and south to Fayetteville, Arkansas, and across the border into Oklahoma.

Waiting for the expedition to start meant that Butrick received requests every day from Christian Cherokees for his presence and prayers. He often arrived at a cluster of families only to find that their child or grandfather had already died. They were living with "only a few barks overhead, though they have been accustomed to warm houses." The coarse food available to them was inedible by their sickest persons, and because of their fear of white people, especially doctors, they were trusting to tribal remedies that were ineffectual against the diseases sweeping the camps.

As word of hardships on the trail filtered back to Butrick, he had entertained—and deplored—a "wild" thought: Perhaps he could scrape together the thousand dollars that would allow him and Elizabeth to "purchase a decent carriage and go in good style to the west." But rereading one bracing passage from John Bunyan's *Pilgrim's Progress* quickly reminded Butrick that he must shun Mr. Money Love. "And may God help me to keep my resolution."

By October 2, 1838, the remaining six hundred members of the Treaty Party awaiting emigration were angry over the better terms that John Ross had negotiated for his faction. Led by John Adair Bell, Stand Watie's brother-in-law, they complained that General Scott was assigning twenty persons to each of their wagons, too many for comfort, and demanded that he cut the number to twelve—fifteen at the most. Scott was eager to accommodate the Cherokees who had accepted Washington's terms and agreed to Bell's conditions.

Scott also assigned a twenty-six-year-old lieutenant, Edward Deas, to accompany the Bell expedition. West Point had accepted Edward at the age of sixteen after his father had squandered the family estate, died, and left his wife and six children destitute. Upon graduating fifteenth in a class of forty-five, Deas was assigned to the Indian Removal.

For his first trip west, Deas's small party had left Georgia in April with Cherokees who agreed to travel by water despite the tribe's innate fear of drowning. When the keelboat he was towing was splashed by water from the Ohio River, the Cherokees panicked, convinced the craft was sinking. Since nothing he said could reassure them, Deas decided that his steamer, the *Smelter*, was large enough to accommodate everyone.

Weighing his passengers' baggage, Deas found that the Cherokees had brought far more belongings than army regulations stipulated. But since they had carried their possessions that far, "it appeared just, and I considered it my duty" to transport the goods to the journey's end.

When his detachment reached Cherokee territory on May 1, 1838, Deas took a muted pride in the fact that only two Indians had died on the river—both children, and both sickly before they left home.

Deas had concluded that "there is never any difficulty in managing Indians, when sober, provided they are properly treated." But "the infamous traffick of whiskey invariably results in rioting, fighting or disorder of some kind." At such times, Cherokees showed their "feelings of hostility."

Deas made another two-week trip the following month before he returned to accompany John Adair Bell in October with a larger detachment that would include John and Quatie Ross.

On October 4, Daniel and Elizabeth Butrick at last left Brainerd—"perhaps never to return"—and set out for a Cherokee camp. Their first night away from home was rendered sleepless by the "almost constant yells of drunkards" who were going to and from "a whiskey shop set up by a white man to ensnare the poor Indians."

On the first Sabbath, Butrick made a forlorn attempt to kindle hope by preaching from the text "There remaineth, therefore, a rest for the people of God."

Many Cherokees still refused to deal with General Scott's office, even though they were due reimbursement for property they were forced to leave behind. They felt that taking the government's money lowered them to the level of the Treaty Party. Others who overcame that sense of shame and went to apply for the money might be turned back by Scott's underlings, who said the general would receive only those Cherokees who could demonstrate that they had permission from a chief in their camp.

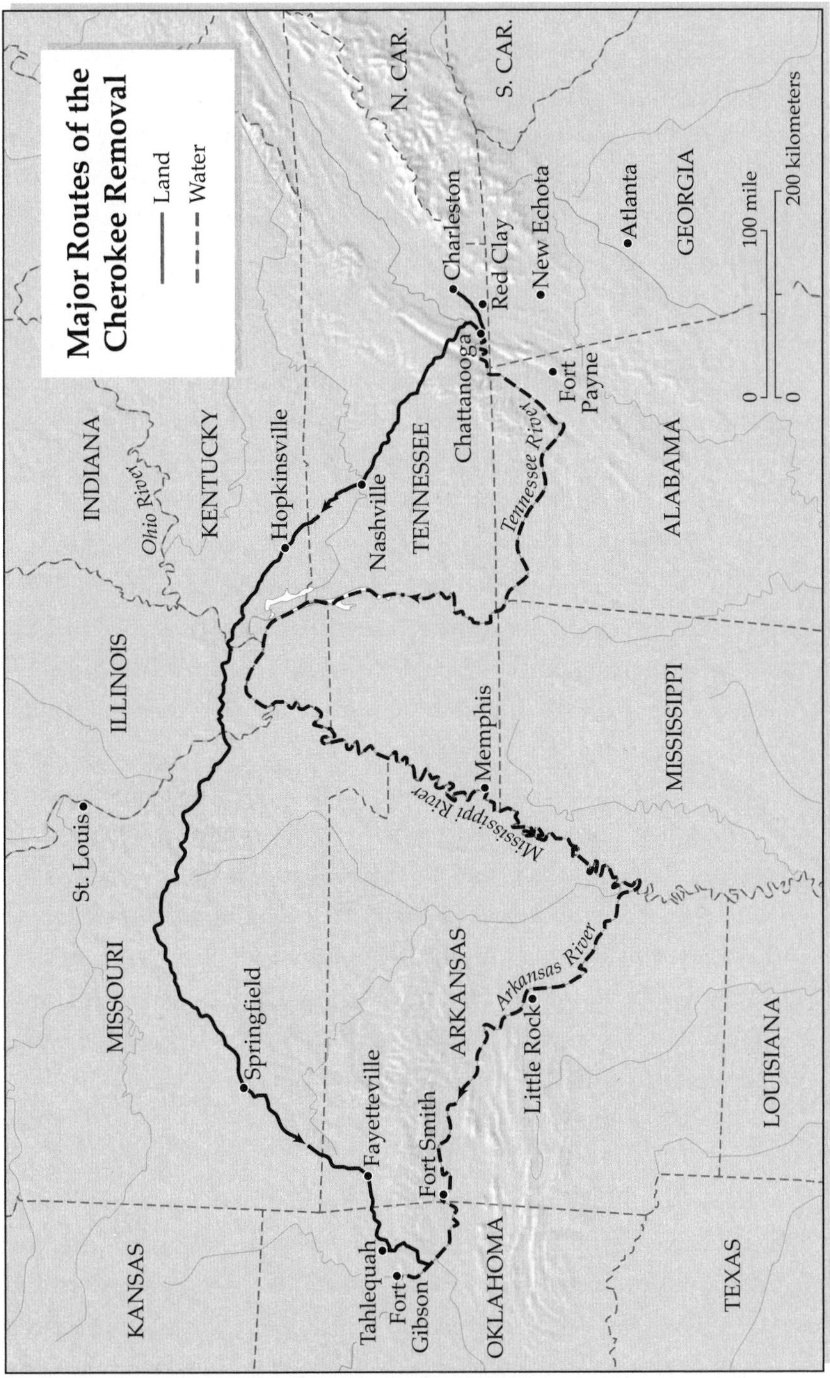

Routes of the Cherokee Removal

Once in a great while, a moment among the prevailing misery raised Butrick's spirit. He visited a Cherokee he called Brother Hawk, who was near death. Two weeks earlier, the missionary had been distressed to find how frightened Hawk had become at the prospect of dying. But now his mood had changed and he wished only to be with his Savior. Hearing of Hawk's new resignation, Butrick wrote, "I could but weep for joy."

After suffering through the nights of drunkenness and blasphemy around them, Butrick assembled a group of Christian Cherokees and adopted a set of resolutions for their upcoming journey: "While on the road they would spend the Sabbath in the worship of God, as far as practicable. They would follow their spiritual inclinations in choosing their home in the west. They would not unite in Christian fellowship with those who had made, signed or executed the New Echota Treaty, without a confession on their part, & they could not recognize Mr. Schermerhorn as a minister, or even as a common Christian."

Reflecting on the division within the tribe, Butrick harked back to the time when Elias Boudinot returned from Cornwall before his marriage and went to a ball play on the Sabbath. Sometime later, when Boudinot had been about to speak at a church in Carmel, Butrick urged him to acknowledge the sin. Butrick had not been in the congregation that day, but he heard that Boudinot had said nothing about his lapse.

From that, Butrick concluded that no one who favored the Treaty of New Echota could ever have had "any true love of God."

When the Butricks finally started on the first leg of their journey on November 1, 1838, the first omens were not good. They had gone only a few miles when one wagon and five horses nearly sank in a river. They then encountered an obstacle even worse—a fence that a white farmer had built to keep the Cherokees from taking a shortcut through his pasture. With Richard Taylor traveling at the rear of the procession, it was left to Butrick to plead with the man. Butrick offered reimbursement for any damage to his property, but "he swore we should not pass through his field," and the caravan was forced to make a long and cumbersome detour.

Being on their way did not end the profane revelry of the camps. When the Butricks settled in for the night, they found that "on one side was a Cherokee by the name of Big Dollar, who had a company with him singing, fighting & yelling almost all night long, and on the other side was a white man by the name of Hog, with another white man from the neighborhood, as I suppose, who were drinking & swearing.

"O the awful oaths we were obliged to hear from their mouths. We could scarcely sleep at all the whole night."

The next evening, Butrick pitched his tent far from the others and "told the people plainly that we would not hear the Name of the Blessed God thus impiously profaned, if we could possibly avoid it." Passing a quiet night, Butrick and Elizabeth prayed together "that the Lord would never shut us up with his enemies."

The ferocity of Butrick's faith could make him seem priggish, especially to those Cherokees who had not converted to Christianity. Other white men might also deplore the prevailing drunkenness but were less shaken by it. Dr. W. J. J. Morrow, a physician traveling with a different detachment, recorded that he, too, was kept awake by the Cherokee roistering. And yet his entry was laconic. He wrote simply, "Many Indians got drunk."

And with the skies clear and calm, Doctor Morrow's spirits were not oppressed by his surroundings: "Did not sleep much. The girls and boys talked and laughed all night. A fine, pleasant day."

The difference was that Butrick's sanctimony had sustained him through twenty bleak years of frontier life. Doctor Morrow was content to minister to Cherokee bodies. Pastor Butrick felt compelled to save their souls.

As the Butricks' detachment moved west, the roundup of resisting Cherokees was winding down. Scott's men had disarmed the tribe and collected mountains of weapons at his headquarters. With Ross now responsible for the move, Scott had cut back his troops to two regiments of the regular army—the Fourth Infantry and the Third Artillery. The remaining regulars were sent either back to Florida or to northern outposts, where a new crisis was developing along the Canadian border.

Accounts of outrages by Scott's men continued to circulate, although they could be hard to verify. One story told of a youth, terrified by the arrival of the militia, who began to run away. Ordered to halt, he continued to run and was shot in the back. Only then, the story went, was the young man discovered to be deaf.

Better documented was the fate of Tsali, a Cherokee called Charley in the white community. Early in the roundup, he was being herded to Fort Cass with his four sons and other relatives when a soldier grew impatient at the slow pace of Tsali's wife and prodded her with his bayonet.

At the moment, Tsali showed no emotion, and his docility led his captors to relax their guard. But Tsali had been speaking in Cherokee to the men in his party. That night, they got up from the ground and stabbed to death the soldier and a companion in their sleep. Tsali's family fled with him back into the Great Smoky Mountains of North Carolina, where they joined other Cherokee families hiding in caves and foraging for food.

Not surprisingly, the report filed with General Scott by a lieutenant who witnessed the attack claimed that it had been unprovoked. On hearing of the soldiers' murder, John Ross sent Scott a contrite letter, eager to convince the general that he had played no role: "As to the particulars which gave rise to it, I am wholly uninformed. But be they what they may, the act can only be viewed as one of those unfortunate individual occurrences which too often takes place among men of every nation, and for which the perpetrators can be held responsible to the laws of the land and to their God."

Hunting down the escapees would require more time and troops than Scott wanted to devote to the task. And yet, men who killed his soldiers had to be punished, and Scott saw an opening for a possible deal with the North Carolina Cherokees.

The general had been informed that holdouts in the caves were under the informal leadership of a respected Cherokee elder named U'tsala or Euchella, with their base somewhere in the mountain range above the head of the Oconaluftee River. Life there was precarious, and Cherokees were dying of starvation and exposure to the harsh November nights.

Scott contacted William H. Thomas, a white trader in his thirties who had grown up among the Cherokees and won their trust. Thomas was already negotiating on behalf of those Indians who lived outside the Cherokee Nation to allow them to stay on in North Carolina. He argued that their land was so rocky and steeply pitched that no white farmers wanted it.

Scott asked Thomas to put a proposition to Euchella: If he would surrender Tsali and the other men responsible for killing his soldiers, Scott would allow the rest of Euchella's fugitives to remain undisturbed in North Carolina. In fact, he would petition Washington for permission for them to make their permanent home there.

Traveling with a few Indians, Thomas had little trouble in locating Euchella. Counting on his good standing with the tribe, Thomas urged the chief to accept Scott's offer. If he did not, Scott would unleash his troops and not rest until every one of Euchella's band was dead or taken prisoner.

On a small scale, Euchella now confronted the choice faced by the Ridges and John Ross—give in or die. Euchella had pledged never to leave his land, but he had already seen his wife and a small son starve to death. He sent Thomas back to tell Scott that he accepted his terms.

Knowing now that Tsali was holed up in a cave near Deep Creek, Thomas asked Scott to hold off from sending troops to capture him. Disregarding Scott's strong recommendation that he travel with guards, he set off for the creek alone.

At the cave, Thomas found Tsali and his sons. As he reported on the agreement between Scott and Euchella, Tsali listened somberly. Then he said, "I will come in. I don't want to be hunted down by my own people."

Tsali came forward with his four sons, and they were taken with their families to appear before Winfield Scott. One son was a teenager, and Scott pardoned him on the spot. On November 25, 1838, the general ordered Tsali and his three adult sons tied to trees and assembled his troops to observe the penalty for Indians who killed American soldiers. The Cherokees refused blindfolds.

Scott left the actual execution to those of Euchella's men who had gone with William Thomas to track down the fugitives. Many Cherokees heard an inaccurate report that the fatal rifle shots had been fired by members of the Treaty Party, and that story became one more source of resentment against Boudinot and the Ridges.

With the Indians executed, Scott upheld his end of the bargain. The colonel who had been in charge of bringing Tsali to justice wrote to recommend formally that Euchella's followers be allowed to remain in North Carolina. They would live beside the Oconaluftees, a tribe already exempt from removal. One month after Tsali and his sons were shot, official permission was granted.

One of Scott's captains informed T. Hartley Crawford, as commissioner of Indian Affairs, that not only had the soldiers' murders been avenged but Tsali's surviving nine family members had been taken to a loading point to be sent west as prisoners. The captain added that John Ross now said his boat was ready for boarding by those Cherokees who chose to go by water.

In freeing his followers from their stockades, Ross had divided them into thirteen groups of roughly a thousand Cherokees each. Several parties were now stalled at Blythe's Ferry, waiting for rains to raise the Tennessee River. Throughout October and the first week of November, individual groups like the one with the Butricks made their way to landings in what became the town of Chattanooga.

To oversee the migration, Ross was staying for a time in Calhoun,

Tennessee. It was there that he learned that as many as fifty North Carolina Cherokees, always the most reluctant to leave, had slipped away to return to the Smoky Mountains.

Scott, who had agreed not to send troops to police the detachments, regretted his decision. He told his superiors that he had "lectured Mr. Ross rather sharply."

The Butricks' detachment had been covering about eight miles a day by the time its members reached the foot of the Cumberland Mountains. Aghast at the behavior of its white settlers, Butrick immediately named it the Vale of Sodom. Although a barrel of cider was rolled out—Butrick suspected it had been "mixed with whiskey, to make the Indians drunk"—he said that the outrageous conduct of the white townspeople shocked the Cherokees into sobriety, and they did not take the bait.

The next day, the group struggled up the steep mountain road to camp in a woods. At night, a cold rain penetrated the Butricks' tent and soaked their bedclothes. But many Cherokees with no protection at all were trying to sleep on the cold, wet ground. In the morning, anyone with a blanket found it covered with snow.

The expedition had been inching through the bitter autumn for five weeks. By the end of November, reaching Nashville, Butrick was deeply impressed by the town's beauty and its abundance of cedars. "I have seen no such place since I left Boston," he marveled. "Here are iron works, a college, penitentiary, female academy, court houses and several very handsome meeting houses, and many very elegant buildings."

Because he was not in charge of the group's finances, Butrick did not know that Nashville merchants were vastly overcharging for their goods and fiddling with the exchange rate for federal currency in order to swell their profits even higher.

Evan Jones, the Baptist missionary traveling with another detachment, noted that ferry owners and keepers of the toll roads hiked their prices whenever the Cherokee wagons came through. "On the Cumberland mountains," Jones complained, "they fleeced us, 73 cents a wagon and 12½ cents a horse without the least abatement or thanks."

In Nashville, an elderly Baptist clergyman volunteered the use of his large brick meeting house, and Butrick was grateful for not being forced to hold his service in the frigid open air. He saw the offer as another sign of God's kindness.

Several hours later, however, when a Cherokee lay down next to an open campfire, his clothes caught fire, and he died from his burns. That same week, a Cherokee woman gave birth to a son while two children died nearby after lingering illnesses. Death was now so commonplace that it merited a line in Butrick's journal but no lamentation.

Neither General Scott nor Chief Ross had expected that Scott would be leaving Cherokee territory before Ross did. But by early November, the general was pressing to return north. He had learned that his wife was suffering from severe bronchitis, and her doctors prescribed a long stay with her daughters in a European spa.

Scott wrote to Secretary Poinsett that he would have already turned over his command to Brigadier General W. K. Armistead, who had been serving in Florida, except for his worry that his successor would agitate for more troops to round up the remaining Cherokees. Scott said he could assure Poinsett that "no country was ever before so thoroughly swept of its red population—at one operation."

But Scott had gotten only as far as Nashville when he received orders from Washington to proceed immediately to the Canadian frontier, where Van Buren needed him to defuse a new crisis. Declining a public dinner in Tennessee to thank him for his success with the Cherokees, the general explained that "I am already hurrying, under the imperious call of public duty, to a distant quarter of the union."

While Scott had been distracted in Georgia, Canadian rebels had expanded their network of U.S. sympathizers along the border. When he reached Cleveland, Scott found that Canada's militia had foiled an attack on the town of Windsor, across the St. Clair River from Detroit, and had shot four of the insurgents.

Once again, Scott drew on his popularity and his high-flown but persuasive oratory as he traveled from Cleveland to pacify crowds in Sandusky and Detroit and in Buffalo and Albany. Then a threat of war arose between the state of Maine and Canada's province of New Brunswick over the rights to valuable forest land south of the St. Lawrence River. Scott was called upon to muffle the cries for war coming from Boston and Portland.

Drawing on his gift for diplomacy, Scott arranged a pullback of forces and presided over a pact that turned the issue over to negotiators from the two countries. Indeed, Scott's success was so impressive that the British representative suggested that his monarch honor the American general for his peacemaking prowess. In refusing, Scott cited the prohibition spelled out in the U.S. Constitution and contented himself with one more public dinner in his honor.

With the northern border tranquil again, President Van Buren could turn his attention to other impediments to his reelection in 1840. Lately one of them looked to be the popularity of a newly ambitious Winfield Scott.

With winter upon them, John and Quatie Ross joined the last detachment heading for Arkansas. It would be the smallest of the groups—about 230 people traveling by boat.

During the past spring, the first detachments had covered the route in about two weeks. But with blizzards and the perils of ice in the river, Ross was facing a hundred days or more.

His detachment sailed around Muscle Shoals, and in Tuscumbia

Ross paid ten thousand dollars for a steamboat called the *Victoria.* Ross left his party briefly to oversee the release of supplies for detachments held up by impassable roads in Missouri and again to mediate in a wrangle between a detachment leader and his assistant. Ross caught up with his boat at Paducah. Then a week later, Quatie Ross died.

John G. Burnett, a twenty-seven-year-old private in the U.S. Army traveling with the detachment, recalled later the night of the death of Ross's "beautiful, Christian wife." When Burnett was relieved from guard duty at midnight, he did not leave his post to sleep "but remained around the wagon out of sympathy for Chief Ross." At daylight, Burnett's captain ordered him to assist in the burial.

According to Burnett, "Her uncoffined body was buried in a shallow grave by the roadside, far from her native mountain home, and the sorrowing cavalcade moved on." Ross wrote, "My children became motherless, and the remains of Mrs. Ross left in a strange land."

Ross continued with his group by water to Arkansas, past Fort Smith to the mouth of the Illinois River. The detachment made the last forty-mile leg of its journey by wagon.

Looking back on the grave of Quatie Ross and the many like it, John Burnett had no doubt that Winfield Scott's soldiers "marched into Indian country and wrote the blackest chapter in the pages of American history."

By the time Ross had set off, the Butricks' expedition had already come within ten miles of the Ohio River. On December 7, 1838, they reached Cumberland College, a Presbyterian school housed in a stately building. A week later, an infant died—the fifteenth death since the expedition crossed the Tennessee River. But on a pleasant winter morning they passed out of the slave states and "reflected on the pleasure of landing where all were in a measure equal and free."

Freedom had not elevated the citizens' vocabulary, however, since "little boys in the streets had already learned to lisp the infernal language." And when a landowner forced the Cherokees to move on, even though it was the Sabbath, Butrick failed to hold a public service for the first time since he left Brainerd.

A few days later, Butrick's own health began to give out. He ran a high fever and took an emetic to induce vomiting. That, in turn, produced a sharp pain in his right side. It got steadily worse until the camp doctor was called and brought Butrick relief by bleeding him and putting a mustard-seed poultice over the pain.

As Christmas approached, Butrick became disillusioned with the residents of the Midwest. When their wagon broke down, the Butricks were forced to share a crude, one-room house with the workman who would repair it. The man was about sixty, drunk most of the time, and as illiterate as the other four adults in his household. They all attended services of a preacher Butrick considered a Schismatic Christian, who drank heavily himself.

"Thus far," Butrick wrote, "the citizens of Illinois appear more & more pitiable. They seem not only low in all their manners, but ignorant, poor, and ill humored. They have no slaves," he concluded, but "because they cannot have slaves, let their work go undone. We see nothing like schools in the country."

Butrick was also disturbed by the news he was receiving from the other detachments. One was stopped at the Ohio River and four others at the Mississippi, all held up by floating ice. Those groups totaled eight thousand Cherokees, beset by "a vast amount of sickness and many deaths.

"And yet all are houseless & homeless in a strange land, and in a cold region exposed to weather almost unknown in their native country. But they are prisoners." They might be led by their chiefs, but the chiefs themselves were in the grip of United States officers.

One of the hardest hit had been the detachment led by B. B. Cannon, whose company had left Calhoun the previous year. Setting out in mid-October, his party had reached Nashville two weeks later. Andrew Jackson was in town, and several Cherokees who knew him went to visit while Cannon issued corn, beans, and fodder.

Resuming the journey, Cannon continued to average fourteen to fifteen miles each day until sickness swept through his wagon train late in November. His traveling doctor recommended that Cannon suspend the march and remain in camp, and for a week the detachment continued to suffer.

On November 29, 1837, Cannon's men buried a surviving child of Corn Tassel, and when the convoy finally pushed on, there was scarcely room in the wagons for the sickest members to ride. In mid-December, the detachment doctor sent to Springfield for medicine, but on December 28, the party finally refused to go forward because of the persistent illness. At that, Cannon gratefully turned the survivors over to a lieutenant from Fort Gibson and filed his final report.

Now, a year later, Daniel Butrick was haunted on the last day of 1838 by a paradox. What had accounted for the misery of the past twelve months? "As coming from God, we know it is just," he wrote. But what had the Cherokees done to the United States?

In Massachusetts, Ralph Waldo Emerson's friend Henry Thoreau had been pondering that question and had come to a conclusion not different from that of Jefferson or even Andrew Jackson. By insisting to live as hunters, Thoreau wrote in his journal, the Cherokees had doomed themselves. He blamed the tribe for not embracing the role of farmer, unaware of the Cherokees who had turned to farming and were being dispossessed all the same.

If they had grasped the plow handle more firmly, Thoreau concluded with certainty, "they would never have been driven beyond the Mississippi."

Butrick, who knew better, spent the last night of 1838 reciting examples of Cherokee suffering: "The year past has been a year of spiritual darkness." Not for the first time, the missionary reproached himself bitterly for letting day-to-day hardships divert him from his prayers. He had lacked, he wrote, "faith & love & zeal."

But the next day, January 1, Butrick's unquenchable faith had asserted itself. "Though we have been distressed on every side, yet we have not been destroyed." And he could thank the Lord for the fortitude of his Elizabeth. Before they left home, she had already been laid low by sickness, and yet "she arose first in the morning, saw to fires being made, and to all the domestic concerns of the house." Then she ran their mission school, which had boarded ten children.

Now for the past three months, "she has slept in a wagon or a tent, & been exposed to cold & wet and at present has to go forward again, and take care of me in my ill health, yet she had not sunk under her burdens." Her husband thanked God for sustaining her and also for not making their journey far worse. There had been no tempests to topple the trees that overhung their path, no flashes of lightning to frighten the travelers. Even the rains had not presented "any special inconvenience."

Some had fallen sick and died along the way, but Butrick preferred to think about those who had survived. "O thou dear Redeemer, do help us to praise Thee, and may thy kindness still attend us."

Later in the week, it appeared that Butrick had counted his blessings too soon. "My dear wife is now unwell, afflicted with ague"—chills from a malarial fever. "Her strength has been declining a number of days. I am also scarcely able to walk."

They struggled on. The drenching rains did not let up and January's weather turned unseasonably warm, which some in their group found debilitating. As Butrick visited the families, he saw many Cherokees who were newly ailing. An old friend known as War Club gave Butrick the bark from a slippery elm tree, which seemed to ease the missionary's bowel complaint.

As the detachment waited to cross the Ohio River, white settlers nearby had devised a new dodge for bilking the Indians. When members of a Cherokee group died, the local residents charged as much as thirty-nine dollars to bury them. If they came upon the corpse of a straggler, they held the body until the next detachment arrived, claimed they had just discovered the body, and demanded payment for a coffin and grave wrappings.

Butrick observed that "the citizens of this state seem thus far to display a more mean & niggardly disposition than I have ever found in any other part of the union."

After two weeks, Butrick's party finally moved on but only for fewer than five miles. Camping out, he was grateful for a quiet night with stars that "sparkled with a peculiar luster." Wind had knocked over an old tree, which supplied firewood that Butrick would have been too weak to chop. "My dear wife and myself are both troubled with a diarrhea. I have also been troubled with a swelling I feared would become dangerous."

The hardships of their travel were severe enough that when Butrick learned that a woman in the Hilderbrand detachment had been killed when a tree fell on her, Butrick thanked the Lord's mercy in allowing her to die while she was asleep.

By the end of January, the party had reached the banks of the Mississippi. Deeply awed, Butrick called it "one of the wonders of creation." Impressive in its own way was the sight of "a large, beautiful & grand steam boat. Neither my dear wife, nor myself had ever seen one before. Of course the appearance was quite imposing. We have long been looking forward to this river; and numbers who crossed the Ohio with us have not lived to arrive at this."

Leading another detachment, George Hicks wrote to a Moravian bishop in North Carolina as he waited twenty miles from the Mississippi for their river crossing. Although Hicks's detachment had been among the last of the thirteen to leave overland for the west, delays by the Butricks' party had put him ahead of them on the trail. Hicks had attended the Moravian church with Boudinot and John Ridge but had opposed removal, and Ross's Cherokees forgave his past associations.

"The fall & Winter has been very cold & we have necessarily Suffered a great deal from exposure, from cold & from fatigue," Hicks wrote. He had started with 1,118 travelers but would lose seventy-nine, mostly women and children, before they reached their goal.

At one point, Hicks thought he was close to dying himself. He recovered sufficiently to continue with his group as they waited for the floating ice to melt and allow them to ford the river.

When the Butricks succeeded in crossing the Mississippi safely, they stopped on its western bank while the rest of their detachment maneuvered past a vast sand bar that cut the river in two. Providentially, men from neighboring households invited the couple to stay with them until they could proceed. Butrick was sure the warmth and shelter had saved his wife's life and probably his own.

Getting the entire group across the river took three weeks, and the death toll continued to rise during that time—"one old Cherokee woman, one black man & three Cherokee children, making in all since we crossed the Tennessee River 26 deaths."

As they proceeded, Butrick was finding a network of clergymen, often Methodists, who would give him and his wife a place to stay. They could not accommodate the throng of Cherokees, however, who continued to camp in the rain and sleep on the ground.

During the next three days, the detachment covered more than thirty-six miles, urged on by John Ross, who met with the leaders of Butrick's party at Jonesborough. Because of the unforeseen delays—and, more important, unexpected expenses—Ross pressed them to push on as quickly as possible, even if that meant traveling on Sundays.

Butrick made a futile protest. "I reminded our Cherokee friends however, that the Lord is here and requires the same observance of the Holy Sabbath as when we are at home." He held firm and traveled ahead twenty-five miles the next Saturday in order to spend the following day quietly with another friendly white family.

On March 4, 1839, Butrick set down the cautionary story of a young man of mixed blood named Lewis Perdue who "had been unrestrained in wickedness and sought pleasure in all forbidden paths." He had been taken ill not long after the detachment crossed the Tennessee River:

"The physician being called, bled him, and it was said that the blood was so impregnated with whiskey as to emit a strong smell of it, as it flew from his veins. He had been intoxicated, it was said, for a number of weeks. At length sores gathered and broke, and worms, it was said, were taken out of the sores.

"He had two uncles and an aunt & many cousins in the detachment, but all left him to suffer; and for sometime before his death he went from one wagon to another begging permission to ride. Last Saturday night a Cherokee went to his uncle and notified him of the distressed condition of his nephew. The uncle then took him into his wagon . . . but the wagoner soon discovered that he was dead.

"The corpse, lying as it was, was carried on to the place of encampment, where a box was made of rough plank, and the remains were interred in the wilderness where we stayed."

In the days that followed, Cherokee children continued to die at a rate of one or two a day, although the March temperature had turned balmy enough that the Butricks wondered if they could soon switch to their summer clothes.

That same night, they were quickly disappointed by a pelting rain that turned to snow and covered the ground to their ankles. Swirling winds kept them from warming themselves by their fire, and Butrick told his wife for the first time that they might not survive.

When they managed to go seven freezing miles through a deep woods, they "arrived at a house which gave us great joy. I hastened to fasten the horse, and we hurried to the door, but on knocking, were told by an unseen voice, we could not warm by the fire, as the house was full, though I believe there were but a few persons by the fire." They camped instead on the bank of the Little Piney River.

The journey seemed to be winding down. The party traveled a desolate stretch along the Osage branch of the Gasconade River. In eighteen miles, they saw only one house. Butrick fretted about the spiritual trials to come when he must confront the Cherokees from the Treaty Party.

"We are now drawing near the Arkansas, that land of spiritual darkness, and I fear I am becoming more & more unfit for the holy warfare. O for an overcoming faith to enable me to withstand wickedness in high places, and obtain a complete victory over myself, the world & the Devil."

Approaching the end of their trail did not mean an end to the dying. On Sunday, March 17, Butrick wrote that just before his service "I visited a family, in which was a boy ten or twelve years old, sick with the bowel complaint. He extended his emaciated hand to take mine, & then pointed to the place of his extreme pain. Before our meeting closed, he was a corpse."

The next two weeks were hectic. A man named Parks, the detachment wagon master, wanted them to get on the road before the Hilderbrand group, traveling a parallel route, could cut over and get ahead of them on their road. To avoid the dust and mire of following behind, Butrick's group rose before dawn and secured the lead. The weather remained snowy and cold, and the Butricks' tent was blown down and their bed soaked.

Weighing the chance for a service the next Sunday, Butrick prayed "before another holy sabbath to be in the country to which we have been so long traveling. O how kind has the Lord been in preserving us thus far, on this tedious journey."

His entreaty seemed to be answered. On Saturday, March 30, 1839, the detachment reached the site presided over by a Mr. Woodhall, whose wife turned out to be a worshipper the Butricks had known. "This is the place of deposit," Butrick wrote, "& also the place where Mr. Taylor is to deliver the detachment over to the U. States officers, who are to supply them with provisions for one year. We arrived about noon, and made arrangements for a meeting tomorrow."

But when Sunday came, the missionary's plan was disrupted. "Mr. Taylor told me that the officers from Fort Gibson had sent word that they should be here today to take the detachment off his hands, and therefore he should not be able to attend the meeting.

"Thus by means of the U. States officers the first sabbath in the country must be profaned by almost every individual in the detachment. We had a meeting, however, and a considerable number of our Cherokee brethren attended. I endeavored to warn them of the dangers & temptations that await them."

On Monday, the first of April, Butrick could make his final entry. He reunited a child from the group with his father awaiting him in Arkansas. Afterward, he "gave our tent to an old Cherokee woman, who had none, & took our leave of the dear detachment with whom we had been wandering these five months past."

Private Burnett could not take his leave so easily. Half a century later, he was still waiting for justice. "Murder is murder, and somebody must answer," he wrote on his eightieth birthday. "Somebody must explain the streams of blood that flowed in the Indian country in the summer of 1838. Somebody must explain the four-thousand silent graves that mark the trail of the Cherokees to their exile.

"I wish I could forget it all, but the picture of six-hundred-and-forty-five wagons lumbering over the frozen ground with their cargo of suffering humanity still lingers in my memory."

The Cherokees who survived the ordeal later wrote of it much as the Choctaws had done before them, as *Nunna Daul Isunyi*—The Trail Where We Cried.

Home of Chief John Ross

15 · Tahlequah (1839)

When John Ross arrived at the new Cherokee territory, he found that his former political enemies posed no immediate threat but that unexpected antagonisms had arisen elsewhere. The Ridges, Elias Boudinot, Stand Watie, and other adherents of the New Echota treaty had found it prudent to avoid politics in their new homeland and had been smoothly absorbed by the Cherokees who had come west in earlier years. But those Old Settlers—fewer than six thousand—worried about being swamped by John Ross's thousands of fresh arrivals.

The two factions agreed to meet in early June 1839 at Takatoka—or Double Springs—a spot four miles northwest of what would become Tahlequah, Oklahoma. Ross was eager to reassure the Old Settlers that his followers wanted only harmony. Although "being compelled by the strong arm of power to come here," Ross said in his formal address, his branch of the Cherokees "have not trespassed or infringed upon any of the rights and privileges of those who were here previous to themselves." As Ross saw it, both groups were equal.

He concluded by quoting the New Testament's Gospel of Mark that "a House divided against itself cannot stand." To underscore the point, he added a line from the "Liberty Song," which dated from the days when America's colonies were fighting their Revolution: "United we stand, divided we fall."

The Old Settlers' response indicated that Ross had achieved only half of his goal. Their chiefs assured him that they already considered the tribe's two branches fully united. But they would not agree that Ross could bring with him the system of laws created by the Cherokees in Georgia. Importing those laws would be "entirely repugnant."

Sounding like Georgia's white officials, the Old Settlers decreed that "to admit two distinct laws or governments in the same country, and for the government of the same people, is something never known to be admitted in any country, or even asked for by any people."

Ross replied to that rebuke by throwing their word back at them. What was "repugnant," he said, was "the attempt of a small minority to enforce their will over a great majority, contrary to their wishes." And yet, Ross added, he hoped "everything will yet be amicably settled" at a further joint meeting at the Illinois Camp Ground on Monday, July 1, 1839.

Before that date, however, a spasm of bloodshed doomed his attempt at reconciliation.

During that debate between the Old Settlers and Ross's group, Treaty Party members had continued to keep out of sight. But while the Old Settlers were rejecting Ross's overtures, a white man named Thomas Hindman reported seeing Major Ridge and his son huddling at the council grounds with Old Settler chiefs. Although Hindman granted that he could not hear their conversation, rumors quickly spread that a deal was in the works, that the Ridges were promising to use their influence to guarantee that the federal government would recognize only the Old Settlers, not Ross, as the legitimate Cherokee government.

The rumors did not trouble Samuel Worcester. With the Ross faction busy with building their new homes, Worcester believed that old hatreds would dissipate and a united Cherokee tribe could live in peace.

Worcester knew many Old Settlers were suspicious of his own motives, and if frictions arose he tried to mediate. When another missionary named Newton lost the Cherokees' confidence and was forced to resign, the Old Settlers commandeered his house and mission school. Since both were property of the American Board, the action was probably illegal. Worcester, however, sided with a colleague who defended it. "We must not blame the Cherokees too much," the man wrote. "Our government have taught them the lesson by a treatment of them in violation of all right, & on an incomparably larger scale."

From Boston, the American Board took an equally tolerant view. Its members admonished Daniel Butrick and other missionaries who had traveled with the tribe that, after "they fairly get through the anxiety & toil of removal," they should endeavor to bring a healing influence to bear on "the sore and troubled minds of the Cherokees."

To Worcester, that meant pressing ahead with his literary pursuits. Lumber being scarce and workmen unreliable, Elias Boudinot's house had not yet been finished, and he was still living with the Worcesters. He and the clergyman passed their evenings translating Bible chapters into Cherokee.

Early on Saturday, June 22, 1839, Boudinot was walking the quarter mile from the Worcester house to the lot where his own house was being constructed when he was accosted by three Indian men. They needed medicine, they said, and asked his help. Since Boudinot had been put in charge of the tribe's store of remedies, he agreed and set off for the mission house. Two of the men walked at his side, the third trailed behind.

They had gone only a short distance when carpenters working at Boudinot's house heard him scream with pain. Rushing to his aid, they found a knife in his back and his skull split open by seven gashes from a hatchet. The murderers had run to a nearby woods where men on horseback were waiting for them.

Boudinot was still alive when Worcester and Delight Boudinot reached his side, but he could not speak and was dead within moments.

The carpenters told a Choctaw working in a nearby field to jump on Worcester's horse—named "Comet" for his speed—and race to warn Stand Watie.

When the messenger reached the store that Watie was operating, he saw several men from Ross's antitreaty faction loitering in front. Calling Watie outside, he bargained loudly with him over the price of sugar while whispering his warning.

Watie returned inside, slipped out a back door, and rode Comet to Worcester's house. Hurrying to the corpse, he lifted the sheet and regarded Boudinot's mutilated face. Solemnly, he promised a reward—men disagreed later whether he had said a thousand dollars or ten thousand—for the names of the men who had killed his brother.

Samuel Worcester, too, was inconsolable. He had spent years seated side by side with Boudinot as they translated scripture. Whoever slew his Cherokee friend, Worcester said, "have cut off my right hand."

That same morning, twenty-five men on horseback and armed with rifles surrounded John Ridge's house at Honey Springs. Three of them dismounted and pried open his front door. They entered quietly, not wanting to alert Ridge's family or his sister-in-law and her husband, who were staying the night.

When they located Ridge asleep, one of the men cocked a pistol and pulled the trigger. It did not fire. They seized Ridge and tried to pull him from the bed. Although he was slightly built, Ridge managed to fight them off for several minutes before they could carry him out to his yard.

By now, Ridge's wife and children were awake and screaming. His assailants had agreed beforehand that they must stop their ears against his arguments for mercy. They deliberately shouted to one another to increase the din and shut out Ridge's pleading.

At the door, other men brandished their rifles to stop Sarah Ridge from running to her husband's side. She saw men holding Ridge by his arms and waist as the designated assassin raised his knife and struck.

He stabbed Ridge methodically twenty-five times, once on behalf of every conspirator looking on. To finish the job, he cut Ridge's throat. Ridge's body fell to the ground, and each of the twenty-five lined up in a single file to kick it.

As they remounted and rode off, Sarah raced to Ridge and found him barely alive. Blood choked his tongue and stopped him from speaking. His twelve-year-old son, John Rollin Ridge, had also seen the attack through the morning gloom and watched his father die.

Ridge's body was wrapped in a sheet and carried into the house. Already his face was pale from loss of the blood that fell drop by drop to the floor. Sarah Ridge sat beside him, hands clasped. Ridge's mother, her loose white hair hanging to her shoulders, cried out to the Great Spirit to give her strength.

Ridge's other children gathered, hardly comprehending what had happened. As the news spread, neighbors came to commiserate, but young John Rollin, a poet in the making, asked himself how many of the mourners had been part of the conspiracy, how many were smiling inwardly to see his father's corpse. With the intensity of a twelve-year-old, he felt that the scene "might make one regret that the human race had ever been created." Truly, the moment "has darkened my mind with an eternal shadow."

Killing Ridge had whetted the conspirators' appetite. They rode south to Beattie's Prairie, where one of John Ross's friends had a hot beef breakfast waiting for them. As they recalled their exertions, a man named Joseph Speak bragged that his had been the knife to deliver the deadly blow.

The morning brought out a third band of assassins. Major Ridge had gone overnight to Cincinnati, Arkansas, to check on a sick slave. Along his return route, his enemies rigged an ambush a mile inside the Arkansas line, at a point on the road near White Rock Creek. From behind trees and bushes, their gunfire picked off Ridge easily as he rode past.

He fell from his saddle with five bullets in his body. His young black servant raced off to alert settlers in nearby Dutchtown. They recovered Major Ridge's corpse and buried him in a small cemetery just inside the new Cherokee Nation.

Sarah Ridge had sent a runner to warn her father-in-law, but the man came back to say that he had been too late.

The Treaty Party's first instinct was for revenge, and their inevitable target was John Ross. In fact, Ross's son, Allen, had been one of the conspirators. But his assignment was to stay close to his father and prevent him from learning in advance about the plot. That, at least, was Allen Ross's version of events some years later.

He said that the leader of a secret meeting had read out the law that John Ridge had first written down for the tribe in 1829, the law that forbade unsanctioned sale of tribal land. When he finished, the conspirators ruled that the Ridges, Boudinot, Watie, and their faction were guilty of signing the Treaty of New Echota.

Forming into three groups, the men drew names from a hat to see who would do the actual killing. Several of them tied on neckerchiefs that they could raise to hide their faces.

Delight Boudinot, in her grief, did not want John Ross killed to avenge her husband. When Ross sent his brother-in-law to hear from her directly what had happened, she quoted Stand Watie's threat and urged that Ross leave his house at once.

John A. Bell, James Starr, and other signers of the New Echota treaty did the same. They fled immediately to Fort Gibson, southwest of Tahlequah in the new Cherokee Nation, to be protected by the fort's commander, General Matthew Arbuckle.

Ross was angry later in the day when he learned that Arbuckle had welcomed the Treaty Party refugees. It turned out that John Ridge had once warned the general that when Ross arrived in Oklahoma, he might cause trouble.

Ross asked a tribal clerk to draft a protest to the general for not upholding the army's neutrality. The young secretary was too upset to write, however, and Ross wrote the letter himself and sent it to the fort with a white soldier who had accompanied Ross's detachment during the removal.

Ross could offer only sketchy details of Boudinot's assassination, but he included the warning he had received from Delight Boudinot. "Why I am to be murdered without guilt of any crime—I cannot conceive." Ross called on General Arbuckle to prevent further bloodshed until an "unbiased investigation might be had in the matter."

Arbuckle responded promptly that Ross should also come to Fort Gibson for protection. In thanking the general, Ross said he had decided he was safer remaining in his own house than in trying to reach the fort. Ross said that his friends were gathering to ward off Watie's expected attack, but he asked Arbuckle to send U.S. Army troops as well.

By then, Ross had learned that John Ridge had also been killed. If the report was true, he wrote, "no one will regret the circumstances more than myself." He alerted Arbuckle that if he did come to Fort Gibson, he would be escorted by two hundred or more armed men. They would be intent only on his safety and would have "no improper feelings" toward the U.S. government. Better yet, however, why not call a meeting of Old Settler chiefs and Arbuckle's representative near Ross's home at Park Hill, since Ross had already scheduled a unity convocation there.

The Old Settlers did not trust his invitation. From Fort Gibson on June 28, 1839, they denounced Ross and his "late Emigrants" for usurping the authority of the Cherokee Nation. Firing back, Ross urged William Armstrong, Van Buren's superintendent of Indian affairs, to visit his assembly and see for himself that "peace and tranquility are restored on a permanent basis."

General Arbuckle was disgusted by that exchange. He was even more dismayed to hear that white settlers in Arkansas feared an Indian uprising and were leaving the state. The menace was also causing those residents who stayed to organize vigilante committees to protect them from the Cherokees.

For his July 1 meeting, Ross now deployed his superior numbers. Close to two thousand Cherokees showed up at the Illinois Camp Ground. Asserting their control over the Cherokee Nation, they presented unyielding demands to the Treaty Party. Its members were required to appear before the convention within eight days and retract all threats of revenge for the killing of Boudinot and the Ridges. And for their "outlawry" in signing the treaty, they were barred from holding tribal office for five years.

That offer of amnesty brought forward only a handful of men, even after the eight-day deadline was extended indefinitely. Stand Watie announced that before he would sign the "infamous oath," he and his allies would rather "fall by the hand of the midnight assassin."

Over the next few days, Ross wrote often to Arbuckle to repeat assurances that his men posed no danger either to the Old Settlers or to the white residents of Arkansas. He persuaded Sequoyah to add his signature—as "Geo. Guess"—to a letter claiming that "our proceedings are altogether pacific and forgiving."

Ross's assurances came at a time when Washington was first learning about the Battle of Neches. On July 16, 1839, Texas Rangers and militia drove from their homes a band of Texas Cherokees who had crossed the Red River as early as 1819 to live in the area that would become the city of Dallas.

Sam Houston had concluded a treaty with those Texas Cherokees in 1836, guaranteeing the tribe a swath of land north to the Sabine River. When Mirabeau Buonaparte Lamar replaced Houston as Texas president, however, the Cherokees' fate seemed sealed; Lamar had once been personal secretary to Governor Troup of Georgia.

Calling the Indians "wild cannibals," Lamar vowed to remove them from Texas. But the Texas tribe was led by a militant chief whose mother was a Cherokee and whose father was a Scotch-Irish trader named Bowles, and he rejected the passive response of the Georgia Cherokees.

About seven hundred Indians fought back unsuccessfully against nine hundred Texans. Among the Cherokee dead was eighty-three-year-old Chief Bowles, whose corpse was scalped and hacked to pieces by Texas militia seeking souvenirs.

By September 12, 1839, Ross could address his tribal council from the new Cherokee capital at Tahlequah. He had won over enough Old Settlers to assert himself confidently as the tribe's principal spokesman, and for past wrongs by the United States he pledged to seek redress only through the U.S. courts. Ross also urged the passage of laws to prevent gambling and to forbid introducing liquor into the territory. When a new constitution was drafted, it duplicated the language of 1827, except that it called for a direct election for chief among all Cherokees.

Ross also laid before the council the applications of various clergymen, including Elizur Butler and Daniel Butrick, for establishing missions within the new territory. Ross welcomed the prospect, describing Butrick's conduct as always following "in the paths of peace, morality and religion."

The last issue to be resolved was the most explosive. General Arbuckle had written to demand that Ross turn over to him all men suspected of the three murders and threatened to dispatch troops to enforce his order.

Ross claimed that U.S. jurisdiction did not extend into Cherokee territory. He sent his brother Lewis to assure Arbuckle privately that the Cherokees had resolved the matter themselves. Federal troops, Lewis Ross warned, would meet with armed resistance.

When Stand Watie took a Treaty Party delegation to plead their case in Washington, he made a side trip to the Hermitage to enlist Andrew Jackson on their side. Jackson obliged him with a letter to President Van Buren that presented the division within the Cherokee Nation in a way that favored the Treaty Party.

Jackson granted that he was indulging in "strong language" when he denounced "the outrageous and tyrannical conduct of John Ross and his self created council." But Jackson also advised Watie to exhaust all peaceful avenues for bringing to justice the murderers of his brother and the Ridges. Only when those approaches failed would "the great and good Spirit smile upon your exertions by force."

At the same time, General Arbuckle was receiving instructions from Washington to tamp down the controversy. He devised a plan for reorganizing the competing Cherokee councils into one body, preferably one that would depose John Ross as its leader.

William Henry Harrison

16 · William Henry Harrison (1839–41)

The presidential election of 1840 was approaching, time again for Henry Clay to see his hopes dashed. He had turned sixty-two, but the weak competition among the Whigs suggested that the nomination was worth pursuing. Clay hoped to persuade Daniel Webster not to run since he had done so poorly four years earlier. And given Clay's distaste for generals who fancied themselves statesmen, he could dismiss William Henry Harrison as too dim to appeal to the intelligent Whig voter.

Certainly, President Van Buren himself looked vulnerable. With the economy still mired in depression, he seemed unlikely to appeal to a changing United States. He sent to political allies at home seventy-five pages of advice that he called "Thoughts on the Approaching Election in New York," which focused entirely on past campaigns. Rather than broaden his appeal to the nation's expanding working class, Van Buren urged fidelity to party principles.

Clay began his campaign by delicately suggesting to Webster that he could best serve his country and his party by withdrawing as a candidate. Webster was equally deft in refusing. Both men saw the peril in an open break and resolved to keep their relations civil.

Clay's boundless sociability had always guaranteed large dinner parties at his boarding house, followed by games of whist that lasted into the early hours. That made him an unlikely recruit for the Temperance

Society when its officers asked for his help in passing their agenda. At his most politic, Clay acknowledged that the temperance crusade "has done great good," but he balked at its coercive aspect. "No man likes to have, or ought to have, cold water or brandy, separately or in combination, put in or kept out of his throat upon any other will than his own."

Clay could afford to alienate the temperance vote. More serious was the resurrection of accusations about the "corrupt bargain" of 1824. A New Yorker wrote to alert Clay that he was being tarred with words like "bribery" and "corruption" and asked to hear Clay's defense. Clay's response blamed Harrison's camp for reviving the charge, and he accused nullifiers in the South of branding him an abolitionist.

To strike back, Clay consulted with such slave-owning colleagues as Senator William Preston of South Carolina. Clay was prepared to sacrifice the admiration of prominent Northerners like the poet John Greenleaf Whittier in order to blur his position on slavery. He promoted his equivocal stand as somehow brave and best for the country, and friendly newspapers printed Clay's declaration in capital letters: "I HAD RATHER BE RIGHT THAN BE PRESIDENT."

In a speech to the Senate in February 1839, Clay condemned extreme voices on either side of the debate. He abhorred slavery itself, Clay declared, and offered a capsule history of its practice. Then he changed direction and accused the abolitionists' zeal of setting their cause back half a century.

"The slaves are here," Clay noted pragmatically. "No practical scheme for their removal or separation from us has been yet devised or proposed."

The only answer was time. Clay concluded with an urgent appeal designed to mollify Southern voters: "I beseech the abolitionists themselves solemnly to pause in their mad and fatal course. Amid the infinite variety of objects of humanity and benevolence which invited the employment of their energies, let them select some one more harmless, that does not threaten to deluge our country in blood."

For the moment, Clay's speech served its purpose. John Calhoun rose on the Senate floor to praise him warmly for alerting the nation to the menace that the abolitionists posed.

Van Buren had also been sidestepping the slavery issue until a maritime incident drew him into the fray. In August 1839, the U.S. Coast Guard boarded the schooner *Amistad* off the coast of Long Island. Two Spaniards aboard said that the forty-nine slaves being transferred from Havana to another Cuban port had risen up, killed the captain and three crew members, and were intending to sail home with their four children and a black cabin boy.

Communicating as best they could, the slaves had demanded that the ship be pointed toward Africa, but their white prisoners duped the leader, Joseph Cinque, and sailed for the United States. Coast Guard crew disarmed the slaves and took the ship as salvage to New London harbor. The slaves were jailed and charged with piracy.

Overnight, the case became a political sensation. Whigs and their abolitionist allies took the side of the slaves. Van Buren's party branded Cinque and the others as murderers.

A slave owner himself, Secretary of State John Forsyth was committed to returning the slaves to their Spanish owner. To fulfill the promise Forsyth made to the Spanish ambassador, Van Buren's attorney general filed suit for possession of the slaves. The ambassador assured Forsyth that his government would make an example of Cinque to ward off future insurrections: Return the slaves to Cuba and they would be put to death.

Van Buren's administration was sure of a favorable ruling by the district court, and the U.S. schooner *Grampus* stood ready off the coast of New Haven to spirit away the slaves immediately.

But before they could be shipped off, New York abolitionists launched a protest campaign, and both the district and appellate courts ruled against the Van Buren position. As the case moved to the U.S. Supreme Court, John Quincy Adams, now seventy-three, agreed to defend the Africans. Even though Adams had never joined the abolitionist movement, he opposed slavery as an inhumane violation of the principles set forth in the Declaration of Independence.

Adams seemed to be allying himself with a losing cause. Public response suggested that most Americans considered their nation's laws to outweigh any natural rights. Nor was the prospect on the Court promising. Of the justices who would be hearing the case, five of them, including Chief Justice Taney, had owned slaves themselves.

As a result, Van Buren could reasonably expect that delay by the Court would resolve his political dilemma. Had he simply used a lower court's decisions to send the slaves back to Africa, he would have outraged his Southern supporters who wanted Cinque dead. Now the delay meant that the case would not reach the Court's docket until January 1841. Abolitionists had petitioned for bail, at least for the children, but were denied.

As he prepared his argument, Adams was acutely conscious of his heritage. In colonial times, British soldiers had fired into a crowd of rebellious Americans, and those killings had become notorious as the Boston Massacre. As a young lawyer, John Adams had defied public opinion and defended the redcoats.

Now his son appealed to his journal: "Oh, how shall I do justice to this case and to these men?"

Like Van Buren, John Ross was devoting his days to keeping his job. While he continued to press for money due the tribe for the removal, he was fighting back against persistent rumors that he had been involved in the Ridge-Boudinot murders. To General Arbuckle, Ross protested, "I am not answerable for the slanderous fabrications of designing Cherokees or vicious whitemen." He was even more irate that John Poinsett had involved himself in the affair, and he demanded from the secretary the names of his accusers.

As tribal chief, Ross was away from Tahlequah, heading a delegation to Washington. In his absence, Arbuckle continued to undercut him. He called a series of meetings with the Old Settlers designed to depose Ross, but he met with no success.

Two other Cherokee factions were also lobbying in Washington—Stand Watie for the Treaty Party and eight men representing the Old

Settlers—and those two blocs united to press Poinsett to recognize them as the Cherokee leadership.

But Ross had the support of wealthy eastern friends. They lent him the money that covered his expenses and allowed him to ask John Howard Payne to come down from New York to help in writing his petitions. Once again, Ross was counting on a change in the presidency. Any successor was certain to be more sympathetic than Van Buren.

Ross wrote to Payne that while the executive door "has been bolted against my admission into the presence of His *transitory Highness* of the White House," he might yet find an entrance through Congress for redressing the wrongs "wantonly inflicted upon the Cherokee people." On reflection, Ross decided that, even for Payne's eyes, that language was needlessly provocative, and he struck it out before he mailed the letter.

In appealing to Congress, Ross recounted horror stories from the removal—"children were abruptly severed from doting parents who never met them more." Most of his petition, however, protested Poinsett's refusal to recognize him as principal chief. Ross's sympathizers on the Committee on Indian Affairs censured the War Department, but the full House refused to make the committee's findings public.

Ross's position was unwittingly sabotaged in a private meeting between Poinsett and Ross's nephew, William Shorey Coodey, an Old Settler who now accepted Ross as chief. When Poinsett referred to the Ross faction as a "murderous majority," Coodey blew up and shouted that the Ridges and Boudinot were traitors under tribal law and deserved to be killed.

Appalled, Poinsett broke off all further talks with the Cherokees and refused to release any further annuities to the tribe until the feud ended.

To Henry Clay's chagrin, two military heroes had joined him as front-runners for the Whig Party's nomination. Not only was there the venerable William Henry Harrison, but Winfield Scott was riding the wave of his successes on the Canadian border. Clay responded with another backroom deal: In exchange for support from Senator John Tyler of Virginia, Clay would back Tyler for the vice presidency.

With the question of slavery dividing the nation, Tyler's career indicated that a man could also be divided within himself. He had inherited moral qualms from his father, John Tyler, Sr., who had voted against the Constitution in 1787 because it had authorized the slave trade to continue for another twenty years. And yet when the senior Tyler died, he bequeathed to his son thirteen slaves and, with marriage, John, Jr., added many more to work his fields and maintain his household. To raise money for his first U.S. Senate campaign, John, Jr., had sold a female slave even though she was a family favorite.

Once in Congress, Tyler claimed to be physically sickened by the sight of slave auctions in the nation's capital, and he tried, unsuccessfully, to have the practice ended. All the same, Tyler could hardly be counted an abolitionist. He opposed federal legislation to outlaw slavery and considered Northern abolitionists a self-righteous danger to the country. His opponents pointed out that they were also dangerous to Tyler's political ambitions.

Clay's presidential prospects seemed to get a boost when Daniel Webster saw his own chances evaporating and decided to sail for England. But Webster left behind a letter expressing a halfhearted backing for Harrison. Webster claimed that "our only chance is with General Harrison," although even that chance was "not a very good one."

On the other hand, John Tyler now pictured himself on the national ticket and was expressing "great solicitude" for Clay's nomination. By the time of the Whig convention in Harrisburg, Pennsylvania, in December 1839, Clay could count on a plurality of the delegates in the hall. Winfield Scott had been touted as an alternative to both Clay and Harrison, but when Scott's candidacy foundered, a clever manipulation of convention rules by the Harrison forces did the rest. The vote was 148 for Harrison, 90 for Clay, 16 for Scott.

Harrison's jubilant supporters offered the sop of the vice presidency to several of Clay's prominent friends, but out of loyalty each of the nominees withdrew his name. Finally, John Tyler, who had been observed with tears in his eyes when Clay was defeated, overcame his disappointment and accepted the nomination.

With that, the convention adopted an imperishable slogan: "Tippecanoe and Tyler, too." A sour Clay loyalist observed that "there was rhyme, but no reason in it."

Clay had been awaiting news from the convention at his boarding house in Washington. The first delegates, back by rail from Pennsylvania, found him there and informed him of his defeat.

Clay could no longer mask his disappointment. Shouting curses, he paced back and forth across his room, reviling so-called allies like Daniel Webster. "My 'friends,'" he said acidly, "are not worth the powder and shot it would take to kill them."

He was sure he was "the most unfortunate man in the history of parties." He had been urged to run for the office when he was certain to lose and now betrayed when he, or anyone else, was certain to be elected.

Clay's fury soon exhausted him. A few days later, he was in his usual debonair form at a dinner in his honor at Brown's Hotel. With every sign of aching sincerity, he offered a pledge and an exhortation: "If I have friends . . . if I have any one that loves me—I assure them that they cannot do me a better service than to follow my example, and vote heartily as I shall, for the nomination which has been made."

When the roar of affection died down, Clay went on to remind his audience that a public man showed his patriotism by sacrificing himself for his country. But for him there had been no sacrifice since his battle had never been with the other candidates. "No! We have been contending for principles." Everyone should tell his constituents to extend all of their energy to the cause of relieving "the land from the curse which rests upon it."

John Ross deplored Clay's loss of the nomination almost as bitterly as the candidate himself. Of the white politicians, Clay had seemed best disposed to the Cherokees. But any Whig would be preferable to another four years of Van Buren and his continuation of Jackson's policies. Awaiting the presidential election, Ross continued to petition John Bell, an influential Tennessee congressman, for support against General Arbuckle and for settlement of the tribe's overdue claims.

Ross was not alone in his discontent. He had arrived in the new Cherokee territory to find Chief Alligator of the Seminoles encamped there with his followers. Weary and frustrated, Alligator poured out his grievances: General Jesup had told the Seminoles, "Your gun is not worth carrying. Leave it. Your Great Father in Washington will order a new rifle to be presented to you when you reach the country which has been assigned to you in the West."

Chief Alligator also quoted Jesup as urging the tribe to leave behind "your old plows, hoes, axes and kettles." Again, "your Great Father will furnish you with new ones."

Nor was that all. "In your new county you shall live in peace, and be protected by the United States. An agent shall be appointed to attend to your wants and to represent your grievances, as in former times. There you will find the country abounding in game, which will enable you to supply your women and children with meat of the buffalo, the bear, the deer, et cetera."

When reality turned out to be very different, Alligator saw no better option than to turn to John Ross and ask that he present this statement to Secretary Poinsett:

"I am in the West—not one of the promises made to me has been fulfilled. I am poor and homeless. I find that all the lands South and West are owned by different tribes of red people and not a spot left for the Seminoles—but I am resting upon the lands of my good brethren, the Cherokees—that the country is scarce of game; and I have no gun to kill squirrels and birds for my children; no axe to cut my firewood—no plow or hoes with which to till the soil for bread—and no agent of the U.S. to whom to represent my wants and grievances.

"In this, my peculiar condition, I am perplexed to conceive the true cause why those fair promises have not been fulfilled—or, whether they were made only to deceive me."

Nearby in Tahlequah that spring, Samuel Worcester was lamenting his own loss, although he remained unshaken in his faith. Writing to the American Board in Boston, Worcester reported stoically on the death of his wife, Ann, in childbirth: "The Lord gave and the Lord hath taken away," he wrote. "Blessed be the name of the Lord."

Ann Worcester had no sooner delivered a healthy baby girl than she was seized by fatal spasms, and her funeral service was joined with the baptismal rites of the infant. Within a year, Worcester had done what was expected and married again. From among the willing candidates within his congregation, he chose Erminia Nash, stolid and pious, to raise his new daughter and five older children.

Replacing a wife proved to be easier than finding an assistant. When Worcester appealed to the American Board for help, David Greene wrote back discouragingly. He said that recruits in New England were dazzled by the challenge of converting hundreds of millions of Chinese. "Going to the Indians seems hardly worth the talents of any but very inferior men. I fear there is some pride in this."

As the 1840 campaign reached its climax, an unlikely political figure attracted national attention by backing William Henry Harrison. Soon after the Democrats nominated Van Buren for a second term, John Eaton broke with his party and endorsed General Harrison.

The years following the Eaton malaria had been largely successful for both husband and wife. On leaving the cabinet, John Eaton had published a book he called *A Candid Appeal to the American People,* in which he rebutted the accusations against Margaret and charged that the real motive had been to drive him from Jackson's side. He also settled scores with Duff Green, the editor who had once been his friend but who now "hates me beyond even the power to extend common justice" because Green had become "an instrument" of John Calhoun.

Jackson was said to have wept when he read Eaton's small volume, and newspapers nationwide called for a truce in the Petticoat Wars. After an unsuccessful run for the Senate in Tennessee, Eaton was appointed governor of the Florida Territory and installed Margaret in the governor's mansion.

The local Democratic Party leader was Richard Call, the captain who had once forced himself on Margaret. She was prepared not only to forget the past but to spare Call's wife any knowledge of the incident, and the two women became good friends.

After Eaton scored a political coup by negotiating a treaty with the Florida Seminoles, Jackson appointed him as the U.S. minister to Spain. In a short time, his wife became a favorite of the twenty-five-year-old Queen Consort Maria Cristina, regent for young Queen Isabella. By the time Margaret Eaton turned thirty-seven in 1836, she could claim to be the most influential foreigner in Madrid.

The political situation deteriorated in Spain, however, as Isabella's uncle, Carlos V, fought for the throne. The resulting tumult caused Eaton to ask Van Buren to recall him and recommend that he not be replaced. By the spring of 1838, Spanish roads were deemed temporarily safe for travel, and Maria Cristina sent a troop from her household cavalry to escort the Eatons to port. But Carlists blocked their route, and they ended up sailing from Paris.

Once home, Eaton encountered a different sort of obstacle. Van Buren did not offer him a new assignment. Outraged, Eaton opened a law office and took his revenge by endorsing Harrison. His switch in allegiance became more striking because Eaton insisted he would not accept an appointment in a Whig cabinet.

From the Hermitage, Jackson regretted Eaton's "ingratitude and depravity" and attributed his defection to heavy drinking. But Margaret Eaton's rehabilitation was complete. One prominent detractor had left the scene when Emily Donelson died of a hemorrhage in 1836 at the age of twenty-nine. Another, Floride Calhoun, was observed at least twice as a guest at the Eatons' house.

Like John Eaton, Clay was being asked to speak on behalf of the Harrison-Tyler ticket, even though he was bone tired and saddened by the death of the young wife of Henry, Jr., who had died ten days after giving birth. Clay knew he was required to make the appearances even if "self respect requires that I should not convert myself into an itinerant Lecturer or Stump orator to advance the cause of a successful competitor."

At a Baltimore rally, Clay reconciled with Daniel Webster and then rang changes on a famous line from Jefferson's inaugural address: "We are all Whigs, we are all Harrison men."

After that, however, the campaign swiftly degenerated into songs and slogans. To the Whigs, the Democratic president became "Martin Van Ruin." Harrison was reinvented as "Old Tip," and his lack of "a ruffled shirt" was rhymed with Van Buren being "a little squirt."

Inexplicably, the populist Democrats denigrated Harrison's backwoods manners in rhymes that also deplored his fondness for liquor:

Rockabye, baby, Daddy's a Whig
When he comes home, hard cider he'll swig
When he has swug
He'll fall in a stu
And down will come Tyler and Tippecanoe.

The Whigs turned that sneer into praise for Harrison as the log cabin candidate who enjoyed his home-brewed cider—a contrast with Van Buren's effete sipping of wine from silver coolers.

When staid Whigs protested that their party had sunk to the frontier vulgarity of the Jackson Democrats, Clay defended the tactics as the only way to defeat the forces of "Corruption, Demagoguism and

Humbuggery." Harrison "may not fulfill all our hopes," Clay wrote privately, but he would return Washington to the rule of law.

Andrew Jackson was bemused by the Whigs' appropriating his party's tactics. He denounced their campaign as proof that the Whigs felt contempt for the masses and were patronizing the average man. Then, outraged by a speech Clay gave in Nashville a few miles from the Hermitage, Jackson brought up again the sixteen-year-old accusation of a bargain between Clay and John Quincy Adams.

By contrast, John Tyler's campaign was drawing little interest. While Harrison would be sixty-eight on inauguration day—the oldest president ever to be sworn in—he seemed healthy enough. Only Daniel Webster seemed to have an intimation to the contrary when he remarked that Harrison would certainly be elected "if an all-wise Providence spares his life."

When Tyler did express a political opinion, the Whig leadership was rarely pleased. After suggesting that a new Bank of the United States charter would require a constitutional amendment, Tyler was told that he had risked party unity and should let the campaign proceed with its catchy campaign songs.

The spirited contest and a growing population resulted in the largest turnout in the nation's history, with the number of eligible voters who went to the polls reaching 80.2 percent. Harrison received 52.9 percent of the total, Van Buren 46.8 percent. Of 2,412,698 votes cast, a third party backed by the abolitionists attracted only 7,053 votes.

In the Electoral College, Van Buren won seven states—Alabama, Arkansas, Illinois, Missouri, New Hampshire, South Carolina, and Tyler's home state of Tennessee. Harrison carried nineteen states for a total of 234 electoral votes, and the Whigs took both the House and the Senate.

In the waning days of the Van Buren administration, the Cherokees were still stymied in receiving the removal monies due them, because Secretary Poinsett continued to use the rupture within their tribe as his excuse for withholding the final payments. To strike back, John Ross sent T. Hartley Crawford, the Indian Affairs commissioner, a detailed list of his personal grievances. Ross began billing Washington fifty thousand dollars for "these most atrocious wrongs & injuries I have suffered."

He was also demanding recompense for his arrest with John Howard Payne in 1834. "And for this incalculable outrage and injury done me by the lawless conduct of the Georgia Guard in my own nation country, where they had no constitutional right of jurisdiction over my person & property . . . I claim damages in this case of $100,000."

As it happened, Payne was visiting Park Hill again late in 1840, collecting more historical material. He found the tribe distracted by putting up its new cabins and fences for their livestock, but when he managed to arrange an interview with George Guess, Payne was tantalized by the prospect of tapping Sequoyah's fund of ancient lore.

They met in an upper section of Ross's log house with an interpreter seated between them. Afterward, Payne supplied a friend in Washington with a detailed description of this most famous of Cherokees—from the flowered turban over his gray hair to the buckskin wrapping around his lame and shrunken leg. To Payne, Sequoyah had the aspect of an ancient Greek philosopher.

As he drew on his pipe, the old man's voice rose, then fell to a whisper. His eyes could grow fiery before his face softened into a benign smile. As time slipped away, his performance was so hypnotic that Payne's interpreter forgot to translate for half an hour at a time.

Understanding nothing, Payne fell back on trying to duplicate the sounds of what he was hearing: "ohsee, turtenuggy, oohsaluanlee, clucky, o—o—o—o—o—o-ogly (dwelling on that note, he observed, before letting it die away)—conesauga, aliquo, naski, whlesstuly, toogah tuhtungh, tawlee—"

All the while, Payne heard the interpreter exclaiming, "as listening Indians always do, at every clause, in a note something between the tone of human lamentation, the voice of Mr. Thomas Cat by moonlight, and the sound of the French word for the month of August—Awe, oooh!"

Belatedly remembering their guest, the interpreter turned periodically to Payne to remark, "Oh, it is beautiful! Oh, how interesting! How *very* interesting!"

Payne said he was left with "the sensation of one who has traveled a couple of thousand miles to plough and plant five hundred acres and reap one single ear of corn!" His consolation was that Sequoyah had now told his story—apparently, it involved the wampum belts of various tribes—and "it will be easy to lead him over it again and slowly enough to get a record."

But the next day, Sequoyah was worried that his account had not been accurate. He "would rather not expose himself to be criticized by the old people, who might say he had not reported the truth."

When months passed with no response to his claims, John Ross sent copies of the removal bills directly to the outgoing president. He assured Van Buren that "the self emigration of the nation was undertaken from purer motives and high considerations than dollars and cents" and asked the president to order a full accounting.

But by the time he addressed the Cherokee Nation at Tahlequah in October 1840, Ross had to confess to an "entire failure" by the tribe's delegates to gain their objectives in Washington. He could report merely that Van Buren had agreed to reexamine their outstanding claim of $581,346.8½. Ross said he was led "to expect that justice will yet be done."

Ross concluded his annual address by urging the Cherokees to treat one another with kindness "and to be gentle and forbearing towards our white neighbors and the surrounding tribes of our red brethren, under whatever circumstances may arise."

Chief Ross soon had a chance to demonstrate forgiveness. One of the signers at New Echota, Archilla Smith, was accused of a murder unrelated to the treaty. In a Cherokee court, Jesse Bushyhead had prosecuted Smith, and Stand Watie had defended him. When a guilty verdict was announced, Smith fled, vowing he would not be taken alive. For some time, he had eluded a sheriff's posse sent to arrest him.

Then one day, while Payne was visiting Ross, a desperate-looking man appeared at the door. When Ross did not recognize him, Archilla Smith identified himself in Cherokee before switching to English.

"How are you?" Smith asked. "It is some time, now, since we met. How long—?"

Ross said, "Some years, I think."

Smith remarked, "You and I are beginning to get into years. We were both of us thought good-looking men."

Ross maintained Smith's ironic tone. "The finest flowers must wither as their season passes."

"You are fatter than when I saw you last," Smith said.

"I am fatter than what I was a short time ago," Ross said regretfully, "but not so fat as I have been. Have *you* been well?"

"Yes." Smith added that there were men after him who had "some purpose in view, for which probably they fancy there is cause."

After a few more exchanges, Smith said, "I thought I would look in to see you. We must be on our way now, and I must journey on and see you no more."

As he prepared to leave, however, horsemen rode up, and the Cherokee sheriff and his posse threw open the door with their rifles leveled. When Smith offered no resistance, the sheriff managed to keep his men from firing.

As Payne watched Smith being led away, he predicted, "I suppose there will be an execution, here, soon, to amuse us."

More than a hundred members of the Treaty Party petitioned Ross to pardon Smith so that "peace and harmony may prevail." Ross refused. Archilla Smith was hanged on January 1, 1841.

Despite the Cherokees' sporadic bloodshed, the election of William Henry Harrison promised a new era for the tribe. In his inaugural address, Harrison called for "liberality and justice" in dealing with "our aboriginal neighbors." He added that "I can conceive of no more sublime spectacle, none more likely to propitiate an impartial and common Creator, than a rigid adherence to the principles of justice on the part of a powerful nation in its transactions with a weaker and uncivilized people whom circumstances have placed at its disposal."

Harrison's listeners might be forgiven if they missed those two sentences in the longest inaugural address in the nation's history. Not only did the new president's exhaustive analysis of the U.S. Constitution run for an hour and forty-five minutes, but it was delivered in a chilling March snowstorm. The sixty-eight-year-old former Indian fighter stood throughout the entire ceremony, then moved on to the White House to welcome his supporters.

For Harrison, the inauguration was the heady culmination of a career that had never again reached the heights of the Indian Wars. His campaign had reminded the nation of that night in 1811, when Harrison defeated the Shawnees led by Tecumseh's brother, and of the battle of the Thames River two years later when Harrison joined with Richard Johnson, Van Buren's recent vice president, in the fighting that killed Tecumseh himself.

After those victories, however, Harrison had fallen out of favor with James Madison's headstrong army secretary, John Armstrong, and resigned his commission. Prodded by Henry Clay, the postwar Congress ruled that Harrison had been mistreated and awarded him a gold medal. In the public mind, Harrison joined Andrew Jackson as a hero of the War of 1812.

Clay continued to champion Harrison's career by arranging his assignment in Colombia. When he had run him for president four years earlier, Harrison had been merely a cog in Clay's scheme to defeat Van Buren. But that campaign had reminded voters of Harrison's heroism from three decades earlier. Now those memories had carried him to the White House, where he stood for hours, still resolute and imposing, as he shook hands and accepted wishes for good health and a long life.

John Quincy Adams was among those who welcomed Harrison's election as a fresh beginning. The new president returned that esteem, assuring people that Adams was a dear friend who "had been so unjustly put out" of the White House in 1828.

Adams was also basking in praise these days for his argument before the U.S. Supreme Court in the *Amistad* suit. He had been nervous about his first appearance before the Court since 1809, but when February 24, 1841, arrived, Adams more than met the challenge. He spoke for four hours and then, when the death of a justice required postponement, spoke for another four hours on the first of March.

Adams's argument ranged widely, sweeping away any claim of property rights and homing in on the moral underpinnings of the case. Reading a roll of the venerated justices who had once served on the Court, Adams said he hoped that the current members would receive the same benediction when they, too, had passed on: "Well done, good and faithful servant. Enter thou into the joy of thy Lord."

Five days later, with Harrison's inaugural barely over, Justice Story read the Court's decision. There was one dissent, but it did not come from Chief Justice Taney, who concurred that the Africans were free men. Several prisoners had died awaiting trial, but thirty-five of the former slaves returned to Africa.

Adams's victory convinced him that he was not yet ready to retire from the Congress.

Since the election, Harrison had been keeping his distance from Henry Clay, determined to show the nation that he was in charge of his administration. In a private meeting, Clay made that goal easier by assuring the president-elect that he preferred to stay in the Senate rather than join the cabinet. Like Jackson, Harrison had pledged to be a one-term president. Unlike Jackson, he seemed to mean it. Clay could wait.

As Clay urged Harrison to appoint Daniel Webster as secretary of state, he tried to exact two pledges from the president in return for his magnanimity: He should recharter the national bank and he should uphold the tariff compromises Clay had hammered out. But Clay was coming to realize that Harrison resented his influence among the Whigs, and he worried that "artful men for sinister purposes will endeavor to foster this jealousy."

It was Clay's high-handed manner, however, that provoked their final break. As Harrison disregarded his advice about other cabinet appointments, Clay's protests grew so strident that Harrison had to bring him up short: "Mr. Clay, you forget that I am President."

In his frustration, Clay began flailing about in the capital. After he provoked a challenge to a duel from an Alabama Jacksonian, Clay could avert it only by posting a five-thousand-dollar bond to guarantee he would maintain the peace.

One appointment that did not distress Clay gave John Ross great satisfaction. John Bell of Tennessee, long a friend to the Cherokees, was named secretary of war, putting him in charge of Indian affairs. Harrison also removed General Arbuckle from Fort Gibson and sent him to Baton Rouge, Louisiana. Ross hoped the president would also name a new Indian commissioner, but for now T. Hartley Crawford was keeping his job.

Secretary Bell personally escorted Ross and his delegation to meet President Harrison. Leaving the White House, Ross's euphoria was intense, but it was destined to be short-lived.

When the new president caught a bad cold, friends blamed his exposure to the cold and snow on March 4. By March 27, his lingering indisposition was diagnosed as "bilious pleurisy, with symptoms of pneumonia and intestinal inflammation." Harrison was ordered to bed. After a week, he seemed considerably improved. But a relapse followed, and Harrison died after midnight on Palm Sunday, April 4, 1841. He had been president a few hours less than one month.

John Tyler

17 · JOHN TYLER (1841–44)

SUCH WAS JOHN Ross's nature that he had to look for some consolation in President Harrison's death. Writing from Washington the following month, he tried to cheer up his niece, Lewis Ross's daughter Araminta: "I can well imagine the shock which you felt, when the sad tidings struck your ear, that *President Harrison was no more!*"

But Ross added that he believed "President Tyler will carry out the measures contemplated by General Harrison, so far as they are known—and that he will act honorably and justly toward the Indians."

In the days after he succeeded to the presidency, however, Tyler had more pressing concerns than seeking justice for the Cherokee Nation. Even Tyler's status was in doubt, since no vice president had ever been asked to fill out a president's term.

John Quincy Adams took to calling Tyler "the Acting President," but Tyler immediately rejected that limitation to his title. In private, Adams was more scathing: Tyler was a mediocrity, a product of the "Virginian, Jeffersonian School," with the vices of slavery rooted in his very being.

As expected, Andrew Jackson at the Hermitage saw Tyler's accession as the result of "a kind Providence" saving "our glorious Union" from "the profligate demagogue Henry Clay."

Clay himself could not yet calculate how this turn of events would affect him. He was particularly concerned about the chartering of a new national bank and confided to friends that he harbored "strong hopes, not however unmixed with fears." But even those friends had noticed Clay's increasingly authoritarian streak. If his hauteur had finally exasperated genial William Henry Harrison, it was sure to provoke stubborn John Tyler.

As Clay concluded his first private meeting with the new president, he pushed for the national bank so persistently that Tyler lost his composure. He told Clay to go back to the Capitol building at his end of Constitution Avenue and let Tyler do his duty from the White House.

Clay took Tyler at his word. He returned to the Senate determined to assert complete control over their Whig Party.

At his end of Constitution Avenue, Tyler did not wield the same authority. In appointing cabinet officers loyal to Clay, Harrison had promised each of them a vote on every subject. Tyler quickly scuttled that notion. He sent a message to Congress that upheld states' rights; pledged to eliminate the national debt; and did not revise the 1833 tariff compromise.

Clay led a movement to recharter the Bank of the United States. Tyler vetoed his bill, and Clay fell one vote short of overriding him. Andrew Jackson, now seventy-four, looked on approvingly as Tyler held firm.

A gang of pro-Bank protesters retaliated by assaulting the White House for the first time in the twenty-eight years since the British set it on fire. Storming the grounds at night, a few dozen men threw rocks at the windows and shouted curses against the new president. The next day Tyler was hanged in effigy near Pennsylvania Avenue.

When Clay introduced another bill to charter the bank, Tyler's advisers laid out the president's options: He could sign it and guarantee the success of his administration. Or he could issue a second veto that would destroy him.

On September 9, 1841, the president sent his son, Robert Tyler, to read the veto message in person. Two days later, Tyler's entire cabinet, except for Daniel Webster, resigned. Looking on glumly, John Quincy Adams predicted the end of the Whig Party.

Clay had expected that the mass resignations would hobble Tyler, perhaps even force his resignation. Instead, Tyler spent a month making new appointments, most of them former Jackson men.

As the Cherokees waited nervously, Tyler sent his first address to Congress on December 7, 1841. "Our brave officers and men" were still fighting the Seminoles, Tyler observed. But "with all other Indian tribes we are enjoying the blessings of peace." The duty of the United States—as well as the nation's own self-interest—lay in strictly fulfilling its obligations so that "the untutored child of the forest be induced to listen to its teachings."

Despite his patronizing tone, Tyler's words reassured Chief Ross. Before John Bell resigned as secretary of war, he had authorized an outstanding Cherokee claim of five hundred thousand dollars and added another eighteen thousand dollars as interest from the tribal trust fund. And Tyler had presented the Ross delegation with a letter promising a new and more generous treaty, one that would guarantee the Cherokee lands "in absolute fee simple" for them and "their remotest posterity."

Tyler wrote, "A new sun will have dawned upon them, in whose brightness their permanent happiness and true glory may be read by the whole world."

During Ross's absence from the Cherokee Nation, an uneasy harmony had allowed him time for a genteel courtship of a white Philadelphia woman named Elizabeth Mulligan. Asking her to marry, Ross anticipated her misgivings. At fifty, he was not too old, Ross assured her, and he enjoyed excellent health. The romance faded, however, and Ross returned to Tahlequah alone.

Meantime, the Tyler administration had sent new representatives to the Cherokees who were unburdened by resentment over Ross's past defiance and could look him over coolly. One special agent, Ethan Allen Hitchcock, noted that Ross's manner was diffident and his speech, unless he became excited, was not fluent. Hitchcock was surprised that Ross spoke only English and relied on an interpreter since he "will not trust himself to address his own people in Cherokee."

Summing up, Hitchcock found Ross a sincere patriot for his

people. Despite an "unlimited opportunity, he had not enriched himself." Hitchcock considered it unfortunate, though, that Lewis Ross should have become wealthy through his brother's patronage. Yet he granted that Lewis's contracts might have been entirely legal.

Another new agent, Pierce Mason Butler, came to much the same conclusions. He wrote that in private Ross was "a retiring, modest, good man." In his public role, he showed "dignity and intelligence." Butler also considered Ross stubborn, however, and sometimes unwisely tenacious in his opinions, and he deplored Ross's favoring friends and supporters for jobs in his administration. Even at that, Butler felt that events of the last decade had confirmed his good opinion: "He looks rather to what he thinks the rights of his people than to what is expedient or to what is to be obtained for them."

In Washington, Henry Clay was satisfied that by reading Tyler out of the Whig Party, he would be its next nominee for president. But to run in 1844, Clay needed to recover his health. Suffering from one persistent cold after another, he had developed a swelling of his upper lip that added to his discomfort, and pains in his chest perhaps signaled a mild heart attack. Friends agreed that, at sixty-four, Clay looked like a far older man.

They also noted that he was ever more short-tempered and autocratic, especially on the tariff question. John Calhoun hit a nerve when he accused the Whigs of deliberately keeping federal spending high so they could undermine the terms of the compromise tariff of 1833. In striking back, Clay attacked the Cherokee removal. He claimed that Jackson's insistence on driving the tribe west of the Mississippi had led to an expense of millions of dollars that was "waste and profligate."

Worse, the costly war against the Seminoles still raged on in Florida. Clay demanded, "What has the nation got to show for its money?" Certainly, national honor would not be stained by allowing the Seminoles to live on a portion of Florida "which will never be occupied, or at least not occupied within the century, by the whites."

Over Daniel Webster's objections, Tyler rejected Clay's latest tariff bill. As excited talk of impeachment spread through the Whigs, Tyler rode out the threat, prevailed, and signed a bill more to his liking.

Clay was not on hand for that presidential victory. During his campaigns, he had sometimes styled himself "the Old Coon from Kentucky." Now, after thirty-six years in the Congress, Henry Clay was retiring. At 1 p.m. on Thursday, March 31, 1842, the Senate gallery was packed for his farewell address.

It was a sentimental valedictory, during which Clay confessed to one shortcoming: "True, my nature is warm, my temper ardent, my disposition in the public service enthusiastic." But that temperament had been placed entirely in the service of "what I at least supposed to be patriotic exertions." Clay bid his colleagues "a long, a last, a friendly farewell," and his audience wept.

Evaluating the scene from the Hermitage, Andrew Jackson remained dry-eyed and exultant. He was convinced that he had finally settled the score from 1824. "The old coon is really and substantially dead," he wrote to Van Buren. "Clay's political career is closed forever."

But John Crittenden, who had been named to replace Clay in the Senate, spoke for much of the country. Clay's leaving Congress, he said, "was something like the soul's quitting the body."

Despite improved relations with Washington, the Cherokees' progress toward a new federal treaty was slow, and Ross was having more rapid success in reconciling with his Indian neighbors. In June 1843, he called together representatives from the four other Civilized Tribes—the Choctaws, Chickasaws, Creeks, and Seminoles—for a meeting at Tahlequah.

Observing the scene, a newly arrived Methodist minister wrote, "The costume of the Indian tribes is greatly varied, from the richest and most genteel style of their white neighbors to the rudest and simplest form of savage dress." The clergyman was dazzled by the "fantastic" display and the "great passion for gay colors." In passing, he also observed that, given their diminutive height and general appearance, John Ross looked very much like Martin Van Buren.

After four weeks, the tribes arrived at a pledge of friendship. They not only promised mutual peace but also agreed to cede no more of their existing territory to the United States. Early in August 1843, the Cherokees held the first general election in their new home, and John Ross won two-thirds of the nearly nine hundred votes cast; George Lowrey was elected as his principal assistant chief.

But as the votes were being counted, the election judges were attacked by six armed men led by two brothers named West. They believed that Archilla Smith had been convicted on evidence rigged by John Ross's men and were set on avenging his hanging. One brother, George West, stabbed Jesse Bushyhead to death while other men severely beat tribal officials, including Elijah Hicks, who had become an associate justice on the Cherokee Supreme Court. Before riding off, the Wests destroyed a number of election ballots.

Ross's supporters rode quickly to his house in Park Hill to form a posse. George West managed to escape, but his brother John and their father, Jacob, were each identified and turned over to the Cherokee sheriff.

At his trial, Jacob West claimed that since he was a white man merely married to a Cherokee woman, he should be tried in federal court in Arkansas. When that defense failed, he was convicted and hanged. John West was found guilty of assault, sentenced to one hundred lashes, and stripped of his Cherokee citizenship.

Bushyhead's murder set off a new round of retaliatory violence. Men from the Starr family who were identified with the Treaty Party killed two white men and the Cherokee wife of one of them. Although their motive was never spelled out, they seemed to be avenging Jacob West.

U.S. Brigadier General Zachary Taylor pursued the murderers, who fled into Arkansas, where they were arrested, then allowed to escape. Taylor concluded that Arkansas's white settlers were making systematic efforts to disrupt Cherokee affairs and undermine John Ross.

Once again, dissident Cherokee delegations arrived in Washington, one from the Treaty Party, the other from the Old Settlers, and both seeking a share of the federal resettlement money. They revived the charges against Ross as a tyrant and an embezzler of tribal funds. Although they did not prevail, they raised enough doubt in the mind of Tyler's new secretary of war, William Wilkins of Pennsylvania, to delay still further a final settlement of the Cherokee claims.

With his election campaign looming, John Tyler's political fortunes looked beyond repair. Under his administration, a U.S. naval officer had occupied Monterey in California, in the belief that Tyler had declared war on Mexico. The next day, the president had to apologize and return control of the area.

But the situation in Mexico required more than apologies. Sam Houston had been serving alternating terms as president of the Republic of Texas, and Tyler was not sure of Houston's plans. By the time Tiana Rogers died of pneumonia in 1838, she had considered herself already divorced from Houston and had remarried. Houston had waited until her death before taking a third wife, Margaret Lea, who was twenty-one to his forty-seven; their family would grow to eight children.

As his Republic's leading politician, Houston had always pressed hard for the admission of Texas to the Union, despite Mexico's warning that annexation meant war. Now with statehood stalled, Tyler suspected that the British might revive their 1814 attempt to hem in the United States between Texas and Canada, and he worried that Houston might be receptive to their overtures. Tyler's suspicions had grown after 1843, when Hawaii's king ceded that nation briefly to Britain.

As the president pondered his strategy for the 1844 election, Andrew Jackson was warming to the prospect of Tyler's remaining in the White House, whatever his party label. But Jackson had more pressing concerns than the election. His son had mismanaged Jackson's fortune to the point that the Hermitage was crumbling and might be lost to creditors.

Jacksonians in the House came to his aid by returning the thousand-dollar fine that a Louisiana judge had once levied to punish Jackson's high-handed defiance of the courts after the Battle of New Orleans. With interest, Jackson collected twenty-seven hundred dollars, plus a personal contribution from President Tyler. All the same, Jackson advised James Polk of Tennessee not to accept a cabinet post with Tyler because his prospects looked hopeless.

Then early in 1844, catastrophe struck. It came after Daniel Webster had finally resigned and Tyler had appointed a replacement as secretary of state. The new man was Abel P. Upshur, a Virginian who was expected to bolster Tyler's reelection chances by annexing Texas. By February 27, 1844, Upshur had negotiated a draft of a treaty that would bring the Lone Star Republic into the Union as a slave territory.

The following day, Upshur was among the dignitaries who joined Tyler for a Potomac River cruise aboard the country's newest and most advanced warship, the *Princeton*. The ship's pride was an imposing fifteen-foot iron cannon with a twelve-inch diameter called the "Peacemaker." As guests drank champagne below deck, the crew fired off jubilant shots.

The morning was the more exhilarating for President Tyler because joining him on board was Julia Gardiner, the young daughter of a former New York state senator. Five years before his inaugural, Tyler's wife, Letitia, had suffered a stroke that left her partially paralyzed. In the White House, she had stayed close to their private quarters before dying in 1842. Since then, Tyler's daughter-in-law, Priscilla, had served as his hostess, but he seemed poised to marry again.

As Tyler lingered below with Miss Gardiner, the *Princeton* was about to pass Mount Vernon. The tipsy guests prevailed on the reluctant captain to fire the Peacemaker in honor of George Washington. The captain had good reason for his reluctance. The big gun exploded, killing Upshur, Julia Gardiner's father, and eight others, including Tyler's personal slave, Henry.

The calamity deprived Tyler of his secretary of state but accelerated his courtship. He married Julia Gardiner four months later. In the aftermath of the disaster, he persuaded John Calhoun to become secretary of state, a post Calhoun had turned down twice.

One more casualty of the explosion appeared to be Upshur's treaty, since Texans were now insisting on stronger guarantees that the United States would defend them against Mexico. And yet, Calhoun was as committed to annexation as Upshur had been. The treaty he negotiated was signed on April 12, 1844.

Tyler pledged to fight for congressional approval, but the outcome was enough in doubt that he could worry that his chance at winning the presidency on his own had exploded on the deck of the *Princeton*.

The crisis in Washington scarcely registered among the Cherokees. Chief Ross took advantage of a new hiatus in tribal affairs to go courting again. This time, his target was an eighteen-year-old Quaker, Mary Bryan Stapler of Wilmington, Delaware. Three years earlier, she had sent him a flirtatious note that left him smitten with the dark-haired white girl. A series of clandestine love letters followed—violating the rules of her strict female academy—and Ross assured her that his feelings were "pure, sincere and ardent." He added, "And once united with yours in the solemn ties of matrimony, I am sure that nothing but the cold hand of death could ever extinguish them from my bosom."

Mary Stapler's father was displeased by the prospect, less because Ross was an Indian or thirty-six years older—about the same as the difference in age between President Tyler and his bride—than because the marriage would take Mary far from home. In the end, Stapler gave his consent. The wedding took place on September 2, 1844, after which the bride was expelled from the Quaker Church for marrying outside her faith.

Local newspapers took a keen interest in the wedding, especially in the rumor that the bridegroom was worth half a million dollars. Indeed, Ross could take his new wife to a home far grander than the log hut he had once shared with Quatie. When Ross first arrived in

Oklahoma, John Howard Payne had found life at Park Hill austere, but over the intervening years, Ross had been able to surround himself with splendor.

Called Rose Cottage, his two-story yellow house was four miles southeast of Tahlequah and furnished with mahogany and rosewood furniture imported from the East Coast. Ross's garden of melon, fruit, and grapes extended almost two acres, tended by the nineteen slaves he had brought from Georgia. Ross's hospitality continued to be as lavish as it had been in New Echota. Now, as then, every traveler could expect a cordial welcome and a hearty meal. Ross's high style fed the rumors, however, that he had enriched himself during the removal.

With the presidential campaign of 1844 raging, Ross believed with Henry Clay that Clay would be elected at last. If so, it would be a "God send to this country, as well as to the poor Indians."

18 · "Manifest Destiny" (1845–52)

Henry Clay was doing his best to deserve Ross's trust. At the height of his campaign, he went to Georgia to remind white audiences that he had voted against ratifying the Treaty of New Echota, and he scolded them for celebrating a treaty that had been "induced by *corruption*."

Despite his harangues, the throng that turned out to greet him in Savannah may have led Clay to confuse affection for him personally with Southern indifference to the annexation of Texas. From Raleigh, North Carolina, Clay issued a warning that any attempt to acquire Texas would set off a war with Mexico.

With age, Clay had lost the martial fervor he had once brought to debates over the War of 1812. Now he wrote, "I regard all war as great calamities to be avoided, if possible, and honorable peace as the wisest and truest policy of this country."

Clay could take that forthright stand because he was sure that Van Buren, his likeliest Democratic opponent, was also opposed to annexing Texas. In that, Clay was correct. But being away from Washington, Clay had missed a shift among his former colleagues. Even before Upshur was killed, many senators had informed Tyler privately that if he could conclude a treaty with Texas, they were ready to ratify it.

Clay had carefully defined his travels as not being a campaign tour, although he ended them in Baltimore by accepting the unanimous nomination of his party for president. To solidify that unity, Clay let the convention select his running mate. Delegates passed over leading

James Polk

contenders, including Millard Fillmore, the New York congressman, to choose Theodore Frelinghuysen.

In the years since his failed crusade on behalf of the Cherokees, Frelinghuysen had lost his Senate seat, then won election as mayor of Newark, New Jersey. The job pitted his religious fervor against his fiscal conservatism, and he tried to prevent ship captains from unloading new immigrants in Newark because they added to his city's budget deficit. All the same, Frelinghuysen's reputation for piety remained so unsullied that the Whigs were accused of cynicism for putting the "Christian statesman" on the same ticket with a reprobate like Henry Clay.

When the Democrats met in Baltimore on May 27, 1844, they upended Clay's expectation of a smooth march to the presidency.

Andrew Jackson had concluded that Van Buren's opposition to annexing Texas made him unelectable, and Calhoun's followers joined a move to deny him the nomination at the convention. When neither Van Buren nor his chief opponent, Lewis Cass, could gain a majority by the eighth ballot, the Democrats settled on James Knox Polk, former Speaker of the House and governor of Tennessee. Their platform included the "reoccupation of Oregon and the reannexation of Texas."

John Tyler held his own convention, largely made up of men who held office in his administration, and chose Van Buren's vice president, Richard M. Johnson, as his running mate. Polk appealed to Jackson at the Hermitage to pressure Tyler to withdraw. Jackson obliged with a letter to a mutual friend warning that Tyler's presence on the ballot would throw the election to Clay and jeopardize the annexation of Texas.

"On Mr. Tyler's withdrawal," Jackson wrote, "every true American will say, Amen to his patriotism in the case of Texas."

Flattered and convinced, Tyler dropped from the race. Then, in the nasty campaign that followed, Jackson resurrected a reliable weapon. The emergence after twenty years of accusations about his corrupt bargain came as a surprise to Clay. He had become convinced that the issue finally had been laid to rest and had acknowledged publicly that agreeing to serve in the Adams cabinet probably had been a mistake.

But the decisive issue was Texas—and, by extension, slavery. When Secretary of State Calhoun put forth his new treaty, he granted that it was intended to protect the institution of slavery in Texas. That declaration inspired the Whigs to join Van Buren's Northern supporters and defeat it in the Senate, thirty-five to sixteen. Jackson suspected that Calhoun had intended just such an outcome in order to consolidate his position with Southerners who were feeling under siege from Northern abolitionists.

Clay did not help himself by softening his position. He suggested that he would not object to admitting Texas but was unwilling to risk the survival of the Union to do it. That wavering upset both North and South. When Clay tried to extricate himself, his further temporizing over slavery—"destined to become extinct, at some distant day"—only aroused more anger. "Confound him," one abolitionist wrote, "and all his compromises from first to last."

Texas and slavery combined to produce the unthinkable. James Polk, long regarded as unimpressive, edged out the most celebrated statesman of his age. Polk's winning margin of the popular vote was 1.4 percent, thirty-eight thousand out of more than 2.6 million votes cast.

The past two decades had given Clay ample practice in being a gracious loser. He told supporters, "Now, I hope to spend the remainder of my days in peace and quiet." Only to intimates did Clay express his pain. He felt the severity of the blow, he wrote, more perhaps because it was so unexpected. He had hoped to "bring the government back to its former purity. . . . That hope is now forever fled."

John Lewis Sullivan, a New York journalist who favored absorbing Texas into the Union, painted a more hopeful vision of the future in an article for the *Democratic Review.* In the process, he also added a popular phrase to the nation's consciousness. His essay of July 1845 predicted that annexation would confirm America's "manifest destiny to overspread the continent allotted by Providence for the free development of our yearly multiplying millions."

As editor of the *New York Morning News,* Sullivan expanded on his point later in the year, arguing that the United States also had the right to claim "the whole of Oregon." America's right of manifest destiny was given to the country "for the development of the great experiment of liberty & federated self-government entrusted to us."

Missouri's Senator Thomas Hart Benton embraced Sullivan's concept with a vengeance. He saw the white race as uniquely blessed by divine command to subdue the earth. Benton had to acknowledge the vast numbers of the "Mongolian or Yellow race" and its past glories in the arts of civilization—although, Benton added, for thousands of years it had been "torpid and stationary." Still, the Caucasians and Mongolians should trade together, even marry each other. That would revive the yellow race and guarantee the ascendancy of the white race.

As for the other races—red, black, and brown—Benton had neither great hope nor interest. He told his fellow senators, "I cannot repine that this Capitol has replaced the wigwam—that this Christian people replaced the savages—the white matrons, the red squaws." Indeed, "I look upon the settlement of the Columbia river by the van of the Caucasian race as the most momentous human event in the history of man since his dispersion over the face of the earth."

Despite his fervor, Benton was less rapacious than many of his colleagues, and he did not endorse seizing the Oregon territory from Great Britain. Ownership of Oregon had been cloudy since a pact between Britain and the United States in 1818 had granted them joint occupancy of the land west of the Rocky Mountains to the Pacific Ocean. But in recent years, American settlers had established a government, and expansionist fervor was urging the United States to claim land as far north as Alaska. Benton preferred that the border stop at Canada with the forty-ninth parallel, and he opposed the cry of "Fifty-four forty or fight."

James Polk entered office ready to settle the question, but he was concerned about protests from his Democratic allies in the West if he did not press for the northernmost border. In time, however, his secretary of state, James Buchanan—with backing from John Calhoun and Daniel Webster—would work out a compromise that settled on the forty-ninth parallel while allowing Britain to retain Vancouver Island.

But with Mexico at stake, the public did not share Benton's caution and seemed ready to plunge into the war he was resisting.

The foremost proponent of annexation did not live to see its drama played out. Andrew Jackson, hardiest of sickly men, had never fully recovered from a duel in 1806 that left a bullet lodged too deeply to be removed. Consumption had destroyed one lung and wracked the other. Three times in the White House, his hemorrhaging had brought Jackson near death, and yet he went on smoking and chewing tobacco despite the headaches they caused him.

By 1845, Jackson's body was alternately swollen by dropsy and laid low by diarrhea. With his thoughts turning regularly to dying, he pondered his future reputation and speculated on the mistakes posterity might charge against him. When asked what he would have done if Calhoun and his faction had persisted with nullification, Jackson answered with his old spirit: "Hang them, sir, as high as Haman," he said, an Old Testament reference to Esther's nemesis, sent to the gallows for plotting against the Jews. "They should have been a terror to traitors of all time, and posterity would have pronounced it the best act of my life."

Crowds of office-seekers continued to descend on the Hermitage to ask for introductions to President Polk. Jackson sent most of them away with a mordant malediction: "I am dying as fast as I can, and they all know it."

To the end, Jackson praised Sam Houston and his actions in Texas. Religion was also much on his mind, and Jackson assured friends, "I am in the hands of a merciful God." He prayed for his family and for the preservation of the Union. Often he concluded, "My work is done for life."

In his last hour on June 8, 1845, family and household staff were brought to him. From a verandah, the slaves looked in on his bedchamber through its windows. Jackson bade them farewell and repeated a phrase he had invoked before. "I want to meet you all, white and black, in heaven."

While debate raged over war with Mexico, the Cherokees were distracted by a resurgence of killing in their nation, much of it due to political strife. To protect her children, Delight Sargent Boudinot had sent them to New England, where General Brinsmade and his wife became their official guardians until they could be farmed out to other relatives. Elias Cornelius Boudinot studied civil engineering in Vermont but stayed in touch with his uncle, Stand Watie. As violence in the territory continued, Watie was maintaining his own small military unit stationed at Beattie's Prairie.

In Washington, President Polk now found three Cherokee delegations bidding for his attention. In October 1845, Walter Medill, who had replaced T. Hartley Crawford as Indian commissioner, sent to the president a negative report on John Ross. Despite the chief's many promises, Ross was not protecting the lives and property of the two rival factions. Medill urged splitting up the Cherokee territory—one-half for the Old Settlers and the Treaty Party, the other for Cherokees loyal to Ross. On April 13, 1846, Polk sent that recommendation to Congress.

Although the idea of dividing his nation alarmed Ross, he did not improve his reputation with a long attack on his opponents as "wholly venal and selfish" men whom a previous U.S. report had branded "a desperate band of banditti."

To stave off the division, however, all of the factions were driven to compromise. Ross had to reassure a presidential commission that he could finally accept the Treaty of New Echota. The Old Settlers renounced their claim to exclusive ownership of the seven million acres of the Cherokee Nation and agreed to accept Chief Ross's government. Watie and others pledged to disband their small private armies.

In financial terms, heirs from the 1839 murders—the Ridge and Boudinot families—would each receive $5,000 from the $115,000 fund Congress had voted to indemnify the Treaty Party. The Ross faction was also compensated—$2,000 for the original *Phoenix* printing press, $5,000 for weapons collected by Winfield Scott, and $25,000 for settling other claims. The major concession by Congress was to reimburse the tribe for any money unfairly deducted from its original $5 million appropriation.

Polk was on hand with twenty ranking Cherokees in mid-August 1846 when Ross and Watie shook hands and signed the treaty. After the president urged the tribe to forget the past, Ross responded as chief: They were satisfied with the new treaty and could now live in harmony. With that, the Cherokees entered upon their own era of good feelings, and former enemies had time to attend to their families.

During the turbulent years, Stand Watie had married Sally Bell, the sister of his allies Jim and Jack Bell, and their family grew to three sons and two daughters. By reconciling with Ross, Watie became a respected voice on the Cherokee national council.

John Rollin Ridge made a different choice. His widowed mother had moved her children to Fayetteville, Arkansas, where the boy came of age, studied law, and took a white bride. His hatred of the Ross faction never cooled. When David Kell, a Ross sympathizer, stole and gelded one of Ridge's stallions, Ridge killed him and ran off, first to Missouri and then, lured by a gold rush, to California.

Before President Polk ordered Brigadier General Zachary Taylor to march the three thousand troops who launched war with Mexico, he first tried to buy the disputed land. In the fall of 1845, Polk had offered $5 million to Mexico if the country would recognize the Rio Grande as the southwestern boundary of Texas. His administration had offered up to an additional $25 million for California and $5 million more for the province of New Mexico, which included land that became Nevada, Utah, and parts of four other states.

When the Mexicans rejected those terms, Polk sent Taylor to the Rio Grande to attempt to blockade the Mexican army at the port of Matamoros. In the fighting that followed, three American dragoons were killed and others wounded.

By the time word of the casualties reached Polk on Saturday, May 9, he was already drafting a message to Congress that accused Mexico of invading U.S. territory and shedding American blood on American soil. In Congress, some members in each party united in their disapproval. A Delaware senator pointed out that sending Taylor's men to the Rio Grande had been "as much an act of aggression on our part as is a man's pointing a pistol at another's heart."

Abraham Lincoln, an Illinois lawyer serving his first term in Congress, called the war immoral and a victory for the forces of slavery.

Since the deaths had occurred on disputed land, Lincoln challenged Polk to identify the exact spot where American blood had been shed on American soil. The true cause of the war, Lincoln claimed, was Polk's desire for "military glory—that attractive rainbow that rises in showers of blood."

But more Whigs in both chambers supported Taylor and Winfield Scott—their two prominent Whig generals. They authorized the war overwhelmingly, and during the first weeks after the declaration, war fever flared throughout the nation. The army asked for fifty thousand volunteers. Two hundred thousand men answered the call.

Henry Clay was heartsick to see his namesake join the ranks as a lieutenant colonel in the Second Kentucky Volunteer Regiment. Ever the politician, however, Clay paid tribute to the regiment's patriotic spirit. He did add that he wished their cause "was more reconcilable with the dictates of conscience." As Clay parted from his son, he presented him with a pair of pistols.

Abolitionist journals were bucking the prevailing mood. William Lloyd Garrison's *Liberator* wished the Mexican people "the most triumphant success." In Massachusetts, Emerson's friend Henry Thoreau joined the protest by refusing to pay his taxes.

Six years had already passed since Thoreau first took his name off the First Parish Church tax rolls. Two years later, he had refused to pay the local poll tax. Now the levy he was protesting supported only the town of Concord, not the Mexican-American War. But when Thoreau set out his reasons for refusing to pay taxes in an essay he called "Civil Disobedience," he invoked the war as his justification.

Comparing the war to the evils of slavery, Thoreau chastised those who claimed not to support the war and yet went on paying their taxes. The local tax collector was flummoxed by that position. He felt personally friendly to Thoreau and asked what he should do.

"Resign," Thoreau said.

Thoreau was jailed for one night before his family defied his wishes, paid his taxes, and set him free. That brief incarceration was long enough to give rise to an enduring story of an exchange with Ralph Waldo Emerson. Emerson was supposed to have passed by the jail and seen Thoreau behind bars. "Henry," Emerson exclaimed, "what are you doing in there?"

To which Thoreau was said to reply, "Waldo, the question is what are you doing out there?"

From Matamoros, reports of military atrocities fed the resistance movement in the Northern United States. George Meade, a young U.S. Army lieutenant, protested that his fellow volunteers were robbing Mexicans, stealing their cattle, and killing civilians "for no other object than their own amusement."

The same Winfield Scott who had blinked away abuses of the Cherokees now said that if even a tenth of those accusations were true, the result was enough "to make Heaven weep, and every American of Christian morals blush for his country."

Yet the war itself was going well for the United States. The troops of General Stephen Watts Kearney had taken Santa Fe and were headed for San Diego in California, and Zachary Taylor bested Santa Anna's forces on February 23, 1847, in the Battle of Buena Vista.

During that fighting, Henry Clay, Jr., was wounded in the thigh. He handed to a friend the pistols his father had given him and asked that they be returned to him. Soon afterward, a Mexican soldier discovered Clay and ran him through with a bayonet.

Expressions of sympathy for Henry Clay poured in from around the country, including one from former president Van Buren. In the depths of his anguish, Clay turned to the religion he had always regarded lightly and, four months after the battle, was baptized in the Episcopal Church.

President Polk would have preferred to send a Democrat to be the conquering general in Mexico, but Winfield Scott's preeminence was as indisputable as his presidential aspirations. The president dispatched him to take Vera Cruz but ordered him to pause there while Polk offered new negotiating terms. Rebuffed once again, Polk charged Scott with wresting Mexico City from Santa Anna. Scott's men raised the Stars and Stripes in the city's plaza on September 14, 1847.

The Treaty of Guadalupe-Hidalgo followed five months later. The United States acquired California and New Mexico, and the Rio Grande became Texas's western and southern boundaries. As compensation, Mexico received substantially less than Polk had originally offered—$15 million in cash and another $3.25 million to settle pending claims against Mexico by American citizens.

The outcome was posthumous vindication for Andrew Jackson, who had claimed for more than a decade that Mexico's behavior would justify war in the world's eyes. For the abolitionists, however, the annexation of Texas represented a triumph for slavery. And yet this war, which many Whigs opposed, had solidified the reputation of Zachary Taylor as a national hero.

The Democrats opened their nominating convention in Baltimore on May 22, 1848, with their most conspicuous politician not in contention. President Polk had committed to serving only one term and now he was almost finished. He had drafted a letter to be read to delegates that made his decision irrevocable.

If his countrymen judged that he had adhered to his principles and faithfully performed his duty, Polk wrote, then he was "amply compensated for all the labors, cares and anxieties which are inseparable from the high station which I have been called to fill."

On their fourth ballot, Democrats named Lewis Cass, now a Michigan senator. He picked as his running mate Major General William O. Butler, who had succeeded Winfield Scott as commander of U.S. forces in Mexico.

Convinced that a fourth attempt by Henry Clay for the presidency would be as unavailing as his last three, the Whigs narrowed the choice to their two successful generals. In early June 1848, they nominated Taylor, a Southern slave owner, over Winfield Scott by 171 to 63. Clay took a diehard 32 votes, Webster 14.

The Whigs considered fourteen men for vice president before settling on Millard Fillmore of New York. Since delegates knew that any statement of principles they might draft would lose votes from one or another bloc in their uneasy coalition, the convention adopted no platform at all.

Zachary Taylor narrowly defeated Lewis Cass because Martin Van Buren had one last political trick to play. Northerners who resented the South's sway over the country were calling it "slave power" and vowing to resist it. As a young Whig wrote to a fellow Yale alumnus, Southerners "have fairly shit upon all our Northern statesmen and are now trying to rub it in."

That spirit permeated the leadership of the Free Soil Party, whose members opposed slavery less on moral grounds than because of the economic benefits to the North in curtailing the influence of Southern oligarchs. Van Buren accepted the Free Soilers' nomination, knowing how heavily the odds were against him. As his running mate, he took Charles Francis Adams, abolitionist son of the sixth U.S. president and grandson of the second. In February that year, Charles had lost his father. John Quincy Adams was stricken at the desk in the Congress where he had served for the past seventeen years.

The Free Soilers attracted moderate abolitionists—Horace Mann, Walt Whitman, William Cullen Bryant—and took fourteen seats in the House and two in the Senate. Van Buren won no electors, but by drawing 10 percent of the presidential total, he contributed to the defeat of Cass and sent Zachary Taylor—nicknamed "Old Rough and Ready"—to the White House.

Zachary Taylor

During a steamboat cruise through Louisiana, the president-elect encountered Henry Clay, and they greeted each other with a semblance of warmth. Taylor did not know that for some months Clay had been considering a return to the Senate. When his replacement, John Crittenden, was elected governor of Kentucky, Clay girded himself for one more joust in the political arena.

In February, the Kentucky legislature elected him to the Senate, ninety-two to forty-five, over his Democratic opponent, former vice president Richard Johnson. Clay, who was recovering slowly from a fall down a flight of stairs, said he felt like a laborer "who having worked hard all day by sunshine is sent again at night into the field to work by moonlight."

But he considered the issues facing the nation too momentous for him to refuse. Horace Greeley had written from New York that the next Congress was sure to decide the status of any new states admitted to the Union.

Millard Fillmore

President Taylor agreed that the great issue would be the expansion of slavery, and he launched his term with a scheme to bypass a congressional debate. Rather than recognize New Mexico and California as territories, Taylor would permit settlers to exercise the option guaranteed to them when they drew up their state constitutions, which meant that they could enter the Union as free states. His plan also would let Taylor duck two other pressing issues: The North wanted to shut down the slave trade in the District of Columbia; the South was demanding stricter fugitive slave laws to stop the increasing number of runaways.

In the Senate, Henry Clay roused himself to work out one last series of compromises, but he found them blocked by Taylor, who put forth his own less popular solutions. When Southerners confronted the president and threatened to secede, Taylor's response was worthy of Andrew Jackson. He would hang anyone who rebelled against the Union, Taylor said, and he would do it with less reluctance than he had hanged spies and deserters in Mexico.

John Calhoun had also been returned to the Senate, but pneumonia confined him to his bed. Following the proceedings closely from home, Calhoun was not won over by Clay's compromises. He was suspicious of Clay's support for a fugitive slave act and of his promise that Congress would not end slavery in the District of Columbia. As the debate raged on, Calhoun feared that the South's very existence was at stake.

On March 4, bundled into a long cloak, he took his Senate seat. Too weak to speak himself, Calhoun listened as his words were read by James Mason of Virginia. He argued that the government had destroyed the nation's equilibrium by deferring to Northern fanatics. The result was transforming the federal republic—as envisioned by the framers of the Constitution—into a "great national consolidated democracy," one as absolute and despotic as czarist Russia.

Calhoun invoked George Washington as "one of us—a slaveholder and a planter." General Washington had drawn his sword in the cause of disunion—by which Calhoun meant separating the colonies from Great Britain. "This was the great and crowning glory of his life."

If Calhoun seemed to be calling for disunion now, he was not ready to go that far. The future, he concluded, was not his to predict. "I shall have the consolation, let what will come, that I am free of all responsibility."

Duty done, Calhoun returned home. On March 30, 1850, he told his son John, a doctor, "I am very comfortable" and died.

Vice President Millard Fillmore was in the Senate chamber three and a half weeks later when the rancor between Senator Benton and a Clay ally, moderate senator Henry S. Foote of Mississippi, reached such a pitch that Foote drew his pistol on Benton. During the entire debate, Fillmore had said nothing publicly about his own position, even after Taylor was rumored to be ill, perhaps fatally. But as a reliable New York state Whig, Fillmore indicated privately that if he were still presiding over the Senate and the vote was tied, he would support Clay.

He was spared the decision. That year, the capital celebrated Independence Day at the Washington Monument amid a stifling heat wave that seemed as menacing to Taylor as cold sleet had been to William Henry Harrison. When Taylor died four days later, however, the most likely cause was cholera. Whatever killed him, Old Rough and Ready had survived in office sixteen months longer than Old Tippecanoe.

After Millard Fillmore took the oath of office, he accepted the resignation of Taylor's cabinet and agreed to Clay's suggestion that he appoint Daniel Webster once again as secretary of state. The debate over Clay's compromises had gone on for six months, and he was past exhaustion, so weak that he could barely get to the Senate chamber. He demonstrated the depth of his fatigue conclusively by declining an offer from last-ditch loyalists to enter his name for the presidency in 1852.

More than a quarter-century had passed since Clay first met in private with John Quincy Adams to advance his ambition. Now that ambition had finally died. "I am here, expecting soon to go hence," the seventy-three-year-old Clay said. He would be answering only "to my own conscience and God."

But in edging his legislation forward, Clay had made his own compromises. He jettisoned an amendment by David Wilmot, a Pennsylvania Democrat, to prohibit slavery in any territory won from Mexico. Called the "Wilmot Proviso," that restriction passed the House but failed in the Senate.

And in maneuvering to pass his bill, Clay denounced both sides—the abolitionists for their recklessness, the Southerners for their continual threats of secession. Challenging Senator Barnwell Rhett of South Carolina, Clay unleashed his old thunder: If Rhett committed overt acts against the Union, then "he will be a traitor, and I hope he will meet the fate of a traitor."

The burst of applause provoked by that flourish showed that Clay could still excite the galleries. But when parliamentary tactics rendered Clay's bill toothless, he rose once more to warn that the failure of his compromises could mean war. He loved his home state, Clay said, but he pledged that if Kentucky joined any secession, "I would go against Kentucky."

On August 2, Clay gave up the fight, resigned his leadership post, and went to Newport, Rhode Island, to repair his health. Taking up Clay's role, Stephen Douglas, the Illinois Democrat and chairman of the Committee on the Territories, worked with colleagues in the House to break Clay's omnibus bill into five separate pieces of legislation.

In the twelve days between September 9 and September 20, 1850, President Fillmore signed bills that admitted California to the Union as a free state; retained slavery in the District of Columbia but outlawed the slave trade there; and organized the Territory of Utah and the Territory of New Mexico—including land that became Arizona—under the rule of popular sovereignty. Congress also agreed to pay Texas $10 million toward its national debt in return for the western land it was claiming. And, by a vote of 109 to 76, legislators passed the Fugitive Slave Act.

The Supreme Court had ruled in 1842 that Northern officials need not violate the due-process provisions in their states by arresting runaway slaves. Now Congress was requiring all U.S. citizens to assist federal marshals in recapturing them. The slaves were then to be handed over to federal commissioners who would receive a double fee for every fugitive sent back to his owner.

The Cherokee Nation immediately felt repercussions from the act, since many Southern slave owners already accused the tribes' lax policing system of encouraging their slaves to take refuge there. Yet few Cherokees were abolitionists. The tribe endorsed laws to prevent marriage between Negro slaves and Indians, and many leaders were turning a substantial profit from slavery.

In Cherokee territory, the slave population had been growing steadily—from 583 slaves at the turn of the century to 1,592 shortly before removal. Lewis Ross was one of those who prospered as a professional slave trader, buying slaves in Little Rock and New Orleans and selling them at a market in Tahlequah. With skilled mechanics valued up to fifteen hundred dollars, Cherokee gangs regularly crossed into Creek, Seminole, and Osage territories to steal slaves and sell them in Arkansas or Missouri.

John Ross had put his own slaves to work at a kiln, making bricks for the expanding number of public buildings and shops along the streets of Tahlequah and Park Hill. The Cherokees still prided themselves on being more humane masters than white owners, but in 1846 Ross had discovered ammunition and guns hidden on his plantation for a possible slave revolt.

A newspaper called the *Cherokee Advocate,* which had replaced the *Phoenix,* carried both advertisements for slaves and news stories about the stealing of entire slave families. In a letter to Washington, Samuel Worcester protested the abduction of five freed blacks, including a child, who had been living in the Creek Nation until they were put up for sale in Tahlequah. After a three-year effort by federal authorities—and lawyers' fees approaching four thousand dollars—the victims were released.

The slavery debate was also straining ties between the Cherokee missionaries and their Northern sponsors. The Congregationalists were urging their clergy to expel slave owners from their churches, and that directive became another source of antagonism within the tribe. Under the banner of states' rights, Stand Watie and many from the Treaty Party were taking up their opposition again to Chief Ross's leadership and seemed ready to cast their lot with the secessionist Southerners.

President Fillmore was making new appointments under the compromise laws that he hoped would shore up his political support. To be Utah's territorial governor, he named Brigham Young, the leader of the Church of Jesus Christ of Latter-Day Saints. Young's government denounced the escaping slaves, but a far more critical issue was plural marriage, which was blocking Utah's application to join the Union.

As the presidential election of 1852 approached, the *Richmond Enquirer* was reporting comparative calm throughout the political world. At first, Fillmore's patient diplomacy had appeared to be serving the country better than Zachary Taylor's blunt ultimatum that he would defend the Union by force.

And yet as he enforced the 1850 Compromise, Fillmore ended up alienating both North and South. He sent army troops to aid federal marshals in rounding up runaway slaves, then sent them again into South Carolina to put down rebels in Charleston who were seizing federal property.

In fact, Fillmore was presiding over the dissolution of the Whigs. His party was split between the "conscience Whigs" of the North and the "cotton Whigs" of the South. Other party members were being lured into such fringe organizations as the Order of the Star-Spangled Banner. The Free Soil Party opposed not only the spread of slavery but also the Compromise of 1850.

When Henry Clay endorsed Fillmore for a second term, it was seen as his last salvo in a presidential campaign. With his physical decline well known, a New York delegation rushed to award him an impressive gold medal. Pointedly, its sponsors noted that the nation's previous medals had gone to war heroes; for the first time, one was being given to a man of peace.

Clay relished the honor. When he helped to draft the list of his accomplishments for the medallion's reverse, the word "compromise" appeared three times: "Missouri Compromise 1821," "Tariff Compromise 1830," and simply "Compromise 1850."

But after the presentation, the gold medal went the way of Clay's presidential aspirations. While it was being returned to New York to improve the engraving of his likeness, the medal was stolen. The substitute that Clay received was made of bronze.

Another friend of the Cherokees was also enjoying recognition for his past achievements. During President Tyler's administration, John Howard Payne had ingratiated himself with his cabinet, and Tyler appointed him U.S. consul to Tunis. The posting eased Payne's habitual money worries, and in an exhaustive letter to his sister on Valentine's Day, 1844, Payne had pronounced himself pleased with his new surroundings. His musician's ear was offended, however, by singers with an "earthquake fury of stentorian lungs in Arabic songs—as I was told, but never should have suspected—of most melting tenderness."

Payne's sinecure ended abruptly when infighting in Washington led to his recall. Eventually Daniel Webster got him reinstated, and the bey of Tunis welcomed him back with all flags flying. But his health soon failed, and on April 9, 1852, in his sixty-second year, John Howard Payne died far from home.

That same spring, Henry Clay was diagnosed with tuberculosis. He fell into an unshakable depression, eating peckishly and, despite a nightly opiate, sleeping badly. He summoned his son Thomas to Washington and, on June 29, 1852, said good-bye. "I believe, my son, I am going." Moments later, Clay died, two months past his seventy-fifth birthday.

His will divided his estate among his wife and surviving children and grandchildren. For his slaves, Clay had devised a complex formula for freeing all children of his female slaves who had been born after January 1, 1850. When the young women reached twenty-five and the young men twenty-eight, they would be paid for the three years of labor before their emancipation. That money was intended to cover the cost of returning them to Africa.

Henry Clay became the first man to lie in state in the Capitol rotunda, and Democrats joined with Whigs in paying him lavish tribute. Theodore Frelinghuysen delivered the official eulogy. John C. Breckinridge extolled the triumvirate of Clay, Webster, and Calhoun.

One of the many national funeral orations was delivered in Springfield, Illinois, by Abraham Lincoln, now returned by unimpressed voters to private practice. Lincoln called Clay "*the* man for a crisis."

Grieving crowds turned out to watch Clay's body being taken back to Lexington by steamboat and railroad. At the gravesite, his coffin was draped with the Masonic apron Lafayette had once presented to him. The Masons had built a temporary vault until a marble sarcophagus could be completed.

The terse wording on Clay's headstone reflected a lifetime devoted to the Union: "I know of no North—no South—no East—no West."

On the first ballot at the Whig convention in Baltimore, Fillmore came within 14 votes of the 147 he needed for the nomination. But that was only 2 more than were cast for Winfield Scott. Daniel Webster's 29 delegates held the balance.

Balloting went on through three days and forty-five roll calls. Webster's delegates held firm until Webster himself agreed to throw his support to Fillmore. As the count continued through another eight ballots, however, Fillmore's lead steadily eroded until on June 24, 1852, Winfield Scott won the nomination. Fillmore's secretary of the navy, William A. Graham of North Carolina, accepted the vice presidential nomination. On October 24, Daniel Webster died at his home in Massachusetts.

Again, Democrats were as badly split as Whigs. It took their delegates in Baltimore forty-nine ballots to nominate little-known Franklin Pierce of New Hampshire. In Concord, Massachusetts, Pierce had become friendly with the resident Transcendentalists and other writers, especially Nathaniel Hawthorne, who had met him when they were students at Bowdoin College. For the campaign, Hawthorne was preparing an admiring biography that would pass over the fact that Pierce drank too much and that he was derided as "Fainting Frank" for alleged cowardice during the Mexican-American War. Pierce loyalists claimed that when he had passed out twice under fire, it was from his wounds.

During the campaign, Pierce would not be enjoying encouragement from his wife. Jane Pierce had detested Washington when Pierce had served in the Senate and thought she had his word that he was not a candidate for president. When she learned that he had accepted the nomination, it was she who fainted.

To the nation at large, Pierce was described as "a Northerner with Southern principles" and, more fancifully, "Young Hickory of the Granite State."

But his home state was causing Pierce problems. Two years earlier, New Hampshire had revised its constitution, intending to eliminate a clause that barred Catholics from holding public office. The repeal of the ban was defeated, however, and both parties were stepping up their pursuit of votes from Irish immigrants, whose ranks had swelled after a six-year potato famine in Ireland.

That increase in the number of foreigners had provoked a backlash among those voters who worried that the country's traditional values were being lost. Such men had first organized in New York as the Native America Party; by 1853, they had become simply the American Party.

The common name for them was less admiring. Within their ranks was an organization so secret that if questioned about it, members were pledged to answer, "I know nothing." The "Americans" became the "Know Nothings."

The party had enjoyed considerable success in races for governor and the state legislature but tended to split ranks for the presidential election, which left Democrats and Whigs to fight campaigns heavy with racial and religious bias.

Democrats accused Whigs of chalking "No Popery" on town walls, while at the same time they expected Scott's campaign to remind Irish voters that Scott had educated his two daughters in Catholic convents.

To counter, the Democrats published correspondence in which Scott had once urged a longer naturalization period for immigrants. Outraging Irish and German voters, the letters united them for Pierce.

But since the 1850 Compromise, the positions of Whigs and Democrats on major issues could seem identical. And with the nation enjoying an economic boom, the result was a widespread lack of interest. One Cincinnati Whig reported that "Genl. Apathy is the strongest candidate out here," and Democrats displayed the same indifference.

The low turnout was catastrophic for Winfield Scott in Georgia, Alabama, and Mississippi. The Whigs took only their four bastions of Vermont, Massachusetts, Kentucky, and Tennessee. Electoral College results from the twenty-seven states translated their failure into stark numbers—254 for Pierce, 42 for Scott.

The period before the inaugural proved personally disastrous to both the new president and his predecessor. Pierce and his wife had already suffered the death of two children from illness. On their way to Washington, they were looking on when a freakish railroad accident killed their third child.

Jane Pierce, at least as reluctant as Rachel Jackson to enter the White House, never recovered from the shock and was fated to spend her days there sickly and miserable.

In the capital, Abigail Fillmore insisted on attending the Pierce swearing-in ceremony even though she had been ailing and the day was marked by heavy rains and snow. Taking the oath of office on March 4, 1853, Pierce pledged his allegiance to the Union and to the Compromise of 1850 designed to preserve it.

The next day, Mrs. Fillmore ran a high fever. The family vacated the White House for Washington's Willard Hotel, and three weeks later she died there.

Franklin Pierce

19 · Prologue (1853–61)

As the two presidents grieved, the Compromise continued to unravel. At first, Pierce's decisive victory and his majorities in Congress seemed to promise a constructive period that would permit a senator like Stephen Douglas to realize his vision of a railroad to connect the nation coast to coast. But Pierce was not a man of bold ideas. He focused instead on cabinet appointments, and they intensified the strains within his party.

Because his secretary of state, William L. Marcy, had opposed the Fugitive Slave Act, Pierce strove for balance by naming as secretary of war Jefferson Davis, a West Point graduate wounded at Buena Vista. Davis had been a Mississippi senator for ten years and a candidate for the state's governorship on the Southern Rights ticket. Further attempts at pleasing everyone wound up alienating every major bloc in Pierce's Democratic coalition.

The new president did pay off his campaign obligation to Nathaniel Hawthorne, however, by offering to appoint him as U.S. consul in Liverpool, England. Hawthorne accepted despite the disapproval of neighbors like Henry Thoreau. Their misgivings seemed justified when, for the next seven years, the author of *The Scarlet Letter* wrote nothing at all.

Stephen Douglas's powerful voice was filling the vacuum in presidential leadership. In trying to deal with Nebraska, Southern Democrats objected to a provision in the 1820 Compromise that "forever prohibited" slavery in that territory. Douglas argued that popular sovereignty—states' rights—took precedence over any such restriction.

In January 1854, Douglas introduced legislation that organized everything north of the thirty-six-degree-thirty-foot parallel to the Canadian border into a single Nebraska Territory. Settlers could decide eventually whether they wanted to legalize slavery or outlaw it. Selling the idea, Douglas made a neat comparison: In 1850, Congress had substituted popular sovereignty for Mexican law. Now he was invoking the same principle to overrule the prohibition against slavery from three decades earlier.

The debate was intensified that spring when the Pierce administration sent federal troops into Boston to guarantee the return to slavery of twenty-year-old Anthony Burns, a fugitive from Virginia. Abolitionists had united three years earlier to block the rendition of another runaway, and this time, Pierce's actions were met by handbills reminding citizens of their proud tradition: "Men of Boston! Sons of Otis and Hancock!" They were exhorted to stand up for freedom, but the verdict in Burns's trial was a foregone conclusion, and he was sent back to his owner.

In Washington, Stephen Douglas said he saw no need to repeal the 1850 Compromise. But leaders on both sides of the slavery issue seized on the opening he had given them. In a showdown on May 30, 1854, Southerners defeated the Northern abolitionists, and Pierce signed the Kansas-Nebraska Act, which created two territories. Rather than an outright repeal, the 1850 Compromise was merely declared "inoperative and void."

For Douglas, the opposition to his proposal had a desirable effect. It ended the torpor in both parties that the 1850 Compromise had produced. By returning slavery to the national debate, Douglas had scored a decisive victory over General Apathy.

Among the Cherokees, the slavery issue needed no ratcheting up. In October 1853, the latest commissioner of Indian affairs in Washington, George Manypenny, had received a report from a federal agent that some missionaries around Tahlequah were behaving "obnoxiously" by "fanatically pursuing" their opposition to slavery, which would necessarily "lead to mischievous and pernicious consequences."

Since the Cherokees benefited from slavery, the agent asked Manypenny for the authority to expel Samuel Worcester and a Northern Baptist, Evan Jones. Manypenny was getting similar warnings from an agent with the Choctaws and Chickasaws, who predicted that if the missionaries were not muzzled, slavery among the Indians would be abolished within five years.

When Manypenny asked for proof, the agents sent him testimony from slaveholders who had been dropped from their congregations by the missionaries who obeyed their Northern boards.

The Reverend Stephen Foreman, with Indian and white ancestors, had graduated from the Princeton Theological Seminary before he became Worcester's Cherokee translator. When Foreman bought his first slaves in 1851, Worcester was dismayed and recommended that he free them and let them work out their indebtedness under a contract for their labor. Foreman refused, and Worcester had to finagle with the American Board to keep Foreman on his payroll. But the incident had left Foreman aggrieved. He reported Worcester for preaching abolition and added that the missionary set a bad example by letting his servants—who had been slaves—eat with his family at their table.

"A slave cannot bear good treatment," Foreman wrote, claiming that Worcester's servants "noise abroad in boasting manner, expatiating on this happy situation" and making Foreman's own slaves dissatisfied.

Rancor over slavery was spreading because of a work of fiction by the daughter of Lyman Beecher, the Boston clergyman who had once celebrated the seeming victory of the Cherokees in the Supreme Court. At twenty-one, Harriet had moved to Cincinnati, where her father was president of a theological seminary, and married Calvin Stowe, a professor there.

As Harriet Beecher Stowe, she had first published *Uncle Tom's Cabin* in July 1851, in serial form in an abolitionist journal, *National Era.* The following year, her novel appeared as a book with the subtitle *Life Among the Lowly.* By then, Mrs. Stowe was a forty-year-old mother of seven children.

She extolled the virtues of her fictional slave Tom, whose African features were "characterized by an expression of grave and steady good sense, united with much kindness and benevolence." In Simon Legree, the cruelest of slave owners, Mrs. Stowe created another enduring stereotype: "How would you like to be tied to a tree," Legree taunts Tom, "and have a slow fire lit up around ye?"

If her characters could seem one-dimensional, her portrayal of Southern life had rounded contours. Evangeline St. Clare—Little Eva, the daughter of Tom's owner—develops a deep love of Tom and other slaves and prefers life on the plantation to time spent with her cousins in the free state of Vermont.

At her novel's end, Mrs. Stowe spelled out her message: Northerners could lay no claim to virtue simply because they owned no slaves. "The people of the free states have defended, encouraged and participated in" the evils of slavery, she wrote, and were the more to blame because they did not have the excuse of their upbringing or the culture around them: "Both North and South have been guilty before God, and the *Christian Church* has a heavy account to answer."

Even apart from the incendiary issue of slavery, Franklin Pierce's first term was ending badly for him. Northerners considered a stillborn plan to buy Cuba from Spain as his attempt to expand slavery. Pierce enjoyed one success when he took Jefferson Davis's advice and spent $10 million for land that would provide a route through southern Arizona for the proposed transcontinental railroad. That development was overshadowed, however, by the shooting war that broke out between Northern and Southern settlers over whether Kansas should be a slave state or free.

Slave owners and their allies had crossed the border from Missouri and set up a government in Leavenworth, Kansas. The usual name for such brazen occupiers was *filibusters,* from a Dutch word for "pirate." In Kansas, they were termed Border Ruffians, and Free Soilers followed their example and established a rival capital in Lawrence. The inevitable violence between the two factions was not confined to their state. In Washington, Congressman Preston Brooks beat Senator Charles Sumner of Massachusetts almost to death for Sumner's insults to Brooks's proslavery uncle.

Nor did Concord, Massachusetts, remain isolated from the carnage in "Bloody Kansas." When a raging abolitionist named John Brown came to town to raise money to foment a slave uprising, he was given a respectful hearing by the Transcendentalists but little money. Henry Thoreau, for one, thought Brown's lecture was sufficiently inspiring that cash contributions were unnecessary.

The passive nature of those Northern abolitionists infuriated Brown, who showed up in Kansas with his four sons and a small group of volunteers determined to replace talk with action.

The caning of Charles Sumner and the raids on Lawrence by the Border Ruffians confirmed for Brown that his crusade against slavery must become more aggressive. Late on the evening of May 24, 1856, five proslavery settlers were confronted in their cabin on Pottawatomie Creek and dismembered with broadswords. Brown's sons took part in the slaughter. To share responsibility, John Brown fired a pistol into the head of a man already dead.

After more skirmishing and an actual battle at Osawatomie, Brown left the Kansas Territory and a new governor achieved a nervous peace.

The bloodshed in Kansas was the final stain on Pierce's administration. His Democrats rejected him and turned instead to sixty-five-year-old James Buchanan, Pierce's minister to Great Britain and formerly Polk's secretary of state.

Buchanan would have nothing to fear from the Whigs. After Millard Fillmore lost his wife in 1853 and then his daughter the following year, he traveled aimlessly through Europe for a year. During his trip, Fillmore was contacted by the Know Nothing Party. With his distaste for "the corrupting influence" of foreigners, especially Catholics, Fillmore endorsed its platform.

He next accepted the presidential nomination of the stragglers from the Whig Party, but even close friends said his chances were too slim for them to waste a vote on him. In the end, Fillmore would carry only Maryland.

Buchanan's true challenge came from the candidate of the emerging Republican Party, John C. Frémont. The Republicans had been organized only two years earlier by men who opposed slavery but also shared a vision for the nation's economic future. Some Know Nothings were drawn to this new movement, along with the Free Soilers, who contributed the campaign's longest slogan: "Free Soil, Free Labor, Free Speech, Free Men, Frémont."

Publishers like Horace Greeley came on board, and Abraham Lincoln attended the first Republican county convention in Jackson, Michigan, the year of the party's founding. Many Quakers, Congregationalists, and Presbyterians enrolled as Republicans. Most Roman Catholics stayed loyal to the Democrats.

Frémont's father-in-law was Thomas Hart Benton, who had arranged government financing for the young man's major surveys of the Oregon Trail, the Oregon Territory, and the Sierra Mountain range. In the Sierras, Frémont had named its highest peak for Zebulon Pike, a casualty in the War of 1812.

His expeditions with his frontier guide, Kit Carson, had made Frémont famous. Then, however, his freewheeling ways during the early tension with Mexico had led to his conviction by a court-martial board that recommended Frémont's discharge from the military. Under pressure from Benton, President Polk had dismissed a charge of mutiny, remitted Frémont's sentence on lesser charges, and restored him to active duty.

Frémont claimed that accepting Polk's terms would mean acknowledging his guilt, and he declined them. In the aftermath, Benton broke with Polk, but during the westward expansion that followed the war, Frémont became one of California's first senators.

Although Frémont was defeated in the presidential election, his Republicans ran successfully in New York, New England, and the northern Midwest. Southern politicians quickly identified the party as their new and potentially most lethal threat.

In one respect, the election proved Stephen Douglas right. Sharpened distinctions between the two parties had led to an unusually heavy voter turnout.

In addition to serving as secretary of state, James Buchanan had been the Pennsylvania congressman whose lazy eye Clay once mocked. A lifelong bachelor, Buchanan was as natty a dresser as Van Buren but less shrewd and less lucky. He came into office expecting to finesse the troublesome slavery question by urging that it be left to the U.S. Supreme Court. As for Kansas, Buchanan assured the audience at his inaugural address on March 4, 1857, that territorial matters were "happily, a matter of little practical importance," since the Court was on the verge of ruling "speedily and finally."

James Buchanan

Two days later, Chief Justice Taney delivered the court's decision in *Scott* v. *Sandford*. The lawsuit stretched back fifteen years to when a slave named Dred Scott had first sued for his freedom. Scott claimed that the army doctor who owned him had kept Scott in slavery illegally while he was stationed in the free state of Illinois and in the Wisconsin Territory. A circuit court in Missouri first ruled in Scott's favor, holding that his residence in free territory had emancipated him. Missouri's appeals court reversed that decision.

By the time the case reached a federal court, the doctor had died and his heir, John A. Sandford, became the defendant. That lower federal court upheld the Missouri decision, and the case moved to the U.S. Supreme Court.

It was then that Buchanan interjected himself. A month before his inaugural, he learned from a friendly justice, John Catron of Tennessee, that the nine justices were split, with five men from slaveholding states against Scott. A narrow ruling based solely on state law might maintain that Scott remained a slave, but it would not help Buchanan politically.

Catron suggested that Buchanan contact Justice Robert Grier of Pennsylvania. If Grier would join the decision, it could be seen as reflecting a national consensus, and Buchanan would be justified in claiming to have resolved the slavery issue.

Grier consulted with Chief Justice Taney. The result was a seven-to-two decision against Scott, buttressed by various concurring opinions. The Court held that since Scott was a slave, he was not a citizen and not entitled to sue in federal court. More critically, the Court ruled that the Missouri Compromise—banning slavery north of thirty-six degrees thirty feet—was unconstitutional. Under the Fifth Amendment, Congress could not deprive slave owners of their property rights without due process.

Buchanan had won the skirmish. If the United States acquired Cuba or moved farther south into Mexico, both areas could welcome slave owners. And he was sure the decision would eviscerate the Republican Party. What was the point of an antislavery movement now that the Supreme Court had ruled that Congress could not ban the expansion of slavery?

If Buchanan expected a supine response, however, the Republicans took another tack. Justice Benjamin Curtis of Massachusetts had pointed out the flaws in Taney's argument, including the fact that five states had granted citizenship to persons of color and that U.S. citizenship had existed before the drafting of the Constitution.

But rather than argue the law, the Republicans charged Buchanan with colluding with the Court to defy the will of Congress. Senator Henry Seward of New York denounced the uninspired Buchanan as "the worst of all the Roman emperors."

Buchanan went on to back the proslavery minority of settlers in Kansas, a decision that lost him his party's Northern support. Not only did he not recover his political influence, Buchanan had exacerbated the battle over slavery and had split the Democrats into two factions.

The president lost further prestige when Brigham Young defied him in Utah. Hostile to outsiders, Young had kept strangers out of Salt Lake City until the day 125 Arkansas emigrants traveled through the area on their way to California. They were set upon and killed by Young's white followers, joining forces with local Paiute Indians.

Buchanan responded by sending twenty-five hundred U.S. Army regulars to assert federal authority. Then a friend of his intervened as peacemaker and the troops were withdrawn. Polygamy, although personally distasteful to Buchanan, persisted.

Since his forays in Kansas, John Brown had been collecting funds, armaments, and disciples. On October, 16, 1859, Brown led nineteen men in an attack on the U.S. armory at Harper's Ferry, Virginia. Emerson and Thoreau had been in his audience for Brown's last round of public addresses, but he had given no hint that he planned to establish a renegade free state and set himself up as its commander. Earlier in the year, however, he did confide his plot to Frederick Douglass, the celebrated fugitive slave, who refused to join his insurrection and discouraged other blacks as well.

Brown intended to seize the armory's hundred thousand muskets, distribute them to slaves throughout the state, and spark a rebellion that would engulf the South. He argued that the weapons were vital for self-defense and would prevent a mass slaughter.

With the armory patrolled by a single watchman, Brown's men seized it easily. But when the Baltimore & Ohio Railroad came rolling past, the rebels opened fire and scored their crusade's first fatality. They killed the train's baggage master, a free black man named Hayward Shepherd.

Alerted to the takeover, local militia surrounded the armory. When Brown's son Watson and another rebel came out with a white flag, the inflamed townspeople shot and killed them.

On the morning of October 18, Army Colonel Robert E. Lee led a company of U.S. Marines to Harper's Ferry and offered Brown terms of surrender. Brown refused them. "No," he said, "I prefer to die here."

Lee's men surrounded and captured him and seven followers. By then, Brown's insurgents had killed four men and wounded nine others; he had lost ten men in a brief gun battle. Besides Watson, another son, Oliver, was killed. A third, Owen, was able to escape with four of the rebels.

At Brown's trial in a Virginia court, his defense attorney reminded the jury that Brown himself had not killed anyone. But jury members took forty-five minutes to find him guilty on three counts of murder, conspiracy, and treason.

On December 2, 1859, John Brown went to the gallows. In his last statement that morning, he predicted that "the crimes of this guilty land will never be purged away but with blood." He was hanged at 11:15 a.m. and pronounced dead thirty-five minutes later.

Brown's religious letters from prison had touched many Northern hearts. After his death, Frederick Douglass came to see him as a martyr: "His zeal in the cause of freedom was infinitely superior to mine," Douglass wrote. "Mine was as the taper light; his was as the burning sun."

Ralph Waldo Emerson went further. He said John Brown would "make the gallows glorious, like the Cross."

In Congress, Republicans were taking advantage of the disarray among the Democrats to offer up their own populist legislation. The Homestead Act would give 160 acres of free public land to every settler in the Northwest who occupied it for five years. Buchanan vetoed that act and another that would have established land-grant agricultural colleges.

By the time of his party's nominating convention in 1860, Buchanan was irrelevant. Stephen Douglas had become the candidate of Northern Democrats and Buchanan's vice president, John Breckinridge, of the Southerners. Buchanan gave Breckinridge his tepid and inconsequential support.

When the Republicans nominated Abraham Lincoln, Southerners warned that his election would mean an end to slavery. Since the days of John Calhoun, South Carolina had been threatening to leave the Union. Calhoun might have been dead for a decade but his nullification spirit lived on.

Under the pretext of strengthening the Union, Buchanan had set off a chain of events he could not control. His final message to Congress absolved himself for creating the crisis and blamed the abolitionists.

By then Lincoln had already been elected president in November 1860, and South Carolina had seceded noisily from the Union on December 20 with fireworks, jubilant cannon fire, and bells ringing from every steeple in Charleston.

Stand Watie

20 · Stand Watie (1861–65)

At seventy, Chief John Ross faced a final test. His instinct was to remain faithful to the Union, despite his years of contending with Washington. As Ross told the *Arkansas Gazette,* the Cherokees considered the Stars and Stripes "the shield of their protection." But Ross warned that if the Union were "wickedly" destroyed, his Nation "will go where their institutions and their geographical positions place them—with Arkansas and Missouri."

As before, Ross was speaking for full-blooded Cherokees, and most of them did not own slaves. He also had the backing of a secret organization with two thousand Cherokees who had adopted the name the Keetoowah Society. Outsiders called them "Pins" for the crossed pins they wore on their shirts. The Pins upheld traditional Cherokee culture and leaned toward supporting the Union.

But Cherokees of mixed blood often sympathized with the Southern rebels. They had their own faction, the Knights of the Golden Circle, and their leadership fell naturally to Stand Watie. The other four members of that loose federation of Civilized Tribes appeared to share Watie's sentiments. When Ross sent delegates to a joint meeting with his neighbors, he warned them against any premature commitments.

Ross was trusting once again to his hopes. He wanted to believe that somehow his Nation could remain neutral, and during the next six months, Ross continued to hold out against the many Southern appeals.

Confederate general Benjamin McCulloch began by asking Ross for one concession: If Union forces invaded the Cherokee Nation, would Ross allow Southern sympathizers to organize a resistance? Ross said he must respectfully decline. Such an armed force would not only jeopardize Cherokee neutrality, it would also revive the tribe's bloody rivalries.

McCulloch's response was to commission Stand Watie as a colonel in the Confederate army.

Ross was pressed further by a lawyer from Little Rock, Albert Pike, who offered attractive terms for joining the Confederacy. Still, Ross remained neutral. At that, Pike undercut Ross's position by signing treaties with elements of the Creeks, Chickasaws, and Choctaws and by working to persuade the Seminoles to join the Southern cause. Pike had adopted Schermerhorn's tactic. When he found that he could not win over full-blooded Indians, he signed separate agreements with each tribe's mixed-blood minorities.

When Chief Ross called a general assembly for August 21, 1861, nearly four thousand Cherokees endured the scorching heat to attend. He began his speech urging tribal unity, but by its conclusion he bowed to reality. The time had come, Ross announced, for preliminary steps toward forming an alliance with the Confederate States.

In Washington, President Lincoln's safety had become an obsession with Winfield Scott, and he hired private detectives to foil any assassination attempts. Now seventy-four, Scott had been the nation's chief general for two decades. But he suffered from gout and vertigo. Combined with his weight of three hundred pounds, they made riding a horse impossible.

To succeed him, Scott's first choice had been his protégé, Colonel Robert Edward Lee of Virginia, the son of the Revolutionary War hero "Light Horse Harry" Lee. When Lincoln offered Lee command of the Union army, however, Lee turned him down and returned home. Although he had first opposed secession, when Virginia left the Union in April 1861, Lee resigned his commission to fight for the Confederacy. More than a third of the army's 1,108 officers joined him, either defecting to the South or dismissed for disloyalty.

By the first of November, 1861, the early stages of the war were going badly for the Union, and Lincoln accepted Scott's standing offer to resign. In his place as general in chief, the president appointed John McClellan, who had been chafing under Scott's command. When Lincoln informed McClellan of his promotion, he replied, "It is a great relief, sir. I feel as if several tons were taken from my shoulders."

The next morning, McClellan showed up at the train station at four o'clock to watch Scott leave Washington for New York. Describing the scene to his wife, he was unsparing: " . . . it was a feeble old man, scarcely able to walk, hardly anyone there to see him off but his successor. Should I ever become vain-glorious and ambitious, remind me of the spectacle."

By the time Benjamin McCulloch designated Stand Watie's men a Confederate regiment, Watie had already recruited three hundred soldiers committed to the South. McCulloch wrote to the Confederate War Department that Watie's men, being half-breeds, were as "educated men and good soldiers" as anywhere in the country. He dismissed any recruits Ross might attract as "full-breeds."

Ross's authority was now jeopardized by Pike's treaties with his neighbors, and he felt increasingly vulnerable to Watie's hostile army within his Nation. The Confederate government's terms began to look irresistible. The Southerners would guarantee the money that Washington still owed to the tribe, which would be forfeited if the Cherokees left the Union. The Confederacy would also enforce the fugitive slave laws within the Territory. And if the Indian nations asked to join the Confederacy as an independent state, they would be welcomed.

Since the Cherokee Nation badly needed money, that generosity was in sharp contrast to Washington's reluctance to pay its lingering debts. A recession had closed the Territory's seminaries and forced the *Cherokee Advocate* to suspend publication. Ross succumbed at last to the Southern blandishments.

By early 1862, however, Albert Pike was arrested on charges of incompetence, and the Confederacy was defaulting on its promised payments. Chief Ross began to have third thoughts about his allegiance.

Although General McCulloch had praised Watie's men for their learning, their leader had grown up keenly aware that the years his brother Boudinot and his cousin Ridge spent in Connecticut had left them better educated. Watie wrote a legible English, but he spoke slowly and made few comments during tribal councils.

Yet on horseback, Watie was commanding. He rode into battle wearing a dark plantation coat over gray flannel trousers and, against the sun, a black slouch hat pulled down to his eyes. Watie was no disciplinarian, but the physical strength and daring that had made him a champion ballplayer now served to inspire his troops.

Almost immediately on taking command, Watie led his Cherokee Mountain Rifles in skirmishes along the Territory's northern border with Osage troops who had remained loyal to the Union. As the war expanded, Watie became invaluable to McCulloch in battles at Wilson Creek and Bird Creek against Creek soldiers fighting for the North.

But it was at the Battle of Pea Ridge in Arkansas on March 6, 1862, that Watie displayed a rash courage bordering on fatalism. His men had barely arrived on the scene when McCulloch sent them to wipe out the enemy's forward position. With no time to plan a strategy, Watie gave a war whoop and led a charge directly into Union guns. His men captured four artillery pieces. But as the hostile barrage grew too intense, Watie shouted, "Charge back, boys! Charge back!"

He survived the engagement, but McCulloch was killed. Although Watie emerged with high praise for bravery, the most telling result at Pea Ridge was the mass defection of many Cherokee soldiers to the Union side. Colonel John Drew, their commander, was Chief Ross's nephew and did not go with them. Drew would stay loyal to the Confederacy even as his uncle was wavering.

In June 1862, Union troops swept south from Kansas toward Cherokee territory with Ross's friend Evan Jones in their ranks. Jones carried a message from the Indian Affairs office in Washington promising that the federal government would honor its past obligations to all loyal tribes. In Tahlequah, Ross declined to meet with the Union commander, Colonel William Weer, because, he explained, he had signed a treaty with the Confederacy.

But Ross was sending conflicting signals. He ignored an order from the Confederate high command to enlist all Cherokee males from ages eighteen to thirty-five. And he sided with his wife's Quaker instincts when she protested raising a Confederate flag over the Cherokee council house.

John Drew had assigned the remnant of his Cherokee regiment to protecting his uncle. But early on the morning of August 3, Ross gathered up his family, along with a host of Northern sympathizers, and set off for Fort Leavenworth, Kansas. Drew's guard followed—adding another fifteen hundred troops to the Union ranks.

In Kansas, Union brigadier general James Blunt encouraged Ross to send a letter to President Lincoln and then go to Washington to explain in person his contradictory actions. Blunt also wrote to Lincoln directly, commending Ross as "a man of candor and forcefulness" upon whose word the president could depend.

Meeting with Lincoln, Ross ran through his catalogue of Cherokee grievances but assured the president of his people's true loyalty to the Union. Although Lincoln seemed cool to Ross's overtures, he agreed to consider his appeal.

Meantime, those who had followed Ross into exile—perhaps as many as six thousand women, children, and elderly men—were facing starvation in Kansas. Those who returned home to the Cherokee Nation fared no better. Their crops had been disrupted, and their hunger became acute. A federal agent noted that the Cherokees, once the most powerful of Indian tribes, had been left "disgraced, humbled, impoverished and demoralized."

Reports of the widespread misery reached Ross in Philadelphia, where he and his family were waiting out the war in a house his wife had inherited. He considered returning to Tahlequah. But his family feared for his life and persuaded him that he could do more for his people by speaking out in Washington.

Had Ross gone back to Park Hill, he would have found a bleak landscape. His son, James, who went there in search of supplies, had been captured by Confederate soldiers and transferred to prisons throughout the South before dying in one of them. In 1863, Confederate troops descended again on Ross's house, where his daughter, Jane, and her husband, Andrew Ross Nave, were living with their children. Nave was shot as he fled, and Rose Cottage was burned to the ground.

In Tennessee, Henry Clay's estate, Ashland, had already been destroyed, but not by warfare. Clay's son James had bought the crumbling house, razed it, and built a replica on the site. When the war began, James enlisted with the Confederacy and took sanctuary afterward in Canada.

Stand Watie had not only deprived Ross of his home, he had also usurped his tribal honors. At an August 1862 meeting, Southern Cherokees elected Colonel Watie as their chief. It took six months before Cherokees loyal to the Union could hold their own conference and restore Ross's title to him in exile.

On the battlefield, Watie went on burnishing his legend. Confederate president Jefferson Davis appointed him a brigadier general on May 10, 1864, making Watie the highest-ranking Cherokee in General Lee's army. The promotion delighted Watie's nephew, Elias Cornelius Boudinot, who had come home to enlist as a Confederate major.

But the war was winding down. Watie's isolation in the West meant that he did not learn for some days that Robert E. Lee had surrendered at Virginia's Appomattox Courthouse in early April 1865. Nor did he hear the following month that Union troops in

Georgia had taken Jefferson Davis into custody. Watie finally capitulated on June 23, 1865. He had become the last Confederate general to surrender.

In peacetime, the struggle for dominance between Watie and Ross moved to arbitration before a peace commission. Its members had been appointed in Washington after Andrew Johnson succeeded to the presidency upon Lincoln's assassination on April 14, 1865. Although Ross continued to protest that he had been forced to sign a treaty with the Confederacy, he was accused of having been an enemy of the United States. In his defense, Ross pointed out that three of his sons had served in the Union army, along with three grandsons and three nephews.

Waite's nephew, the former Major Boudinot, remained unforgiving, still blaming Ross for the murder of his father twenty-six years ago. "I will show," he testified, "the deep duplicity and falsity that have followed him from his childhood to the present day, when the winters of sixty-five or seventy years have silvered his head with sin: and what can you expect of him now?"

Cornelius Boudinot went on to work for railroad interests, acquiring rights through Cherokee territory. Driving in the first spike in the territory in 1870, Boudinot made brief remarks. He said his tribe had benefited from contact with the white man: "I stand in no fear of the railroad. It will make my people richer and happier. I feel that my people are bound closer together and to the government by these iron bands."

John Ross could take heart from a White House meeting with Andrew Johnson although, like Lincoln, Johnson promised only to review the case and act justly.

In July 1865, Ross's second wife, Mary, died of lung congestion. Within six months, Ross himself was confined to his bed with severe stomach pains. But he lived long enough to see President Johnson agree to a treaty that vindicated Ross's behavior and upheld his title as chief.

The treaty was signed on July 19, 1866. On August 1, Ross died in Washington at the age of seventy-four. His body was returned to Park Hill, where he was buried near the ruins of Rose Cottage.

Stand Watie lived another seven years, still leader of the dissidents but without political influence. When he died at sixty-four on September 9, 1871, he left his widow and family deeply in debt.

The first civil war—fought with angry words in Congress over the Cherokee removal—had pitted North against South and ended in defeat for the North. The second civil war—fought with cannon and guns—had crushed the South. The victims in both wars included the men, women, and children of the Cherokee Nation and their Native American neighbors. When the costs of the second civil war were calculated, the Five Civilized Tribes had lost a higher percentage of their citizens than any Southern state.

Throughout the early years of the twenty-first century, members of the U.S. Senate Committee on Indian Affairs introduced a resolution calling on the federal government to make a formal apology to the nation's 564 tribes for its past policies. The senators cited similar apologies made to Japanese Americans in 1988 for their internment during World War II and to native Hawaiians five years later for the illegal overthrow of the Hawaiian Kingdom in 1893.

A preamble to the Senate resolution listed the wrongs committed against Native Peoples by the United States and deplored the suffering and death of Native Peoples during a policy of forced removal, "including the infamous Trail of Tears."

The resolution concluded that the United States, acting through its Congress, "apologizes on behalf of the people of the United States to all Native Peoples for the many instances of violence, maltreatment and neglect inflicted on Native Peoples by citizens of the United States."

That resolution died annually in Congress until October of 2009, when it was passed as an amendment to the 2010 Defense Appropriations Bill and signed into law by the president on December 19, 2009.

As enacted, the bill stripped away the Senate preamble with its litany of abuses by the United States, among them the Trail of Tears, "the theft of tribal lands and resources," the breach of treaties, and the massacres at Sand Creek in 1864 and at Wounded Knee in 1890.

The apology ended with a disclaimer that nothing in its language "authorizes or supports any claim against the United States."

ACKNOWLEDGMENTS

Near the end of his life, Arthur M. Schlesinger, Jr., granted that his celebrated study of Andrew Jackson had severe shortcomings. Writing in 2006, Schlesinger praised the work of Princeton professor Sean Wilentz for giving "slavery and the Indians their proper place in the Age of Jackson."

Schlesinger explained that more than sixty years earlier he had been writing as "an ardent New Dealer" whose aim was to link the current president, Franklin Roosevelt, to the venerable strain of American populism that Jackson represented. He was hardly alone in his enthusiasm for Roosevelt; this book is dedicated to a friend from Arkansas whose family named him Franklin Delano. Schlesinger remembers being entirely absorbed by the economic struggles of that era. It was only much later that he came to feel he had "underplayed and ignored" the less admirable aspects of Jackson's presidency.

Writers and historians who are still assessing Jackson will sympathize with Schlesinger's attempt to define so complex a figure. At best, one may have to settle for praising Jackson's strengths, including his indomitable courage, before deploring his failings.

Certainly it was an odd twist that Jackson, a man fervently committed to preserving the Union, should have strengthened the states' rights movement by refusing to uphold the Supreme Court against the state of Georgia. He bought time against the secessionists of South Carolina but at a price he did not foresee.

If interpreting Jackson calls for caution, defining the two factions of the Cherokee Nation is even riskier. The fatal split between the Treaty Party and the Ross Party may have represented realism versus idealism. But which was which? In Oklahoma last year, I found that question still being debated.

What seems undeniable after 180 years is that John and Quatie Ross, Major and Susannah Ridge, John and Sarah Ridge, Elias and Harriet Boudinot, and Stand and Sally Watie all acted in what they took to be the best interests of their people.

Driven West represents my third attempt to tell our nation's early years as a living story, and once again I have been intrigued by men and women who often had been relegated to supporting roles—James Otis and Samuel Adams in *Patriots*, Tecumseh and Zebulon Pike in *Union 1812*.

This time, Margaret Eaton threatened to take over whole chapters just as she had dominated Jackson's first year as president. If she deserves full treatment now it is because few episodes in his life show so clearly the point at which Jackson's admirable loyalty crossed over into mulishness. Telling her side of the affair was also a twenty-first-century response to Mrs. Eaton's pained cry that her "heartless persecutors" had "put into American history statements that are likely to be perpetuated hundreds of years after I am dead."

But Margaret complicated the restoring of her reputation. Four years after John Eaton died in 1856, she married Antonio Buchignani, an Italian musician and dancing teacher.

The bride was about to turn sixty, the groom was forty years younger. Margaret signed over to him Eaton's sizable estate, and when he ran off to Italy with her granddaughter in 1866, she was left penniless. Working as a dressmaker, Margaret supported herself until her death in 1879, a month before her eightieth birthday.

Apart from the Cherokees themselves, the other memorable characters to emerge from my research included, of course, Clay, Webster and Calhoun, along with John Howard Payne; Winfield Scott; and especially the Christian missionaries, men and women who left the comforts of New England to serve their god on a rough, often hostile, frontier. One can question the wisdom of inducing a people to sacrifice their native beliefs in favor of an alien creed and yet admire the conviction and bravery of Samuel and Ann Worcester and Daniel and Elizabeth Butrick.

In traveling to the Cherokee capitals in Georgia and Oklahoma, I was given invaluable assistance at many libraries and archives. Among the people to whom I owe great thanks are Dr. Donna J. Myers, president of "Friends of New Echota" in Georgia; Dawn Hampton, Rome–Floyd County Library, Rome, Georgia; Bill Montgomery, Special Collections, Atlanta Central Library; Kitty M. Rutherford, Calhoun, Ga.; April Miller, Sarah Erwin Library, Gilcrease Museum, Tulsa, Okla.; Delores Sumner, John Vaughn Library, Northeastern State University, Tahlequah, Okla.; Tom Mooney, Cherokee Heritage Center, Park Hill, Okla.; John Lovett, Western History Library, University of Oklahoma, Norman, Okla.; Jack Baker and Curtis Rohr, Claremont, Okla.

My hope is that this book leads readers to the excellent earlier works that explore these events and central figures in greater detail. At the head of any list would be the lifetime of indispensable scholarship by Robert V. Remini. Gary E. Moulton has served John Ross well, both in his biography and in editing his papers. Among the other writers whose books have made the Trail of Tears indelible are John Ehle, Grant Foreman, Gloria Jahoda, Francis Paul Prucha, and especially Thurman Wilkins.

Lynn Nesbit at Janklow & Nesbit has represented my writing for forty-five years now, and my gratitude only grows.

And once more, it is a pleasure to thank the team at Simon & Schuster for its amiability and total professionalism: A meticulous and forbearing copy editor, Sean Devlin; editors Roger Labrie and Karen Thompson; art director Jackie Seow; production editor Al Madocs; Toby Greenberg for picture research; Judith Hancock for the comprehensive index; and from publicity, Alexis Welby and executive director Victoria Meyer.

As for Alice Mayhew, there's nothing left to say. As an editor and a friend, she is the best, and all of her grateful writers know it.

NOTES

CHAPTER 1. HENRY CLAY (1825)

2 The boy's early education was entrusted: Schurz, I, 4.
3 "Kissing is like the presidency": Remini, *Clay*, 252.
4 Clay had "snickered" over the mistake: Nagel, 257.
5 But he had also demanded of his Northern colleagues: Forbes, 36–37.
5 Jefferson was attuned more viscerally to slavery: Schurz, I, 193; Jefferson to John Holmes, April 22, 1820.
6 A serious setback then arose, however, when Missouri proposed: Forbes, 119.
6 Missouri's new senator, Thomas Hart Benton: Remini, *Clay*, 192.
6 As bankruptcies and unemployment roiled the nation: Baxter, 22.
7 Into that ambitious vision: Baxter, 27.
8 "the most haughty period of imperious Rome": Watson, 137.
8 "I cannot believe," Clay said, "that killing two thousand five hundred": Schurz, I, 239.
8 For years afterward, men used the phrase: Dangerfield, 8.
8 In his fury, Adams also reneged on his earlier vow: Nagel, 291.
9 Defeat, he felt, "would be equivalent to a vote of censure": Nagel, 286.
9 Hugely disappointed, Clay thrashed about: Clay, *Papers*, III, 891.
10 Even before the national election: Niven, *Van Buren*, 148.
10 "substantially well": Niven, *Van Buren*, 157.
11 "to show our strength": Cole, 138.
11 By the time Van Buren moved to the state senate: Niven, *Van Buren*, 17.
12 "I am enjoying, while alive": Rogers, 129.
12 He deplored the fact that Clay's "morals": Rogers, 133.
12 "Well, gentlemen," Clay announced, "since you are both": Remini, *Clay*, 257.
13 Earlier in the day, Adams got a note: J. Q. Adams, *Diary*, 6, 464.
13 Meeting with Jebediah Morse, a prominent evangelical: Nagel, 261.
14 Letcher responded that "the Speaker now entertained": Clark, 223.
14 "To give a decent time for his own funeral solemnities": J. Q. Adams, *Diary*, 6, 465.
14 Clay "wished me, as far as I might think proper": J. Q. Adams, *Diary*, 6, 465.
15 But John Quincy Adams worried that winning: Nagel, 293.
15 He warned a Kentucky congressman that if his state: Van Buren, 199–200.

15 The man who made the accusation was "a dastard and a liar": Remini, *Clay*, 261.
16 When suspicion settled on Congressman George Kremer: Schurz, I, 243.
16 Asked about the rumors, Adams said merely that "the object": Nagel, 293.
16 "That I should vote for Mr. Crawford?": Clay, *Papers*, IV, 54–55.
17 "I said," Adams recorded that night: J. Q. Adams, *Diary*, 6, 494.
18 The son agreed with their family friend Rufus King: J. Q. Adams, *Diary*, 6, 504.
18 "Well, Mr. Van Buren," he said, "you see that I could not": Niven, 161.
18 "What a farce!": Remini, *Jackson*, II, 95.
18 And Jackson himself concluded that the "rights": Remini, *Jackson*, II, 96.
19 Other guests moved closer to watch their meeting: J. Q. Adams, *Diary*, 6, 503.
19 "How do you do, Mr. Adams?" Remini, *Jackson*, II, 97.
19 One man observing their exchange was struck: Goodrich, II, 403–4.
19 But since the Constitution did not provide for that alternative: Nagel, 297.
20 Steeped in the classics, Adams praised "the magnificent": Nagel, 299.
20 Adams called them "lighthouses of the skies": Remini, *Adams*, 80.
20 Although the president sensed that such erudite projects: Hargreaves, 166.
21 He made overtures to his recent opponents: Schurz, I, 250.
21 And Clay desperately wanted the job: Nagel, 298.
21 "I told Sullivan that I would some day call upon him": J. Q. Adams, *Diary*, 6, 507.
22 He called it "the most dangerous stab which the liberty": Niven, *Calhoun*, 109.
22 "So you see," he shouted, "the *Judas* of the West": Remini, *Jackson*, II, 98.
22 At least, Adams said, he could now be sure: Nagel, 298.
22 After Jackson calmed down, he had written: Remini, *Jackson*, II, 99.
22 When Harvard's president declined to reinstate his son: Nagel, 280.
22 To remove the Indians "by force, even with a view": Cresson, 466.

CHAPTER 2. MAJOR RIDGE (1825)

25 By the early 1800s, the Choctaw tribe lived in a swath: Phillips, 62.
26 For Cherokee women who had farmed together: McLoughlin, 18; U. B. Phillips, 64.
26 For the time being, a worrisome contradiction was ignored: Cotterill expands on the point, 165–70.
26 The Cherokees may have signed away: Walker, 4.
26 William Fyffe, a white South Carolinian traveling among the tribe: William Fyffe Papers, Thomas Gilcrease Library, Tulsa, Oklahoma.
27 Within four years, America's secretary of war was complaining: Walker, 12.

27 He predicted a clash between the tribes and "a few avaricious men": Prucha, ed., *Documents*, 1.

28 In 1792, Washington issued a proclamation: Ehle, 42.

28 Long before he became president, Thomas Jefferson had tried: Jacqueline Greb, *Cherokee Advocate,* February 1989, II.

28 "We shall push our trading houses," Jefferson suggested: Harrison, W. H., 1, 71.

29 The Europeans who followed William Fyffe: Timberlake, 75–78.

29 Records indicated that as far back as 1690: Starr, 24.

29 When they got hold of liquor, the men might drink: Timberlake, 79.

30 Throughout his teens, he had sometimes joined: Woodward, 86.

30 At about the time that she gave birth to a son: Confer, 9.

31 Doublehead had promised to spare the post: Horan, 266.

31 In the darkness, Ridge shot him: Wilkins, 40.

31 Some Indians had been accepting Jefferson's offer: Starkey, 22.

32 "I scorn this movement of a few men to unsettle the nation": Wilkins, 46.

32 Give up the plows and the looms, Tecumseh exhorted them: Starkey, 23.

33 Setting off for battle, the Cherokees stuck two white feathers: Wilkins, 67.

33 Meigs showed the same spirit when the first white Moravian: Ehle, 67.

33 In 1809, Meigs had overseen a meticulous census: Douglas C. Wilms, "Cherokee Land Use in Georgia" in W. L. Anderson, 6.

34 Their switch from hunting to farming: Ehle, 199.

34 In return, he said, "it will be expected that you will be obedient": Wilkins, 68.

35 When Colonel Meigs testified to the plundering: Wilkins, 85.

35 As a concession, his agreement called for friendly Creeks: Debo, 83; Buchanan, 300.

35 Meeting with the chiefs, President Madison offered: W. L. Anderson, xi.

36 Ridge boycotted the subsequent meeting with Jackson: Wilkins, 94.

36 As he pondered their future, Jackson ended a statement: Minges, 35.

37 "A country of tall trees, many water courses": Remini, *Jackson,* I, 394.

37 Pushmataha, a revered Choctaw chief: Barrett, 400–402.

37 At fifty-six, Pushmataha was three years older: Remini, *Jackson,* I, 395.

37 In two highly lucrative deals: Wallace, 5.

38 He retained his belief in the Immortals: Gabriel, 16.

38 "I've resolved never to do such a thing again": Wilkins, 105.

38 "Because for all his skill for learning": Wilkins, 106.

38 Publishing a report from Cherokee country: *Boston Record,* October 24, 1818.

39 The Cherokees' final judgment on Meigs: Ehle, 395, cites Rights, *American Indian,* 186.

40 Half of McIntosh's ancestors were Creek: Hargreaves, 202.

40 "By and by, he will take them": Wilkins, 144.

41 Georgia's agents had set aside twelve thousand dollars: McIntosh Papers, Library, Gilcrease Institute, Tulsa, Oklahoma.
41 McIntosh assured Ross that "nobody shall know it": Wilkins, 144.
41 When McIntosh stumbled over his explanation: Wilkins, 145.
41 He warned that his federal delegation might not be coming: Wilkins, 145.
42 His family traced their bloodline to a Scot: Moulton, 2.
42 He never forgot his humiliation during a green corn dance: Gabriel, 135.
42 Joining with other men of mixed blood, Ross founded: Gabriel, 137.
43 "Sir," the Indian delegation wrote to Calhoun in English: Wilkins, 155, cites *American State Papers, Indian Affairs,* II, 474.
43 Addressing the Georgia legislature, Governor Troup: Eaton, 50, cites Hardin's *Life of George M. Troup,* 469.
43 In a letter to President Monroe, Georgia's officials underlined: Wilkins, 15.
43 "It is a very hot talk": Wilkins quotes the *Illinois Intelligencer* (Vandalia), August 20, 1824, 2, col. 5.
44 "They write their own state papers": Adams, *Memoirs,* 6, 272.
44 That would mean "Indians be looked upon as human beings": Horan, 51.
45 In an effort to persuade official Washington to see the chieftains: Ehle, 178.
45 McIntosh's allies represented only eight of the forty-six towns: Remini, *Adams,* 92.
45 A fellow chief said to him, "My friend": Remini, *Adams,* 92.

CHAPTER 3. JOHN QUINCY ADAMS (1825–27)

47 The agreement went on to reward the citizens of Georgia: Foreman, 318.
47 The treaty gave the Creeks a year and a half to evacuate: Bemis, 80.
47 A provision also promised that the federal government: Remini, *Adams,* 92.
48 Short but husky, Troup was a striking figure: Cook, 100.
48 "Welcome, Lafayette!" Troup cried: *Biographical Directory of the American Congress.*
48 When Troup urged his cousin, General McIntosh: Hargreaves, 202.
49 "I say *satisfaction*": *Niles' Weekly Register,* XXIX, Oct. 15, 1825.
49 The governor couched his letter in extravagant language: Remini, *Adams,* 93.
50 He had decided that receiving them made better use of his time: Lipsky, 121.
50 The general was another officer who had fought: J. Q. Adams, *Diary,* 7, 8.
50 Adams was beginning to accept Troup's warning: J. Q. Adams, *Diary,* 7, 5.
51 For now, Adams and Barbour agreed not to answer: J. Q. Adams, *Diary,* 7, 11.
52 The Carters were from old English stock: Wooten: 62–63.
52 They amassed a few hundred acres of land: Boney, 112.
52 *"All I want in this creation":* Brinkley, 785.
52 *"Way up yonder in the Cherokee Nation":* Ehle, 213.
52 They would travel with the Creek leader: Wilkins, 167.

52 Good Shouting Child: *American Indian Biographies,* 350.
52 But after they had inspected them at a public ceremony: Bass, 75, cites *Chronicles of Oklahoma,* vol. VII, No. 3 (Sep. 1929), 246.
53 There, John fell violently in love with the red-haired: Parins, 5.
53 When Sally's mother learned that the girl returned: Wilkins, 133.
54 The missionary agreed, pointing out that taking a white-skinned: Wilkins, 134.
54 John considered their conversion one more way: Ehle, 172.
54 Speaking to raise money for the mission school: Wilkins, 136.
54 When Major Ridge came to visit the Cornwall school: Bass, 76, cites *Chronicles of Oklahoma,* vol. VII, No. 3 (Sep. 1929), 247.
55 "She would be disappointed of her home": Gabriel, 185.
55 Hostile crowds jeered at the couple: Ehle, 189.
56 That was how Buck Watie had arrived at Cornwall: M. W. Anderson, 12.
56 Since the school encouraged Indian students to retain: Ehle, 146.
57 "The eloquence of Herman Vaill," one began: Gabriel, 52.
57 "Poor Harriet, I am so sorry": Gaul, 80.
57 When Stephen finished her letter, he began to scream, "Harriet!": Gaul, 81.
57 "The dye is cast, Harriet is gone": Gaul, 81.
58 Many friends had dropped her, but "the few friends I have": Gaul: 85.
58 Another of Harriet's brothers-in-law: Gaul, 89.
59 "When first we met we were taking the red path": Wilkins, 163.
59 The eloquence of their pledge moved even Gaines: Wilkins, 167.
60 "The subject is embarrassing": Wilkins, 171, cites National Archives, RG 75, *Letters sent by the Office of Indian Affairs,* Letter Book II, 269–74.
60 "We may as well be annihilated": Wilkins, 171–72, cites National Archives, RG 75, T-494, Roll 1, frames 0777–81.
61 One morning, Samuel Pooley, a New Yorker who made mathematical: J. Q. Adams, *Memoirs,* 6, 537; April 27, 1825.
61 "The whole science of diplomacy": J. Q. Adams, *Memoirs,* 6, 539; April 30, 1825.
61 "There is much to correct and reform": J. Q. Adams, *Memoirs,* 6, 539; May 1, 1825.
61 Henry Clay dismissed Barbour's idea: J. Q. Adams, *Memoirs,* 7, 89.
62 That evening, he confessed to his diary: J. Q. Adams, *Memoirs,* 7, 90.
62 Adams responded in his loftiest manner: J. Q. Adams, *Memoirs,* 7, 92.
62 Opothle Yoholo, not yet thirty years old, was despondent: J. Q. Adams, *Memoirs,* 7, 106.
63 The final terms left the Creeks with almost no territory: Wilkins, 173.
63 Adams thought the delay would prevent the "excitement or debate": J. Q. Adams, *Memoirs,* 7, 110.
64 Reading Barbour's proposal, Adams found it "full of benevolence": J. Q. Adams, *Memoirs,* 7, 113.
64 Portraying himself as a disinterested observer, Tazewell made: Wilkins, 174.

CHAPTER 4. SEQUOYAH (1828)

67 Many traders lived with two or three squaws: U. B. Phillips, 64.
67 One night in 1770, he packed up his few belongings: Foster, 20.
67 She called the infant by the cryptic name: Foster, 26.
67 Cherokee mothers had developed an effective way: Foster, 28.
68 White comrades called him George Gist: *American Indian Biography,* 454.
68 His wife agreed with their neighbors: Wilkins quotes Peter Jones, *History of the Ojebway Indians,* 187–88.
68 "What I have done, I have done": Ehle, 160, quotes Major George Lowery. "Notable Persons in Cherokee History: Sequoyah or George Gist," Introduction by John Howard. *Journal of Cherokee Studies* 2.4 (1977) 385–93.
70 Then he collected the results, shuffled them: Samuel Carter, 51.
70 In 1825, the Cherokee legislative council voted twenty dollars: Ehle, 306.
70 Three years later, when the Old Settlers: T. Mooney, *Generations,* 7.
71 At first, Gallatin was incredulous: Gabriel, 103.
71 John thought that his father's gracious two-story house: Wilkins, 190.
72 The event was surprisingly violent: Abbot, 44; Underwood, 19.
72 But he was angry about the anonymous death threats: Gaul, 20.
73 "To those who are unacquainted with the manners" Boudinot, 3.
73 "You here behold an Indian!": Wilkins, 193.
73 "I am not as my fathers were": Boudinot, 4.
73 "Must they perish? Must they all, like the unfortunate Creeks": Boudinot, 16.
74 Samuel's wife had been born Ann Orr: Bass, 21.
74 "To make the whole tribe English in their language": Bass, 31.
74 The child was the latter—a girl—and Cherokee women: Bass, 68.
75 The press, boxes of type, and office furniture were shipped by steamboat: Bass, 78.
75 They caulked chinks in the log walls: Shadburn, *Blood,* 2.
75 When Harriet delivered another blond child: Bass, 88.
76 But in a letter to his brother-in-law: Gabriel, 111.
76 The Cherokees "would not return any abuse from Georgians": Ehle, 217.
76 "We, the Representatives of the people of the Cherokee": Ehle, 205, quotes Starr, 55–56.
78 But Boudinot expected their religious influence to continue: Gabriel, 108.
78 The idea of a written constitution drafted by the tribe's wealthiest: Ehle, 211.
79 As Ross had predicted, poor Indians, who seldom participated: Perdue, 62, in W. L. Anderson, *Removal.*

CHAPTER 5. JOHN C. CALHOUN (1828)

81 As the seventh vice president in American history: Calhoun, *Papers,* X, xiii.
81 A neighbor who avoided his company explained: Thomas, 77.
81 Even an admiring hostess summed up Calhoun: Coit, 70.
82 "The moment we engage in confederations or alliances": Remini, *Jackson,* II, 111.
83 Patrick Calhoun had always spoken of "my family": Bartlett, 279.
83 Floride Calhoun preferred white servants and felt she had: Bartlett, 281.
83 "We must send and receive ministers": Niven, *Calhoun,* 115.
83 Randolph was newly elected as senator: Remini, *Adams,* 83.
83 To enliven his insults, Randolph drew on the novel: Dangerfield, 357 note.
84 It was against his principles, Randolph said, to "make a widow and orphans": Remini, *Clay,* 295.
84 "You owe me a coat, Mr. Clay": Dangerfield, 358.
84 He contended that the president should not accept: Bartlett, 130.
85 To send along with the delegation, Clay prepared: Remini, *Clay,* 299.
85 He was particularly annoyed by Congressmen: Remini, *Adams,* 111.
86 Southerners complained that they sold their cotton: Remini, *Jackson,* II, 136.
86 General John Cocke saw reason for optimism: Wilkins, 202.
87 He maintained that "Georgia is sovereign": Remini, *Adams,* 98.
87 "From the first decisive act of hostility": Cook, 100.
87 But since the result could be civil war, he was submitting the question: Remini, *Adams,* 99.
87 Despite the talk of benevolence and humanity: Remini, *Adams,* 100.
88 "Indeed, I tremble for my country": Jefferson, 288.
88 "They are crying sins for which we are answerable": Remini, *Adams,* 100.
88 Georgia's senators decided that the new Cherokee constitution: Wilkins, 204.
88 Instead, the senate ruled that land could be taken on any terms: Williams, 17.
88 A handsome, highly gregarious congressman: Cook, 102.
89 Adams understood that his cabinet officers would soon find excuses: Parsons, 195.
89 President Adams glanced through the extended coverage: Parsons, 196.
90 "Fellow citizens, I thank you for this kind": Parsons, 196.
90 Adams appreciated the value of having a Georgian: Hargreaves, 282.
90 Adams had made it clear that he would reappoint: Hargreaves, 282.
90 One paper accused the president of polluting the White House: Parton, III, 141.
91 "It is from that trivial incident": Remini, *Adams,* 119.
91 Then he gave up even that pastime: Remini, *Adams,* 119.
91 "We are both guilty or innocent of the calumnies": Clay, *Papers,* VI, 76.
92 But he believed that "suspicion has been kindled": Remini, *Clay,* 321.

92 Writing to one federal agent, Hugh Montgomery: Ross, *Papers,* I, 136.
92 Ross warned that "the Cherokee nation objects to making": Ross, *Papers,* I, 139.
92 They described the *Cherokee Phoenix* as a "powerful auxiliary": Ross, *Papers,* I, 141.
92 They also addressed head-on the accusations: Ross, *Papers,* I, 144.
93 His group from Tammany Hall was labeled the Bucktails: Remini, *Van Buren,* 7.
93 One Presbyterian churchgoer in Rochester: Cole, 172–73.
94 A victorious Jackson was sure to offer him: Cole, 174.
94 Binns's "Coffin Handbill" showed six coffins: Dangerfield, 418.
94 One of them had been pardoned, he said: Remini, *Jackson,* II, 123.
95 "COOL AND DELIBERATE MURDER": Parton, *Jackson,* III, 144.
95 The impecunious proprietor of a St. Louis newspaper: Parton, *Jackson,* III, 180–81.
95 "Let Mrs. Jackson rejoice": Dangerfield, 419.
96 "The General always treated her as if she were his pride": Brands, 404.
96 "Ought a convicted adulteress and her paramour husband": Dangerfield, 419.
96 "General Jackson's mother was a COMMON PROSTITUTE": Remini, *Clay,* 325.
96 To John Coffee, he wrote, "How hard it is": Jackson, *Correspondence,* III, 409.
96 He expressed his bitterness to a friend: Burke, 117.
97 The same officer's daughter who praised Rachel's devotion: Brands, 403.
97 When she permitted herself a rare lamentation: Dangerfield, 420.
97 The boy surprised the Jacksons when, at age five: Remini, *Jackson,* II, 144.
97 "The persecution she has suffered," he wrote: Remini, *Jackson,* II, 149.
98 The focus of the *Cherokee Phoenix* remained resolutely local: *Cherokee Phoenix,* vol. 1, no. 39, Nov. 26, 1828.
98 At one point, Elias Boudinot tendered his resignation: *Cherokee Phoenix,* vol. 1, no. 40, Dec. 3, 1828.
98 The boy had not been named for the Quaker: Gabriel, 100.
98 "The majority of these Indians do not wish to remain": *Cherokee Phoenix,* vol. 1, no. 42, Dec. 29, 1828.
98 Samuel Worcester weighed in against a Georgia newspaper's: *Cherokee Phoenix,* vol. 1, no. 37, Nov. 12, 1828.
99 By now, Boudinot was editing his journal with an eye: Gabriel, 123.
99 Although it denied that the Cherokees were an independent nation: *Cherokee Phoenix,* vol. 1, no. 43, Jan. 7, 1829.
99 "It smelled so much of deception": Bassett, 500–501.
100 But throughout all of Tennessee, Adams and Rush got fewer than three hundred votes: Parton, *Jackson,* III, 151.
100 "We are beaten": Clay, *Papers* VII, 552–53.

100 He "has done me much injustice": Parton, *Jackson,* III, 172–73.
101 Once again, an election had thwarted Clay's dream: Remini, *Clay,* 337.
101 From New York, Van Buren solicited Washington news: Niven, *Van Buren,* 215–16.
101 He called for a program to house the growing number: Cole, 177.
102 Since he did not intend to live there long: Niven, *Van Buren,* 216.
102 To avoid any echo of the Adams-Clay deal: Parton, *Jackson,* III, 164.
102 One neutral Massachusetts congressman noted: Niven, *Van Buren,* 223.
102 As Calhoun wrote to one of his former professors: Niven, *Calhoun,* 157.
102 Otherwise, Calhoun assured his correspondents that "we are quiet": Calhoun, *Papers,* X, 542.

CHAPTER 6. ANDREW JACKSON (1829)

105 "Well, for Mr. Jackson's sake, I am glad": Parton, *Jackson,* III, 153.
105 "Mistus and Marster done elected President": Burke, 119.
105 Unaware that Nashville's matrons had gathered: Parton, *Jackson,* III, 153.
106 No, Rachael replied, "I'll never forget it": Burke, 120.
106 Jackson spent the night sitting next to her body: Remini, *Jackson,* II, 152.
106 "They have got more land than they use": Perdue, *Removal,* 50.
106 Although Montgomery had failed to negotiate: Moulton, 38.
107 He complained that too few of its residents observed the Sabbath: Moulton, 27.
107 "The people always supported Mr. Adams' cause": Parton, *Jackson,* III, 165.
109 Writing to Albany, Jackson said that he needed: Cole, 179.
111 "Young lady, you remind me of my wife": L. Phillips, 30.
111 But she preferred to think of the Franklin as "a first-class": P. Eaton, 2.
111 When Jackson returned to stay at Franklin House: Pierce, *American History,* 3.
111 As for Rachel, when Margaret met her: P. Eaton, 69.
111 Next she tried to elope with a dashing aide: P. Eaton, 18.
111 "Come here, Mother": P. Eaton, 20.
112 President Monroe's secretary of the navy: P. Eaton, 23.
113 The ship's log listed the cause of death: L. Phillips, 52.
113 Eaton said he was prepared to save Margaret: L. Phillips, 54.
113 "If you love Margaret Timberlake": Eaton, 48; L. Phillips, 55.
113 Margaret thought he represented "a great match": P. Eaton, 48.
114 "They are fine fellows," Jackson said.: Remini, *Jackson,* II, 160.
114 Except for Van Buren, the appointments were summed up: Parton, *Jackson,* III, 179.
114 Britain's minister reported to London: Cole, 180.
114 Jackson was pleased to have surrounded himself: Remini, *Jackson,* II, 165.
115 "Persons have come five hundred miles": Parton, *Jackson,* III, 170.

115 "It is beautiful!" Key exclaimed: *United States Gazette* (Phila.), March 6, 1829.
116 The Constitution required "that the great interests of agriculture, commerce": Parton, *Jackson,* III, 171.
116 Then, in a gesture to critics who had deplored: Jackson, *First Inaugural Address,* 1829.
116 "It will be my sincere and constant desire": Jackson, *First Inaugural Address,* 1829.
116 He would undertake "the task of *reform*": Jackson, *First Inaugural Address,* 1829.
116 Reform was vital because of abuses: Parton, *Jackson,* III, 172.
117 "All sorts of people," Story complained to his wife: Parton, *Jackson,* III, 170.
118 He described the mob as "spirits black, yellow and grey": Dangerfield, 424.
118 John Quincy Adams was preparing to devote: Nagel, 328.
118 Like many Virginians, his family had moved to the frontier: Cook, 109.
119 Most recently, as a member of the House Committee on Indian: Lumpkin, 45.
119 He deliberately kept silent on other matters: Lumpkin, 46.
119 "I was now applauded," he said, "for what I had then been": Lumpkin, 41.
119 Lumpkin fretted over the delay because "Northern fanatics": Lumpkin, 47.
120 "It is quite idle, at this time, to talk of coercion": *Cherokee Phoenix,* vol. 1, no. 48, Feb. 11, 1829.
120 "Braver men never lived," Story declaimed: *Cherokee Phoenix,* vol. 1, no. 45, Jan. 21, 1829.
120 As a small consolation for his people's losses: *Cherokee Phoenix,* vol. 2, no. 2, March 25, 1829.
120 Wilson Lumpkin found the onslaught from Northerners: Lumpkin, 47.
120 Although Rachel was no longer by his side: Remini, *Jackson,* II, 181.
121 "To the victor belongs the spoils of the enemy": Remini, *Jackson,* II, 185.
121 But Colonel McKenney soon learned that disloyalty: McKenney, *Memoirs,* 201–5.
121 "You know, Colonel McKenney": McKenney, *Memoirs,* 202.
122 George Washington had originally set up the posts: Ehle, 236.
122 Missouri's Senator Thomas Hart Benton had long been promoting: McKenney, *Memoirs,* 285.
123 "Well, then," he said, "the office will not suit me": McKenney, *Memoirs,* 205.
124 The Indians "must remove, or perish!": Satz, *American Indian Policy,* 15.
124 Traveling to speak on behalf of removal: Satz, *American Indian Policy*, 15.
124 "Mr. Jones," Van Buren began when the clerk appeared: Parton, *Jackson,* III, 236.
125 "No matter how you dispense it, you make enemies": Parton, *Jackson,* III, 237.
125 Looking ahead to his first message to Congress: Remini, *Jackson,* II, 192.
126 Eaton suggested that the emissaries should not waste: Moulton, 38–39.
126 Rather than appearing conciliatory, the Georgia legislature responded: Forbes, 231–32.

126 Congress had outlawed the African slave trade: Forbes, 221.
127 When John Ross appealed to Agent Montgomery: Moulton, 39.
127 It urged the tribe to "walk in the straight-forward path": Wilkins, 207.
127 But since his return, Hicks seemed disoriented and erratic: Wilkins, 208, cites Payne Papers, Ayer collection, Newberry Library, Chicago, II, 86–87.
127 Invoking his age, Womankiller said, "When I sleep": Bass, 112, cites *Cherokee Phoenix,* vol. II, no. 29, Oct. 28, 1829.
128 The killing could be "in any manner most convenient": Dale and Litton, 8.
129 For Parks, "It was more than my eyes could believe": Williams, 23.
129 Parks recalled that they were "acting more like crazy men": Williams, 26.
130 The *Phoenix* reported instances of white prospector's: *Cherokee Phoenix,* Feb. 11, 1829.
130 Parks had once hoped to marry a Cherokee girl: Williams, 30.
130 In the days when she was Mrs. Timberlake, Margaret had been assaulted: L. Phillips, 43.
130 But she had not learned just how widespread: P. Eaton, 56.
130 "Margaret Eaton," Jackson told her fondly: P. Eaton, 93–94.
131 "I can fight your battles and my own": P. Eaton, 91.
131 Unappeased, Margaret traced the rumor: L. Phillips, 76.
132 "You ought to have been here a little sooner": P. Eaton, 103.
132 Campbell said he was positive it was in 1821: L. Phillips, 78.
132 And he claimed that Craven's widow had other: L. Phillips, 79.
132 She considered these eccentricities her "little fooleries": P. Eaton, 86.
133 As she was growing up, her mother occasionally: P. Eaton, 32.
133 "We know, *here,* that none are spared": P. Eaton, 120.
133 "I tell you, Margaret, I would rather have": P. Eaton, 83.
133 Jackson prompted, "Nor Mrs. Eaton, either": L. Phillips, 81.
134 Seeking him out, she said, "If you told Dr. Ely": P. Eaton, 107.
134 Later, she recalled with considerable satisfaction: P. Eaton, 107.
134 He had "lied about me years before and was gone": P. Eaton, 104.
134 Navy Secretary John Branch, Attorney General John Berrien: Marszalek, 117.
134 He lived openly with Julia Chinn, a mulatto slave: Widmer, 119.
134 But when he brought one daughter: Marszalek, 116.
135 When a friend tried to fill him in: Van Buren, 342.
135 Van Buren, however, found Eaton "a man of moderate": Van Buren, 352.
135 But whenever the president was within earshot: P. Eaton, 82.
135 "But," Van Buren added, "don't tell General Jackson": Alexander, 262.
135 Van Buren was "the most frank man I've ever known": Alexander, 262.
136 To Jackson's dismay, his family became caught up: Burke, 149.
136 Instead, she faulted Mrs. Eaton for "possessing a bad temper": Van Buren, 344.
136 From her silence, Van Buren's reliable instincts: Van Buren, 345.

137 "Mrs. Donelson said, 'Mr. Van Buren'": J. Q. Adams, *Memoirs,* VIII, 185.

137 As the night approached, however, every cabinet officer: Marszalek, 110.

CHAPTER 7. THEODORE FRELINGHUYSEN (1830)

139 Jackson turned to writing: *Inaugural Addresses,* Jackson.

139 The Eaton affair had severely drained: Remini, *Jackson,* II, 224.

141 He wrote to Nicholas Biddle, the president of the Bank: Clay, *Papers* VIII, 166.

141 Since Indian Removal offered a promising target: *Cherokee Phoenix,* II, 44, Feb. 17, 1830.

141 He recommended merely that Hammond's newspaper: Clay, *Papers* VIII, 111–12.

141 Emboldened by President Jackson's speech, Georgia's legislators: Wilkins, 270.

142 White settlers had only to guarantee: Wilkins, 270.

142 Gilmer claimed that Ridge had induced "some old drunken": Wilkins, 271.

142 "You are too near to my white children": *Cherokee Phoenix,* II, 45, Feb. 24, 1830.

143 In authorizing the retaliation, John Ross had instructed: *Cherokee Phoenix,* II, 45, Feb. 17, 1830.

143 They left behind four Cherokees who had discovered a keg: *Cherokee Phoenix,* II, 45, Feb. 17, 1830.

144 But when he tried to refuse to go, he was struck: *Cherokee Phoenix,* II, 52, April 14, 1830.

144 Sarcastically, its editor suggested that a portrait: Wilkins, 212.

144 Gilmer assured Washington that it had been difficult: Wilkins, 213.

145 Wirt wrote to a friend that "very far beyond": Kennedy, 1, 108.

145 *The Letters of the British Spy* would still be in print: Wirt, xxii.

145 But as Wirt's authorship became known: Kennedy, 1, 108.

146 "I go for the Constitution as it is": Remini, *Jackson,* II, 233, quotes Register of Debates, 21st Congress, 1st Session, 31–41, 43–80.

146 Jackson had once expressed himself trenchantly: Remini, *Jackson,* II, 233.

147 When the evening arrived, Van Buren watched a keyed-up Jackson: Niven, *Van Buren,* 255.

147 "Our Union: It must be preserved": Remini, *Jackson,* II, 235.

148 "Are you willing—are my friends willing": Remini, *Jackson,* II, 253.

148 In another round of cost cutting, Jackson vetoed: Meacham, 139.

148 In some cases, Jackson simply killed a bill: Remini, *Jackson,* II, 256.

148 The authors of the House report left no doubt: Cave, 1333.

148 Presidential allies, like Pennsylvania congressman James Buchanan: Cave, 1334.

149 "I send him to another lawyer": Eells, 11.

149 Political opponents painted Frelinghuysen as an intolerant zealot: Schlesinger, 351–52.
149 He regretted that the present chief magistrate "did not pursue": U.S. Congressional Documents, 309, recorded April 9, 1830.
150 "I admire the ingenious clothing of a most odious": U.S. Congressional Documents, 311, recorded April 9, 1830.
150 As his speech entered a second day: U.S. Congressional Documents, 314, recorded April 9, 1830.
151 "For, sir, after the first day of June next": U.S. Congressional Documents, 318, recorded April 9, 1830.
151 To underscore his resistance: Eells, 21.
151 But he believed that "defeat in such a cause": U.S. Congressional Documents, 320, recorded April 9, 1830.
152 Forsyth's rebuttal was aimed at reminding senators: D. Brown, 7.
152 "A most unfortunate allusion, sir," Sprague said: U.S. Congressional Documents, 345, recorded April 17, 1830.
152 Under that theory, he said, "Britain has done no wrong": U.S. Congressional Documents, 354, recorded April 17, 1830.
153 "And what security do we propose to them?": U.S. Congressional Documents, 356, recorded April 17, 1830.
153 "If, sir, in order to become such, it be necessary": U.S. Congressional Documents, 357, recorded April 17, 1830.
153 In rising, Adams claimed he was embarrassed: U.S. Congressional Documents, 359, recorded April 20, 1830.
154 "If gentlemen are really in earnest in the opinions": U.S. Congressional Documents, 361, recorded April 20, 1830.
154 As a delaying tactic, Frelinghuysen called for putting off the vote: Remini, *Jackson,* II, 261.
155 Not only had a public outcry arisen: Van Buren, 288–89.
155 "If the friends of state rights propose to sanction": U.S. Congressional Documents, 1001, recorded May 15, 1830.
156 "What will be the decision of the Executive in the next case?": U.S. Congressional Documents, 1002, recorded May 15, 1830.
156 "We came to these people with peace offerings": U.S. Congressional Documents, 1014, recorded May 15, 1830.
156 In a somewhat transparent ploy, Storrs downplayed the stakes: U.S. Congressional Documents, 1015, recorded May 15, 1830.
158 The president had "staked the success": Remini, *Jackson,* II, 263.
158 Wilson Lumpkin acknowledged the South's deepest fears: U.S. Congressional Documents, 1020, recorded May 17, 1830.
158 He said he "opposed it from the purest motives": Conley, *Cherokee Nation,* 134.
159 "Cupidity and Avarice by sophistry, intrigue and corruption": Moulton, 42, cites Ross to Crockett, Jan. 13, 1831, Ross Papers, Newberry Library.

159 He acknowledged that except for the unusual circumstances: *Cherokee Phoenix,* III, 19, Sep. 18, 1830.

159 Two weeks later, Gilmer sent back a snide response: *Cherokee Phoenix,* III, 19, Sep. 18, 1830.

160 In fact, Marshall was already on record: Hobson, 172.

161 The Georgia legislature claimed that Marshall's order: Wilkins, 215–16.

161 On Christmas Day, Tassel was driven to the scaffold: Abbot, 10.

161 Their name came had been bestowed by the Choctaw: Jahoda, 162.

162 Afterward, Jefferson's administration subdued the survivors: Jahoda, 14.

162 By the time of the removal legislation: Foreman, 22.

162 The Choctaws had also negotiated a treaty: DeRosier, 116.

162 Light-skinned, comfortable in dark suits with stiff collars, Leflore had named: Jahoda: 82.

163 Eaton also resorted to the time-honored tactic of bribes: Foreman, 27–28.

163 Margaret Eaton recalled later in life: P. Eaton, 162.

163 "Indians are coming to town": P. Eaton, 165.

164 "Let him go," Eaton said. "Let him go": P. Eaton, 169.

165 "A considerable portion of them are poor": Foreman, 39.

165 "Two hundred and fifty head of horses have died": Jahoda, 86.

165 Alexis de Tocqueville, a twenty-five-year-old Frenchman: *New York Times,* C1, Nov. 9, 2009, quotes from Tocqueville's letters to be published by Yale University Press.

165 The march was being made "under pressure of hunger": Jahoda, 86.

165 One team leader agreed with that bleak report: DeRosier, 146.

165 Rough calculations concluded that one of every five Choctaw: Jahoda, 88.

166 It had been, he said, "a trail of tears and death": *Bishinik,* article by Len Green, Nov. 1978, 8–9.

166 In Washington, it was the financial cost: DeRosier, 149.

166 "The mass of the Cherokee people," Worcester wrote: David A. Wishart, "Evidence of Surplus Production in the Cherokee Nation Prior to Removal," in Shoemaker, 131.

166 Adventurous and physically fit, he had traveled south: Walker, 219–21.

167 At their meeting, the clergymen insisted that the debate: *The Missionary Herald,* XXVII, March 1831, 80–84.

167 In his second annual message to Congress, on December 6, 1830: Richardson, 2.

CHAPTER 8. JOHN MARSHALL (1831–32)

169 While Jackson had been pressuring the Choctaws: McKenney, *Memoirs,* 255.

169 Randolph seemed surprised. "Why, the General said": McKenney, *Memoirs,* 259.

169 "Colonel," Berrien began, "do you not know that this is not what": McKenney, *Memoirs,* 260.

170 James Barbour wrote in three thousand dollars and penciled a notation: Horan, 69.

170 More fatefully, McKenney had run afoul of the president: Satz, *American Indian Policy,* 156.

170 McKenney calculated that the individual rations would cost: Carter, 98.

170 "Will *you* take it at *ten*?": Parton, *Jackson,* III, 386.

171 Disappointed and angry, drinking heavily, Houston left Washington: Parton, *Jackson,* III, 388.

171 "Sir," he concluded, "they ought to be destroyed": Wilkins, 220.

172 They met in a room at Brown's Hotel: Wilkins, 221.

172 On his way home, McKenney stopped at a post office: McKenney, *Memoirs,* 262.

172 It took until November 1833 for him to wring exoneration: McKenney, *Memoirs,* 263.

172 The missionaries were modest about their own role: Wilkins, 225.

173 Its members passed a law to ban all whites: Moulton, 45.

173 To Elias Boudinot, John Ridge wrote, "From private": Wilkins, 220.

173 And Ridge assured his father that, even within Jackson's party: Wilkins, 220.

173 "Although representing the Cherokees would": Wirt, *Memoirs,* II, 292.

174 "It is so evident that they can never be tranquil": Wirt, *Memoirs,* II, 299.

174 He quoted to Madison his letter to John Ross: Wirt, *Memoirs,* II, 300.

174 Marshall survived the winter at Valley Forge: Newmyer, 23.

175 In the landmark case of *Marbury* v. *Madison*: Newmyer, 165.

175 The chief justice cherished the Constitution: S. Carter, 112.

175 On March 12 and March 14, 1831, Wirt repeated: Wilkins, 222.

175 "The whole affair is settled": Remini, *Jackson,* II, 305.

176 Jackson wrote to a friend that Calhoun had cut his own throat: Jackson, *Correspondence,* 4, 246, March 7, 1831.

176 A New Hampshire senator called Jackson "an ignorant": Remini, *Jackson,* II, 305.

176 When Van Buren seized the reins, Jackson responded: Marszlek, 159.

177 "Never, sir! Even you know little of Andrew Jackson": Marszlek, 159.

177 "Mr. Van Buren, I have made it a rule": Marszlek, 159.

177 After Van Buren had pledged to stay on: Niven, *Van Buren,* 267.

177 "I am the man about whom all the trouble has been made": Van Buren, 401–8.

178 Margaret Eaton appreciated his concern: P. Eaton, 170.

178 As a senator during John Quincy Adams's administration: Niven, *Van Buren,* 427.

178 To him, the removal bill was a "most generous: Cole, 214.

178 Henry Clay firmly opposed Georgia's attempt: Clay, *Papers,* VIII, 358–59, June 6, 1831.

179 Next, the Kentucky legislature elected Clay: Remini, *Clay,* 370–71.

179 He left home "with no anticipation of pleasure": Clay, *Papers,* VIII, 425.

179 Once there, Clay began to strengthen a coalition: Widmer, 87.

179 "It is, sir, as I have said, a small college. And yet": William H. Rehnquist, Foreword, in Shewmaker, xiii.

180 "If courts were permitted to indulge their sympathies": J. E. Smith, 516.

180 Marshall believed that the tribe constituted a "distinct": Hobson, 176.

180 Finally, Marshall apologized for not having time: Hobson, 176.

181 "Sooner than ask the President": Wilkins, 222.

181 "I'm particularly glad to see you at this time": Wilkins, 222.

181 "They took some of the Cherokee warriors prisoner": Wilkins, 223.

182 He urged Taylor to tell his people that "you can live": Wilkins, 223.

182 Clay decided that Wirt must have been bought off: Remini, *Clay,* 374.

183 They first picked up Isaac Proctor from the American Board: Foreman, 234.

183 Only a month earlier, Worcester had become a father: Gabriel, 130.

183 Worcester explained that taking the oath as a citizen: Bass, 134.

184 "My own view of duty is, that I ought to remain": Bass, 135.

184 While Worcester was temporarily free, the *Phoenix* published: Gabriel, 130.

184 But when the colonel saw that Ann Worcester and her infant: Rozema, *Voices,* 52.

184 John Ridge described "these unoffending and guileless": Wilkins, 227.

185 When Dickson McLeod, a feisty missionary: Rozema, *Voices,* 56.

185 "Fear not, little flock," he jeered: Rozema, *Voices,* 56.

185 "Here is where all the enemies of Georgia have to land": Bass, 138–39; Rozema, *Voices,* 59.

185 "If you leave, I fear the Cherokees will make no stand": Bass, 141.

186 Instead of the money being paid to the council, Wirt explained: Wirt, *Memoirs,* II, 303.

186 "But the Indian question is a cord of insanity": Wirt, *Memoirs,* II, 303.

186 In his personal life, Wirt suffered a loss: Wirt, *Memoirs,* II, 331.

187 By the end of the year, John Marshall had joined the ranks: J. E. Smith, 517.

187 In court, Wirt observed that, as a widower, Marshall now neglected: Masur, 113.

187 John Quincy Adams had picked up alarming rumors: Masur, 116.

187 His wife, Louisa, and son Charles had opposed: Nagel, 336.

187 When Edward Everett had taken up the issue: Parsons, 206.

188 He was informed that whenever he chose to take: Gabriel, 131.

188 John Ross, who had recently survived one assassination attempt: Moulton, 47.

189 One reporter noted approvingly that "his metaphors": Wilkins, 234.

189 After appearing at the Old South Church: Wilkins, 235.
189 "Expectation has for the last few days": Gabriel, 132.
189 Beecher had been a strong ally: Gabriel, 62.
189 "God be praised!" Wilkins, 235.
189 John Ridge was convinced that the Marshall Court: Wilkins 235–36.
190 "John Marshall has made his decision": Conley, *Cherokee Nation,* 135; Garrison, 193.
190 "If I had known that Jackson would drive us": Bass, 162.
190 Legal opinion was divided, in fact, over the extent: Satz, *American Indian Policy,* 49.
190 Declaring flatly that he would not intervene: Wilkins, 236.
191 He found Boudinot's blunt news reports: Bass, 164.
191 In Washington, Justice Story was clearly relieved when he wrote: Satz, *American Indian Policy,* 49.
191 Rather than being persuaded, however, Ross denounced: Wilkins, 238.
191 On their side, the Georgians had resurrected their investigation: Moulton, 47.
192 Jackson could frame his removal argument as one more populist issue: W. L. Anderson, 68.
192 He was simply following what he termed "the dictates of humanity": Remini, *Jackson,* II, 265.
192 Filing a hopeful report, Currey said that, yes, some Cherokees wanted: Foreman, 236–37.
193 "Extensive prairie badly watered": Moulton, 49.
193 As he waited for volunteers, Currey received sixteen U.S. flatboats: Foreman 242.

CHAPTER 9. ELIAS BOUDINOT (1832–34)

195 His final total was 380: Foreman, 242.
195 But by the time they landed, they had neither provisions: Foreman, 243–44.
196 In his letter, Ridge acknowledged Ross's position: Moulton, 51.
197 "Resolved by the National Committee and Council": Gabriel, 139.
197 As the leading Cherokee voice against removal: Moulton, 51, cites U.S. Senate, "Documents in Relation to the Validity of the Cherokee Treaty of 1835," 25th Cong., 2nd sess. Document 121 (serial 315), 3–11.
197 Working through the Cherokee Council, he forced out: Moulton, 51–52.
197 He believed in the free expression of ideas, he wrote: Wilkins, 244.
198 Ridge said then that although he was not ready: Wilkins, 137.
198 "I am still a bad man," Ridge said: Wilkins, 246.
198 "Many of my countrymen are now Christians": Wilkins, 246, cites Oochgelogy Diary, Moravian Archives, Winston-Salem, North Carolina, March 4, 7, 1830.

198 Ridge's conversion did not deflect: Wilkins, 246.

198 "Now, as a friend of my people, I cannot say *peace, peace*": Wilkins, 247.

199 If his appointment was rejected, the result "would cripple": Remini, *Clay,* 380.

199 Van Buren knew he was called "the magician": Van Buren, 446.

199 Meantime, he considered his most important priority: Van Buren, 452.

199 As his first point of attack, Henry Clay castigated Van Buren: Schurz, I, 367.

200 "It will kill him, sir, kill him dead": Curtis, 37.

200 "You have broken a minister: Remini, *Clay,* 385.

200 One predicted, "You will be V.P.": Van Buren, 454.

200 For tactical reasons, Van Buren wanted to delay: Niven, *Van Buren,* 298.

201 "No one can doubt," wrote the champion: Van Buren, 480.

201 Just before Van Buren boarded the packet *New York*: Niven, *Van Buren,* 301.

201 "I am a member of no religious sect": Remini, *Clay,* 397.

201 One critic claimed that if Clay could gain votes: Remini, *Clay,* 397.

203 "It is to be regretted," Jackson wrote: Remini, *Clay,* 398.

204 Clay greeted him cordially, and Van Buren: Niven, *Van Buren,* 308.

204 Defending the veto, Thomas Hart Benton chastised Clay: Remini, *Clay,* 400.

204 "False! False! False!": Remini, *Jackson,* II, 373.

205 "Are you Mr. Stanbery?": Parton, *Jackson,* III, 390.

205 He struck Stanbery repeatedly with a hickory stick: Gregory, 94 note.

206 The president told a friend that after a few more examples: Parton, *Jackson,* III, 391.

206 He remitted Houston's fine and gave him a small contribution: Gregory, 163.

207 As for the Cherokee removal, the pamphlet briefly mentioned: Remini, *Jackson,* II, 378.

208 The parade would stop at the doors of Jackson supporters: Brands, 474.

208 Since they were residents of Henry Clay's home state: Remini, *Jackson,* II, 385.

208 Soon afterward, however, Clay's candidate for governor: Remini, *Clay,* 403.

209 Biddle was sure that Jackson's argument was so flimsy: Remini, *Clay,* 404.

209 If he lost both Pennsylvania and Ohio, however: Clay, *Papers,* VIII, 588.

209 To the end, Clay expressed confidence: Remini, *Clay,* 409.

209 He wrote to a friend, "Whether we shall ever": Clay, *Papers,* VIII, 607.

209 But within days, Clay was writing, "We must bear it": Remini, *Clay,* 410.

210 "It makes me weep to think of it": Wilkins, 240.

210 The difference was that so far South Carolina: Ross, *Papers,* I, 268.

210 He was convinced that the early release of Worcester: Coleman, 133.

210 Then six days later, Jackson issued a proclamation: M. D. Peterson, 47–48.

211 The erratic John Randolph announced, "There is one man": M. D. Peterson, 51.

211 Clay—his ally in 1812, his opponent thereafter: M. D. Peterson, 61.

212 Giving up that center of joy and prayers, he wrote: Gabriel, 142.

212 "Tall, thin, cadaverous-looking animals": Wilkins, 251, quotes volume 2, 226, George W. Featherstonhaugh, *A Canoe Voyage up the Minnay Sotor, With an Account of . . . the Gold Region in the Cherokee Nation,* 2 vols., London, 1847.

212 In Milledgeville, Shadrach Bogan, a white commissioner, was discovered: Wilkins, 249.

212 Bogan's offense was minor, the newspaper observed: Wilkins, 250.

212 By now, however, the sentiments of the Ridge faction: Wilkins, 250.

213 Under the new legislation, Cherokees could no longer sell: Foreman, 246.

213 Cass rejected new terms under which the tribe would give up: Moulton, 55.

213 The Indians would "be perpetually made drunk by the whites": Wilkins, 261.

213 From 1829, his assurances of goodwill: Jackson, Second Annual Message to Congress, December 6, 1830, Richardson, II, part 3.

214 Georgia's Cherokees, Jackson wrote, "have neither the intelligence": Jackson, Fifth Annual Message to Congress, December 3, 1833, Richardson, III, part 1.

214 On June 19, 1834, Andrew Ross, claiming to speak for: Moulton, 56.

214 That sum included allotments for schools: Foreman, 264.

214 John Ross lobbied strenuously against his brother's: Ross, *Papers,* I, 299.

215 "These men have good clothes on": Ehle, 269.

215 "Let's kill them!": Wilkins, 262.

215 By leaving, they missed John Ridge's impassioned praise: Wilkins, 262; Ehle, 269.

215 When Major Ridge spoke on his own behalf: Ehle, 269.

216 "If some men did not take care they would drop": Ehle, 270.

216 The council voted that the three were indeed guilty: Wilkins, 263.

216 What he knew about Walker was that he had married a niece: Foreman, 265 note.

216 At that time, Walker had been promised protection: Wilkins, 264.

216 After leaving the council meeting, Walker and his companion had been riding: Ehle, 271.

216 Questions would arise later about whether the motive: Foreman, 265 note, cites James S. Mooney, *Myths of the Cherokee,* Nineteenth Annual Report, Bureau of American Ethnology, Part I.

217 "The Government of the U.S. has promised": Wilkins, 264.

217 "By God, sir, I was let out with a silver key": Ehle, 272.

217 "Don't pay them one dollar": Parton, *Jackson,* III, 280.

CHAPTER 10. JOHN HOWARD PAYNE (1835)

219 But if that was impossible, the tribe would accept $20 million: Moulton, 61.

219 Ross was shaken enough by the latest setback: Moulton, 62.

221 Schermerhorn made good use of that position: Schermerhorn, 93–96.

221 Women of the tribe quickly formed a different: Moulton, 84.
221 Seeking out the Ridge faction, Schermerhorn proposed terms: Foreman, 266.
221 John Ridge wrote to assure his father: Wilkins, 268.
221 He paid the president the ultimate compliment: Wilkins, 269.
222 Zillah Brandon considered the winter weather disagreeably cold: Perdue and Green, *Removal,* 94.
222 She concluded that "when they were sober, we were not afraid": Perdue and Green, *Removal,* 98.
223 That anxiety went on until "to our great comfort the liquor store was demolished": Perdue and Green, *Removal,* 99.
223 But the vote rejecting individual annuity payments: Moulton, 64.
223 That session promised to be harmonious for the first time: Gabriel, 145.
224 "Ross holds out the olive branch of peace": Wilkins, 276.
224 John Ridge wrote despairingly that "it is dreadful": Wilkins, 277.
224 To keep the press out of Ross's hands: Moulton, 65.
225 He already had developed a knack for adapting: Harrison, 58.
225 He admired Junius Brutus Booth as the Iago: Harrison, 72.
225 But Payne was a notoriously bad manager: Brainard, 24.
226 *"'Mid pleasures and palaces though we may roam"*: Brainard, 28.
226 But Payne's luck ran true to form: Brainard, 31.
226 The house sold out at a steep five dollars: Brainard, 38.
226 Heading back to New York, Payne resolved to publish: Wilkins, 281.
227 He had heard about the murder of William McIntosh: Harrison, 172.
227 Reluctantly, Payne rode on to his next destination: Harrison, 176.
227 At their meeting, Payne found Ross shorter, milder: Moulton, 66.
227 They agreed to work together to confirm the Cherokees' Hebrew ancestry: David J. Tackett, in a thesis proposal dated Oct. 2009, cites Papers of John Howard Payne, Edward E. Ayer collection, Newberry Library, Chicago, Illinois.
227 He noted that Boudinot had "married a Gold": Wilkins, 282–83.
228 "Their dress was neat and pictureqe": Foreman, 267.
228 Schermerhorn considered John Ross the "Devil in Hell": Moulton, 67.
228 The Cherokees played off Schermerhorn's name: Moulton, 63; Rozema, *Voices,* 75.
228 "I'll have a treaty within a week": Wilkins, 283.
228 But he resented Payne's presence and wrote angrily: Wilkins, 283.
229 He concluded that their opposition was the inevitable result: Wilkins, 280.
229 "The Lord is able to overrule all things for good": Gabriel, 147, cites Schermerhorn to Commissioner of Indian Affairs, Oct. 27, 1835, manuscript file of the Bureau of Indian Affairs.
230 "Well, gentlemen, I shall not resist. But what have I done?": "The Captivity of John Howard Payne by the Georgia Guard," *The North American Quarterly Magazine,* Jan. 1836, 112.

230 "Hold your damned tongue," the leader said: Moulton, 69.
230 "What song was that I heard you humming?" *The North American Quarterly Magazine,* Jan. 1836, 113.
230 "That might have done very well once": *The North American Quarterly Magazine,* Jan. 1836, 115.
231 Ross secured his own release by pointing out: Moulton, 69.
231 "The minute you hear the tap of the drum": *The North American Quarterly Magazine,* Jan. 1836, 120.
231 which Ridge called "diametrically opposite" to his own: Moulton, 70.
231 As Ross's delegation prepared to leave for Washington: Moulton, 70.
232 Schermerhorn had worked during the past two months: Gabriel, 152.
232 Even so, only a small number of Cherokees were on hand: Foreman, 269.
232 Although he had converted to Christianity, Boudinot could appreciate: Gabriel, 153.
232 One of Ross's men, present to monitor the event, described: Moulton, 72.
233 The provisions that followed were little different from those: Moulton, 75.
233 The Cherokees might be entitled to a delegate: Article 7, original draft, Treaty of New Echota, Dec. 29, 1835. OKGenWeb Project, Cherokee Nation, Indian Territory Research.
233 "I have hunted the deer and turkey": Abbot, 16.
234 When Boudinot spoke next, he struck a different note: Abbot, 18.
234 On December 28, 1835, that committee announced its unanimous approval: Moulton, 73.
234 A thirty-year-old Methodist circuit rider, Robert R. Rogers: Shadburn, *Unhallowed,* 124.
235 John Ridge shared with Schermerhorn his feeling: Moulton, 114.
235 Major Ridge said, "I have signed my death warrant": Wilkins, 289.

CHAPTER 11. JOHN ROSS (1836)

237 Delivering that news, Cass bemoaned the fact: Moulton, 73.
237 While he was staying in Washington, Ross heard of the Treaty: Ross, *Papers,* I, 407.
238 In Georgia, federal advisers to the Ridge faction were urging: Moulton, 73.
238 Even those two, according to Ross, had come "from curiosity": Ross, *Papers,* I, 410.
238 Compiling a chronology of recent events: Ross, *Papers,* I, 412.
239 "Alas! Poor Indians, what rights can they assert": Clay, *Papers,* VIII, 811.
239 Once more John Quincy Adams sided with his former: Wilkins, 292.
239 The final vote came on May 18, with thirty-one in favor: Moulton, 77.
239 Harriet Boudinot had always been able to reassure her family: Gabriel, 157.
240 She told Boudinot, "I hope this is the last night": Gabriel, 159.

240 Addressing his adversary directly, Boudinot wrote: Gabriel, 161.
241 Although the two years were slipping away, he could not believe: Gabriel, 164.
241 When the British had stymied the Americans at Queenston Heights: Langguth, *Union* 1812, 215.
242 John H. Garrett, a white man who had claimed: Wilkins, 295.
242 At the time, Jackson ordered that "no council should be permitted": Foreman, 269.
242 As Wool was faced with Ross's disobedience, his letter: Wilkins 297.
242 He wrote to the Office of Indian Affairs: Moulton, 79.
242 Wool believed that the tribe should move: Moulton, 79.
243 Lumpkin passed the days sorting through claims: Wilkins, 298.
243 Lumpkin wrote to Washington that he "shall never cease": Lumpkin, II, 85–86.
244 Schermerhorn had been "a most unfortunate selection": Moulton, 76.
244 At about that time, another commander, General R. G. Dunlap: Foreman, 273.
244 He said it was futile to talk with the overwhelming number: Foreman, 271.
244 "They will die before they will leave the country": Foreman, 271.
245 "About fifteen hundred or two thousand Indians": Wilkins, 299.

CHAPTER 12. MARTIN VAN BUREN (1836–37)

247 Federal land sales rose in the West during Jackson's administration: Cole, 256–57.
247 An 1835 biography attributed to David Crockett: Crockett, 80–81.
249 Speaking courteously but with an undertone of mockery, Van Buren said: Remini, *Clay,* 453.
250 During a debate, Clay complained that the Jacksonians: Remini, *Clay,* 477.
250 "Never, never can its wounds be healed": Clay, *Papers,* VIII, 809.
251 "God knows I have suffered enough for my Southern partialities": Cole, 261.
251 although he was also drawing new followers from the West: Cole, 262.
252 But "if compelled to vote, they must take a man": Niven, *Van Buren,* 396.
252 Tennessee's chief justice derided the woman for: Cole, 262.
253 When Calhoun described Andrew Jackson in the Senate: Cole, 264.
253 Clay agreed with John Quincy Adams: N. L. Peterson, 17.
253 "The United States," Bolívar wrote, "seems determined": Bolívar, 732.
253 As Clay surveyed the field, he decided: Remini, *Clay,* 479.
253 "The only condition upon which it would have been acceptable": Remini, *Clay,* 480.
254 But Protestants in Philadelphia were alarmed by an influx: Cole, 269.
254 He called slave owners "sincere friends to the happiness": Cole, 270.

254 "I have no confidence in a People who can elect": Remini, *Clay,* 491, cites Thurlow Weed, former leader of the Anti-Masons and Whig chief in New York, in letters, Nov. 25, 31, William H. Seward Papers, University of Rochester Library.

254 Benjamin Currey had died: Moulton, 82.

255 And General Wool had become increasingly frustrated: Moulton, 83.

255 Just as Wool was requesting a transfer: S. Carter, 214.

255 Poinsett . . . had gone to Mexico as America's first ambassador: Niven, *Van Buren,* 407.

255 But as an honor, it could not match the naming: Horan, 266.

256 A Jacksonian from New York brought a wheel of cheese: Parton, *Jackson,* III, 626.

256 "And filled with gratitude for your constant and unwavering": Parton, *Jackson,* III, 627.

256 "Happily it is the last humbug": Parton, *Jackson,* III, 627.

257 Jackson's bearing was still erect: Niven, *Van Buren,* 409–10.

257 Because of the hush, many in the audience of twenty thousand: *Inaugural Addresse,* Van Buren.

257 The reception that followed at the White House: Parton, *Jackson,* III, 626.

257 Fellow tribesmen refused to speak to him: Jahoda, 225.

258 The army general in charge of the passage had been allotted: Wilkins, 304.

258 But not only had they recovered, no other passenger had died: Wilkins, 306.

258 "It seems to me as if these beautiful regions": Wilkins, 307.

259 In a letter to her brother, he described his "deeply wounded heart": Gaul, ed., 196–97.

259 When Boudinot wrote again to the Golds: Gaul, ed., 199.

259 Ridge had received $19,741.67: Wilkins, 310.

260 As for now, "perfect friendship": Letter to John Kennedy, Jan. 16, 1838, National Archives, RG 75, First Board of the Cherokee Commissioners, Letters of the Cherokee Commission, quoted in Wilkins, 310.

261 Initially, Van Buren thought he might have to challenge: Cole, 295.

261 Rather than provoke a face-to-face showdown, he solicited: Cole, 296.

261 At last, Van Buren decided he must take responsibility: Niven, *Van Buren,* 414.

261 A New York City lot at Broadway and 100th Street: Lynch, 406.

261 Unemployment rose to one-third—in some areas, one-half: Pessen, 147.

262 "Are you authorized by the President": Moulton, 88.

263 Ross went with a Cherokee delegation to St. Augustine: Ross, *Papers,* I, 544.

263 "I know that a brave people when driven": Moulton, 88.

264 Ross's discussions with local white soldiers: Ross, *Papers,* I, 545.

264 Not only would Poinsett not support Ross: Moulton, 89.

264 To Ross, it was proof that newly installed officials: Moulton, 90.

265 Two days after Christmas, Poinsett wrote to chastise Ross: S. Carter, 224.
265 The American Board of Foreign Missionaries sent a printing press: S. Carter, 174–75.
265 Applying for permission to establish himself: Worcester File 4027; 8431 Library, Gilcrease Institute, Tulsa, Oklahoma.
266 In mid-December 1836, he wrote a plaintive letter: Worcester quotes from his earlier letter in a Feb. 8, 1839, letter to James Orr. Worcester Archives, Library, Gilcrease Institute, Tulsa, Oklahoma.
266 He was certain that the tribe's resentment: Gabriel, 175–76.
266 Boudinot conceded that the Ridge faction might have been small: S. Carter, 211.
267 The council "respectfully requests you not use": S. Carter, 222.
267 *"We will not fight with guns or swords"*: Cherokee *Almanac,* 1856, 4026.8432, Library, Gilcrease Institute, Tulsa, Oklahoma.
268 He implored Poinsett to send to Cherokee country: S. Carter, 229.
268 "There is a great many of our people here every mail day": Ross, I, 615.
268 and he gave the Cherokees two more years in Georgia: S. Carter, 229.
268 If Van Buren did not reverse his extension: Gilmer, 423.

CHAPTER 13. WINFIELD SCOTT (1838)

271 Unwilling to accept that she was gone: Cheever, 33.
271 she addressed her husband as "Mister Emerson": Cheever, 35.
272 Six years earlier, he had become acquainted: Emerson, "To Charles," 346.
272 In a lecture the following year titled "Manners": Emerson, *Early Lectures,* 135.
272 "I can do nothing. Why shriek?": Emerson, *Journals,* 5, 477; cited by Jennifer M. Wing, endnotes, *American History Through Literature,* "Trail of Tears."
272 "By right and natural position, every citizen is your friend": Emerson, *Prose and Poetry,* 543.
274 In fact, as Ross recounted the conversation to his brother: Ross, *Papers,* I, 623.
274 Ross responded with his latest terms: Ross, *Papers,* I, 641.
274 Even in the North, memories persisted of the slave revolt: McDougall, 63.
275 Ross's correspondent concluded that "this mixing of white and black": Ross, *Papers,* I, 639–40.
275 Handsome, dark-haired, standing six-foot-five: Peskin, 4.
275 Serving under corrupt Major General James Wilkinson: Elliott, 33.
276 He awoke to find his countrymen comparing his exploit: Peskin, 55.
276 What Jackson got back was a patronizing letter: Peskin, 73.
277 He wrote in his journal that "Scott's vanity": J. Q. Adams, *Memoirs,* 4, 322.
277 To recruit Americans to their cause, the rebels: Cole, 322.
277 Stumping along the disputed frontier, Scott persuaded upstate New Yorkers: Niven, *Van Buren,* 438.

278 "I like difficulties!": Elliott, 347.
278 "Cherokees!" Scott began. "The president of the United States": Mansfield, 306.
279 Mobilizing at New Echota, members of the Georgia militia: Howden Smith, 214.
279 "Every possible kindness," Scott decreed: Peskin, 106.
279 Outraged by the Treaty of New Echota: Butrick, Foreword.
280 Or, as Pastor Butrick put it, the soldiers "now commenced": Butrick, 1.
280 Before his arrival, the federal government had built: Wilkins, 320.
280 "Infants, superannuated persons, lunatics": S. Carter, 234.
281 "Poor creatures!" Scott wrote later: Rozema, *Voices,* 188.
281 Before the Cherokees could be led away: Moulton, 96.
281 "The soldiers rushed in," according to one letter: Elliott, 351, quotes letter in *Niles' Weekly Register,* LIV, 385.
282 One old man, about to be marched off: Moulton, 96.
282 "They say they prefer death to Arkansas": Jahoda, 228.
282 The clergyman had no doubt the children would soon die: Butrick, 2.
283 If they went directly to General Scott's headquarters: Butrick, 3.
283 "The distress caused the emigrants by their want of bedding": Elliott, 352, quotes letter to Smith, June 8, 1838, *Executive Documents,* 25th Congress, 2nd session, 453.
283 On June 16, a Baptist preacher named Evan Jones: Jahoda, 232, quotes Foreman, 289ff.
284 At one stockade, John Ross's ailing wife, Quatie: Jahoda, 233.
284 On July 27, 1838, he informed Scott that his council: Ross, *Papers,* I, 652.
284 His goal, he said, was "the comfortable removal": Ross, *Papers,* I, 654.
285 Lewis Ross was expected to deliver at various points: Ross, *Papers,* I, 658.
285 Possibly because his brother would be the supplier: Ross, *Papers,* I, 654.
285 Agreeing with the criticism, Scott wrote: Ross, *Papers,* I, 660.
285 After three days of brooding, John Ross responded: Ross, *Papers,* I, 662.
285 "It seems strange that these economical projectors": Ross, *Papers,* I, 664.
286 Buttressing Ross's argument was the offer white speculators: Moulton, 95.
286 Before Ross took charge, the federal government had already: Moulton, 97.

CHAPTER 14. DANIEL AND ELIZABETH BUTRICK (1838–39)

287 When a soldier approached, they fled: Butrick, 9.
287 "It is said," Butrick wrote in his journal, "that many old women": Butrick, 9.
287 Some Cherokees refused to shake his hand: Butrick, 8.
288 He had watched white gamblers "strolling through": Butrick, 11.
288 "He was seized and bound, but two of his brothers": Butrick, 34.
289 a young married woman had been raped: Butrick, 10.

289 "After abusing her in this manner": Butrick, 14.
289 "We understand that a letter has been received": Butrick, 26.
289 He likened the white agents who had skimmed: Butrick, 27.
289 "Suppose the President of the United States had ordered": Butrick, 27.
289 "The plan for getting the Cherokees away": Butrick, 28.
290 His missionary service in Georgia had confirmed Butrick's view: Butrick, 33.
290 Butrick wrote of a slave named Nanny, who belonged to a white man: Butrick, 32–33.
290 "This is all we could desire": Butrick, 33.
290 "The Chickamauga creek is probably lower": Butrick, 33.
291 They were living with "only a few barks overhead": Butrick, 34.
291 "And may God help me to keep my resolution": Butrick, 36.
291 the remaining six hundred members of the Treaty Party: Moulton, 98.
292 Their first night away from home was rendered sleepless: Butrick, 37.
292 "There remaineth, therefore, a rest for the people of God": Butrick, 37.
292 Others who overcame that sense of shame and went to apply for the money: Butrick, 37.
294 "I could but weep for joy": Butrick, 38.
294 "While on the road they would spend the Sabbath": Butrick, 41.
294 From that, Butrick concluded that no one who favored the Treaty: Butrick, 41.
295 But "he swore we should not pass through his field": Butrick, 42.
295 When the Butricks settled in for the night, they found: Butrick, 42.
295 The next evening, Butrick pitched his tent far from the others: Butrick, 42.
295 "Many Indians got drunk": Rozema, *Voices,* 152.
295 "Did not sleep much. The girls and boys talked": Rozema, *Voices,* 152.
296 With Ross now responsible for the move, Scott had cut back: Elliott, 354 note.
296 One story told of a youth, terrified by the arrival of the militia: S. Carter, 234.
296 Better documented was the fate of Tsali: Jahoda, 226; Rozema, *Voices,* 154. Finger, 23–27, challenges aspects of the Tsali legend, including the mistreatment of Tsali's wife and his voluntary surrender to Thomas.
296 On hearing of the soldiers' murder, John Ross sent Scott: Ross, *Papers,* I, 687.
297 Scott contacted William H. Thomas, a white trader in his thirties: Rozema, *Voices,* 158.
297 He argued that their land was so rocky and steeply pitched: Jahoda, 227.
297 Then he said, "I will come in": Rozema, *Voices,* 160.
298 On November 25, 1838, the general ordered Tsali and his three adult sons: Rozema, *Voices,* 162.
298 With the Indians executed, Scott upheld: Finger, 24–28, quoted in Rozema, *Voices,* 158.
298 One of Scott's captains informed T. Hartley Crawford: Rozema, *Voices,* 162.

299 Scott, who had agreed not to send troops: Moulton, 99.
299 Although a barrel of cider was rolled out—Butrick suspected: Butrick, 43.
299 "I have seen no such place since I left Boston": Butrick, 46.
299 Because he was not in charge of the group's finances: Moulton, 105.
300 "On the Cumberland mountains," Jones complained: Moulton, 105.
300 Scott said he could assure Poinsett: Elliott, 355, cites Scott's letter of Oct. 23, 1838, Poinsett Papers, Pennsylvania Historical Society.
300 Declining a public dinner in Tennessee: Elliott, 355, cites *Niles' Weekly Register,* LV, 239.
301 In refusing, Scott cited the prohibition spelled out in the U.S. Constitution: Elliott, 366.
302 John G. Burnett, a twenty-seven-year-old private: Underwood, 23.
302 "My children became motherless": Rozema, *Voices,* 36.
302 Looking back on the grave of Quatie Ross: Underwood, 25.
303 Freedom had not elevated the citizens' vocabulary: Butrick, 49.
303 He ran a high fever and took an emetic: Butrick, 50.
303 "Thus far," Butrick wrote, "the citizens of Illinois": Butrick, 51.
303 "And yet all are houseless & homeless": Butrick, 52.
304 He blamed the tribe for not embracing the role of farmer: Thoreau, *Journal,* 444.
305 "she arose first in the morning": Butrick, 53.
305 "O thou dear Redeemer": Butrick, 53.
305 "My dear wife is now unwell": Butrick, 53.
306 Butrick observed that "the citizens of this state": Butrick, 55.
306 Camping out, he was grateful for a quiet night with stars: Butrick, 56.
306 "My dear wife and myself are both troubled": Butrick, 56.
306 Deeply awed, Butrick called it "one of the wonders": Butrick, 57.
307 "The fall & Winter has been very cold": Perdue and Green, *Removal,* 177.
307 "one old Cherokee woman, one black man": Butrick, 58.
308 Butrick made a futile protest: Butrick, 59.
308 On March 4, 1839, Butrick set down the cautionary story: Butrick, 59.
309 When they managed to go seven freezing miles: Butrick, 60.
309 "We are now drawing near the Arkansas": Butrick, 61.
309 On Sunday, March 17, Butrick wrote that just before his service: Butrick, 61.
310 "O how kind has the Lord been": Butrick, 63.
310 "This is the place of deposit,": Butrick, 63.
310 "Mr. Taylor told me that the officers from Fort Gibson": Butrick, 64.
310 He reunited a child from the group with his father: Butrick, 64.
310 "Murder is murder, and somebody must answer": Underwood, 27.
311 The Cherokees who survived the ordeal later wrote: McDougall, 53.

CHAPTER 15. TAHLEQUAH (1839)

313 The Ridges, Elias Boudinot, Stand Watie, and other adherents: Moulton, 109.

313 Although "being compelled by the strong arm of power": Ross, *Papers,* I, 712.

313 He concluded by quoting the New Testament's: Ross, *Papers,* I, 713.

314 "to admit two distinct laws or governments in the same country": Ross, *Papers,* I, 714–15.

314 that the Ridges were promising to use their influence: McLoughlin, 13.

315 "We must not blame the Cherokees too much": Bass, 254.

315 From Boston, the American Board took a similarly tolerant view: Bass, 255.

315 Early on Saturday, June 22, 1839, Boudinot was walking: Gabriel, 177.

315 The carpenters told a Choctaw working: Wilkins, 336.

316 Whoever slew his Cherokee friend, Worcester said: Bass, 256.

316 That same morning, twenty-five men on horseback: Wilkins, 335.

317 With the intensity of a twelve-year-old, he felt: Wilkins, 335.

317 Killing Ridge had whetted the conspirators' appetite: Wilkins, 336.

317 The morning brought out a third band of assassins: Wilkins, 338.

318 In fact, Ross's son, Allen, had been one of the conspirators: Moulton, 112.

318 When he finished, the conspirators ruled: Wilkins, 334.

318 Several of them tied on neckerchiefs: S. Carter, 270.

318 Ross asked a tribal clerk to draft a protest: Moulton, 113.

318 "Why I am to be murdered without guilt": Ross, *Papers,* I, 717.

319 If the report was true, he wrote, "no one will regret": Ross, *Papers,* I, 718.

319 Firing back, Ross urged William Armstrong: Ross, *Papers,* I, 725.

319 General Arbuckle was disgusted by that exchange: Moulton, 115.

319 Its members were required to appear: Moulton, 115.

320 Stand Watie announced that before he would sign: Moulton, 116.

320 He persuaded Sequoyah to add his signature: Ross, *Papers,* I, 743.

320 Calling the Indians "wild cannibals," Lamar vowed: Moore, 81.

320 Among the Cherokee dead was eighty-three-year-old Chief Bowles: Moore, 156.

321 Ross welcomed the prospect, describing Butrick's conduct: Ross, *Papers,* I, 763.

321 Ross claimed that U.S. jurisdiction did not extend: Moulton, 121.

321 Jackson granted that he was indulging in "strong language": Dale and Litton, 17.

CHAPTER 16. WILLIAM HENRY HARRISON (1839–41)

323 He sent to political allies at home seventy-five pages: Cole, 353.

323 Webster was equally deft in refusing: Remini, *Clay,* 524.

324 "No man likes to have, or ought to have, cold water or brandy": Clay, *Papers* IX, 219.

324 "I HAD RATHER BE RIGHT THAN BE PRESIDENT": Remini, *Clay,* 527, cites *National Intelligencer,* March 30, 1839, and *Niles' Weekly Register,* March 23, 1839.
324 "I beseech the abolitionists themselves solemnly to pause": Clay, *Papers,* IX, 248.
325 Coast Guard crew disarmed the slaves: Cole, 363.
325 A slave owner himself, Secretary of State John Forsyth: Niven, *Van Buren,* 467.
325 The ambassador assured Forsyth that his government would make: Jones, 109.
326 Of the justices who would be hearing the case: Jones, 135.
326 "Oh, how shall I do justice": J. Q. Adams, *Memoirs,* 10, 383.
326 To General Arbuckle, Ross protested: Ross, *Papers,* I, 769.
326 He was even more irate that John Poinsett: Ross, *Papers,* II, 4.
327 Ross wrote to Payne that while the executive door: Ross, *Papers,* II, 6.
327 In appealing to Congress, Ross recounted horror stories: Ross, *Papers,* II, 7.
327 When Poinsett referred to the Ross faction: Moulton, 123.
328 He had inherited moral qualms from his father: Crapol, 59.
328 To raise money for his first U.S. Senate campaign: Crapol, 61–62.
328 Tyler . . . was expressing "great solicitude": N. L. Peterson, 25.
329 A sour Clay loyalist observed that "there was rhyme": Remini, *Clay,* 553.
329 "My 'friends,'" he said acidly, "are not worth the powder and shot": Remini, *Clay,* 554.
329 "If I have friends . . . if I have any one": Clay, *Papers,* IX, 363–64.
330 General Jesup had told the Seminoles, "Your gun": Ross, *Papers,* II, 80–81.
331 Ann Worcester had no sooner delivered: Bass, 261–62.
331 "Going to the Indians seems hardly worth": Bass, 299.
332 He also settled scores with Duff Green, the editor: L. Phillips, 128–29.
332 The local Democratic Party leader was Richard Call: L. Phillips, 137.
332 By the time Margaret Eaton turned thirty-seven in 1836: L. Phillips, 144.
332 From the Hermitage, Jackson regretted Eaton's "ingratitude": Meacham, *Lion,* 349.
333 Emily Donelson died of a hemorrhage in 1836: Burke, 303; L. Phillips, 154.
333 Clay knew he was required to make the appearances: Remini, *Clay,* 561.
333 "We are all Whigs, we are all Harrison men": Remini, *Clay,* 561.
333 To the Whigs, the Democratic president became "Martin Van Ruin": McDougall, 100.
333 Harrison was reinvented as "Old Tip": Remini, *Clay,* 563.
333 "Rockabye, baby, Daddy's a Whig": Wikipedia, United States Presidential Election, 1840; Martin Van Buren.
333 When staid Whigs protested: Remini, *Clay,* 563.
334 Harrison "may not fulfill all our hopes": Remini, *Clay,* 563.
334 "if an all-wise Providence spares his life": N. L. Peterson, 28.

334 The spirited contest and a growing population: N. L. Peterson, 29; Remini, *Clay,* 567.

335 To strike back, John Ross sent T. Hartley Crawford: Ross, *Papers,* II, 62.

335 As it happened, Payne was visiting Park Hill again: Letter from Payne to George Watterson, Dec. 2, 1840. John Howard Payne Papers, Box 13, Folder 10b, Library, Gilcrease Institute, Tulsa, Oklahoma.

336 He assured Van Buren that "the self emigration": Ross, *Papers,* II, 65.

336 But by the time he addressed the Cherokee Nation at Tahlequah: Ross, *Papers,* II, 74–75.

337 "How are you?" Smith asked. "It is some time": Letter from John Howard Payne to George Watterson, Dec. 2, 1840. Payne Papers, Box 13, Folder, 10b, Library, Gilcrease Institute, Tulsa, Oklahoma.

338 More than a hundred members of the Treaty Party petitioned: Ross, *Papers,* II, 77.

338 In his inaugural address, Harrison called: *Inaugural Addresses,* Harrison.

339 John Quincy Adams was among those who welcomed: Nagel, 381.

339 "Well done, good and faithful servant. Enter thou": First published by S. W. Benedict in 1841; historycentral.com/amistad.

340 As Clay urged Harrison to appoint: Remini, *Clay,* 569.

340 But Clay was coming to realize that Harrison resented his influence: Remini, *Clay,* 570.

340 "Mr. Clay, you forget that I am President": Remini, *Clay,* 573.

340 Clay could avert it only by posting a five-thousand-dollar bond: Remini, *Clay,* 574.

340 John Bell of Tennessee, long a friend: Ross, *Papers,* II, 78.

341 By March 27, his lingering indisposition was diagnosed: N. L. Peterson, 41.

CHAPTER 17. JOHN TYLER (1841–44)

343 "I can well imagine the shock which you felt": Ross, *Papers,* II, 82–83.

343 Tyler was a mediocrity, a product of the "Virginian": Nelson, 39.

343 As expected, Andrew Jackson at the Hermitage: Nelson, 39; Remini, *Clay,* 576.

343 He was particularly concerned about the chartering: Clay, *Papers,* IX, 532.

344 A gang of pro-Bank protestors retaliated: Nelson, 40–41.

344 Looking on glumly, John Quincy Adams predicted the end: Nelson, 41.

345 "Our brave officers and men" were still fighting the Seminoles: Nelson, 52.

345 Before John Bell resigned as secretary of war: Moulton, 129.

345 Asking her to marry, Ross anticipated her misgivings: Moulton, 128–29.

345 One special agent, Ethan Allen Hitchcock, noted that Ross's manner: Moulton, 131.

346 Another new agent, Pierce Mason Butler: Moulton, 132.

346 He claimed that Jackson's insistence on driving the tribe west: Remini, *Clay,* 605.

347 "True, my nature is warm": Remini, *Clay,* 608.

347 "The old coon is really and substantially dead": Remini, *Clay,* 610, cites Jackson to Van Buren, Nov. 22, 1842, *Van Buren Papers,* Library of Congress.

347 But John Crittenden, who had been named to replace Clay: Remini, *Clay,* 609.

347 Observing the scene, a newly arrived Methodist minister wrote: Moulton, 135.

348 Early in August 1843, the Cherokees held their first general election: Moulton, 135–36.

348 They believed that Archilla Smith had been convicted: McLoughlin, 44.

348 Taylor concluded that Arkansas's white settlers: McLoughlin, 45.

349 Although they did not prevail, they raised enough doubt: Moulton, 138.

350 With interest, Jackson collected twenty-seven hundred dollars, plus a personal contribution: Nelson, 108.

350 The following day, Upshur was among the dignitaries: Crapol, 207.

351 Three years earlier, she had sent him a flirtatious note: Moulton, 143.

352 Ross's garden of melon, fruit, and grapes: Moulton, 144; Kraychir, 10.

352 If so, it would be a "God send to this country": Ross, *Papers,* II, 251.

CHAPTER 18. "MANIFEST DESTINY" (1845–52)

353 At the height of his campaign, he went to Georgia: Remini, *Clay,* 636.

353 Now he wrote, "I regard all war as great calamities": Remini, *Clay,* 639.

354 The job pitted his religious fervor against his fiscal: Eells, 39.

354 All the same, Frelinghuysen's reputation for piety remained so unsullied: Eells, 37.

355 the Democrats settled on James Knox Polk: Merry, 94.

355 "On Mr. Tyler's withdrawal": Borneman, 119.

356 When Clay tried to extricate himself, his further temporizing: Merry, 109.

356 "Now, I hope to spend the remainder of my days": Remini, *Clay,* 666–67.

356 His essay of July 1845 predicted: Sullivan, "Annexation," *United States Magazine and Democratic Review,* 17 (I), 5–10.

356 Benton had to acknowledge the vast numbers of the "Mongolian or Yellow race": *Congressional Globe,* 29:1 (1846), 917–18.

357 but he was concerned about protests from his Democratic allies: Merry, 203.

358 "Hang them, sir, as high as Haman": Parton, *Jackson,* III, 670.

358 "I am dying as fast as I can": Parton, *Jackson,* III, 671.

358 He prayed for his family and for the preservation: Parton, *Jackson,* III, 673.

358 "I want to meet you all, white and black": Parton, *Jackson,* III, 678.

358 Delight Sargent Boudinot had sent them to New England: Gabriel, 178 note.

359 "wholly venal and selfish" men: McLoughlin, 56.
359 The major concession by Congress was to reimburse: Moulton, 152.
359 Polk was on hand with twenty ranking Cherokees: McLoughlin, 157.
360 During the turbulent years, Stand Watie had married: M. W. Anderson, 22.
360 John Rollin Ridge made a different choice: Parins, 21.
360 In the fighting that followed, three American dragoons: Merk, *Manifest Destiny,* 87.
360 A Delaware senator pointed out that sending Taylor's men: Mintz, *The Mexican War,* 2.
361 Lincoln challenged Polk to identify the exact spot: Mintz, *War Fever and Antiwar Protests,* 1.
361 But more Whigs in both chambers: Merk, *Manifest Destiny,* 91–92.
361 The army asked for fifty thousand volunteers: Mintz, *War Fever and Antiwar Protests,* 1.
361 Clay paid tribute to the regiment's patriotic spirit: Remini, *Clay,* 681.
361 That brief incarceration was long enough to give rise: Cheever, 60.
362 George Meade, a young U.S. Army lieutenant: Mintz, *War Fever and Antiwar Protests,* 1.
362 The same Winfield Scott who had blinked away abuses: Mintz, *War Fever and Antiwar Protests,* 1.
362 During the fighting, Henry Clay, Jr., was wounded: Remini, *Clay,* 655–56.
362 President Polk would have preferred to send: Borneman, 256.
363 If his countrymen judged that he had adhered: Merry, 446.
365 Clay, who was recovering slowly from a fall: Remini, *Clay,* 717.
365 Horace Greeley had written from New York: Remini, *Clay,* 715.
367 Calhoun invoked George Washington: Bartlett, 372, cites Calhoun, *Works,* vol. 4, 542–74.
367 On March 30, 1850, he told his son John, a doctor: Bartlett, 374.
368 After Millard Fillmore took the oath of office: Schurz, vol. 2, 354.
368 If Rhett committed overt acts against the Union, then: Schurz, vol. 2, 357.
368 But when parliamentary tactics rendered Clay's bill: Schurz, vol. 2, 360.
369 The Supreme Court had ruled in 1842 that Northern officials: McDougall, 228.
369 In Cherokee territory, the slave population had been growing: McLoughlin, 125.
370 but in 1846 Ross had discovered ammunition and guns: McLoughlin, 135.
370 In a letter to Washington, Samuel Worcester protested: McLoughlin, 131.
370 To be Utah's territorial governor, he named Brigham Young: Hamilton, 174.
371 As the presidential election of 1852 approached: Hamilton, 176, cites the *Richmond Enquirer,* July 6, 1852.
371 for the first time, one was being given to a man of peace: Remini, *Clay,* 779.
371 When he helped to draft the list of his accomplishments: Schurz, vol. 2, 407.

372 His musician's ear was offended, however: Harrison, 197.
372 But his health soon failed: Harrison, 208.
372 "I believe, my son, I am going": Remini, *Clay,* 781.
372 His will divided his estate among his wife: Remini, *Clay,* 772.
373 One of the many national funeral orations: Remini, *Clay,* 786.
373 The Masons had built a temporary vault until a marble sarcophagus: Remini, *Clay,* 785 note.
373 On the first ballot at the Whig convention: Farrell, 61.
373 Again, Democrats were as badly split as Whigs: McDougall, 325.
373 In Concord, Massachusetts, Pierce had become friendly: Cheever, 44.
375 But since the 1850 Compromise, the positions of Whigs and Democrats: Holt, 127.
375 Pierce and his wife had already suffered: McDougall, 326.
375 In the capital, Abigail Fillmore insisted on attending: Farrell, 63–64.

CHAPTER 19. PROLOGUE (1853–61)

377 But Pierce was not a man of bold ideas: Hamilton, 188.
377 Further attempts at pleasing everyone wound up alienating: Holt, 141.
377 Hawthorne accepted despite the disapproval of neighbors: Cheever, 151.
378 "Men of Boston! Sons of Otis and Hancock!" Forbes, 283.
378 Rather than an outright repeal, the 1850 Compromise: Holt, 147.
378 In October 1853, the latest commissioner of Indian affairs: McLoughlin, 141.
379 "A slave cannot bear good treatment": McLoughlin, 143.
380 whose African features were "characterized by an expression of grave": Stowe, 29.
380 "How would you like to be tied to a tree": Stowe, 400.
380 "Both North and South have been guilty before God": Stowe, 472.
381 The usual name for such brazen occupiers was *filibusters*: McDougall, 344.
381 In Washington, Congressman Preston Brooks beat Senator Charles Sumner: McDougall, 375.
381 Henry Thoreau, for one, thought Brown's lecture was sufficiently: Cheever, 155.
381 Late on the evening of May 24, 1856, five proslavery settlers: Rhodes, 385.
381 Brown's sons took part in the slaughter: McDougall, 682, note 33.
382 With his distaste for "the corrupting influence": Grayson, 151.
382 his freewheeling ways during the early tension: Merry, 423–24.
383 As for Kansas, Buchanan assured the audience: McDougall, 365.
385 Justice Benjamin Curtis of Massachusetts had pointed: McDougall, 366.
385 Senator Henry Seward of New York denounced: Holt, 203.
385 Not only did he not recover his political influence: Baker, 117–18.
387 When the Republicans nominated Abraham Lincoln: Baker, 118.

CHAPTER 20. STAND WATIE (1861–65)

389 As Ross told the *Arkansas Gazette*: Ross, *Papers,* II, 488.
389 He also had the backing of a secret organization: Moulton, 163.
390 Ross said he must respectfully decline: Confer, 55.
390 McCulloch's response was to commission Stand Watie: M. W. Anderson, 26.
390 He began his speech urging tribal unity: Moulton, 170.
391 More than a third of the army's 1,108 officers: Howden Smith, 367.
391 When Lincoln informed McClellan of his promotion: Elliott, 743.
391 ". . . it was a feeble old man, scarcely able to walk": Elliott, 744, cites William Starr Myers, *A Study in Personality: General George Brinton McClellan,* 226, but notes that Myers incorrectly gives the day of Scott's departure as Nov. 3.
391 The Southerners would guarantee the money: Cunningham, 45.
391 A recession had closed the Territory's seminaries: Moulton, 164.
392 By early 1862, however, Albert Pike was arrested: Moulton, 174.
392 He rode into battle wearing a dark plantation coat: Waugh, 39–40.
392 But as the hostile barrage grew too intense: M. W. Anderson, 29.
392 Although Watie emerged with high praise: M. W. Anderson, 29 note.
393 But Ross was sending conflicting signals: Cunningham, 45.
393 Drew's guard followed—adding another fifteen hundred: Moulton, 175.
393 Blunt also wrote to Lincoln directly: Moulton, 175.
393 Meantime, those who had followed Ross into exile: Moulton, 176–77.
393 A federal agent noted that the Cherokees: Confer, 123.
394 His son, James, who went there: Moulton, 177.
394 In Tennessee, Henry Clay's estate, Ashland: Remini, *Clay,* 773 footnote.
395 In his defense, Ross pointed out that three of his sons: Ross, *Papers,* II, 647.
395 "I will show," he testified, "the deep duplicity": Moulton, 187; Parins, *Boudinot,* 71.
395 John Ross could take heart from a White House meeting: Ross, *Papers,* II, 666.
395 But he lived long enough to see President Johnson agree: McLoughlin, 307.
396 His body was returned to Park Hill: Moulton, 195.
396 When he died at age sixty-four on September 9, 1871: Parins, *Boudinot,* 107.
396 When the costs of the second civil war were calculated: Cunningham, 5.

Bibliography

Abbot, Isabella K. *The Cherokee Indians in Georgia.* University, Ala., 1980.

Abel, Annie Heloise. *The American Indian in the Civil War, 1862–1865.* Lincoln, Neb., 1992.

Adams, John Quincy. *Diary,* Allen Nevins, ed. New York, 1929.

———. *Memoirs: Comprising Portions of His Diary from 1795 to 1848,* Charles Francis Adams, ed. Philadelphia, 1876.

Alexander, Holmes. *The American Talleyrand: The Career and Contemporaries of Martin Van Buren, Eighth President.* New York (1935), 1968.

American Indian Biographies, Carole Barrett, ed. Pasadena, Calif., 2005.

Anderson, Fred. *The War That Made America: A Short History of the French and Indian War.* New York, 2005.

Anderson, Mabel Washbourne. *The Life of General Stand Watie and Contemporary Cherokee History.* Pryor, Okla., 1931.

Anderson, William L. *Cherokee Removal Before and After.* Athens, Ga., 1991.

Andrews, John A. III. *From Revivals to Removal: Jeremiah Evarts, the Cherokee Nation and the Search for the Soul of America.* Athens, Ga., 1992.

Baker, Jean H. *James Buchanan.* New York, 2004.

Bancroft, George. *Martin Van Buren: To the End of his Public Career.* New York, 1889.

Barrett, Carole, ed. *American Indian Biographies.* Pasadena, Calif., 2005.

Bartlett, Irving H. *John C. Calhoun: A Biography.* New York, 1993.

Bartley, Numan V. *The Creation of Modern Georgia.* Athens, Ga., 1983.

Bass, Althea. *Cherokee Messenger.* Norman, Okla., 1966.

Bassett, John S. *The Life of Andrew Jackson,* 1 vol. New York, 1911.

Baxter, Maurice G. *Henry Clay and the American System.* Lexington, Ky., 1995.

Bealer, Alex W. *Only the Names Remain: The Cherokees and The Trail of Tears.* 1972.

Bemis, Samuel Flagg. *John Quincy Adams and the Union.* New York, 1956.

Beveridge, Albert J. *The Life of John Marshall,* 4 vols. Boston, 1919.

Biographical Directory of the American Congress. Washington, D.C., 1989.

Birkner, Michael J., ed. *James Buchanan and the Political Crisis of the 1850s.* Cranbury, N.J., 1996.

Bishinik. Newspaper of the Choctaw Nation in Oklahoma. Durant, Okla.

Bobbe, Dorothie. *Mr. and Mrs. John Quincy Adams: An Adventure in Patriotism.* New York, 1930.

Bolívar, Simón. *Selected Writings of Bolívar,* trans. Lewis Bertrand; Harold A. Bierck, Jr. ed. New York, 1951.

Boney, F. N. *Southerners All.* Macon, Ga., 1991.

Borneman, Walter R. *Polk: The Man Who Transformed the Presidency and America.* New York, 2008.

Boudinot, Elias. *An Address to the Whites, Delivered in First Presbyterian Church, 26 May 1826.* Philadelphia, 1826.

Brainard, Charles H. *John Howard Payne: A Biographical Sketch.* Boston, 1885.

Brands, H. W. *Andrew Jackson: His Life and Times.* New York, 2005.

Brinkley, Douglas. "A Time for Reckoning: Jimmy Carter and the Cult of Kinfolk." *Presidential Studies Quarterly* 29, no. 4 (Dec. 1999).

Brown, Charles H. *Agents of Manifest Destiny: The Lives and Times of the Filibusters.* Chapel Hill, N.C., 1980.

Brown, Dee. *Bury My Heart at Wounded Knee.* New York, 1991.

Buchanan, John. *Jackson's Way.* New York, 2001.

Burgan, Michael. *Henry Clay: The Great Compromiser.* Chanhassen, Minn., 2004.

Burke, Pauline Wilcox. *Emily Donelson of Tennessee,* Jonathan M. Atkins, ed. Knoxville, Tenn., 2001.

Butrick, Daniel S. *Journal: Cherokee Removal.* Park Hill, Okla., 1998.

Byers, Ann. *The Trail of Tears.* New York, 2004.

Calhoun, John C. *Papers,* vol. X, Clyde N. Wilson and W. Edwin Hemphill, eds. Columbia, S.C., 1977.

Cannon, B. B. "An Overland Journey to the West." Office of Indian Affairs, "Cherokee Emigration," C-553, Special File 249. Transcribed and edited by R. Raymond Evans. National Archives. Washington, D.C.

Carter, Graydon, ed. *Presidential Profiles.* New York, 2010.

Carter, Samuel III. *Cherokee Sunset: A Nation Betrayed.* New York, 1976.

Cave, Alfred A. "Abuse of Power: Andrew Jackson and the Indian Removal Act of 1830." *The Historian,* vol. 71, 2009. Tampa, Fla.

Cheever, Susan. *American Bloomsbury.* New York, 2006.

Cherokee Mission Records 1800–1804 and 1815–1836. Rome, Ga., Public Library.

Cherokee Phoenix. New Echota, Ga., 1829, 1831–33.

Chidsey, Donald Barr. *And Tyler Too.* Nashville, Tenn., 1978.

Clark, Bennett Champ. *John Quincy Adams: "Old Man Eloquent."* Boston, 1933.

Clay, Henry. *The Papers of Henry Clay.* Lexington, Ky. 1959–.

Coit, Margaret L. *John C. Calhoun.* Englewood Cliffs, N.J., 1970.

Cole, Donald B. *Martin Van Buren and the American Political System.* Princeton, N. J., 1984.

Coleman, Kenneth, ed. *A History of Georgia.* Athens, Ga., 1991.

Confer, Clarissa W. *The Cherokee Nation in the Civil War.* Norman, Okla., 2007.

Conley, Robert J. *Cherokee.* Photographs by David G. Fitzgerald. Portland, Ore., 2002.

———. *The Cherokee Nation: A History.* Albuquerque, N.M., 2005.

Cook, James F. *The Governors of Georgia.* Macon, Ga., 2005.

Corps, Terry, ed. *Historical Dictionary of the Jacksonian Era and Manifest Destiny.* Lanham, Md., 2006.

Cotterill, R. S. *The Old South: The Geography, Economics, Social, Political and Cultural Expansion, Institutions and Nationalism of the Ante-Bellum South.* Glendale, Calif., 1936.

Cottrell, Steve. *Civil War in the Indian Territory.* Gretna, La., 1998.

Crapol, Edward P. *John Tyler: The Accidental President.* Chapel Hill, N.C., 2006.

Cresson, W. P. *James Monroe.* Chapel Hill, N.C., 1946; reprinted, 1971.

Crockett, David. *The Life of Martin Van Buren.* Philadelphia, 1835.

Cunningham, Frank. *General Stand Watie's Confederate Indians.* Norman, Okla., 1998.

Current, Richard N. *John C. Calhoun.* New York, 1963.

Curry, Jabez L. M. *Georgia in the 1840s.* University, Ala., 1980.

Curtis, James C. *The Fox at Bay: Martin Van Buren and the Presidency, 1837–1844.* Lexington, Ky., 1970.

Dale, Edward Everett, and Gaston Litton, eds. *Cherokee Cavaliers: Forty Years of Cherokee History As Told in the Correspondence of the Ridge-Watie-Boudinot Family.* 1995.

Dangerfield, George. *The Era of Good Feelings.* Gloucester, Mass., 1973.

Deas, Edward. "Emigrating to the West by Boat (April–May 1838)." Office of Indian Affairs, "Cherokee Emigration" C-553, Special File 249, National Archives. Washington, D.C.

Debo, Angie. *Road to Disappearance.* Norman, Okla., 1941.

Denson, Andrew. *Demanding the Cherokee Nation: Indian Autonomy and American Culture, 1830–1900.* Lincoln, Neb., 2004.

DeRosier, Arthur H., Jr. *The Removal of the Choctaw Indians.* Knoxville, Tenn., 1970.

Dusinberre, William. *Slavemaster President: The Double Career of James Polk.* Oxford, 2003.

Eaton, Peggy. *Autobiography,* Annette K. Baxter, ed. New York, 1932.

Eaton, Rachel Caroline. *John Ross and the Cherokee Indians.* Menasha, Wisc., 1914.

Eells, Robert J. *Forgotten Saint: The Life of Theodore Frelinghuysen.* Latham, Md., 1987.

Ehle, John. *Trail of Tears: The Rise and Fall of the Cherokee Nation.* New York, 1988.

Elish, Dan. *The Trail of Tears: The Story of the Cherokee Removal.* New York, 2002.

Elliott, Charles W. *Winfield Scott: The Soldier and the Man.* New York, 1937.

Ellis, Jerry. *Walking the Trail.* New York, 1991.

Ellis, Richard E. *The Union At Risk: Jacksonian Democracy, States' Rights, and the Nullification Crisis.* New York, 1987.

Emerson, Ralph Waldo. *The Early Lectures,* vol. 1, Stephen E. Whicher, Robert E. Spiller, and Wallace E. Williams, eds. Cambridge, Mass., 1964.

———. *The Journals and Miscellaneous Notebooks,* vol. 5, Merton M. Sealts, Jr., ed. Cambridge, Mass., 1965.

———. "To Charles Chauncy Emerson," Boston, March 4, 1832. In *Letters,* Ralph L. Rusk, ed., pp. 345–47. New York, 1939.

———. "To Martin Van Buren, Concord, April 23, 1838." In *Emerson's Prose and Poetry.* Joel Porte and Saundra Morris, eds. New York, 2001.

Emmons, William. *Biography of Martin Van Buren, Vice President of the United States.* Washington, D.C., 1835.

Etcheson, Nicole. *Bleeding Kansas: Contested Liberty in the Civil War Era.* Lawrence, Ks., 2004.

Falkner, Leonard. *The President Who Wouldn't Retire.* New York, 1967.

Farrell, John J., ed. *Zachary Taylor and Millard Fillmore: Chronology, Documents, Bibliographical Aids.* Dobbs Ferry, N.Y., 1971.

Faulkner, Cooleela. *The Life and Times of Reverend Stephen Foreman.* Tahlequah, Okla., 2006.

Filler, Louis, and Allen Guttmann, eds. *The Removal of the Cherokee Nation: Manifest Destiny or National Dishonor?* Boston, 1962.

Finger, John R. *The Eastern Band of Cherokees 1819–1900.* Knoxville, Tenn., 1984.

———. "The Saga of Tsali," *North Carolina Historical Review* 56, 1–18.

Fleischmann, Glen. *The Cherokee Removal, 1838.* New York, 1971.

Forbes, Robert Pierce. *The Missouri Compromise and Its Aftermath.* Chapel Hill, N.C., 2007.

Foreman, Grant. *Indian Removal.* Norman, Okla., 1972.

Foster, George E. *Se-Quo-Yah: The American Cadmus and Modern Moses.* Philadelphia, 1885.

Freehling, William W. *Prelude to Civil War.* New York, 1965.

Gabriel, Ralph Henry. *Elias Boudinot: Cherokee and His America.* Norman, Okla., 1941.

Garrison, Tim Alan. *The Legal Ideology of Removal: The Southern Judiciary and the Sovereignty of the Native American Nations.* Athens, Ga., 2002.

Gatell, Frank Otto, ed. *Essays on Jacksonian America.* New York, 1970.

———, and John M. McFaul, eds. *Jacksonian America 1815–1840.* Englewood Cliffs, N.J., 1970.

Gaul, Theresa Strouth, ed. *To Marry an Indian: The Marriage of Harriet Gold and Elias Boudinot in Letters, 1823–1839.* Chapel Hill, N.C., 2005.

Gibson, Wayne Dell. "Cherokee Treaty Party Moves West," *The Chronicles of Oklahoma,* vol. LXXIX, no. 3, Fall 2007.

Gilbert, Joan. *The Trail of Tears Across Missouri.* Columbia, Mo., 1996.

Gilmer, George R. *First Settlers of Upper Georgia.* Americus, Ga., 1926.

Goodrich, S. G. *Recollections of a Lifetime,* 2 vols. New York, 1956.

Grant, Donald L. *The Way It Was in the South: The Black Experience in Georgia.* Athens, Ga., 1993.

Grayson, Benson Lee. *The Unknown President: The Administration of President Millard Fillmore.* Washington, D.C., 1981.

Gregory, Jack, and Rennard Strickland. *Sam Houston with the Cherokees, 1829–1833.* Norman, Okla., 1967.

Guinn, Jeff. *Our Land Before We Die: The Proud Story of the Seminole Negro.* New York, 2005.

Gunderson, Robert Gray. *The Log-Cabin Campaign.* Louisville, Ky., 1957.

Hamilton, Holman. *Prologue to Conflict: The Crisis and Compromise of 1850.* Lexington, Ky., 1964.

Hargreaves, Mary W. M. *The Presidency of John Quincy Adams.* Lawrence, Ky., 1985.

Harrell, Sara Gordon. *John Ross.* Minneapolis, Minn., 1979.

Harrison, Gabriel. *John Howard Payne: His Life and Writings.* Philadelphia, 1885.

Harrison, William Henry. *Messages and Letters.* Logan Esarey, ed. Indianapolis, Ind., 1922.

Hobson, Charles F. *The Great Chief Justice: John Marshall and the Rule of Law.* Lawrence, Ks., 1996.

Hoig, Stanley W. *The Cherokees and Their Chiefs in the Wake of Empire.* Fayetteville, Ark., 1998.

Holt, Michael F. *The Political Crisis of the 1850s.* New York, 1978.

Horan, James D. *The McKenney-Hall Portrait Gallery of American Indians.* New York, 1972.

Horr, David Agee, ed. *Cherokee and Creek Indians.* New York, 1974.

Horsman, Reginald. *Race and Manifest Destiny: The Origins of American Racial Anglo-Saxonism.* Cambridge, Mass., 1981.

Howden Smith, Arthur D. *Old Fuss and Feathers: The Life and Exploits of Lt.-General Winfield Scott.* New York, 1937.

Hurt, R. Douglas. *The Indian Frontier 1763–1846.* Albuquerque, N.M., 2002.

Inaugural Addresses of the President of the United States, Washington, D.C., 1989.

Indian Removals, The. Doc. 512. U.S. Senate, 23rd Cong., 1st Session, 2 vols. New York, 1974.

Ishii, Izumi. *Bad Fruits of the Civilized Tree: Alcohol & the Sovereignty of the Cherokee Nation.* Lincoln, Neb., 2008.

Jackson, Andrew. *Correspondence,* 6 vols., John S. Bassett, ed. Washington, D.C., 1926–33.

———. *Papers,* 7 vols., Daniel Feller, Harold D. Moser, Laura-Eve Moss, Thomas Coens, eds. Knoxville, Tenn., 2007.

Jahoda, Gloria. *The Trail of Tears: The Story of the American Indian Removals 1813–1855.* New York, 1975.

Jefferson, Thomas. *Jefferson,* Merrill D. Peterson, ed. New York, 1984.

Johnson, Richard Malcolm. *Autobiography.* ReadHowYouWant.com, 2006.

Johnston, Carolyn Ross. *Cherokee Women in Crisis.* Tuscaloosa, Ala., 2003.

Jones, Howard. *Mutiny on the* Amistad. New York, 1887.

Kansil, Joli Quentin. *John Quincy Adams and Latin America.* Honolulu, Hawaii, 1983.

Kennedy, John P. *Memoirs of the Life of William Wirt,* 2 vols. Philadelphia, 1851.

Koestler-Grack, Rachel A. *Chief John Ross.* Chicago, 2004.

Kraychir, Hank. *Chief John Ross: Opportunist During the American Civil War.* Scotts Valley, Calif., 2008.

Langguth, A. J. *Union 1812.* New York, 2006.

Latner, Richard B. *The Presidency of Andrew Jackson: White House Politics.* Athens, Ga., 1979.

Lipsky, George A. *John Quincy Adams: His Theory and Ideas.* New York, 1950.

Littlefield, Daniel F., Jr. *The Cherokee Freedmen: From Emancipation to American Citizenship.* Westport, Conn., 1978.

Loizeau, Pierre-Marie. *Martin Van Buren: The Little Magician.* New York, 2008.

Long, Laura. *Fuss 'N' Feathers: A Life of Winfield T. Scott.* New York, 1944.

Lumpkin, Wilson. *The Removal of the Cherokee Indians from Georgia,* 2 vols. New York, 1907; 1 vol. reprint, New York, 1969.

Lynch, Denis Tilden. *An Epoch and a Man: Martin Van Buren and His Times.* New York, 1929.

Magoon, E. J. *Living Orators in America.* New York, 1849.

Magruder, Allan B. *John Marshall.* Boston, 1899.

Malone, Dumas. *Jefferson the President: Second Term, 1805–1809.* Boston, Mass., 1974.

Malone, Henry Thompson. *Cherokees of the Old South: A People in Transition.* Athens, Ga., 1956.

Mansfield, Edward D. *The Life and Services of General Winfield Scott.* New York, 1852.

Marszalek, John F. *The Petticoat Affair: Manners, Mutiny and Sex in Andrew Jackson's White House.* New York, 1997.

Masur, Louis P. *1831: Year of Eclipse.* New York, 2001.

May, Ernest R. *The Making of the Monroe Doctrine.* Cambridge, Mass., 1975.

May, Gary. *John Tyler.* New York, 2008.

Mayer, Henry. *All on Fire: William Lloyd Garrison and the Abolition of Slavery.* New York, 1998.

Mayo, Bernard. *Henry Clay: Spokesman of the New West.* Boston, 1937.

McDougall, Walter A. *Throes of Democracy: The American Civil War Era 1829–1877.* New York, 2008.

McKenney, Thomas L. *Memoirs, Official and Personal,* Herman J. Viola, ed. Lincoln, Neb., 1973.

McKenney, Thomas L., and James Hall. *The Indian Tribes in North America,* 3 vols., 2nd ed. Edinburgh, 1933–34.

McLoughlin, William G. *After the Trail of Tears: The Cherokees' Struggle for Sovereignty 1839–1880.* Chapel Hill, N.C., 1993.

———. *Champions of the Cherokees.* Princeton, N. J., 1990.

———. *Cherokees and Missionaries, 1789–1839.* New Haven, Conn., 1984.

———. *Cherokee Renascence in the New Republic.* Princeton, N. J., 1986.

Meacham, Jon. *American Lion.* New York, 2008.

Merk, Frederick. *Manifest Destiny and Mission in American History.* Cambridge, Mass., 1963.

Merry, Robert W. *A Country of Vast Designs: James K. Polk, The Mexican War and the Conquest of the American Continent.* New York, 2009.
Minges, Patrick N. *Slavery in the Cherokee Nation: The Keetoowah Society and the Defining of a People 1855–1867.* New York, 2003.
Mintz, S. *Digital History.* Houston, TX, 2007.
Monroe, James. *Autobiography,* Stuart Gerry Brown, ed. Syracuse, N.Y., 1959.
———. *Writings,* 8 vols., S. M. Hamilton, ed. New York, 1898–1902.
Mooney, James. *Historical Sketch of the Cherokee.* New Brunswick, N. J., 2006.
Mooney, Tom, and I. Mickel Yantz and contributing artists. *Generations: Cherokee Language Through Art.* Tahlequah, Okla., 2009.
Moore, Stephen L. *Last Stand of the Texas Cherokees: Chief Bowles and the 1839 Cherokee War in Texas.* Garland, Tex., 2009.
Morse, Jedediah. *A Report on Indian Affairs.* New Haven, Conn., 1822.
Morse, John T., Jr. *John Quincy Adams.* Boston, 1886.
Moulton, Gary E. *John Ross, Cherokee Chief.* Athens, Ga., 1978.
Mushkat, Jerome, and Joseph G. Rayback. *Martin Van Buren: Law, Politics and the Shaping of Republican Ideology.* DeKalb, Ill., 1997.
Nagel, Paul C. *John Quincy Adams: A Public Life, A Private Life.* New York, 1997.
National Park Service. *New Echota: Birthplace of the American Indian Press.* Washington, D.C., 1941.
Nelson, Lyle. *John Tyler: A Rare Career.* New York, 2008.
Nevins, Allan. *American Press Opinion, Washington to Coolidge.* Boston, 1928.
Newmyer, R. Kent. *John Marshall and the Heritage of the Supreme Court.* Baton Rouge, La., 2001.
Niven, John. *John C. Calhoun and the Price of Union.* Baton Rouge, La., 1988.
———. *Martin Van Buren: The Romantic Age of American Politics.* New York, 1983.
Norton, A. B. *Reminiscences of the Log Cabin and Hard Cider Campaign.* Mount Vernon, Ohio, 1888.
Parins, James W. *Elias Cournelius Boudinot: A Life on the Cherokee Border.* Lincoln, Neb., 2006.
———. *John Rollin Ridge: His Life and Works.* Lincoln, Neb., 1991.
Parsons, Lynn Hudson. *John Quincy Adams.* Madison, Wisc., 1998.
Parton, James. *Life of Andrew Jackson,* 3 vols., New York, 1860–61.
Perdue, Theda. *Cherokee Women: Gender and Culture Change, 1700–1835.* Lincoln, Neb., 1998.
———. *Slavery and the Evolution of Cherokee Society, 1540–1866.* Knoxville, Tenn., 1979.
Perdue, Theda, and Michael D. Green. *The Cherokee Nation and the Trail of Tears.* New York, 2007.
———. *The Cherokee Removal: A Brief History with Documents.* Boston, 2005.
Peskin, Allan. *Winfield Scott and the Profession of Arms.* Kent, Ohio, 2003.
Pessen, Edward. *Jacksonian America: Society, Personality, and Politics.* Urbana, Ill., 1985.

Peterson, Merrill D. *Olive Branch and Sword—The Compromise of 1833.* Baton Rouge, La., 1982.

Peterson, Norma Lois. *The Presidencies of William Henry Harrison & John Tyler.* Emporia, Ks., 1989.

Phillips, Leon. *That Eaton Woman: In Defense of Peggy O'Neale Eaton.* New York, 1974.

Phillips, Ulrich B. *Life and Labor in the Old South.* Boston, 1939.

Pierce, J. Kingston. "Andrew Jackson: The Petticoat Affair." In *American History,* The History Net.

Pinheiro, John C. *Manifest Ambition: James K. Polk and Civil-Military Relations During the Mexican War.* Westport, Conn., 2007.

Pollack, Queena. *Peggy Eaton: Democracy's Mistress.* New York, 1931.

Pound, Merritt B. *Benjamin Hawkins—Indian Agent.* Athens, Ga., 1951.

Proceedings. *Trail of Tears Symposium.* Little Rock, Ark., 1996.

Prucha, Francis Paul. *Documents of United States Indian Policy.* Lincoln, Nebr., 2000.

———. *The Great Father,* abridged ed. Lincoln, Nebr., 1986.

———. *The Indians in American Society.* Berkeley, Calif., 1985.

Reed, Marcelina. *Seven Clans of the Cherokee Society.* Cherokee, N.C., 1993.

Remini, Robert V., ed. *The Age of Jackson.* Columbia, S.C., 1972.

———. *Andrew Jackson: Volume One: The Course of American Empire.* New York, 1975. *Volume Two: The Course of American Freedom, 1822–1832.* Baltimore, Md., 1981. *Volume Three: The Course of American Diplomacy, 1833–1845.* Baltimore, Md., 1984.

———. *Andrew Jackson & His Indian Wars.* New York, 2001.

———. *Henry Clay: Statesman for the Union.* New York, 1991.

———. *John Quincy Adams.* New York, 2002.

———. *Martin Van Buren and the Making of the Democratic Party.* New York, 1959.

Rhodes, James F. *History of the United States from the Compromise of 1850.* New York, 1892.

Richardson, James D. *A Compilation of the Messages and Papers of the Presidents,* 20 vols. Washington, D.C., 1908.

Rogers, Joseph M. *The True Henry Clay.* Philadelphia, 1904.

Rogin, Michael Paul. *Father and Children: Andrew Jackson and the Subjugation of the American Indian.* New York, 1975.

Ross, John. *Papers,* 2 vols., Gary E. Moulton, ed. Norman, Okla., 1984–85.

Rozema, Vicki. *Cherokee Voices: Early Accounts of Cherokee Life in the East.* Winston-Salem, N.C., 2002.

———. *Footsteps of the Cherokees: A Guide to the Eastern Homelands of the Cherokee Nation.* Winston-Salem, N.C., 2007.

———. *Voices From The Trail of Tears.* Winston-Salem, N.C., 2006.

Ruskin, Gertrude McDaris. *John Ross, Chief of an Eagle Race.* Decatur, Ga., 1963.

Satz, Ronald N. *American Indian Policy in the Jackson Era.* Norman, Okla., 1975.

———. "The Cherokee Trail of Tears: A Sesquicentennial Perspective." *The Georgia Historical Quarterly,* Fall 1989. Savannah, Ga.

Schermerhorn, Richard A. *Schermerhorn Genealogy and Family Chronicles.* New York, 1914.

Schlesinger, Arthur M., Jr. *The Age of Jackson.* Boston, 1946.

Schurz, Carl. *Life of Henry Clay,* 2 vols. Boston, 1915.

Sellers, Charles. *James K. Polk,* 2 vols. Princeton, N.J., 1957, 1966.

Seward, William H. *Life and Public Service of John Quincy Adams.* Auburn, N.Y., 1849.

Shadburn, Don L. *Blood Kin: Pioneer Chronicles of Upper Georga Centered in Forsyth County.* Cummings, Ga., 1999.

———. *Cherokee Planters in Georgia 1832–1838.* Roswell, Ga., 1989.

———. *Unhallowed Intrusion: A History of Cherokee Families in Forsyth County, Georgia.* Alpharetta, Ga., 1993.

Sharp, James Roger. *The Jacksonians versus the Banks.* New York, 1970.

Shepard, Edward M. *Martin Van Buren,* American Statesmen series, vol. 18. Boston, 1899.

Shewmaker, Kenneth E., ed. *Daniel Webster: "The Completest Man."* Hanover, N.H., 1990.

Shoemaker, Nancy, ed. *American Indians.* Malden, Mass., 2001.

Silbey, Joel H. *Martin Van Buren and the Emergence of American Popular Politics.* Lanham, Md., 2002.

———. *Party Over Section: The Rough and Ready Presidential Election of 1848.* Lawrence, Ks., 2009.

Smith, Elbert B. *President Zachary Taylor: The Hero President.* New York, 2007.

Smith, Jean Edward. *John Marshall: Definer of a Nation.* New York, 1996.

Spencer, John D. *The American Civil War in the Indian Territory.* New York, 2006.

Starkey, Marion L. *Cherokee Nation.* North Dighton, Mass., 1995.

Starr, Emmet. *History of the Cherokee Indians and Their Legends and Folk Lore.* Oklahoma City, Okla., 1921.

Stephanson, Anders. *Manifest Destiny: American Expansion and the Empire of Right.* New York, 1995.

Stowe, Harriet Beecher. *The Annotated Uncle Tom's Cabin.* New York, 2007.

Sullivan, Roy. *Scattered Graves: The Civil War Campaigns of Confederate Brigadier General and Cherokee Chief Stand Watie.* Bloomington, Ind., 2006.

Thomas, John L., ed. *John C. Calhoun: A Profile.* New York, 1968.

Thoreau, Henry David. *The Journal of Henry D. Thoreau, 1837–1846,* Bradford Torrey and Francis H. Allen, eds. Boston, 1949.

Thurmond, Michael. *Freedom: Georgia's Antislavery Heritage, 1733–1865.* Atlanta, Ga., 2002.

Timberlake, Henry. *Memoirs 1756–1765.* Marietta, Ga., 1948.

Traveler Bird. *Tell Them They Lie: The Sequovah Myth.* Los Angeles, Calif., 1971.

Underwood, Thomas Bryan. *Cherokee Legends and the Trail of Tears: Adapted from the Nineteenth Annual Report of the Bureau of Indian Ethnology.* Cherokee, N.C., 2006.

U.S. Congressional Documents and Debates. *A Century of Lawmaking for a New Nation.* Library of Congress, Register of Debates, Senate 21st Congress, 1st Session.

Van Buren, Martin. *Autobiography,* John C. Fitzpatrick, ed. Washington, D.C., 1920.

Van Deusen, Glyndon G. *The Jackson Era: 1828–1848.* Long Grove, Ill., 1959.

———. *The Life of Henry Clay.* Boston, 1937.

Wait, Eugene M. *The Second Jackson Administration.* New York, 2002.

Walker, Robert Sparks. *Torchlights to the Cherokees: The Brainerd Mission.* New York, 1931.

Wallace, Anthony F. C. *The Long, Bitter Trail: Andrew Jackson and the Indians.* New York, 1993.

Wardell, Morris J. *A Political History of the Cherokee Nation: 1838–1907.* Norman, Okla., 1938.

Warren, Mary B., and Eva B. Weeks. *Whites Among the Cherokees, 1828–1838.* Athens, Ga., 1987.

Watson, Harry L. *Andrew Jackson vs. Henry Clay: Democracy and Development in Antebellum America.* Boston, 1998.

———. *Liberty and Power: The Politics of Jacksonian America.* New York, 2006.

Waugh, John C. *Sam Bell Maxey and the Confederate Indians.* Abilene, Tex., 1995.

Widmer, Ted. *Martin Van Buren.* New York, 2005.

Wilentz, Sean. *Andrew Jackson.* New York, 2005.

———. *The Rise of American Democracy.* New York, 2005.

Wilkins, Thurman. *Cherokee Tragedy: The Ridge Family and the Decimation of a People.* Norman, Okla., 1983.

Williams, David. *The Georgia Gold Rush: Twenty-Niners, Cherokees, and Gold Fever.* Columbia, S.C., 1993.

Wilson, Major L. *The Presidency of Martin Van Buren.* Lawrence, Ks., 1984.

Wirt, William. *The Letters of the British Spy.* Chapel Hill, N.C., 1970.

———. *Memoirs,* vol. 2, John P. Kennedy, ed. Philadelphia, 1849.

Woodward, Grace Steele. *The Cherokees.* Norman, Okla., 1963.

Wooten, James. *Dasher: The Roots and Rising of Jimmy Carter.* New York, 1979.

Wright, Amos J., Jr. *The McGillivray and McIntosh Traders of the Old Southwest Frontier, 1716–1815.* Montgomery, Ala., 2001.

Young, Mary. "The Exercise of Sovereignty in Cherokee Georgia." *The Journal of the Early Republic,* vol. 10, no. 1 (Spring 1990).

Zinn, Howard, and Anthony Arnove. *Voices of a People's History of the United States.* New York, 2004.

INDEX

About the Author

A. J. Langguth is emeritus professor in the Annenberg School of Communication & Journalism at the University of Southern California and has published three novels and eight works of nonfiction, including *Patriots, Union 1812,* and *Our Vietnam*. His Web page is ajlangguth.com.